TRANSITIONAL CITIZENS

Voters and What Influences
Them in the New Russia

Timothy J. Colton

HARVARD UNIVERSITY PRESS

Cambridge, Massachusetts

London, England

2000

To H. Gordon Skilling

Library of Congress Cataloging-in-Publication Data

Colton, Timothy J., 1947–
Transitional citizens : voters and what influences them in the new Russia /
Timothy J. Colton.
p.   cm.
Includes index.
ISBN 0-674-00277-6 (cloth : alk. paper) — ISBN 0-674-00153-2 (pbk. : alk. paper)
1. Elections—Russia (Federation)   2. Voting—Russia (Federation)
3. Political participation—Russia (Federation)
4. Political culture—Russia (Federation)
5. Public opinion—Russia (Federation)   I. Title.
JN6699.A5 C65   2000
324.947′086—dc21   00-021216

TRANSITIONAL CITIZENS

8/11/00

Contents

Preface

Subjects obey. Citizens choose. The signal accomplishment of the epic "transition" in the former Soviet Union—in counterpoint to a sorry economic record—is the political feat of having converted so many subjects into citizens. This book takes a look at the people of the Russian Federation as they make democratic choices they could not have dreamed of being allowed to make a few years back. The venue is the electoral arena, where they periodically pass judgment on their governments and would-be governments. Voting is the consummate act of citizenship.

One hundred and nine million strong and straddling two continents, eleven time zones, and eighty-nine constituent regions, the Russian electorate has from the moment of inception been one of the biggest on earth.[1] Comprehending the way its members stand up and are counted will be critical to debates within political science about mass politics and about regime change and consolidation.

The fascination of this gigantic collectivity lies less in sheer size than in its very enfranchisement, which cuts against the grain of a singularly autocratic past. Russia's citizens now go to vote in what used to be the citadel of the dictatorship that embodied the main alternative to liberal democracy. This brave new world of competitive elections is thinly mapped. Peaceful jousting among political parties, seating thresholds and runoff formulas, the arcana of *reitingi, politicheskiye konsul'tanty, polstery, fokus-gruppy, press-konferentsii,* and *imidzh-meikery*—all were unheard of not so long ago. Most exotic of all is the idea that the man or woman on the street can every so often have a voice in picking state personnel and policy. "We are not accustomed to holding the country's destiny in our hands," Mayor Yurii Luzhkov of Moscow remarked grandiloquently of his compatriots in the last-stretch drive of the presidential race of 1996. "The bosses always did it for us. But now, and this is our achievement, the vote of any of us may prove to be decisive."[2] The mayor spoke the truth, if—as a latter-day boss himself—with some disingenuousness in his resort to the first person plural.

A related anomaly of the Russian vote is the enormity of the potential winnings and losses in post-Communist elections. Office seekers in the quiescent West fuss over tuning up social systems in working order and over whether to shave a percentage point or two off the budget deficit or add pennies to the gasoline tax. In Russia the battle is about graver and more incendiary concerns—dysfunctional and insolvent institutions, individual freedom, nationhood, property rights, provision of the basic necessities of life in an economic downswing worse than capitalism's Great Depression of the 1930s. The idiom of Russian electoral campaigns is that of apocalypse, deliverance, and mutual "Satanization."[3] When Boris Yeltsin was fending off rivals for the presidency in the summer of 1996, his archantagonist Gennadii Zyuganov of the KPRF (Communist Party of the Russian Federation) intoned that Russia was "under threat of self-annihilation"; only he and his socialistic nostrums could rescue the country "from falling into the abyss" to the brink of which Yeltsin's misbegotten reforms had led it. The then pro-Yeltsin Luzhkov rejoined by summoning up the nightmare of retrogression to Stalinism were Zyuganov to be victorious: "One thing would follow another, according to the logic of the totalitarian system . . . until we were cut off by an iron curtain from the rest of mankind and here in our land people were forced to labor out of fear and not out of economic interest." The choice, he insisted, was "either chaos and tyranny [with Zyuganov] or hope [with Yeltsin]."[4] The rhetorical grandstanding does not erase the point that in Russian voting the stakes—declared, perceived, and real—are spectacularly out of the ordinary.

The Russian electoral saga was quick to catch the eye of area experts and generalist students of democratization, the latter sometimes in partnership with the former. Stephen White, Richard Rose, and Ian McAllister's groundbreaking *How Russia Votes*,[5] Jerry F. Hough's and my edited volume recapping a major collaborative project,[6] and a spate of journal articles, papers, and monographs[7] are the first tender shoots of a scholarly literature.

The output thus far contains fine accounts of the prehistory, administration, and results of elections in transitional Russia, from the half-free elections in the twilight of Soviet power to the inauguration of multiparty voting for parliament in 1993 and Yeltsin's re-election triumph in 1996.

Anyone wishing to be educated about these things should consult the published narratives, which I shall not duplicate. (As a reference, Appendix A compiles returns from the post-Soviet elections to date—parliamentary in 1993 and 1995 and presidential in 1996.) Nor do I propose to clone the worthwhile material already on the library shelf describing the substance and the roots of public opinion in the post-Soviet states. Much as it can teach us about attitudes toward democracy and economic reform, it scarcely dips into their impact on voting or other forms of political participation.[8]

The pioneer scholarship on Russian elections has tracked events, reconnoitered avenues of inquiry, and spawned an assortment of insights which complement the work on citizen beliefs. It is ripe for extension and revision in several regards:

- Most of it recapitulates a single election or, as with *How Russia Votes,* successive elections seriatim.[9] Taking elections one at a time was unavoidable at the outset; now it is time to stress overarching questions and topics.
- The literature is skimpy in its coverage of the electoral process per se. It skips lightly over political phenomena such as voter immersion in campaigns, attachments to parties, candidates' personalities, and the role of the news media.[10]
- In explaining the vote, analysts underutilize quantitative techniques and are unambitious about sorting out causal relationships through statistical modeling.[11]
- Odd for so turbulent a country, the commentary is static. Granted the danger of reaching prematurely for the long-range dynamics of electoral choice, this still leaves ample shorter-term dynamics to tend to.
- Authors have not made maximum use of their findings to contribute to theories of how democracies are built.

Transitional Citizens aims to decipher why suddenly enfranchised Russians vote as they do and to further the study of the grassroots politics of democratization by proceeding as follows:

- The text is structured by theme and not by election, tabling evidence from several elections as required. It chiefly exploits individual-level data culled in coordinated pre- and post-election surveys of a large

probability sample of the electorate, done under my, William
Zimmerman's, and Russian colleagues' supervision in 1995 and 1996.

- It tackles the electoral process and election-related organization head
  on. Whole chapters profile engagement in campaigns and with Russia's teeming political parties. Political actors remain central throughout.
- To make voting preferences intelligible, I work with a wide range of
  determinants and with a statistical tool kit capable of drawing them
  into a unified synopsis. Methodologically, I am indebted to the magis-
  terial *The New American Voter,* by Warren E. Miller and J. Merrill
  Shanks, and to the "multistage, bloc recursive model" of origins of the
  presidential vote adumbrated there.[12] The particulars and mechanics I
  have tailored to a society which is starkly different from the United
  States, and which faces choices exceedingly more harrowing than
  those in the charmed circle of established democracies. (A rundown
  of survey data, methods, and models employed in the book is given in
  Appendix B.)
- The survey data were obtained in a format that taps into certain dynamic properties of popular behavior. Three waves of face-to-face interviews over ten months in 1995–96—before and after a parliamentary election and on the heels of a presidential election—were
  mustered as a panel, that is, through repeated interviews of the same
  persons. Panels fix changes in attitudes and action more faithfully
  than standard cross-sectional surveys and are more informative about
  linkages among the elements of public choice.
- As best I can, I tease out lessons for overall conceptions of political behavior and development.

The learned discourse about transitions away from authoritarianism,
and especially away from Communism, has stressed the unsettled tenor of
politics and government during such periods. There is much to be said for
that characterization. Beyond a doubt, caprice and coincidence do enter
into Russians' principal mode of civic action, the vote, and some aspects of
it are indeterminate and mercurial.

My research brings out, however, that voting in post-Soviet Russia must
also be understood as *highly patterned behavior.* Despite the unfamiliarity
of subjects-turned-citizens with democratic procedures and despite the
myriad uncertainties that besiege them publicly and privately, their elec-

toral choices manifest a degree of purposiveness and systematic variation which, I suspect, will surprise a fair number of readers. There is plenty about Russians' voting decisions that continues to baffle the observer; I lay emphasis on how much we can manage to say about the forces that shape them.

I say "forces" advisedly because, contrary to claims that in the wake of Communism voters react to one commanding factor—ethnicity, temptation by charismatic leaders, and comparisons of the new regime with the old have all been put up for the honor—I find that it is the interplay of multiple factors which produces the outcome. I frame an argument about them in cross-national perspective and by and large define the components generically, capitalizing on the shared vocabulary and theoretical advances of the field. I infuse the common-use categories with empirical content that has verisimilitude in contemporary Russian conditions.

Variables in reasonably clear-cut categories—electors' social traits, their appraisals of the health of the economy and polity, budding affinities for parties, convictions about systemic reform and other disputed issues, leadership evaluations, and assessments of the performance and promise of incumbents and opposition—all have a significant bearing on how post-Soviet Russians vote. Thanks to the exigencies of the transitional environment, some of these variables are haler predictors of voting choice than others. Moreover, influences on voting have their effects in combinations and sequences that differ plainly from one immediate political context to another.

The electoral politics of post-Communism, in short, has in a historical instant grown into a multicausal and multiphased game of great richness and intricacy. In dissecting it, I will be happy if I can begin to match the participants in subtlety.

1

Subjects into Citizens

The ongoing transformation of Russia and its neighbors in Eurasia and Eastern Europe is as far-reaching a revolution as any in modern times. Precisely because of its magnitude, it has yielded a turmoil of results a bare decade into its trajectory. That the countries of the region are in convulsive transition away from Soviet Communism is crystal clear; just where they will transit to, singly and collectively, is murky.[1]

Readers undoubtedly hope, as do I, that the trek ends in vibrant democratic regimes. Democracies are governments whose "actions have been in relatively close correspondence with the wishes of relatively many of their citizens for a long period of time."[2] By that principle, the Russian Federation is at best a protodemocracy, a work in progress that may some day evolve into a full-grown democracy. Its population is a transitional citizenry.

Emblematic of this limbo polity is the awkwardness its denizens have in characterizing it. Boris Yeltsin has lamented that, although Russia has adopted "a new political system," those at its helm "have not yet learned how to govern in a new way." "We are stuck halfway," he goes on. "We have shoved off from the old shore, but flounder in a stream of problems [that] carries us along and keeps us from making it to the far shore."[3] Ordinary people confess consternation, too. When my survey sample of voting-age Russians was asked in 1996 if they thought their political system "is a democracy," rather more opposed the statement (34 percent) than approved it (29 percent); the largest group of all (37 percent) was unable to say.[4]

In a well-ordered democracy, political sophistication on the part of the public generally fosters respect for the governmental setup. That this does not occur in Russia is a telltale sign of the makeshift and fragile nature of its protodemocracy. The Russian electorate can readily be stratified by knowledge of political facts, begetting a scale of citizen awareness similar to scales devised in the venerable Western democracies (cf. Appendix B for the procedure).[5] When we then plot citizens' civic consciousness against their positions on Russia's regime, we find that greater consciousness leads to greater denial of democratic governance (see Figure 1.1). Persons in the politically most aware fifth of the population, who have the same probability of grading Russia a democracy as the least aware fifth, are nearly three times as likely as the least aware to claim it is not a democracy.[6]

The most cogent reason to grant Russia the benefit of the doubt and rank it a democracy-in-the-making is its record of staffing high offices and adjudicating conflicts through passably free and inclusive elections. The Russian demos may not have many levers over public policy, but it can at least throw the rascals out if all patience is exhausted.

Momentous electoral reforms that eliminated single-candidate charades and instituted competitive campaigns and a secret ballot were the brainchild of the last secretary-general of the CPSU (Communist Party of the Soviet Union), Mikhail Gorbachev, in the late 1980s. Multicandidate elec-

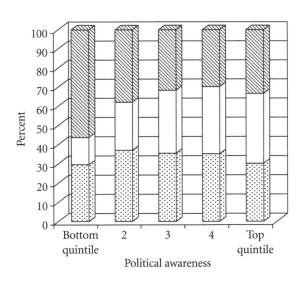

⊡ A democracy   ☐ Not a democracy   ▨ Cannot say

Figure 1.1. Assessments of the Russian Political System by Level of Political Awareness, 1996

tions more than any other innovation let his *perestroika* get out of hand and brought on the subversion and ruination, not the rejuvenation, of the Soviet system. Boris Yeltsin, once Gorbachev's protégé and Politburo comrade, turned into his radical nemesis outside the CPSU as he seized the opening to gain the chairmanship of the Russian republic's legislature in May 1990. In June 1991 Yeltsin won popular election as Russian president in a landslide over five other candidates.[7]

Since becoming a sovereign state in December 1991, Russia has staged parliamentary elections in December 1993 and December 1995 and a presidential election in June–July 1996. (As this book goes to press, preparations are under way for another pair of parliamentary and presidential elections.) The State Duma, the lower chamber of the Federal Assembly chartered by the constitution of 1993, is elected by writ of a split formula.[8] One-half of its 450 seats are distributed by proportional representation to national lists nominated by the political parties and equivalent organiza tions, subject to a 5 percent threshold. The other half are filled by simple plurality in single-member territorial districts. Sixty percent of the district candidates and 66 percent of the winners were partisan nominees in 1995, and the rest were independents with no party imprimatur.[9] I delve into voting for the national party lists only. Regrettably, not much can be learned from the obtainable data about the 225 district races. Besides their national component, they sway to local vagaries liable to elude a survey with sampling units strung from the Gulf of Finland to the Sea of Japan.[10] The upper house of parliament, the Federation Council, elected for only its maiden term from 1993 to 1995, is excluded outright from the study.[11]

Choice of the kingpin of Russia's federal government, the president, is our other action focus. Russia is one of those atypical countries which directly elect their head of state.[12] The president is elected to a fixed four-year term separate from the legislative branch. A runoff between the top two finishers settles the score if no one secures 50 percent the first time, as happened in 1996. As in the district leg of Duma elections, nomination by a party is optional, not mandatory.

Russia's first multiparty vote, in 1993, was instigated by the Yeltsin administration as an "engineered founding election"[13] which would give its allies ascendancy in the State Duma and, in an accompanying plebiscite, ratify the president's draft constitution. Except for narrow confirmation of the constitution, the results were a letdown, as Russia's Choice, the one party wholeheartedly for Yeltsin, finished well behind the raucously nationalist LDPR (Liberal-Democratic Party of Russia) in the popular vote.[14] Progovernment forces were embarrassed again in 1995, with the neo-Communist KPRF overtaking the LDPR in votes for the party lists and forming the largest caucus in the Duma. In 1996, though, Yeltsin, whose chances for re-election many handicappers had belittled the preceding winter, outpolled nine rivals to win a second term and perpetuate divided government in Russia.

Much will be imparted on these pages about political parties. In the Soviet dispensation, there was only "the" party: the CPSU leviathan which monopolized decisions and treated the machinery of state and the population as executors of its will. To an interplanetary pilgrim who docked in Russia today after a decade's absence, no change would be more astonishing than to find the CPSU in its grave and Moscow and the provinces awash in parties of all sizes, viewpoints, and temperaments.

I define a political party functionally—as "any group, however loosely organized, seeking to elect governmental office-holders under a given label," to quote Leon D. Epstein.[15] Russian rules of the political road have not set duly certified and titled parties *(partii)* apart from quasi-parties. These may have more circumspect name tags—ranging from the most common, "movement" *(dvizheniye)*, to "association" *(ob"edineniye, obshchestvo,* or *assotsiyatsiya)*, "union" *(soyuz)*, "league" *(liga)*, "congress" *(kongress)*, "foundation" *(fond)*, and "front" *(front)*—but in elections they all pursue the same core political purpose of drumming up votes for candidates. Russia's electoral laws bring both quasi-parties and parties under the tent of "electoral associations" *(izbiratel'nyye ob"edineniya)* and afford them the same prerogatives to nominate and promote candidates. Under prevailing legislation, the Central Electoral Commission will in principle license any group to participate in a national election, so long as it has registered as a bona fide public organization with the Ministry of Justice,[16] its bylaws authorize it to take political action, it does not propound violent overthrow of the government, and it submits petitions with the required quantity of signatures by eligible voters.[17] The law also enables "electoral blocs" *(izbiratel'nyye bloki)*, alliances of several parties or public organizations, to campaign for parliamentary seats as quasi-parties. Setting the official terminology aside for convenience, I will regularly speak of all these bodies as "parties."

The number of parties and quasi-parties in transitional Russia is exorbitant. Twenty-one of 35 associations entitled to enter the 1993 election to the State Duma put up slates of candidates and signature sheets; 13 got onto the ballot, of which 5 were juridically parties.[18] In 1995 the set of organizations permitted to nominate slates for the Duma had billowed to 273. Of the 111 that gave it a try, 38 were parties; 40 of the 111 acted autonomously, and 71 made their bids within 29 electoral blocs. Forty-three lists of candidates were eventually registered and presented to the electorate—10 cobbled together by parties, 15 by stand-alone quasi-parties, and 18 by multipartner electoral blocs.[19]

For the most part I will handle Russian parties (and quasi-parties) as discrete entities. Occasionally it will be beneficial to group them into programmatically contiguous "families" of parties, which also help sort the individual politicians associated with the parties or with the parties' issue stances.[20] Six party families may be demarcated (cf. Tables A.1, A.2, and A.3 in Appendix A for the taxonomy and for 1993 and 1995 vote totals).

A privileged subset as of the mid-1990s contained but one movement, Our Home Is Russia (Nash Dom—Rossiya). Convened at President Yeltsin's instigation in May 1995 and chaired by his prime minister from 1992 to 1998, Viktor Chernomyrdin,[21] it replaced Russia's Choice as the *government* party.[22] Our Home's goal on the hustings was unabashedly to shore up the political and policy status quo. The *liberal* opposition or, as its proponents relish saying, the "democratic opposition," has also preached reform, but promises to prosecute it more cleanly and humanely. Russian liberals are renowned for their internecine feuding and for calving splinter groups. Parties in the *centrist* family act the part of angels of moderation and compromise, maneuvering what they say is a middle way between the government and the militant currents in the opposition. The *nationalist* or self-styled "patriotic" parties chafe at Russia's humiliations and vow to restore it to grandeur and to stamp out threats to internal order. The *socialist* opposition, its powerhouse the KPRF, trumpets its fidelity to many of the collectivist values of the defunct Soviet regime. Unclassifiable *miscellaneous* groups round out the directory of parties.

Uncertainty and Elections

Uncertainty—the "lack of sure knowledge about the course of past, present, future, or hypothetical events," in the words of Anthony Downs[23]—is inherent in all politics. The hallmark of a transitional environment is the presence of this universal element in aberrant doses.

Abundant uncertainty characterizes the "third wave" of democratization that has swept many parts of the globe since the 1970s.[24] One of the most oft-cited overviews of the process, by Guillermo O'Donnell and Philippe C. Schmitter, underlines "the extraordinary uncertainty of the transition, with its numerous surprises and difficult dilemmas." "Few moments," they say, "pose such agonizing choices and responsibilities, ethical as well as political."[25]

When right-wing despots and juntas bowed out in Latin America and southern Europe, change and its companion uncertainty centered on political arrangements. Economic adjustments were enacted in most countries, but questions about the role of the military, civil rights, censorship, and unfettered elections were at the crux of the transfer of power. In the Soviet Union and its satellites, what melted down was an entire civilization.[26] Its backbone an apparatus of political repression and control, the *ancien regime* also paid homage to a messianic ideology and acted out all-embracing blueprints for "scientific socialism" in economics, social organization, and international relations. Its legitimacy withered largely because it failed to deliver the material prosperity it pledged. Chronic economic ills had been exacerbated by Communism's death pangs; hence programs to leap from Marx to market—to scrap socialist planning and replace it with a free-enterprise economy—crowned the agenda of successor governments. In Yeltsin's Russia economic "shock therapy" began in the winter of 1991–92.

As if that and the revamping of the central state were not enough, the retreat of the overextended Russians from empire and the dismemberment of the three Communist ethnofederations (the USSR, Yugoslavia, and Czechoslovakia) raised vexing questions about community and national cohesion. Unrehearsed, Russia, a pseudo-federation inside the Soviet Union until 1991,[27] had to learn to act like a genuine federal state. The attempt to squelch a separatist rebellion in the North Caucasus republic of Chechnya, when tens of thousands of civilians and troops were killed between December 1994 and August 1996, is proof (if proof were needed) of the potential for deadly violence.

As a catchword for the post-Communist panorama, it would be hard to improve upon "uncertainty." Yeltsin writes in his memoirs that the demise of the old order ushered in "a time of troubles and uncertainty, forcing us to rack our brains to find a way out of desperate stalemates."[28] Scholars agree, seeming at times to be trying to outdo the practitioners in dramatizing the mayhem. In a brilliant essay taking Hungary as a springboard, Valerie Bunce and Maria Csanádi talk of the "enormous uncertainty" of the time: "The basic structure of post-communism is the absence of much structure . . . Fluidity and uncertainty are the fundamental characteristics of the transitional period."[29] Kenneth Jowitt colorfully compares the annihilation of the Leninist regimes to the "mass extinction" of a biological species, such as the dinosaurs at the end of the Cretaceous age; its aftermath is a "traumatic Genesis environment" typified by "the dissolution of existing boundaries and related identities and the corresponding potential to generate novel ways of life."[30] Mary McAuley observes that the dismantling of the USSR and of one-party rule, long held to be "part of the natural order of things," saddled Russia with changes equal "in American terms to the disappearance of the office of the presidency, the flag, the Constitution, together with California, Texas, and New Mexico."[31] David D. Laitin calls the downfall of the Soviet Union a "cataclysm . . . devastating to many in the Russian Federation." For the Russian diaspora outside the federation, it was often "as if . . . New Yorkers were suddenly faced with the prospect of learning Iroquois or being deported to England."[32]

In mass politics, and especially in elections, there is no escaping uncertainty about the morning after—about who will come out ahead and who will not—in the most granite-solid of democracies.[33] But suspense is abridged there because, as Adam Przeworski says, "the possible outcomes are entailed by the institutional framework" and the protagonists have proven knowledge of each other's desires and abilities. "That uncertainty is inherent in democracy does not mean everything is possible or nothing is predictable . . . Democracy is a system of ruled open-endedness, or organized uncertainty."[34]

It is a safe bet that electoral uncertainty will loom larger in transitional countries that are "stuck halfway" between systems, in Yeltsin's pithy phrase. What with their rickety institutions, the plasticity of their laws, and the brevity of their acquaintance with nonviolent political contestation, vote choice there could hardly ride the well-worn grooves it does in a consolidated democracy. Voting cannot be sequestered from the crisis that inundates society as a whole, exemplified during the Russian election cycle audited in this book by economic deprivation, state weakness, moral anomie, savage political infighting, and the bloodbath in Chechnya.[35]

Four Kinds of Electoral Uncertainty

One token of Russia's electoral uncertainty is the *volatility* of behavior. Volatility reflects both effervescence within the elites and the fickleness of the citizens they woo. The election-fighting organization par excellence, the political party, illustrates this behavior pattern. Parties and quasi-parties have germinated, renamed and reclassified themselves, coalesced, and dissolved with abandon in Russia from the day they were legalized under Gorbachev's auspices in 1990. As mentioned earlier, thirteen entered the début multiparty election to the State Duma in December 1993. Nine of them had been hatched that year, some scant weeks before; five had perished by the time the next parliamentary election rolled around two years later. The eight holdover parties procured 82.30 percent of the valid votes cast in 1993,[36] which dwindled to 55.42 percent in December 1995. Thirty-five parties not on the scene in 1993—thirty-one of them born only in the election year 1995—feasted on 41.75 percent of the proportional-representation vote in 1995.[37]

The ups and downs of the vote shares of the eight parties (cf. Tables A.1 and A.2 in Appendix A) are vivid testimony to the tempestuousness of the transition. Only for the liberal Yabloko party and KEDR, an obscure ecological faction in the centrist fold, did 1995's share fall within one percentage point of 1993's. The KPRF leapfrogged from 12.40 percent to 22.73 percent of the total vote, or from third to first place. The vote base of the pacesetter in 1993, the LDPR, was halved, from 22.92 percent to 11.40 percent. The second-ranked Russia's Choice movement, the darling of the Yeltsin administration in 1993 (and known as Russia's Democratic Choice in 1995), shed three-quarters of its base, and PRES (the Party of Russian Unity and Accord) lost 95 percent, both of them undershooting the 5 percent bar.[38] Lumping the parties into programmatic families (cf. Table A.3) dampens the variability without eliminating it. The socialist parties, the KPRF in their van, fattened their share of the popular vote by 12.45 percent (from 20.39 percent to 32.84 percent), at the expense of the government party (now Our Home Is Russia) and the liberal, centrist, and nationalist oppositions.

Much brisker is electoral turnover in Russia at the level of the individual citizen. *Seventy-one percent* of 1995 voters who had participated in the 1993 election and could remember how they chose at the time said they had jumped ship to another party in 1995, our survey data disclose.[39] The defection rate in an established democracy will usually hover between 15 and 25 percent.[40] Six in seven supporters of Russia's Choice in 1993 did not vote for it again, and the interviewers were hard put to find anyone who voted a second time for PRES or KEDR, while nearly three KPRF supporters in four stayed put (see Figure 1.2). Sixty percent of our respondents changed partisan family, a more abrupt move than changing party (Figure 1.3). Again, there is a discrepancy between the socialist parties, disowned by about one-quarter of their previous supporters, and the government and centrist parties, from which about three-quarters defected.

A second and disturbing way in which uncertainty manifests itself is in discord over the *integrity* of the electoral process. Lacking ingrained norms of fair play and impartial courts to arbitrate disagreements, emerging democracies are prone to conflict over the rules and machinery for nominating candidates, filing ballots, and tallying the votes. In post-Soviet Russia's brief history, the surliest campaign was for the parliamentary election and constitutional poll of December 1993. Precipitated by the president's peremptory dissolution of the sitting parliament, the shelling of its headquarters by army tanks, the arrest of its leaders, and street fighting in downtown Moscow, with more than 100 fatalities, the election was followed by charges of vote fraud at the hands of Yeltsin's lieutenants.[41]

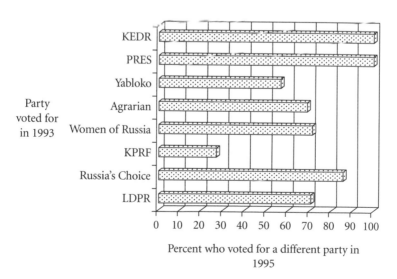

Figure 1.2. Vote Switching among Parties, 1993 to 1995

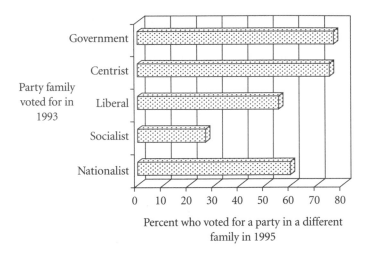

Figure 1.3. Vote Switching among Party Families, 1993 to 1995

Threats to cancel or disrupt the voting and accusations that the Kremlin coterie was again conniving for illicit advantage accompanied both the State Duma election of 1995 and the presidential campaign of 1996.[42]

Suspicion about the integrity of elections is widespread in Russia. Approximately half of the electorate in both 1995 and 1996 believed on balance that elections in those years had been fairly conducted (see Table 1.1), leaving large minorities either giving them a flunking or lukewarm grade or having no opinion. Doubts about electoral justice nourish misgivings about the country's democratic credentials. A mere 17 percent of the citizens who were most critical of the 1996 presidential election said Russia was a democratic system, versus 55 percent among those who accepted the vote as fully democratic.[43]

Worries over electoral formulas and issues phase into concern about—or, for reactionaries, hope for—the *reversibility* of the systemic reforms to which untrammeled campaigning and voting are life-giving oxygen. In a mature democracy it would be incredible to learn that citizens walked into a polling place frightened that the future of their social and political systems may be on the line. Not so in a transitional society. Boris Yeltsin set the tone in 1993 by thundering from his presidential pulpit that refusal by the electorate to seat sympathetic lawmakers and parties in the Duma or ratify his draft constitution would wreak havoc with Russia's "peace and calm."[44] In 1995 one opposition spokesman commented ominously that

Table 1.1 Citizen Assessments of the Fairness of National Elections (Percentages)

Assessment on 5-point scale	1995 parliamentary election[a]	1996 presidential election[b]
1—Completely undemocratic	4	10
2	4	8
3	21	21
4	25	19
5—Completely democratic	25	28
Don't know	21	14

a. Post-election survey (N = 2,774 weighted cases). Some respondents were interviewed in January 1996.

b. Post-election survey (N = 2,472 weighted cases).

postponement of that year's parliamentary election might ice it "for centuries."[45] Similar bombast reverberated during the presidential race of 1996, as the two leading candidates, Yeltsin and Gennadii Zyuganov, "artificially pumped up political tensions and injected them with . . . nearly sacral meaning."[46]

Electoral doom-saying strikes a chord with rank-and-file Russians. Quizzing citizens after the 1996 presidential vote, we asked if they had entertained the possibility during the runup to it that sundry disasters would befall Russia "as a result of the election." The answers are a revelation. About one-fifth feared that religious persecution would follow the election, one-fourth worried about a spike in emigration, and one-third expected problems in foreign policy. Most discomfiting is the degree of concurrence in 1996 in the three most drastic outcomes referred to in the questionnaire. Fifty-three percent of our respondents agreed it had crossed their minds that the Russian economy would slump, 33 percent that there would be a hemorrhage of political freedoms, and 45 percent that a *civil war,* no less, would erupt.[47]

Uncertainty takes form, fourthly, in voter *hesitancy.* People unsure of themselves and of their surroundings often procrastinate as long as possible in making decisions. So it has been in Russia's transitional electorate. Dithering attained heights unthinkable in a developed democracy in the parliamentary election of 1993, which came after months of political strife and was the first national election in Russia coordinated by parties. A post-election survey[48] divulged that only about one voter in three had decided which party list to support as of a month before election day, and one in two deferred decision until the dying days of the campaign or until polling day. Sixty percent waffled until the last moment on whom to choose as the deputy from their single-member district.[49]

The Limits of Uncertainty

If it is something of a truism to say that elections in a transitional setting are steeped in uncertainty, the thought would be incomplete if it did not allow for the complexity of that uncertainty. The syndrome is not unchanging, as the fuller data about decision timing in Table 1.2 clarify. Compared to 1993, the group of citizens who settled on a party list by one month before the 1995 Duma election doubled, and the group that sat on the fence into the closing days of the campaign was halved; there was a fainter trend in the same direction in the territorial districts. By the time Russians elected a president in 1996, almost 80 percent of voters had decided as of the one-month mark. The rhythm of choice in 1993 resembled that of a U.S. presidential primary, whose result may teeter in the balance until the last weekend of stumping in the state; in 1996 it was closer to that of a general presidential election in the United States.[50]

Table 1.2 Timing of Voting Decisions Recalled in Post-Election Surveys (Percentages)

Timing	1993 parliamentary election		1995 parliamentary election		1996 presidential election (first round)[e]
	Party list[a]	District[b]	Party list[c]	District[d]	
Over one month before election	18	9	44	23	64
One month before election	13	10	19	14	14
Two weeks before election	16	19	11	15	7
Final days of campaign	39	42	18	28	9
Election day	12	18	6	17	3
Don't know	2	3	3	3	3

a. N = 2,365 weighted cases.
b. N = 1,715 weighted cases.
c. N = 2,116 weighted cases.
d. N = 1,691 weighted cases.
e. N = 2,016 weighted cases.

Electoral uncertainty in Russia is not unidimensional, either. Volatility, mistrust, catastrophism, and hesitancy are quite dissimilar phenomena, and not always symbiotic. The most hair-raising uncertainty, about social peace and the viability of reforms, need not paralyze transitional citizens or stifle their involvement in elections. On the contrary, this angst can coincide with a keen sense of stake in a campaign and lure citizens into the electoral process, rather than repel them. The survey data show that Russians to whom it was "very important" personally who was elected president in 1996 were twice as likely as the most blasé to fear economic disruption or civil war and four times as likely to be alarmist over forfeiting civic freedoms (see Figure 1.4).[51]

Furthermore, electoral uncertainty in transitional Russia is not unlimited. To say, with Bunce and Csanádi, that the trademark of post-Communism is "the absence of much structure" is not to say *all* structure is absent. Were there to be no structure conferred by institutions, rules, and joint expectations, people would have no way of knowing that an election would indeed take place on the day scheduled, that the parties and candidates listed on the ballot would be the same ones publicized in the campaign, that the official vote count would have any resemblance to the votes cast, that the winners would be sworn into office, and so on. Under absolute uncertainty or something approaching it, citizens would not want to have anything to do with elections and, for that matter, governments would not bother running the election gauntlet.

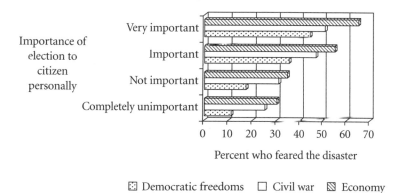

Figure 1.4. Fears of Disaster Resulting from the 1996 Presidential Election: Percentages by Degree of Importance of the Election to Citizen

The fact is that Russia's leaders, disregarding whatever siren songs urge them to act differently, have held national elections on time and in rough compliance with preset procedures.[52] And, as will be demonstrated in Chapter 2, most Russians are interested in these elections, follow them through multiple information channels, and turn out to vote in them. A post-Communist election may be an amateur and indecorous occasion, but it is not a maelstrom empty of rhyme or reason. A democracy, as Przeworski has it, is the incarnation of organized uncertainty; democratizing societies live with *semi-organized uncertainty* in which constraints are weak but not altogether absent.

Can uncertainty in and of itself explain citizen behavior in elections? Some recent work on Western political systems, inspired by Anthony Downs, links uncertainty, knowledge, and information to voting decisions. But scholars have used these variables to supplement and perfect inherited models resting on other, more essential factors, not to fabricate alternate models.[53]

In the former Soviet Union, uncertainty as such will not move us very far toward a picture of the mainsprings of voting. Consider what we know from Figures 1.2 and 1.3 about volatility in the Russian vote. The hopscotching from party to party and from one party family to another between 1993 and 1995 signifies massive uncertainty. But it begs the question why some parties and party families fare better than others and what the impetus is for individuals to act. Uncertainty may explain why switching is rife but not why, say, a large majority of Russia's Choice and LDPR supporters switch in 1995 when only a small minority of KPRF supporters do the same. Nor does uncertainty give us a grip on the switchers' destinations. It might assign voters such-and-such a probability of abjuring the party or party family they used to favor; it could not foretell which among the plethora of alternatives they would choose. All the more so for first-time voters, who were legion in 1995: uncertainty would not prescribe the place they would alight, only that the search might be arduous.[54]

Scholars of post-Soviet affairs have attempted to deduce more concrete predictions about mass politics and voting from their reading of the transition's high-uncertainty ambience. Bunce and Csanádi, for instance, point out the social homogenization effectuated by Communism and the inconclusiveness of economic and socioeconomic change under new governments, and go from there to sound a general note of skepticism:

Liberal politics cannot materialize before liberal economics. This is because the socioeconomic base of political pluralism—that is, a capitalist
economy that defines interests—is not yet in place . . . What this means in
practice is that politics is not anchored in the social and economic structure and is, as a result, extraordinarily fluid. Thus it is quite difficult for
citizens to "attach" in any enduring way to the system-in-the-making in
general or to parties and interest groups in particular; political participation lacks structure; and politicians find it very hard to be accountable
when they find it hard to determine either their own interests or the interests of their constituents.

In the absence of structure Bunce and Csanádi see only one beacon: "The
usual bases for political identity and for political activity are missing—for
example, class and functionally based interest groups and thus unions and
parties based on them. What this leaves, of course, is *religion and ethnicity*,"
two cultural markers.[55]

Richard Sakwa, in the elections chapter of his textbook on Russian society and politics, likewise plays up flux and disconnectedness. Where institutions are weak and new social classes have not cohered, support for a
political party is "friable and susceptible to rapid changes," while opposition to the government "cannot be taken as a stable political position but
[as] a reflection of temporary antipathies." Voters' reflex in this morass,
Sakwa says, will be to tune in to political personalities, not broader programs. Yeltsin's runaway victory in 1991 and the later success of Vladimir
Zhirinovskii bespeak "the degree to which support for *charismatic personal
leadership* is structured into Russian politics."[56] Geoffrey Evans and Stephen Whitefield have written similarly of "signs across eastern Europe that
the politics of personality and charisma may be more important in struc-
turing political attitudes than that of party competition."[57]

Stephen White, Richard Rose, and Ian McAllister, in the only book-
length study of Russian voting, take yet another tack. They fault some
scholars for organizing opinion research in Russia around seeing how the
natives "measure up to Western standards of democracy." Better, they
say, to assume an "origins model" of behavior in the interregnum, where
uncertainty-burdened citizens fall back on what they know about the former regime and compare it with the new through the prism of tangible experience:

Even though this [old] regime has formally disappeared, it is an axiom of socialization research that many attitudes and patterns of behavior learned in the first decade or two of life persist subsequently . . . [Our] surveys are concerned with how people are reacting to the political and economic transformations around them, of which free elections are but a part. The critical issue for ordinary Russians is not, Would you rather live like Swedes or Californians? but, What do you do to keep body and soul together here and now? . . . In politics, the critical question concerns the *change in regimes.* The old communist regime was a fact that everyone had experienced; the new regime, whatever its character, can thus be compared with the old. The more negative the old appears, the more a change may be welcomed, if only as a lesser evil.[58]

In their analysis of voting, White, Rose, and McAllister underscore citizens' summary evaluations of regimes and, as a subsidiary theme, discuss how the voters apportion blame for economic ills among the government, alien and domestic capitalists, and Communists.

Here we have divergent predictions of what will galvanize the transitional voter. One fixes on ethnic and religious identities, a second on mesmerizing leaders, and a third on evaluations of regimes. All are interesting and believable. But are they correct? Are they bound to be incompatible and competing explanations? Do they exhaust the possibilities? And where do these and other possible explanations stand in relation to the wider comparative enterprise of studying elections?

Comparative Perspectives on Determinants of the Vote

Scholars, in assembling what "may well be the largest literature in all of political science,"[59] have ferreted out and argued the pros and cons of a congeries of factors associated with voting decisions in countries that freely elect their leaders. Revisionism in the field tends to be gentle and absorptive. Variables from once-regnant paradigms live on merrily in backup formation long after new paradigms have climbed to prominence. Consensus is elusive.[60]

Table 1.3 inventories the explanatory variables headlined in two generations of analyzing and theorizing about voting. The horizontal rows define the object whose relationship with the citizen is the cynosure of the inves-

Table 1.3 Principal Explanatory Variables in the Comparative Study of Voting
Behavior

Analytical focus	Time frame	
	Long term	Short term
Social structure	Social and socioeconomic characteristics	Current conditions
Political parties	Partisan identification	Party performance Party promise
Issues	Ideology and principles	Opinions on current issues
Candidates	Founder figures	Incumbents' performance Personal qualities Candidate promise

tigation: social system, parties, public issues, or statesmen. The vertical columns set off long-term manifestations of the variables, operating over
many years or a lifetime, from short-term manifestations during the campaign or at most in the hiatus between elections.

Long-range explanations have predominated in the Americanist and
comparative literatures. The topmost cell has the hoariest pedigree, going
back to the 1940s. As the earliest survey-based study of a U.S. presidential
election, by Paul F. Lazarsfeld and his Columbia University colleagues, put
it, the premise is that "a person thinks, politically, as he is, socially," so that
voting alignments mimic the divisions between groups in society delineated by attributes such as occupation, income, place of residence, and religion.[61] Citizens' psychological identification with political parties, a second
long-range variable, has held pride of place in work on elections in the
United States since the publication of *The American Voter* by four University of Michigan professors in 1960. Skeptics question its centrality and its
portability to other countries; a larger faction keeps the faith.[62] "Issue voting" or "policy voting," highlighted in V. O. Key, Jr.'s *The Responsible Electorate* in 1966, came into its own in electoral studies in the 1970s, as researchers picked up signs of partisan "dealignment" in many polities and
of the rise of self-sufficient voters impelled by life-style and value concerns.[63] "Founder figures" being rarities, the bottom cell in the first column
is underpopulated. It is in France, the only industrial democracy to have
had its constitution torn up and rewritten twice since World War II, that a

perspicacious study spotted "the uniquely central position" of attitudes toward a patriarchal leader—Charles de Gaulle—even in years when he was not himself up for election.[64]

Short-term versions of the same quartet of themes, in the second column of Table 1.3, have garnered many adherents over the last twenty years. On the upper right, voters are said to be guided by current assessments of private and social well-being, chiefly material and financial. In "economic voting," citizens cool on governments when times are hard and warm to them when times are good.[65] The second and fourth cells allude to summary evaluations of how adequately specific parties and politicians satisfy what citizens see as their immediate, down-to-earth needs, as opposed to earning their permanent love and affection (the gist of party identification theory). These evaluations, more focused on governmental performance than are diffuse appraisals of current conditions, can gaze backward to what incumbents have done in the recent past or forward to what they and the opposition might do down the road. Vis-à-vis issues (in the third cell down), scholars have sought to decouple the effects of opinions on matters of present dispute (such as a budgetary measure or law) from more abstract and philosophical questions (such as social egalitarianism or state intervention in the economy).[66] Popular appraisal of the personal magnetism of leaders may also enter into the tableau (viz. the fourth cell). Presidential scholars have said for years that it does, and students of prime ministers and parliamentary systems have lately followed suit.[67]

Obviously, the menu of possible influences on the vote is mammoth. Which factor or factors *actually* steer voting in any given country or countries is resolvable only by appeal to high-quality individual-level data gleaned from voters themselves.

Astute analysts of elections have always grasped that in considering such data they cannot deal with explanatory factors in isolation. Inferences about voting choice normally are distilled from quantitative estimates of the relationships between variables measured numerically over many observations. Estimates of the effect on the vote of any one independent variable or subset of variables will be distorted if other factors correlated both with it and with the outcome are excluded from the analysis—a caveat about "omitted variable bias" which applies to any quantitative or qualitative analysis. A major choice has to do with the order in which variables are deemed to exert their effects. A computer will winkle out statistical associations among a multitude of variables at lightning speed, but the numbers will be hollow if the analyst at the keyboard has no coherent and credible conception of how the pieces of the puzzle interlock.

One answer to the design dilemma is to arrange all explanatory factors of interest in a single batch and relate them to the voting outcome all at once, solving the mathematical problem in one equation. This single-stage procedure is deficient because it dodges questions of causal order and glazes over the prospect that some independent variables will have indirect effects on the political outcome, filtered by variables that are more proximate to the voting decision. Inattention to indirect effects will suppress the impact of variables found toward the beginning of the causal chain.

Specialists on public opinion and elections in the United States have worked up more elaborate statistical models of the formation of voting preferences than the single-stage type. Some of the better known make provision for plural causal stages and take pains to remedy the complications of "endogeneity" or "feedback," whereby the causal dependence of some predictor variables on other variables in the model confounds estimations of forward effects. A sizable number of scholars have subscribed to a statistical technique called "two-stage least squares," which forecasts the values of endogenous variables from designated "exogenous" or "instrument" variables (usually demographic) and then employs the predicted scores to analyze voting behavior.[68]

As a statistical template for analyzing voting choice, the bloc-recursive scheme expounded by Warren E. Miller and J. Merrill Shanks in *The New American Voter* is more realistic and more capacious, and will help frame the analysis in the present volume.[69] It makes room for mediating effects and for multiple causal stages, not limiting their number to two. It incorporates explanatory variables hierarchically in thematic blocs, "each of which may include several specific factors that share the same kind of content and may influence the vote through similar processes or mechanisms."[70] The Miller-Shanks approach is "recursive," that is, unidirectional; features of earlier models inviting two-way "non-recursive" analysis have been discarded.[71] Social and economic indicators, introduced at the initiatory stage, are exogenous to the model but not immaterial to the outcome. As "first causes," they have political effects "as the result of political interaction with the external world"; these interactions show up in the examination of variables in subsequent phases.[72] All explanatory variables are posited to have direct effects on the voting decision, *and* indirect effects relayed by variables following them in the causal progression. Excepting the first-bloc social and economic variables, all variables are affected by antecedent causes; estimates of their direct and indirect effects have to be adjusted for the influence of antecedent and simultaneous causes.

A Voting Model for Transitional Russia

Where does this ratiocination take us with regard to voting decisions in protodemocratic Russia? It would be a mistake to take insights cultivated in the United States or any other contemporary political system and casually repot them in Russian soil, unamended and unadapted. A transitional society is not yet a perennial democracy, and Moscow is not Minneapolis or Manchester. History supplies contingencies that parallel certain aspects of Russian life in the 1990s more closely than present examples. How exciting it would be if in pursuit of our theoretical interests we could rigorously compare party formation and voting in Russia with embattled new democracies in the past—in Jacksonian America, let us say, or pre-World War I France or Italy, Weimar Germany, or India after the partition. But we immediately run into a dearth in such places of the individual-level data that are necessary for modeling the vote. Accidents of timing and resource endowment have forever robbed us of the opportunity.[73]

Any conclusion, however, that we should start an inquiry into a late democratizer like Russia from scratch would be foolhardy. To blindfold ourselves to the accumulated social science is just as futile as to import extraneous findings uncritically. The smart strategy is to utilize the comparative literature, not ignore it—but utilize it as a store of hypotheses and hunches and not of canned answers.

It will disappoint anyone looking for pat answers that there is no unanimity among scholars about how strongly the causal factors recited in Table 1.3 shade voting decisions in all democracies or even in any one democracy. Instead of a synthetic theory of electoral behavior to which a study such as this must conform, the received knowledge consists of:

- A set of priority questions about origins of the vote, generally taking the form of propositions about the absolute importance of a particular variable or assemblage of variables;
- Understandings about which variables rank highest in impact;
- Constantly evolving empirical investigations, most often into circum-

scribed facets of electoral behavior (such as party identification, economic voting, or leadership effects), which then spin off refinements of previous understandings; and

- Recurrent and at times circular controversies about facts and method.

For the purposes of opening up a subfield like the study of transitional voting, the crucial contribution is the first—the questions to be asked. Here we do not have to pick and choose before lining up the evidence. Unraveling the determinants of the vote is not an all-or-nothing project: many variables may fit the bill to a greater or lesser degree. In the United States, whose voters have been poked and prodded the most by researchers over the years, the exhaustive study by Miller and Shanks decided that variables in almost all the cells in Table 1.3 had some significant impact on how citizens voted in the 1992 presidential election. The Miller-Shanks volume is not in the slightest an outlier in the breadth of its interests and findings. For example, a superb study of the Canadian federal election of 1988 concluded that "virtually every imaginable element in the calculus of voting exhibited dynamics and virtually every element mattered in the final choice."[74]

The explanations I abstracted above from works on post-Communist politics and elections can easily be slotted into the panoply of theoretical explanations propounded in the comparative literature. The Bunce-Csanádi thesis about religious and ethnic influences would fit in the upper left cell of Table 1.3. Sakwa's exegesis of the charismatic appeal of Russian leaders belongs in the fourth cell on the right. And White, Rose, and McAllister's position on the decisive effect of evaluations of regimes and of blame for economic hardship would go in the upper right-hand corner, and in the third cell down on either the left or the right.

There is nothing wrong with these several assertions, as far as they go. But to test for the applicability of any one of them the analyst risks finding spurious relationships if he expunges correlated variables. And, if we aim for an overall reconstruction of voting in a transitional democracy, it makes no sense to leave off our rota of potentially useful explanations factors which the comparative research has found to be compellingly predictive of electoral behavior. Without being encyclopedic, we are close enough to square one in the study of post-Communist citizenship to be glad to err on the side of catholicity in drawing up our hypotheses. Whether the hypotheses are confirmed or disproved by the data is a separate question. Research on post-Soviet elections has until now been unduly selective in this connection.[75]

A final caution we may take from the U.S. and comparative literature is about the importance of sequence in pulling explanatory variables into the analysis. Studies of Russian elections until now have by and large used single-stage statistical models of the vote—with all of the predictable headaches in terms of neglect of causal ordering and of mediated effects.[76] A more exacting method is required.

Variables and Causal Stages

What, then, are the explanatory variables to be included in a model of voting in Russia, and in what order should they be examined?

In scrutinizing quadrennial U.S. presidential elections, Miller and Shanks for their own good reasons rely on eight clusters of variables, which they bale into six stages or blocs. They alertly pry clues about causal order from the accrued knowledge about temporal sequencing. They assert that social and economic attributes, party identification, and policy-related predispositions all predate the passions stirred in the heat of an American campaign and can be "treated as 'givens' for the current election—on the assumption that they were already 'in place' before the current campaign began and were generally not changed by short-term forces based on campaign issues or candidate personality."[77]

Unless and until experience instructs us otherwise, broad-gauged variables in determinate categories implanted in comparative theory are the best point of departure for analyzing elections in Russia or any protodemocracy. The conceptual categories they set forth are commodious enough to cope with new cases, just as a powerful theory of the origins of war can be adapted to study a great variety of international conflicts, or a theory of language acquisition can be put into use in Kenya or Catalonia.[78] It goes without saying that the variable types must be applied with sensitivity to historical and cultural facts and amended as needed to ensure that factors or sequences integral to transitional mass politics are not shortchanged. The variables are shorthand for multiplex conditions, attitudes, and behaviors, not bloodless abstractions. We should not hesitate to bring out the sometimes staggering differences between Russian and Western conditions within the ambit of the factor types. In-category comparisons, after all, may silhouette dissimilarities as starkly as they do similarities. For example, historians have shown that leaders' ideas of the good society, and the way they put them across to mass publics, helped determine the very different responses to the Great Depression in North America and Germany. Political opinions decisively shaped electoral and policy outcomes in each country, but the opinions and outcomes themselves could hardly have been more disparate—regulated capitalism in the United States' New Deal, agrarian socialism on the Canadian prairies, and Nazism in Germany.[79]

Figure 1.5 is a schematic rendering of the variable types and presumptive sequences that form the causal model of transitional voting I will probe in this book. The model at this juncture is heuristic only. Whether the associations diagrammed here pertain in real life, and their relative strength, will be ascertained through quantitative analysis. The construct contains one fewer variable type than Miller and Shanks' but the same number of causal rungs. Following bloc-recursive logic, the multistage model assumes that influence is unidirectional and that clusters of explanatory variables exert direct influence on voting choice and indirect influence transmitted by other variables.

As the boxes and directional arrows in Figure 1.5 indicate, I propose for testing purposes that the background social characteristics of Russia's transitional citizens may enter into the causal flow culminating in the vote at its first and most elementary stage, that their assessments of current and economic and political conditions may join in at a second stage, and fondness for a party and issue opinions at a third stage. The fourth through sixth stages of the model are reserved for other blocs of factors—Russians' retrospective evaluations of the job governmental incumbents have done (in stage four), their assessments of the leadership qualities of politicians (in stage five), and their prospective evaluations of how parties and candidates will govern (in stage six)—that are progressively closer to the electoral choice.

A prefatory word is in order about our explanatory variables and sequencing.

SOCIAL STRUCTURE AND SYSTEM TRANSFORMATION.   Russia, like all modern countries, has a multidimensional social structure within which individuals can be located on the strength of recognizable demographic traits. There should be no impediment to verifying with survey data assertions about the connection (or connections, or lack thereof) between that

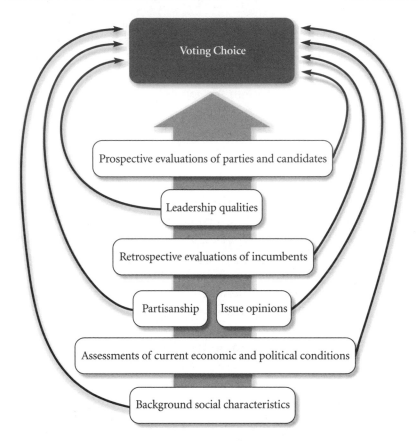

Figure 1.5. Schematic Causal Model of Russian Voting

structure, still mostly a bequest from the Soviet period, and electoral behavior. The persistent social characteristics of individuals cannot be derivatives of those individuals' attitudes and beliefs.[80] Such characteristics must accordingly be located at the front end of any causal sequence terminating in the vote. Not all social cleavages are frozen in place, even in a stable society. Since Russia is midpassage in a revolution, a sea change that has frayed and torn many ties between persons and groups, it behooves us to give thought to changing as well as unchanging personal characteristics and social relationships.

The current conditions of life for the average Russian are appalling beyond the experience of most Westerners. Russians have pronounced views on the transformation and, some would say, the degradation of their country which they are not reticent to share with survey personnel. In the transitional milieu, perceptions of society's current predicament should enter into the determination of electoral preferences at an earlier phase than in seasoned democracies. Miller and Shanks maintain that in the tranquil United States the effects on political behavior of short-term citizen concerns (chiefly pocketbook economic concerns) mostly "occur through the activation of relatively longstanding predispositions," including partisan identification and issue stances;[81] ergo, they put them in the third of their six blocs. For Russia, underinstitutionalized and in dire straits economically and politically, it is more credible that impressions of the status quo would govern attitudes toward parties and public issues—and affect the vote through them—than vice versa. That is how I will set up the problem. A similar sequence has been put to fruitful use for some years now by scholars studying mass satisfaction with political and economic change in post-Communist countries.[82]

In analyzing the electoral effects of perceptions of current conditions, I will make another modification to the stock sequence: to subsume an expressly political element under voter assessments. The metamorphosis of Russia and other once Communist countries is about politics no less than about economic welfare and social structure. There is every reason for citizens, in sizing up the country's plight, to be moved by political perceptions in addition to economic and social issues.

POLITICAL PARTIES.   Almost all electoral scholars in the West put much theoretical stress on psychic bonds to political parties, which they find to be among the most durable of all political phenomena and to be intimately linked to voting preference. Miller and Shanks state that apart from its large direct influence on the presidential vote, party identification in the United States "exerts a pervasive indirect influence by shaping many of the other mediating political attitudes that have an impact on the vote."[83] So taken are they by the sweep and power of partisan loyalty that they consign it to the second-from-the-beginning of their causal stages.

We can be under no illusion that stable partisan identification in its classic Western guise exists in the Russian Federation so soon after the dawn of democratic politics. The data will bear out, nonetheless, that a sizable segment of the electorate betrays evidence of a precursor of party identification, an elective affinity which I label "transitional partisanship." To test for the effects it may have on the vote, I consign it to the third of our six explanatory stages, giving it a place in my interpretation but not imagining it in the strategic, formative role it assumes in interpretations of American or British electoral politics.

Many Russian citizens do not yet have affective ties to political parties. But that should not disqualify them from making instrumental assessments of government and opposition parties. Short-term retrospective evaluations of the incumbent party are encapsulated in the fourth stage of Figure 1.5; prospective evaluations of incumbent and opposition parties, and of what they should be able to accomplish for the voter and the country, are in the sixth stage.[84] My imperfect measures of these variables furnish some basis for judgment of electoral impact. The analysis is complicated in Russia by the proliferation of parties, by their lesser involvement in presidential than in parliamentary electioneering, and by placing the responsibility for governmental performance with the president, an act which pushes parliament and its party fractions toward the margins of high politics.

ISSUES.   Another cog that may conceivably drive Russian voters is their normative opinions on the issues of the day. Theories of voting in the West differentiate between ideational and moral predispositions on the one hand and preferences on issues of tighter scope and more fleeting duration on the other. The first set ought to have some influence on the second, and so be situated upstream from it in any causal model. Miller and Shanks roost policy-related predispositions, which they take to be resistant to change, in the second of their blocs of variables, together with partisan identification, and relegate current policy preferences to the third bloc, alongside perceptions of current conditions.

For post-Soviet Russia, as we shall see, this bifurcation of issues is insupportable. Formal ideology is impoverished and does not provide a compass to most voters. Russians' attitudes toward the most basic questions prove to be no sturdier than their other political attitudes. More telling, in a country in transition the border between fundamental predispositions and current controversies is porous. In a sense, the hot short-term issues are about whether and on whose terms the long-term reworking of society is to go forward. Therefore we will look for the electoral consequences of issue opinions not at two stages but at one stage of the analysis, in the third of our six blocs—the same stage as partisanship.[85]

CANDIDATES. Candidate effects, which have tweaked the interest of some scholars of the transition but have not been carefully studied, are taken up in the last three stages of my retracing of the Russian vote. Post facto evaluations of the sitting president and government fit into the fourth stage; the personalities and styles of party leaders and presidential contenders, which are apt to be affected by retrospective evaluations, into the fifth stage; and forward-looking evaluations of politicians, which will be affected by both of the foregoing blocs, into the sixth stage.

As with policy issues, long-term and short-term modes are entwined here. So long as the architect of the new Russian state, Yeltsin, has lingered on the podium, popular perceptions of him have overlapped percep-tions of the whole epoch of change over which he has presided. In explain-ing his capture of a second term in 1996, the task is to disentangle this iconic status from the more pedestrian ingredients that go into the images of individual candidates anywhere—approval of record in office, persona, and anticipated performance after the election—and to stack up all candi-date-related factors against other variables. This needs to be done also for Yeltsin's adversaries.

In the 1995 parliamentary contest the imperial presidency was not at is-sue, but we still wanted to find out if attitudes toward the overweening Yeltsin intruded on the contest. The parties on the ballot, too, all flaunted leaders of their own. Many of these politicos were household names, and most had headed their organizations since their inception. To what extent, we wish to learn, do voters relate to them as individuals and not as symbols of their parties, and how important are leadership effects as compared to other causal variables?

Preview of the Book

My choices about the content and mode of presentation of the book have been made in the interests of cohesion, clarity, and readability.

Parties and Candidates

For most of *Transitional Citizens,* I will elaborate explanations of voter choice in two consecutive Russian elections—the State Duma vote of De-cember 1995 and the two-round presidential election of June-July 1996. I do not have the Americanist's luxury of having only a neat pair of national parties and their presidential standard bearers to reckon with. Political parties and presidential candidates come by the bushel in Russia. It is not feasible to put equal emphasis on them all; even if it were, few readers would wade through the written product.

When it is appropriate to look at the embryonic party system as a whole or at groupings within it, as in the perusal of partisanship in Chapter 4, I do that. Since proportional-representation votes are cast for parties and not for party families as catalogued by the external observer, fine-grained analysis of voting decisions is doable only for parties.[86] My choice is to target the quartet of parties that overcame the 5 percent threshold in the 1995 PR vote—the KPRF, the LDPR, Our Home Is Russia, and Yabloko:

- The KPRF, the largest by a country mile of the four socialist parties competing, got almost one-quarter of the valid votes in 1995. Registered in February 1993 as the successor to the outlawed CPSU,[87] it has the most élan and the most active local branches of any Russian party and has offered the bluntest alternative to the nascent post-Soviet regime. The KPRF houses social democrats in company with hard-line Marxist-Leninists, and laces its propaganda with vehement anti-Americanism and anti-Westernism, fervent Russian patriotism, and nostalgia for the Soviet Union.[88]
- The comically misnamed "Liberal-Democratic" LDPR, the noisiest of the six nationalist parties registered in 1995 and the most proficient at bagging votes, won 11.40 percent of the popular vote, two years after it sent shockwaves when its party list finished first in the inaugural Duma election.[89] A thorn in the side of the government and Westernizing liberals since March 1990, it is one of the oldest post-Communist parties. Its "leader for life," the irrepressible demagogue Vladimir Zhirinovskii, campaigns under the slogan "No to the Breakdown of Russia!" (*Net—razvalu Rossii!*).
- Our Home Is Russia, the party of government or, as Russians nickname it, "the party of power" *(partiya vlasti)*, was slapped together only seven months before the 1995 election, in which it took 10.33 percent of the votes. Its leader, then Prime Minister Chernomyrdin, for most of his career a bureaucrat in the Soviet petroleum industry, packed its ticket with functionaries, businessmen, and entertainment celebrities.

- Yabloko, the most popular of the twelve liberal factions registered in 1995, received 7.02 percent of the party-list vote that December. It was set up on the eve of the 1993 election by the economist Grigorii Yavlinskii, Vladimir Lukin, a former Russian ambassador to Washington, and Yurii Boldyrev, a corruption-fighting intellectual from St. Petersburg who soon quit it in a huff. Yavlinskii was the paramount leader from the beginning. The appellation Yabloko, Russian for "apple," is a play on the first letters of the triumvirate's names.

These organizations collected 51.48 percent of the popular vote between them in 1995 and were awarded 100 percent of the party-list seats owing to the 5 percent cutoff. They represent all but one of Russia's six party families. The only parts of the spectrum left out are the Lilliputian miscellaneous parties, which took in a puny 2.54 percent of the votes between them in 1995, and the centrist grouping, which got 14.59 percent all told. No centrist party made it over the 5 percent barrier. The feminist Women of Russia, the most successful, made the grade in 1993 but was held to 4.70 percent in 1995.

For the presidential election of June-July 1996, when the choice was about politicians and not parties, I draw a bead on the four who led the pack—Boris Yeltsin, Gennadii Zyuganov, Aleksandr Lebed, and Grigorii Yavlinskii:

- Yeltsin (b. 1931), the federation's one and only president, campaigned for reelection in 1996 as the paladin of the political and economic establishment, declaring that only he could prevent Russia's return to the Gulag concentration camps and rationing coupons of Communism. He took 35.79 percent of the valid votes in the qualifying round and 54.40 percent in the runoff duel with Zyuganov.
- The head of the KPRF, Zyuganov (b. 1944), drew 32.49 percent in the first round and 40.73 percent in the runoff. He had masterminded the party's phoenix-like rebirth and entry into electoral politics in 1993. In appearance almost a caricature of the stolid Soviet *apparatchik,* Zyuganov has considerable skills as a polemicist and organizer. He was officially nominated in 1996 by a "Bloc of Popular-Patriotic Forces of Russia" under KPRF tutelage.
- From the nationalist camp we will spotlight the former paratroop general, Aleksandr Lebed (b. 1950), who eclipsed Zhirinovskii in 1996, gaining 14.73 percent of the ballots in the first round and finishing

third. The plain-spoken Lebed had been co-leader of the nationalist KRO (Congress of Russian Communities) in the 1995 Duma election. On record as extolling Chilean strongman Augusto Pinochet, he spoke out for a crackdown on crime and corruption but was a moderate on Chechnya and had little by way of an economic program. He was to endorse Yeltsin in the runoff and work for three months as his national security adviser, brokering a truce and interim pact with the Chechen guerrillas. According to our data, 57 percent of Lebed's first-round supporters voted for Yeltsin in the second round.

• Yabloko's Yavlinskii (b. 1952), well known as one of the drafters of the "500 Days" program for marketizing the Soviet economy in 1990, came fourth in 1996 with 7.45 percent of the votes. He campaigned on promises to step up economic reform, bring the boys home from Chechnya, and improve human rights. Although he did not endorse Yeltsin, 67 percent of those who voted for Yavlinskii in the first round voted for Yeltsin in the runoff.

We again address most of the main tendencies in Russian electoral politics. Left out are only fringe elements and centrists, who were all but blanked in the presidential vote.[90] The big four presidential contenders harvested 90.45 percent of the first-round popular vote, 39 percentage points more than the four most proficient parties had in 1995. This alone should awaken us to the refracting role of electoral rules and context, a recurring motif in the book.[91]

Statistical Method

An ever-expanding arsenal of statistical methods has been deployed to calculate influences on modern electorates. Miller and Shanks relate individual attributes and attitudes to the vote in the United States through the familiar device of linear or ordinary least squares (OLS) regression. Linear regression may be a defensible method for the analysis of simple choices, such as whether to support the Democratic or the Republican nominee in a U.S. presidential race.[92] It would misrepresent the convoluted decisions voters are compelled to make in a country like Russia, which does not have a disciplined party system or other institutions or protocols that would order or streamline their options.

For digging into the statistical relationships underpinning voting in transitional Russia, I use the method of multinomial logit, a maximum likelihood algorithm which reliably estimates the effects of explanatory variables on outcomes comprising multiple nonordered categories. (See the more detailed discussion of estimation and testing in Appendix B.)[93] To make the findings intelligible and interpretable, I work not with the raw regression coefficients, which are obscure quantities low on intrinsic value, but with fitted probabilities of specific outcomes occurring under counterfactual conditions simulated by the investigator. The key parameters I adduce state the change in the probability of obtaining a given voting outcome that is associated with a change in an explanatory variable from its minimum to its maximum value. In its simplest form, such a statistic describes the bivariate relationship between a particular explanatory variable and electoral choice, without reference to any other variables. Usually, though, it is necessary to go on to estimate an explanatory variable's influence on voting behavior as other causal factors are brought into the equation. Typically, I present a series of such statistics, organized into a table. The analytical strategy is close to that codified by Miller and Shanks, whose statistics are OLS regression coefficients:

> [These] coefficients [come] from a sequence of multivariate analyses which allow the analyst to consider statistical controls for different combinations of the other explanatory variables in our model. The more important of these analyses are designed to remove the confounding effects of other explanatory variables that we have assigned to a prior stage, or to the same stage, in our model. These analyses take into account or control for variables whose apparent influence on the vote might otherwise be confused with that of the explanatory variable being examined. From those analyses, we have designated one coefficient for each explanatory variable as our preferred estimate of its "apparent total effect" on the vote . . . [That] coefficient . . . should be regarded as an approximation of the overall extent to which differences between voters on that variable were in fact responsible for "producing" differences between them in their vote.[94]

I retain the term "total effect" for the reduced-form statistic, although, to repeat, the quantities I adduce are logit-based first differences in predicted probabilities, not linear regression coefficients. Statistical control for other variables is achieved by holding them constant at their medians as values are fitted. Once total effects have been computed, additional statistics perform a different but related service:

> Several additional coefficients [to excerpt Miller and Shanks again] . . . suggest the ways in which that total effect may have been mediated by variables which we have assigned to causal stages lying between it and the vote. In general, each of the total effects for an explanatory variable in "earlier" stages in our model may include a variety of indirect effects, based on that variable's influence on other explanatory variables that are more proximate to the vote.[95]

Although my measures differ mathematically from Miller and Shanks' coefficients, their function is fundamentally the same.

Chapter Plan

The questions framed in this introduction reel systematically through the length of the book. Chapter 2 gives a bottom-up view of electoral participation and electoral campaigns in Russia, as they appear to its citizens; the extant literature scans these phenomena mostly from the top down, as they appear to parties and candidates. This chapter lays a descriptive groundwork for the analysis of the microfoundations of the vote, which is our main preoccupation.

In carrying out that analysis, I will proceed from blocs of variables that come into the molding of Russians' voting preferences at earlier stages to variables that come in at later stages. Chapter 3 takes up the electoral influence of social structure and current conditions in the country. Chapter 4 concerns the genesis and ramifications of partisan attachments in the Russian electorate. Chapter 5 discusses the influence of voters' opinions about normative issues. Chapter 6 moves on to their retrospective and prospective evaluations of incumbents and oppositionists and their appreciations of the personal charisma and competence of leaders.

In each of these chapters I review the theoretical reasoning that upholds the relevance of the explanatory variables, specify their observable implications, report the distribution of indicators of the variables in the Russian population, and generate statistical measures of their impact on the vote. As we shift from one knot of explanatory variables to another, I keep the full suite of variable types in play, eschewing ad hoc analysis.

The cause-by-cause, stage-by-stage layout of the book puts the onus on

Chapter 7 to weave the threads together into a succinct overview of voting in Russia. In it I group variables by type and come to tentative conclusions about which blocs are most important to citizen decisions in the transition. I go on to ponder the signature qualities of transitional citizenship and the future of electoral politics as society and polity continue to change. In the end, good social science is about "explaining as much as possible with as little as possible."[96] Confronted with a multicornered research problem as rich and as poorly charted as this one, we can reach the terminus only through way stations where we systematically encounter the principal pieces of the whole.

2

Transitional Citizens and the Electoral Process

The sight of Russians streaming into their local precincts to pronounce on who is fit to rule them is as startling a transposition of conventional imagery as a takeover by Maoist guerrillas would be in the United States. They are citizens neither by birthright nor by considered choice. Their political entitlements were handed to them on a silver platter—revocably by a fading Soviet regime and then (supposedly) irrevocably in post-Soviet laws adopted with much fanfare but little public deliberation. Article 3(3) of Russia's constitution proclaims free elections "the supreme direct expression of the people's authority." That document, bristling with inconsistencies and lame clauses,[1] does not give guidance on how the people's authority is to be exercised and respected.

Before examining influences on Russians' voting preferences, we would do well to form an impression of citizen involvement in the climactic act of voting and in the campaign pageant that precedes it. The Soviet system, until Mikhail Gorbachev stood it on its head, stripped its subjects of discretion on both counts. Showing up to vote in ersatz elections was for ablebodied adults a nonnegotiable obligation, enforced through moral suasion, intimidation, and the bribe of snacks and beer at the polling place. Once on site, failure to vote for the one name on the ballot, the anointed candidate of the "Bloc of Communists and Non-Party Members," was to invite reprisal from the powers-that-be.[2] The *agitprop* "pre-election campaign," so-called, was programmed to wring out a numerical result specified to specks of the last percentage point. From start to finish, the populace was cast as an adoring chorus, "a purely demonstrative and supportive force with no real opportunity of indicating policy preference."[3]

For a decade now, Russians have been electoral grownups, deciding for themselves in secret whether and for whom to vote and hooking up with campaigns of their own volition. All this would seem to put them on a par with voters in the long-lived democracies of the West. But does it really? From some portrayals of the rampant uncertainties of post-Communism, one would have to guess the opposite, that individuals will be overtaxed by the electoral process and by their political habitat in general. When they "feel defenseless in the face of a bombarding environment," and decision making "tends to be frenzied and irrational,"[4] how could it be otherwise?

The first section of this chapter outlines the extent and the correlates of Russians' electoral participation, situating it in the portfolio of political action routines available to them. Although behavioral options in their infant democracy deviate little in the abstract from other modern countries, the balance among options taken is more heavily weighted than usual toward electoral endeavors. Competitive elections, which only a few years ago knocked the Soviet government to its knees, now provide the most steadily trod path for input into the ramshackle system that replaced it. We need to understand what kinds of citizens participate in and decline to participate in elections and why.

The second and third sections of the chapter recap from a comparative vantage point the extent of public involvement in the campaign prologue to the vote.[5] The aim here is to ask what the conduits are through which Russians learn about elections, share in the hoopla of campaigning, and receive voting cues, and what this implies about the resources they have in their possession as they set about voting: does the electoral process give them the information they need to act responsibly, or does it leave them hostage to desultory and one-sided communication?

Campaigners in Russia have their work cut out for them. They must whet the interest of humble folk who have many preoccupations other than politics, a familiar enough story in many countries. But those extrapolitical diversions are exceptionally pressing in such a stressed-out society, and the members of the audience, previously captive but now emancipated, can be ornery: after all, they are no longer forced to hang on the words of politicians. The organizations that back particular candidates are so hit-and-miss that many voters have very little or no direct contact with them or their emissaries during a campaign. Hence much of the information surrounding a Russian election percolates through indirect channels: places of work and secondary associations to a minor extent; interactions with fellow citizens and the mass media to a major extent. Dependency on the media and above all on television kindles misgivings about the quality and heterogeneity of voters' intake. The inverted sequence in which campaign technologies have been put into play—with slick broadcast methods being introduced at a dazzling pace while traditional, low-technology methods languish at a primitive level—leads me to earmark a section of this chapter for the media and campaigns, bringing the discussion to land on the issue of voter competence.

Voting as Political Participation

Let us begin with voting turnout. In national elections turnout spans a broad gamut among democratic polities, from about one-half of the qualified population to more than 90 percent. A review of voting in twenty-four industrial democracies since World War II calculated average rates to be 82 percent in the 1950s and 76 percent in the 1990s. The United States was consistently near the bottom of the list and Australia and several West European countries near the top.[6]

Russian voting on preliminary showing makes it onto the democratic continuum, though at its apathetic lower end. All nonincarcerated citizens aged eighteen and over are eligible to vote at the polling station in their urban neighborhood or rural administrative center. There is no registration procedure beyond the Stalinist system of compulsory registration *(propiska)* of one's place of residence with the police; citizens abroad may vote at a Russian consulate.[7] Officially announced participation in elections since independence was heaviest in the first round of the 1996 presidential ballot (69.70 percent) and lightest in the parliamentary election cum constitutional plebiscite of 1993 (54.37 percent); in the 1995 parliamentary election it came in about midway between them (at 64.38 percent) and in the presidential runoff in 1996 it was a tad short of the first round (at 68.89 percent).[8] Mean turnout in the four polls, 64.34 percent, surpasses only two industrial democracies in the 1990s—Switzerland (46 percent) and the United States (53 percent)—and is 12 percent beneath the average.[9] Russia's most ebullient turnout, in June 1996, straggles behind eighteen of the twenty-four country averages.[10]

No one would tout the Russian Federation as a sparkling paragon of voter participation. But it would be wise to refrain from too reproachful a verdict. It is poignant to document that Russia's rookie citizens, meager as their experience of democracy is, put the franchise to fuller use than members of the world's oldest democracy. Moreover, the favorable longitudinal comparison with the pre-Gorbachev USSR[11] should count as much as the unfavorable cross-national comparison with the bulk of the institutionalized democracies. Uncoerced, two-thirds of the Russian electorate, in round numbers, has voted in any one federal election and one-third has not. The contrast with Soviet practice, where spontaneous participation in elections was designed out of the system, is crisper than with normal Western levels.

The vote should be assessed in the company of other modes of democratic participation. Behavioral scholars distinguish four chief modes aside from voting: pitching in on a political campaign; communal activity through neighborhood and other associations; contacting officials on matters bearing on the individual or household; and acts of protest such as signing a petition or taking part in an anti-government march or strike.[12]

Civic exertion other than voting can as a rule be gauged only through a sample survey. Surveys are also indispensable for determining the incidence of all modes of participation, voting among them, and for explaining participation and nonparticipation. They invariably overstate the frequency of voting, often by 10 to 20-plus percentage points, for several reasons: the winnowing of many apolitical individuals out of the survey sample through their refusal to be interviewed; artificial incitement of political interest by the interviews themselves; and the propensity of some informants to "exaggerate or lie about their political involvement and the frequency of their voting in order not to appear to be violating social norms."[13] Nonetheless, scrupulously gathered survey data have enabled political scientists to assemble composite profiles of citizen activism.[14]

Electoral surveys in Russia, as elsewhere, over-report voting. The discrepancy between the participation claimed by members of our 1995–96 survey panel and turnout in the official communiqués was 17 percent for the parliamentary election and 15 percent and 13 percent for rounds one and two of the presidential election.[15]

That having been said, the data leave no doubt that voting towers over all other participatory modes in Russia, and that it does so more than it would in an established democracy. Participation in the basic modes of civic action, as imparted to interviewers after the State Duma election of 1995, is itemized in Table 2.1.[16] On three of the five dimensions, Russia does not much undershoot the international norm. Two of the three—the vote and campaign activism, official and unofficial—are bound up with

Table 2.1 Political Activity in Russia, as Reported in 1995 Survey (Percentages)[a]

Mode and activity	Participation
Voting	
In 1995 election[b]	82
In 1993 election (among age-eligible)[c]	65
Campaign activity	
Participated in 1995 campaign, tried to persuade others how to vote	28
Member of political party or movement	1
Communal activity	
Member of community improvement, environmental, or women's organization	1
Contacting officials "on problems that concern you and your family"	
At least several times a year	12
Less often	25
Protest	
Ever signed a petition	8
Ever participated in a demonstration, strike, or boycott	3

a. N = 2,774 weighted cases (post-election survey), except for voting in 1993. Some respondents were interviewed in January 1996

b. For party lists only. Seventy-five percent said they voted for a candidate in their territorial district.

c. Question asked in 1995 pre-election survey. Includes only respondents who were eighteen years of age or older in December 1993 (N = 2,756 weighted cases).

elections. The third is particularized contacts with officials. About one in three Americans make these no less than once a year;[17] nearly 40 percent of Russians make them now and then.[18] For the fourth and fifth modalities, communal activity and protest, there is more of a gulf between Russian and Western levels of participation. Only 1 percent of Russians belong to a community action, ecological, or women's group, whereas 18 percent of Americans and 11 percent of Britons and Germans did in the early 1990s. More than half of those polled in the United States and many West European countries had put their names to a petition and 20 to 40 percent had partaken of a more strident act of civil disobedience. Russia, where about 10 percent of our sample ever in their lifetimes joined in a protest action, again trails behind them.[19]

Figure 2.1 sums up what we know about rates of political participation in post-Soviet Russia, mining the same survey data from 1995 and giving overlaps among the modes. Less than 10 percent of its transitional citizens are totally inactive. Two in five confine themselves to voting[20] and a smidgen over one-half to voting plus campaign activity. Another two-fifths of the population combine some other mode, typically particularized contacting, with election-linked activity. Only several percent participate exclusively outside the electoral realm. The repertoire is skewed toward election-related acts.

Voting and Nonvoting

Excepting those few democracies that legislate compulsory voting, citizens have the right not to vote. No one should begrudge Russians this right; not having had it until so late, they would be loath to part with it now. So long as it does not become the prevalent mode, nonvoting can coexist on quite a large scale with a lively democratic politics. American turnout statistics constantly remind us this is so.

Nonvoting is pernicious to citizenship and political cohesion when it is repetitive, willful, and proselytizing. Among Russians, such behavior has thus far been the exception and not the rule, with no large reserve of chronic abstainers or electoral dropouts. True, more than 60 percent of the age-eligible members of our survey panel who opted not to vote in the 1995 Duma election recollected that they had not taken part in the low-turnout election of 1993 either (see Table 2.2). Yet most of these same per-

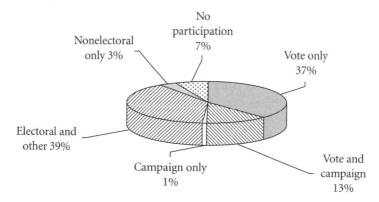

Figure 2.1. Voting in the Participatory Mix, 1995 Data

Table 2.2 Behavior of 1995 Nonvoters

Behavior	Percentage
Recalled voting in 1993 parliamentary election[a]	37
Intended to abstain in pre-election interview[b]	36
Decided to abstain in final days of campaign or election day[b]	53
Voted in 1996 presidential election[c]	
Either round	73
Both rounds	52
Urged others to abstain in 1995[b]	3

a. Only respondents of voting age in 1993 (N = 477 weighted cases).
b. N = 483 weighted cases.
c. N = 434 weighted cases.

sons did not indicate that their abstention in 1995 was premeditated. Only about one in three abstainers said in the pre-election interview that they had made up their minds to boycott.[21] When interrogated after election day, more than half of them said they had come to the decision not to vote during the last few days of the campaign. And three-quarters of the 1995 nonvoters returned to vote in one or both rounds of the presidential election six months later.

Nor do we find much evidence of Russian abstainers, habitual or casual, acting as evangelists for nonparticipation. Hardly any nonvoters—3 percent in December 1995—bestir themselves to coax their peers into following their lead. And those who do are ignored: the abstention rate among persons urged by others not to vote in 1995 was less than 1 percent higher than among persons who got no such advice.

Who tends to vote in democratizing Russia and who does not? Comparative studies of participation find variation in turnout by demographic group and social position. Especially common are differences along the lines of age and educational attainment.[22] Both these characteristics prove to be bound up with Russian voting—a sign of normalcy of sorts.

The connection between electoral participation and age in Russia has already assumed the curvilinear shape it takes in most democracies. As Figure 2.2 traces it for the 1995 parliamentary election, voting is about 20 percentage points higher among persons in middle age and the early retirement years than among the under-thirties, and about 10 percent higher than among people over the age of sixty-nine.[23] This ordinariness is some-

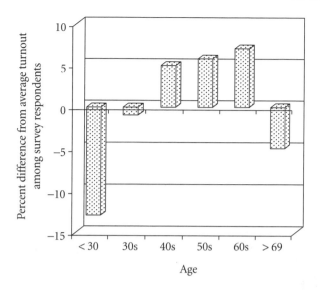

Figure 2.2. Age and Voting Turnout, 1995

thing of a disappointment: the young adults who suffered the least from Soviet repression are the most lethargic about taking advantage of the democratic suffrage. It is unlikely to be a coincidence that younger persons also had the least exposure to Soviet political socialization, which elevated voting in single-candidate elections into a sacrosanct duty.[24] It is too soon to judge if age gradations like these connote life-cycle, generational, or period effects and whether they will dim with time.[25]

The tie between electoral participation and education in Russia is generally positive, as comparative findings about the acquisition of politically relevant knowledge, cognitive skills, and personal poise during formal schooling would foresee,[26] but it has historically conditioned complexities. While better-educated Russians are on average more likely to vote than the poorly educated,[27] the correlation with higher education vanishes among individuals in their forties and fifties, who earned their diplomas during the conservative Kremlin reign of Leonid Brezhnev in the 1960s and 1970s (see Figure 2.3). It is understandable that studying at a university or institute in the liberal 1980s and 1990s would have equipped someone for democratic participation better than being a student under Brezhnev, when cynicism flourished among Soviet youth, and that this might also hold for individuals (now in their sixties) educated in the decade or so after Joseph

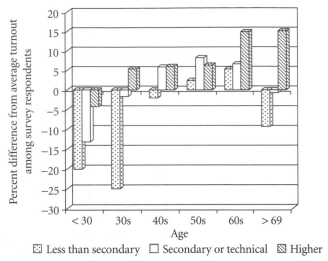

Figure 2.3. Education and Voting Turnout by Age Group, 1995

Stalin's death in 1953, when hope still flickered for reform of the Soviet system from within. What is counterintuitive is the benevolent effect of elite schooling upon participation in the group of elderly Russians reared in the ultra-oppressive Stalinist atmosphere. Two interpretations are equally plausible: that so conformist an upbringing instilled an ethic of duty to cooperate with officially sponsored political events which has survived the fall of Communism; or that educated Russians from this generation, starved of an outlet for their civic energies, pounced on the chance when it presented itself.[28]

Recent scholarship on democracies has discovered that, irrespective of personal background and status, "socially connected" citizens who are well integrated within the surrounding nonpolitical community are better disposed to civic activity, voting included, than loners.[29] This very same nexus exists in transitional Russia, despite all the differences in social structure with the Western prototype. Two good indicators of connectedness—neighborliness and marriage—are yoked to voting turnout in Russia (see Figure 2.4, with 1995 data).[30] Married persons who are friendliest with their neighbors are about 25 percentage points more likely to vote than are single persons who see none of their neighbors. The tendency applies in all age groups and to the ill-educated and well-educated alike. It may be speculated that, as happens in the United States and Japan, Russians who

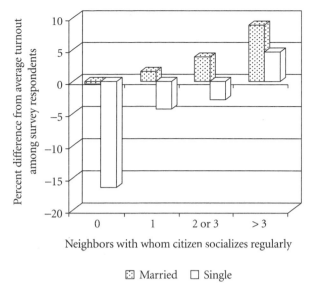

Neighbors with whom citizen socializes regularly

⊡ Married   □ Single

Figure 2.4. Social Connectedness and Voting Turnout, 1995

interact frequently with others from day to day make "secondary contact" with political elites seeking to mobilize their support in elections, and may be targeted by candidates for office because they are able to sway their peers.[31]

Important though these sociological correlations are, they leave out the motivations and sentiments bolstering voting and nonvoting. We made open-ended requests to nonvoters in the surveys after the 1995 and 1996 elections to tell in their own words why they had abstained. Table 2.3 lays out the coded responses.[32]

Russians' motives for abstaining from the vote sort out into two broad categories: personal and family circumstances and expressly political sensitivities. The more innocent, circumstantial motives crop up slightly more often than political motives; a small fraction of abstainers give both circumstantial and political reasons for their choice. Circumstantial abstainers, we find from the 1995 data (where we can match the answer on nonvoting with attitudinal information from the same respondents in a pre-election interview), are less inclined than political abstainers to plan their nonparticipation well in advance of the election. Conversely, 70 percent of political abstainers tell interviewers before election day that they will sit out the vote; less than one-third say afterwards they came to the decision

Table 2.3 Circumstantial and Political Reasons Given for Nonvoting, 1995 Parliamentary
Election and 1996 Presidential Election (Percentages)[a]

	1995[b]			1996 (First Round)[c]
Type of reason	All nonvoters who gave a reason	Nonvoters who gave a reason and who intended to abstain in pre-election interview	Nonvoters who gave a reason and who said in post-election interview they decided to abstain late in campaign	All nonvoters who gave a reason
Circumstantial	57	23	73	52
Political	49	56	30	50

a. Columns total more than 100 percent because some respondents mentioned two reasons.
b. N = 446 weighted cases.
c. N = 343 weighted cases.

to desist in the waning days of the campaign. All of which is to say that circumstantial abstainers are more impulsive and political abstainers more purposive.

A more detailed breakdown of the rationales for nonvoting may be found in Table 2.4. The circumstantial causes, starting with ill health (the bane of frosty December) and travel (more of a temptation in summertime), are mostly humdrum. Sign-up formalities enter into 5 to 7 percent of the abstentions and are nowhere near the hurdle they are in the United States.[33]

Political justifications for abstention in Russia single out shortfalls in three areas: political interest, political efficacy, and political trust. None of these will be a stranger to the comparativist, since they have many referents in the literature on democracies. About 10 percent of Russian abstainers in 1995 and in 1996 charge their failure to vote to a dearth of interest in political affairs or in the just ended election campaign, with another 1 or 2 percent saying they are so ill-informed that they cannot participate. About one of every four abstainers allude to a low sense of efficacy, dividing into roughly equal subsets troubled by deficits of what political psychologists call "internal efficacy"—the feeling of competence about raising one's voice—and of "external efficacy"—assurance that officials will listen to what is said.[34] Around 20 percent of all nonvoters advert in their answers to the deeper malaise of lack of confidence in the fundamental integrity of

Table 2.4 Detailed Reasons Given for Nonvoting, 1995 and 1996 (Percentages)[a]

Reason	1995[b]	1996[c]
Circumstantial		
Illness	27	14
Family and personal responsibilities	9	7
Travel	6	18
Work	7	8
Registration formalities	7	5
Weather	1	0
Other	0	1
Political		
No interest in politics or election	11	10
Insufficient knowledge to decide	1	2
Internal efficacy—individual's voice does not count	13	10
External efficacy—election will not change anything	12	9
Distrust of political system	3	2
Distrust of electoral system	7	9
Distrust of parties or candidates	10	10
Other	1	2

a. Columns total more than 100 percent because some respondents mentioned two reasons.

b. N = 446 weighted cases.

c. N = 343 weighted cases.

the institutions of the state or, more often, of the electoral system itself and of political parties and politicians.

In the interviews in 1995–96 respondents often meandered from one grievance to another. Verbatim quotations will telegraph the flavor:

1995 parliamentary election:

"I can't stand a single one of the parties. The only ones who need all these elections are our government and our president" (factory foreman, age thirty-seven, Saratov oblast [region]).

"I didn't bother voting because, whether I do or not, nothing is going to change. I'm against all these parties and candidates. It's all the same to me who is at the government trough" (lathe operator, age forty-six, Stavropol krai [territory]).

"I don't believe in anything or anyone. Nothing is going to make life any easier. We've had all kinds of elections, and look how the price of a subway ticket has just gone up again" (messenger, age thirty-six, Moscow).

1996 presidential election:

"You know nothing is going to change. Put anyone you like up there and we will still slide downhill. We now live worse than the [American] Negroes do. They all make promises, but I'm convinced nothing will come of it" (truck driver, age forty-one, Orenburg oblast).

"I have no faith in any election. I was sure Yeltsin was going to become president [again]. All this is the latest swindle. I didn't see any deserving candidate I could give my vote to" (traffic policeman, age twenty-four, Altai krai).

"My vote isn't going to decide a thing. Nobody is going to improve or change my life. I am doomed to live in poverty and die. All four of us get by on 440,000 rubles a month [about $95 at the time]. What kind of a life is that, and what is the point of voting? They [the politicians] are all fighting it out so that they, and not the simple person, can live better" (pensioner, age seventy, Komi republic).

Such is the spontaneous testimony of the nonvoters. To buttress it, we have harder measures of interest, efficacy, and trust from closed-ended questions put to Russian voters *and* nonvoters at the time of the 1995 election. Question wording is given in the notes to Table 2.5, discussed below.[35] The picture is motley. On the bright side, about 70 percent report medium to high interest in political events and in the Duma campaign. This is comparable with, or somewhat higher than, levels of interest found in consolidated liberal democracies.[36] Most Russians score low on internal efficacy, about 70 percent agreeing that government is so complicated "that people like me cannot understand what is going on"—but this is the same proportion as in the United States.[37]

So far as external efficacy and trust in institutions are concerned, though, Russia suffers by comparison with the outside world. Only small minorities of those we polled would quarrel with assertions that people like them "have no say in what the government does" (29 percent demur) and that officials "do not especially care what people like me think" (6 percent against); the proportion of Americans spurning such statements is about 40 percentage points higher.[38] More Russians distrust their central political institutions than trust them; faith in regional and municipal governments is a jot higher.[39] The differences with Western mass publics are less here than in some other areas.[40] Finally, we must note the skepticism a multitude of Russians nurse about the utility of elections themselves. Forty-two percent of respondents surveyed in 1995 accepted the statement that "nothing will change" in Russia because of how people vote, as against 35 percent disagreeing. And half of Russian citizens, it will be recalled from Chapter 1, could not bring themselves to vouchsafe the 1995 and 1996 elections "democratic." Questions about whether elections make a difference, and especially about whether they are fair or fraudulent, would not so much as be asked in an opinion poll in a stable democracy.[41]

Comparing the closed-ended responses of Russian nonvoters and voters corroborates the responses to the open-ended questions put to nonvoters only, yet with some differences in emphasis. The thrust of the correlation coefficients in Table 2.5 is that the best predictors of willingness to turn out to vote are indicators of political interest—interest in public affairs generally and in elections. Remember that it is in the realm of interest, and not of efficacy or trust, that the distribution of attitudes in Russia is closest to that in mature democracies. In all probability, political interest is less obtrusive in the nonvoters' verbal responses than in the voter/nonvoter comparison only because many abstainers, when put on the spot by an interviewer about why they did not vote, would have taken their disinterest as self-evident. Of the three other explanatory variables that generate correlations higher than .10, one sums up trust in the political authorities but two have to do with evaluations of elections as such—of the procedural fairness of this political device and of its capacity to change things for the better in Russia.

Involvement in Campaigns

On election day Russians rarely go into the voting booth empty-handed. Few will have been unaware of the campaign and its assorted attractions and sideshows. The parties and candidates will have directed copious promotional material at the prospective voters and laid on a variety of public spectacles. Some voters, though relatively few, will have been dunned by their employers and by members of secondary associations to which they belong. Practically everyone will have chatted about issues and personalities with kin and friends. The present section of the chapter discusses con-

Table 2.5 Associations between Voting Turnout and Political Interest, Efficacy, and Trust, 1995[a]

Measure	Correlation (r) with casting a party-list vote[b]
Interest	
In politics[c]	.30**
In campaign[d]	.28**
Efficacy[e]	
Government is complicated[f]	−.01
People have no say[g]	−.08**
Officials don't care[h]	−.01
Nothing will change because of vote[i]	−.18**
Trust	
In authorities[j]	.14**
In fairness of 1995 election[k]	.15**

**p ≤ .01 (two-tailed test). Missing values deleted pairwise.

a. Questions on interest in campaign and "Nothing will change because of vote" asked in pre-election survey (N = 2,841 weighted cases). All others asked in post-election survey (N = 2,774 weighted cases).

b. Casting a vote is a dummy variable.

c. Four-point index (follow politics not at all, very rarely, sometimes, all the time).

d. Four-point index (completely uninterested, uninterested, interested, very interested).

e. All are five-point indices (strongly disagree with statement, disagree, indifferent, agree, strongly agree).

f. Statement reads: "Sometimes the activity of the government looks so complicated that people like me cannot understand what is going on."

g. Statement reads: "People like me have no say in what the government does."

h. Statement reads: "It seems to me government officials do not especially care what people like me think."

i. Statement reads: "Nothing will change in this country as a result of how people vote."

j. Average of four-point indices (complete distrust, distrust, trust, complete trust) for six institutions (Russian government, parliament, president, regional government, local government, courts).

k. Five-point index (see Table 1.1).

testant-initiated, citizen-initiated, and organization-initiated inclusion in Russian campaigns, leaving the other main source of involvement—the mass media—for a separate segment.

Contestant-Initiated Involvement

The engine of any election campaign is the push by political parties and candidates to identify potential backers, stretch out a hand to them, and solidify their support. Two tangible forms of outreach have been present in Russian elections since the onset of democratization: the dissemination of literature and visual propaganda, and canvassing in the residential set-ting.[42] Both are weapons in the campaign armory of parties and candidates everywhere. The scope with which they are deployed is a discerning barometer of the strength and professionalism of the combatants and their capability to penetrate Russia's changing society.[43]

Statistics about campaign activities in Table 2.6 speak both kindly and unkindly of their perpetrators. Each type of political self-promotion

Table 2.6 Contestant-Initiated Involvement in Campaigns (Percentages)

Activity	1995[a]	1996[b]
Received campaign literature in mailbox		
From party	48	—
From district candidate	48	—
From party or district candidate	56	—
From presidential candidate	—	49
Came across leaflets or posters		
From party	48	—
From district candidate	47	—
From party or district candidate	55	—
From presidential candidate	—	56
Was canvassed in person or on telephone		
On behalf of party	3	—
On behalf of district candidate	4	—
On behalf of party or district candidate	5	—
On behalf of presidential candidate	—	5

a. N = 2,774 weighted cases.

b. N = 2,472 weighted cases.

through the written word and pictures, as paraphrased in the table's first and second main entries, got through to approximately one-half of the body politic in 1995 and again in 1996. Courtesy of the hybrid rules for the Duma election, voters were targeted in 1995 by a dozen individual candidates per territorial district (a good many of them party nominees) as well as by the forty-three Russia-wide party lists. In the ten-candidate presidential election the following summer, the torrent of propaganda was less fragmented than in the parliamentary campaign and slightly larger. All told, 69 percent of our survey respondents in 1995, and 72 percent in 1996, encountered campaign materials on the streets or, more often, in their mailboxes.[44]

Keeping in mind that Russia's parties were no more than a few years old in the mid-1990s, and that the district and presidential candidates were also political greenhorns, this performance is workmanlike if less than stellar. Contestants conveyed their promotional materials to millions while completely passing over almost one-third of the electorate, more people than cast a vote for any one party or candidate in 1995 or 1996.

Professional organizers, amateur helpers, and commercial contractors alike participate in the job of cranking out, circulating, and displaying campaign-related paper and posterboard. Of survey respondents who received materials in their mailboxes before the first round of the presidential vote in 1996, 53 percent recalled seeing many pieces from Yeltsin's polished and very well funded campaign; but 47 percent also got much material from the Zyuganov campaign, which relied more on volunteers. Money apparently talks louder in the distribution of leaflets by hand and the plastering up of placards, since here 67 percent of the interviewees said they had come across many Yeltsin materials, versus 31 percent who had for Zyuganov.[45]

The labor-intensive chore of home canvassing, which entails enlisting amateur or mercenary activists, familiarizing them with a political program, and marshaling them to ring voters' doorbells or call them on the telephone, is probably a more stringent test of the experienced campaigner's capacity than the distribution of visual materials. And indeed this is so in Russia: parties and politicians have been incomparably less adept at getting in personal touch with voters (see the third main entry in Table 2.6). They made overtures in person or by telephone to a mere 5 percent of citizens in 1995 and in 1996. Neither monetary resources nor the vaunted grassroots organization of the Communists have varied the pattern much. Four percent of supporters of the cash-rich Our Home Is Russia movement reported being canvassed by the representatives of a party in 1995, about the average rate. Persons who voted for the liberal Yabloko had the highest rate of contact (7 percent), while, surprisingly, KPRF voters had one of the lowest rates (2 percent). In the presidential campaign, the Zyuganov team did just a bit more to live up to the KPRF's image as an organizational juggernaut. Five percent of first-round Zyuganov voters were canvassed, and among them 3 percent were canvassed by agents of Zyuganov; 7 percent of Yeltsin voters were canvassed, and 3 percent by representatives of his.

Whatever the distribution, the 5 percent mean rate of personal contacting is extremely low. Russians canvassed in 1995 and 1996 were about one-tenth of the number who saw leaflets, signs, and the like, and a small fraction of the voters importuned in an American or British national election.[46]

The geography of the largest country on the planet—sprawling and northerly, with tens of millions of people still inhabiting villages and towns with poor and seasonally unreliable transport links and erratic postal service—adds a grueling aspect to the logistics of a Russian campaign. The politicians' patchy success in the assignment underscores the immaturity of the structures they command.

The larger the local settlement, and so the closer it is to transportation and communication nodes, the more efficiently parliamentary and presidential contenders dispense political materials to the electorate in Russia (see Figure 2.5). Campaign managers are well on the way to industrializing this part of the process. But human canvassing is more of an uphill slog.[47] Organizers make many fewer forays into out-of-the-way communities in person than through booster materials, as could perhaps be predicted. Less predictable is that economies of scale in contacting would turn out to be so negligible in the metropolitan areas, where telephones are much more widely installed than in villages and small towns and where population density works in foot canvassers' favor. Computer-aided dialing for canvassing and spot polling still lies in the future, even for Moscow and St. Petersburg. In the 1995 parliamentary election, the difference between the fraction of citizens canvassed and the much larger number reached by campaign literature, posters, and billboards—41 percentage points in the countryside and the smallest towns—rises to 74 points in the biggest cities. For the presidential campaign, the disparity in contacting rates is 52 per-

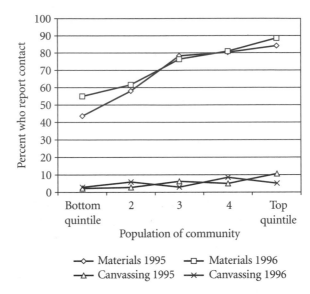

Figure 2.5. Penetration of the 1995 and 1996 Campaigns by Community Size

centage points in the least urbanized quintile but 84 percent in the most urbanized.

Citizen-Initiated Involvement

Rank-and-file citizens can get involved in campaigns without waiting for the elite players to do it for them. They can sign on in a formal sense, by collaborating with the parties and candidates and their entourages, or informally, in the fellowship of their social peers and acquaintances.

On the first point, the data about Russians in the transition are unpropitious: seldom do they come forward on their own to lend a hand within an election's official framework. Of the four subclasses of activity on which we have a reading—soliciting signatures for nomination papers, assisting with a campaign, attending a rally, and donating funds—none encompasses more than 5 percent of the citizenry in 1995 or 1996, and their merged share is 9 percent both years (see Table 2.7). Individuals are decidedly less likely to contribute to these errands than are citizens in the West. There is as yet no culture of political volunteerism and cheerleading in post-Soviet Russia.[48]

The lassitude that reigns in the official domain is anything but the whole story, for there is intense informal engagement at the ground level in Rus-

Table 2.7 Citizen-Initiated Involvement in Campaigns (Percentages)

Activity	1995[a]	1996[b]
Official framework		
Collected signatures for nominations	3	5
Agitation or other campaign work	3	4
Attended rally or meeting	5	5
Donated money	0.1	0
Any activity	9	9
Unofficial framework		
Conversed about politics during one week of campaign		
Never	29	—
Once	4	—
Several times	25	—
Almost daily	21	—
Daily	20	—
Conversed about election in course of campaign		
With family	81	85
With other relatives	52	63
With neighbors	47	59
With workmates	52	56
With other friends and acquaintances	59	70
With anyone	91	95
Respondent tried to convince someone else how to vote		
For party or candidate	22	29
Abstain or vote against all	3	2
Any advice	24	30
Someone else tried to convince respondent how to vote		
For party or candidate	32	43
Abstain or vote against all	8	12
Any advice	33	44
Respondent followed advice		
Proportion of respondents who were given advice	15	12
Proportion of electorate	5	5

a. N = 2,774 weighted cases, except for "Conversed about politics during one week of campaign" (N = 2,841 weighted cases).

b. N = 2,472 weighted cases.

sian campaigns. Almost all citizens discuss election issues at least sporadically, and many do it with great frequency (see Table 2.7 again). Seventy percent of persons interviewed during the hurly-burly of the 1995 Duma campaign said they discussed politics with family or friends in the preceding week, and 41 percent had such conversations every or almost every day. Better than 90 percent said after the 1995 and 1996 elections that they had conversed about the campaign at some time with members of primary groups: their immediate and extended families, neighbors, co-workers, and friends.

This gregariousness is not limited to the exchange of politically neutral information. Oftentimes the discussions stray into advocacy. About one-quarter of Russians in 1995 and 30 percent in 1996 said in interviews that they had mounted an attempt to influence some other person's vote during the campaign.[49] More than that number—one-third in 1995 and 44 percent in 1996—recalled being pressured by *their* confrères. The incongruity between the two figures can only mean that some would-be persuaders try to sell their wares to more than one customer.

Unrehearsed political crossfire in the kitchen, around the neighborhood, and at the office is thus a pervasive feature of the same Russian election campaigns which have failed abjectly to entice citizens into the officially choreographed ballet of activities. It builds on the tradition of whispered private conversation about taboo subjects that Soviet authoritarianism grudgingly tolerated. Now out of the closet, so to say, the informal colloquy about electoral politics is quantitatively and, to all appearances, qualitatively in the same league in Russia as in full-grown democracies.[50] Like voting, fraternization is most regular among the better-educated, the middle-aged, the socially connected, and those most interested in and best informed about public affairs and election campaigns.[51] Russians are better at giving personal electoral advice than taking it. Only 15 percent of those buttonholed by their peers in 1995, and 12 percent in 1996, amounting to 5 percent of the entire electorate each time (see the bottom two rows in Table 2.7), said subsequently they had gone along with the advice given.

Organization-Initiated Involvement

Over and above campaign machinery and the blandishments of friends and neighbors, a naive observer might prophesy that two kinds of formal but nonpolitical organizations—work units and voluntary associations—

would help post-Soviet Russians adjust to the electoral process and color their voting choices.

Factories, farms, and other workplaces provided the glue in the every-day life of Soviet Communism. Directors of such organizations allocated apartments, social services, vacation vouchers, and petty perquisites along with wages, and it was here that the CPSU had its membership cells. Managers in the privatizing economy of the 1990s, who still must curry governmental favor to stay afloat, might have reason to want to deliver their workers' votes to accommodating politicians. Off the job, Russians now have the right to band together into secondary associations for the pursuit of some collective goal. Such groups either were forbidden under the old regime or, if condoned, were under the thumb of the ruling party. Today they could in theory be a seedbed of civic virtue and "social capital."[52]

Neither brand of organization, the data say resoundingly, has as yet played a serious role in Russian elections. Diffidence on the part of organizational executives, wariness among members, and, for voluntary associations, the stunted development of the organizational form itself jointly produce this null outcome.

Most Russian adults are gainfully employed in some branch of the economy. And yet, no better than 5 percent of persons in the labor force recalled in the post-election interview in 1995 that the head of their firm or office had touted any party or candidate in the parliamentary election (see Table 2.8).[53] Furthermore, less than 10 percent of them "followed the advice of management" on voting day—fewer than took the counsel of

Table 2.8 Work Units and the 1995 Campaign

Activity	Percentage
Employed as proportion of electorate[a]	62
Management of individual's work unit favored a party or candidate	
Proportion of employed[b]	5
Proportion of electorate[a]	3
Individual followed advice	
Proportion of employed who were given advice[c]	9
Proportion of employed[b]	0.4
Proportion of electorate[a]	0.3

a. N = 2,774 weighted cases (post-election interview).

b. N = 1,687 weighted cases.

c. N = 84 weighted cases.

friends and neighbors. The upshot is that employer influence affects a microscopic fraction, less than 1 percent, of the electorate.[54]

Secondary associations, a more auspicious avenue for popular induction, have been equally inconsequential in the Russian electoral game. Although 44 percent of citizens belong to one or several voluntary organizations as of 1995 (see Table 2.9), the great majority are in trade unions, which are mostly ossified remnants of the Soviet power structure. Effusive talk of the rebirth of "civil society" to the contrary, the social base for associational activity after Soviet Communism is painfully slim. Eight persons out of every hundred in our sample, no more, were affiliated with a non-union body like a school parents' association, athletic club, or religious congregation.[55] Looked at against the thicket of secondary associations that has grown up in the United States and many older democracies, this is no better than scraggly underbrush.[56]

As with work units, more than 90 percent of association members got no coaching from the organization on how to behave in the 1995 election.[57] Those who did were rather more amenable than employees were to listen to their bosses—almost 30 percent said they took the cues lent—but the organizational factor still touched a minuscule portion, about 1 percent, of the Russian electorate.[58]

Table 2.9 Voluntary Associations and the 1995 Campaign

Activity	Percentage
Members of associations as proportion of electorate[a]	
Trade union	41
Other	8
All associations	44
Association favored a party or candidate	
Proportion of members[b]	8
Proportion of electorate[a]	3
Individual followed association's advice	
Proportion of members who were given advice[c]	28
Proportion of members[b]	2
Proportion of electorate[a]	1

a. N = 2,774 weighted cases (post-election interview).

b. N = 1,226 weighted cases.

c. N = 109 weighted cases.

The Mass Media Versus the Rest

A standout feature of democratization in Russia and Eastern Europe has been the reversal of developmental sequences observed in the West. The role of the mass media in electioneering is a case in point.

In the United States and Western Europe, parliamentary factions, local political clubs and electoral committees, and eventually national parties, all of them creatures of oral and print communication, antedated the expansion of the suffrage. Electronic communication, first by radio and then by television, came about only generations later. The "television revolution" in campaigning in the West, progressing gradually from free election broadcasts and telecast leaders' debates to paid advertising, broke out only in the 1970s and 1980s.[59] In the Soviet Union, where open elections arrived in one fell swoop, political parties and campaign machines took the stage decades *after* the populace had been wired in to radio and, especially, to television. Russia in 1994 had 323 television sets per 1,000 people, only 66 fewer than Spain and 111 fewer than Great Britain.[60]

Starting with the maiden multiparty election in 1993,[61] the Russian electoral authorities have given candidates regulated access to the mass media. Media proprietors, of their own accord and in response to political and market pressures, have made campaign stories staple ingredients of the news. From mid-1995 to mid-1996, for example, the Duma and presidential elections were covered and editorialized nonstop.

How long a shadow the mass media throw in Russian elections is apparent from Table 2.10. For sheer volume of information exchange about campaign issues, the media surpass all the alternatives, even the giant lattice of horizontal, person-to-person conversations.[62] As a pipeline for input from the world of high politics, they are in a class by themselves. In a typical week of the 1995 and 1996 campaigns, roughly half of the electorate read about the election in a newspaper—most likely in a local, not a national one—while about 55 percent heard about it on the radio, and a thumping 85 percent watched television broadcasts about it, with about 50 percent tuning in daily or almost daily. The post-Soviet media in general and the TV screen in particular verge on saturation of the electoral marketplace, with fewer than one person in ten evading them altogether.[63] Of the several forms in which the media monger political information, news reporting ranks well ahead of both paid political advertising and the free air time and newspaper space given to office seekers by Russian law. On

Table 2.10 Exposure to Campaigns through the Mass Media, Times per Week (Percentages)

Frequency	Television	Radio	Press Regional	National	Either
1995[a]					
Never	15	42	58	79	51
Once	4	3	6	3	6
Several times	28	19	25	12	28
Almost daily	23	16	7	4	9
Daily	30	20	4	3	5
1996[b]					
Never	13	45	55	69	48
Less than once	3	1	3	2	3
Once	6	3	11	9	12
Several times	29	17	24	13	27
Almost daily	27	18	5	4	7
Daily	23	16	2	2	4

a. Question asked in pre-election interview about media exposure in the week preceding the interview (N = 2,841 weighted cases).

b. Question asked in post-election interview about media exposure in a typical week of the campaign (N = 2,472 weighted cases).

television, frequent viewing of news programming about campaigns is one-and-a-half times more common than of advertising clips *(agitatsionnyye roliki)* or public-service broadcasts.[64]

Media audiences cross-cut in Russia, as in other industrial countries. Only one-quarter of the electorate, most of them television viewers, depend exclusively on a single source; most additionally patronize one or both of the alternative media (see Figure 2.6). Russians also have some consumer choice within specific media. "Surfing" through television channels is as customary in Russian as in American living rooms. The average television viewer in 1996 got campaign information with some regularity from 1.8 channels. Channel One (ORT), controlled by a board representing the state and business interests, was by a fat margin the most popular, followed by government-owned Channel Two (RTR) and NTV, Russia's first commercial network.[65] Newspaper readers consulted a mean of 1.5 national papers each in 1996. Of the fifty central newspapers identified by members of our survey panel as sources of news about the presidential

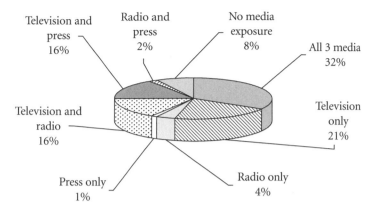

Television and
press
16%

Radio and
press
2%

No media
exposure
8%

All 3 media
32%

Television and
radio
16%

Television
only
21%

Press only
1%

Radio only
4%

Figure 2.6. Overlapping Media Audiences for Information about the Campaign,
1996

campaign, two-thirds of all mentions were of four that were industry leaders in the liberalized late Soviet era: *Komsomol'skaya pravda* (Komsomol
Truth), formerly the Communist youth league's daily paper; the weekly
Argumenty i fakty (Arguments and Facts); *Trud* (Labor), once put out by
the USSR trade union federation; and *Izvestiya* (News), for decades the
mouthpiece of the Soviet government.[66]

Contact with campaigns through the Russian mass media, like interest
in politics and voting turnout, varies by age and education.[67] Different
from the parties' and candidates' efforts to propagate their own advertising
materials, media use does *not* taper off in the towns, hamlets, and villages
of provincial Russia. Only for radio is regular exposure to political information more than 10 percent higher in the big cities than in the countryside (see Figure 2.7, with 1996 data). Readership of the central press swells
slightly in bigger communities, but for the local press it decreases com-
mensurately, and for the nonpareil medium, television, frequency of viewing is flat across the population spectrum.[68]

The Media and Voter Sophistication

The impact of the news media on public opinion and electoral choice—
in the presence of a congeries of other causal variables—is notoriously
hard to pluck out of survey data. Analysts of American politics have experimented recently with techniques for knifing through the methodologi-

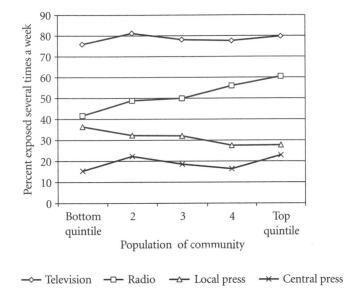

Figure 2.7. Exposure to Campaign Information in the Mass Media by Community Size, 1996

cal knot, among them laboratory experimentation and aggregate time-series work.[69]

The question of media impact is more piquant in protodemocratic Russia than in a settled democracy because of the disproportionate leverage the state, and business interests affiliated with it, have over mass communications. Privatization of ownership of the Russian media has been under way since the early 1990s, yet the federal government retains equity in some outlets, particularly in television, and wields subtler influence on many others through licensing authority, favoritism in the awarding of advertising accounts, and selective leaks of information.[70] Although all campaigners benefit from complimentary presentations, only those few with bulging purses benefit from paid ads. During the 1995 Duma campaign, the government party, Our Home Is Russia, bought almost seventy-five times more advertising time than the KPRF, eight times more than Yabloko, and 40 percent more than the LDPR. Worse than that, Russian television *news* coverage often kowtows to members or friends of the current administration. In 1995 about one-quarter of all news coverage on the national TV networks was devoted to the government party, Our Home Is

Russia, and only 6 percent to the heatedly anti-government KPRF. Prior to the qualifying round of the 1996 presidential election, the 9 P.M. newscast on Channel One brought up President Yeltsin in 55 percent of its stories on the campaign; the underdog Gennadii Zyuganov figured in 35 percent, frequently in a derogatory or sinister light, and no other candidate appeared in more than 20 percent. Igor Malashenko, the general manager of NTV, made no pretense of even-handedness, serving as a media adviser to Yeltsin's campaign staff.[71]

Are we to infer, then, that Russia's transitional voters have nothing to say in the matter, that they are docile couch potatoes who absorb every sound bite fed to them in the mass media? Such a picture would be a caricature for several reasons. One is that popular awareness of media favoritism is widespread in the Russian Federation. Many citizens doubted the veracity of the state-controlled mass media since Soviet times—as the wits put it, "There is no truth [pravda] in [the newspaper] Pravda and no real news [izvestiya] in Izvestiya." Many distrust the post-Soviet media today, just about as many as distrust the institutions of government, and distrust of the media is correlated with distrust of state institutions.[72] Almost 40 percent of citizens espied distortions in media coverage of the 1995 Duma campaign; the next summer more than 50 percent sensed it in the race for the presidency, almost all of them seeing the media product as warped in Yeltsin's favor.[73] Alertness to media discrimination increases with political consciousness. In both 1995 and 1996, the politically most aware fifth of the Russian electorate was about 25 percentage points more likely than the least aware to perceive imbalance in media treatment of the campaign (see Figure 2.8).[74] Citizens who recognize media manipulation for what it is stand a greater chance than the gullible of resisting it.

The diversity of the information channels to which Russians have access is another mitigating circumstance. Most clients of the mass media, as noted above, obtain political information through several media and, within any one medium, from several outlets. The data also underline that media use, far from being an isolated activity, goes together with exploitation of *other* dispensers of information, hard and soft, about politics and campaigns. Especially strong is the link with the informal peer circles in which almost all citizens are enmeshed. The more attentive Russians are to the media, the thicker those social networks tend to be. In 1996 the difference in the rate of recurrent exposure to television broadcasts about the campaign between the most cloistered individuals and those who inter-

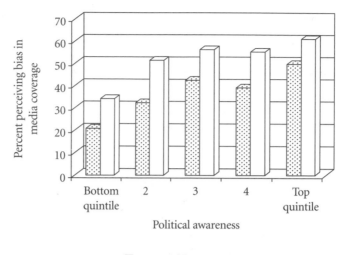

Figure 2.8. Political Awareness and Perception of Media Bias, 1995 and 1996 Campaigns

acted with the maximum number of primary groups (family, relatives, neighbors, workmates, and friends) was 58 percentage points; for radio the lag was 28 points, for the local press 31 points, and for the national press 26 points (see Figure 2.9).

Several simple measures give us a handle on the connection between media dosage and voting behavior. In both 1995 and 1996, we inquired of Russian respondents whether television broadcasts and newspaper stories had "influenced your decision on whether to participate [vote] in the election and for whom to vote." Approximately two interviewees in five gave positive answers for television and one in five for the press—many more than those who admitted being influenced by other citizens (5 percent), employers (0.3 percent), or voluntary associations (1 percent).

But the responses do not sustain a black-and-white interpretation of the direction of media effects. Although Prime Minister Chernomyrdin's Our Home Is Russia was lavishly favored by television and press in the 1995 parliamentary campaign, it finished third in that election to an opposition movement, the KPRF, which was discriminated against in news coverage and purchased almost no television advertising.[75] Supporters of the government party in 1995 were no more likely than the supporters of opposition party families to say in interviews that they had been influenced by ei-

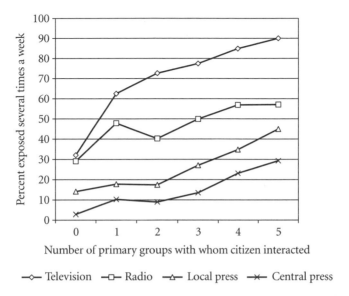

Figure 2.9. Media Exposure by Density of Face-to-Face Interactions in the Campaign, 1996

ther TV or the press (see Table 2.11). In 1996, when television coverage was brazenly pro-Yeltsin, his voters were just several percentage points more likely than the average to believe they had been budged by the media. Almost one-third of first-round *Zyuganov* voters thought something they saw on television had affected their vote—meaning, most likely, that they were reading between the lines of the official message or were recoiling against some piece of it.

Substantiation of citizen autonomy can also be read into the personal attributes of the individuals susceptible, by their own admission, to media influence. The small minority of Russians who say they accept electoral advice from other individuals are slightly more often found in the politically less literate strata. But receptivity to television and press input, a far more prevalent pattern, is more frequent among the more politicized citizens who have the acumen to treat incoming information with care. These are some of the last people in Russia you would expect to be dupes or knee-jerk voters. The contrary patterns for interpersonal and media persuasability can be found in Figure 2.10 (using 1996 data to illustrate).[76]

It is instructive, finally, to appraise the relative influence of the mass media and of other factors on citizens' grasp of election campaigns, their par-

Table 2.11 Citizen Perceptions That Mass Media Had an Influence on Their Voting Behavior (Percentages)

Year and group	Television	Press
1995[a]		
All respondents	38	22
Nonvoters	20	7
Voters	43	25
Voters by party family:		
Government	43	25
Liberal	44	24
Centrist	54	29
Nationalist	45	29
Socialist	39	25
1996[b]		
All respondents	36	16
Nonvoters (first round)	20	7
Voters (first round)	38	18
Voters (first round) for:		
Yeltsin	42	20
Zyuganov	30	18
Lebed	45	18
Yavlinskii	42	17
Others	47	15

a. N = 2,774 weighted cases.
b. N = 2,472 weighted cases.

ticipants, and their stakes. The more they know about what is going on in an election, the more responsibly they can make civic choices. Table 2.12 presents standardized regression coefficients that estimate influences on five indicators of voter knowledge in Russia. Three of the dependent variables register the ability to evaluate key electoral players on a 101-point feeling thermometer: ten national political parties (1995), all candidates in the person's territorial district (1995), and all ten presidential candidates (1996).[77] The two location variables represent ability to state (or, more correctly, to try to state) the positions of ten parties and five presidential candidates on selected issues debated during the campaign (two issues in 1995, four in 1996). Education and age are run as controls for background personal sophistication and life experience.

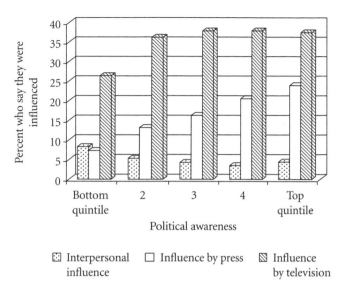

Figure 2.10. Perceptions of Influence on Personal Voting Decision on the Part of the Media and Fellow Citizens: Percentages by Level of Political Awareness, 1996

The first thing the multivariate analysis demonstrates convincingly is that contacts with the Russian mass media, far from being detrimental, have positive effects on people's understanding, as gauged by the capacity to evaluate electoral actors and impute policy positions to them. Three times out of five, television is the most potent media influence. The national press is the best media predictor for one knowledge index (giving the parties' positions on campaign issues in 1995), while the regional press comes out ahead for the one measure with strong local content (judging candidates in Duma single-mandate districts). Radio is not tops in influence for any sector.

The second lesson of the analysis is that a plentitude of forces other than the mass media condition what Russians think about elections. For none of our information outcomes in 1995 or 1996 is a media variable the leading determinant. Contestant-initiated involvements (campaign materials and canvassing), citizen-initiated involvements (conversations with members of primary social groups), and educational level and age come into play in each and every case. It speaks volumes about the strength of interpersonal networks in Russia that, for four of the five knowledge measures, the innocuous, behind-the-scenes conversations in which citizens swap

Table 2.12 Media and Other Influences on Knowledge about Campaigns (Standardized Regression Coefficients)

Explanatory variable	1995[a]			1996[b]	
	Parties evaluated[c]	Parties located[c]	District candidates evaluated[c]	Candidates evaluated[c]	Candidates located[c]
Campaign materials[d]	.04**	.02	−.02	.11**	.09**
Canvassed[d]	.07**	.06**	−.00	.01	.01
Conversations about campaign[e]	.14**	.10**	.20**	.17**	.17**
Media exposure[f]					
Television	.19**	.10**	.03	.17**	.15**
Radio	.04**	.08**	.03	.06**	.05*
Regional press	.05**	.03	.13**	.02	.02
National press	.07**	.12**	.02	.09**	.07**
Education[g]	.25**	.14**	.07**	.21*	.09**
Age[h]	.00	−.02	−.03	−.04	−.11**
Adjusted R^2	.226	.124	.096	.263	.171

**$p \leq .01$
*$p \leq .05$

a. Sample N = 2,738.

b. Sample N = 2,421.

c. Maximum of dependent variable ten for parties and presidential candidates evaluated, twenty for parties and presidential candidates located, and twenty-two for district candidates evaluated. The raw score for the last indicator has been adjusted for the size of the field by dividing by the number of candidates in the respondent's district.

d. Binary measure.

e. Six-point index, one point for conversations with each primary group (see Table 2.7).

f. Five-point index (see Table 2.10). Missing values coded at lowest score. Exposure in 1996 at less than once a week coded at a half-point.

g. Five-point index (values for zero to four years of school, five years through incomplete secondary education, secondary, secondary specialized or incomplete higher, and higher education).

h. Six-point index (values for eighteen to twenty-nine years, thirties, forties, fifties, sixties, and seventies and older).

tales and exhortations with relatives, neighbors, work colleagues, and friends have as much explanatory power as any media-exposure measure.

Conclusions

I referred at the outset of the chapter to the fears of some analysts that transitional citizens might be overwhelmed by the confusion and flux engulfing society and either eschew political participation or take part without much relish or sense of purpose. For the Russian Federation, such trepidation is exaggerated, if not totally misplaced.

Post-totalitarian political decompression and the opening of opportunities for voluntary electoral participation in Russia have occasioned a response that is on balance more positive than negative. The quicksilver quality of public affairs, the past decade's manifold letdowns and debacles, and the sullen powerlessness so many feel in their bones have not kept a majority of the electorate from turning out at the polls. The electoral franchise is the participatory lever Russians pull in their evolving political system much more frequently than any other, and it dominates other participatory modes more than voting does in older democracies. Some do balk at taking part, but voting is the default setting, and few are irrevocably alienated. We have identified circumstantial and political reasons for electoral participation, prime among the latter being feelings of political interest, efficacy, and trust. The crucial point about the origins of voting and nonvoting in this protean polity is not determining the exact contribution of any one attitude but realizing that *some* palpable logic lies behind the variation. Russians vote, and foreswear voting, for finite reasons that yield to empirical investigation. It follows that their rates of participation will be subject to change in future, upward or downward, to the extent that the forces influencing the proclivity to vote themselves change.

In the bustling campaign runup to voting day, post-Soviet Russians enter extensively into direct and indirect contact with political entrepreneurs. Direct solicitation and recruitment into formal events and shows of support are flimsy by Western standards, but with so brief a time electoral machines had to gear up, it is to their credit that they get even this small yield. Unmediated encounters with politicians and their agents pale in importance before indirect engagement in the cozy setting of the primary group and through the impersonal outpourings of the mass media. The press and the airwaves bathe citizens in the sights and sounds of political struggle, yet no one communication medium, or the news media in the aggregate, approaches a monopoly of influence. We can say with some conviction that the pictures in the Russian population's heads, in Walter Lippmann's lapidary phrase,[78] are not painted by any one brush alone.

3

Society in Transformation

Now that we are briefed on how transitional citizens come into contact with the electoral process and why they turn out to vote, we can set about probing the choices they pencil onto their ballot slips. It is reasonable to start the quest at the beginning of the hierarchy of causal influences postulated in the first chapter. All roads in the study of political behavior, one might say, lead back to the social environment in which the behavior unfolds.

In theory, there are two principal ways social and socioeconomic factors can be injected into electoral analysis. The raw material for the first is knowledge of voters' place *in* the group structure of society, a structure which may be inert, evolving gradually, or, as in Russia today, in the throes of transformation. For the second route, the nub of the inquiry is voters' appraisals of the current well-being *of* society and its members. These assessments in post-Soviet Russia are more often than not etched in gloom and doom, especially on the economic plane.

It is worth noting in the first connection that Russian politicos, as they learn their craft on the stump, can give every impression of wanting to please identifiable social groupings. They eagerly toss campaign bouquets at agrarian producers, women, ethnic Russians, trade unionists, Muslims, pensioners, and youth, among others. Occasionally, they go so far as to name their parties and movements after the group.[1] The roster of targets, mind you, is incomplete—there is a rural party and a women's party but no urban party or men's party[2]—and, whoever the intended supporters, there is no guarantee they will be won to the cause. Russian office seekers also harp on the costs and the benefits, individual and collective, of the changes wrought to the social fabric since national independence in 1991. Again, this does not necessarily sway voters.

In this chapter I sift the evidence on both counts. The first two segments lay out measures of citizens' location in the social structure and relate them to the calculus of voting. The third takes up mass perceptions of current Russian realities. These find egress not only in "economic voting," a syndrome common to many countries, but in "political voting," which is peculiar to societies whose governmental orders are being remade.

Mapping the Russian Demos

The idea that electoral alignments are essentially functions of underlying sociological realities has a long and honorable ancestry in political science, stretching back to the trailblazing work on U.S. national elections done out of Columbia University in the 1940s and 1950s and to earlier research on Europe by André Siegfried and Herbert Tingsten. Voting decisions in this lineage "are basically seen as reflecting broadly based and long-standing social and economic divisions within society, and the cleavage structure is thought of in terms of social groups and of the loyalties of members to their social groups."[3] These group boundaries vary from society to society, making it a challenge to mount cross-national generalizations about them and their political repercussions. The canonic statement remains Seymour Martin Lipset and Stein Rokkan's essay from the 1960s on the social foundations of democratic party systems. Using West European examples, Lipset and Rokkan linked partisan differences to fissures opened up by the worldwide process of modernization, which, they said, time after time pitted urban against rural interests, capital against labor, state against church and religion against religion, and homogenizing center against ethnic minorities and local authorities on the periphery.[4] More recent work has pegged electoral realignment in advanced democracies to the advent of formations like the "new middle class," emancipated women, baby boomers, and Evangelical Protestants.

The serviceability of the sociological paradigm has been debated for years. Critics brand it deterministic, insensitive to the entrepreneurial and alliance-building powers of political elites, and a diversion from the task of understanding how attitudes and states of mind define the act of voting. Some also maintain that the approach is losing what validity it once held as atomistic self-absorption grows in affluent societies and the "fragmentation of life spaces" erodes group coherence.[5]

Even skeptics, however, concede the descriptive value of gathering intelligence about the social ecology of electoral preferences. Such a mapping expedition, write the authors of *The New American Voter*, tells us much about the lives and circumstances of citizens, which ought to be of concern to the analyst "even if we were certain that [these variables'] impact on the vote was ultimately interpreted or entirely mediated by . . . explicitly political . . . and attitudinal variables." What is more, it would be wrong to assume that each social characteristic will have its impact only through intervening variables. That being so, they say, social traits cannot be dropped from a general explanatory model, since "any effect estimate for a political variable, at any given stage, which is based on an analysis that does not include social and economic characteristics, may be at least partially spurious . . . because of its 'origin' in the confounding impact of prior variables."[6]

Students of post-Soviet politics, with the odd exception, take the standard critique of the sociological approach up another notch. Social leveling under Communism, the eradication of private property and of social institutions separate from the ruling party, the jolt of the transition itself, and its half-finished character have, so the argument goes, loaded the dice against a social-based mass politics after the breakdown of the old regime.[7] Seldom, though, do observers take the absolutist stance that post-Communist society is so putty-like that social variables can have no relevance at all for voting behavior. Most ask with an open mind about the electoral consequences of a certain handful of social variables.[8] Some, as we have said, anticipate that primordial ethnic and religious identities will be foremost, while others, working mainly on East Central Europe, explore the role of incipient stratification by social class.[9]

The questions for us, then, are many. A study of transitional citizenship would be incomplete, and the multistage statistical analysis in which it is grounded faulty, unless we look into the concordance between voting choice and social structure.

Sketching the contours of any big, multifaceted society is an arduous task. For Russia it is compounded by a tortured history which this century alone has witnessed: revolutions, civil war, famine, foreign invasion, state terror, social engineering with the goal of building an earthly paradise, the dethroning of the engineers, the severance of a rump Russian Federation from the rest of the USSR, and after all that a ragged crusade to transfigure Russia into a capitalist democracy. To pinpoint individual citizens and to generate apposite variables for electoral analysis, multiple slices through Russia's complex social milieu are required, begetting multiple, cross-cutting indicators of social position.

Seven of the indicators I will utilize (falling under six demographic headings) are compatible with Lipset and Rokkan's master modernization scheme, some referring to ingrained qualities of all industrial societies, others to idiosyncrasies of the Soviet model of development. These measures are relatively static, if not cast in stone, in present-day Russia. Four indicators (in three categories) delimit aspects of social structure that have been set in agitated motion by the change of regimes and the policy course of post-Communist governments. And three social indicators (in two categories) describe stable relationships unconnected to modernization or to the logic of the transition. All fourteen variables are creditable candidates for influencing voting behavior in the transition.

Modernization-Related Variables

URBANIZATION.   The growth of cities, a universal symptom of modernization, sets up a first measuring stick. Overwhelmingly a land of farms and villages when the Soviet leaders seized power, Russia was three-quarters urbanized when they relinquished it, thanks largely to government-abetted industrialization and the influx of peasants into factories and towns.[10] Rural folk mostly inhabit the collective and state farms which Joseph Stalin imposed by duress in the 1930s. Urban settlements themselves run from crossroads hamlets of a thousand souls to Moscow, a megacity of 9 million. Median community size in our 1995 sample of the Russian electorate is 109,000.

EDUCATION.   The Soviet leadership promoted mass literacy, the training of a technically proficient work force, and post-secondary education as assiduously as it did urbanization. Large groups are now at very disparate steps on the educational ladder. At the bottom, around one-quarter of adult Russians never finished secondary school; about half have a standard secondary education and about 10 percent a "specialized secondary" (vocational or paraprofessional) diploma; at the top, about 15 percent have completed a higher, college-level or better education.[11]

OCCUPATION.   Although the Russian labor market is evolving, most people's occupations are bounded for the moment as they were in the socialist command economy. We should be most curious about two occupational groups.[12] It was manual *workers* whom the Soviet "dictatorship of the proletariat" claimed to represent; there may plausibly be a cache of support there for defenders of the old order. Active and retired blue-collar personnel in primary and secondary industries constitute 47 percent of the electorate as of 1995, our survey data say. In countries weathering an economic liberalization, low-skill workers have cause to fear displacement in the event they are left to the mercy of unbridled market forces. Among white-collar employees, *managers and professionals,* making up 18 percent of Russia's eligible voters, still rank high in prestige and workplace clout.[13] Their professional chances in the new economy ought to be better, and they and fledgling subgroups could eventually be the nucleus of a Russian middle class.[14]

RELIGION.   Some scholars have forecast that religious and ethnic subcultures and feelings will surge to the forefront in transitional politics. The Russian Orthodox Church would be a natural beneficiary. The church was the premier nonstate institution in tsarist Russia; under atheistic Communism it proved the strongest of all traditional social forces. Slightly more than half of the populace is Orthodox, brandishing differing degrees of devotion and observance.[15] The other faiths have flocks too small to test for electoral effects.

ETHNICITY.   Ethnic Great Russians *(russkiye),* a hair over 50 percent of the Soviet population, are 80-plus percent in the de-Sovietized Russian Federation.[16] More than one hundred minority nationalities, living inside and outside designated homelands, comprise the remainder. The Russians' lopsided majority precludes a party or presidential candidate riding to power on the shoulders of any community but theirs, but rapport with non-Russians, all or some, could furnish the margin of victory in a close election or lift a party over the Duma's 5 percent entry bar.

MEMBERSHIP IN THE CPSU.   The Communist Party of the Soviet Union was so ever-present before it crumbled in the 1980s that it is classifiable as a social as well as a political institution. One could imagine past enrollment in the party, and the habits and relationships associated with it, having political aftereffects in the post-Soviet system. Millions of Russians belonged to the CPSU in its heyday. Fourteen percent of our survey respondents, their mean age fifty-three in 1995, said they held a party card before its liquidation in 1991.[17]

Transition-Related Variables

INCOME.   The pyramid of pecuniary and nonpecuniary compensation under Soviet socialism was flat by comparison with capitalist economies. That has gone by the boards: "money sings" in marketizing Russia, as Blair A. Ruble puts it.[18] Consumer goods and services are no longer in short supply and rationed by queuing, and money is much more unequally held, as wages diversify and private capital accumulation commences. Average family earnings divulged to our interviewers in 1995 were 960,000 rubles a month, or about $210 at the posted exchange rate. For households in the best-off quintile, mean intake was 2,570,000 rubles; in the worst-off quintile, it was 158,000 rubles, or one-sixteenth as much.[19]

PARTICIPATION IN THE NEW ECONOMY.   Russia's newfangled capitalist economy was just getting started in the mid-1990s. We have two good indicators of induction into it: holding down a *job* as self-employed or in a private business started from scratch,[20] a foreign-owned firm, or a joint venture; and enlistment in the government's program to privatize public *housing,* a giveaway which doubled the housing stock in nonstate hands between 1992 and 1995. Nine percent of our respondents, or about 15 percent of those in the labor force, were in private or foreign employ in 1995; 28 percent had acquired legal title to their dwellings since 1992.[21] Other countries' experience intimates that changes like these can have an electoral effect. In Britain in the 1980s, Margaret Thatcher's "popular capitalism" divested state corporations and housing estates and gave or sold property to upwardly mobile members of the lower classes, "shift[ing] their electoral support from Labour to the Conservatives as a result of their new economic interests."[22]

AGE. An oversight of Lipset and Rokkan's was not to foresee the political potentiality of generational differences in societies rocked by sudden change. Russia's transition intersects with the life passage of cohorts possessing sharply different experiences and memories, creating the possibility of different conceptions of self. Roughly one-fifth of the electorate came of age under Stalin and was fifty or older when Gorbachev ignited reforms in the USSR in 1985. At the youthful pole, every fifth citizen was twenty or younger that same year, and so knew Stalin only from the history textbooks and faced the ferment of the Gorbachev and Yeltsin years as a young adult. An apt parallel might be with Japan and Germany, after defeat in World War II shattered their authoritarian regimes. In Japan, "older people retained an emotional attachment to the emperor . . . [and] tended to support the conservative parties," while younger citizens sympathized with "the 'modern' values of the postwar era of individualism, equality, and fear of military buildup and war" and with parties that touted those values.[23] In Germany, the shifting social environment stimulated the greatest change among younger voters, "because their values [were] more receptive to this new environment and because they [were] less locked in to long-standing patterns of behavior."[24]

Other Variables

GENDER. Russian women, who have been less affected by demographic disasters than men and live to a riper old age, outnumber them in the electorate.[25] In the first multiparty election, the one to the State Duma in 1993, the Women of Russia movement gleaned 8.13 percent of the votes, primarily from females. The nationalist party which led the polls, the LDPR—whose head, Vladimir Zhirinovskii, has a swaggering, macho style—was shunned by women.[26] Most parties and presidential candidates, all ten of whom were male in 1996, have not customized their solicitations to either sex.

GEOGRAPHY. The other social characteristics that do not mesh smoothly with either modernization or transition dynamics have to do with geography. Published election returns since 1991 show reformist candidates running best in the northern and central provinces of European Russia and in the Urals zone on the Europe-Asia seam (Boris Yeltsin's native region), while the socialist opposition thrives south of Moscow and along the southern rim of Siberia, and nationalists do well in eastern reaches of the country.[27] Scholars who remark upon the regional breakdown of the vote in Russia work mostly with territorially aggregated data, which they exploit as a proxy for individual-level data; this procedure skirts the question of the autonomous impact of the spatial factor.[28] Our survey data from 1995 and 1996 permit us to take the question up. To streamline the analysis and conserve statistical degrees of freedom, I use indicators for *north-south* and *east-west* location.

Social Structure and the Vote

What connections could we expect between these manifold markers of social position and Russians' voting decisions? Modernization theory, the classics of political sociology, and analogies with partially comparable environments abroad would on principle predict a plenitude of ties. Contrarily, prevalent notions about the democratization of Communist systems augur no relationship to speak of or at most associations with one or two ascriptive characteristics. Both schools of thought cannot be right.

If sociological circumstances did affect the vote, we may hypothesize that they would work in these ways:

- Urbanization: as in much of the world, Russians in big cities should be more amenable to a modernizing administration and to the fellow-traveler liberal parties, and people in villages and small towns should be drawn to the opposition parties most hostile to central policy.
- Education: better educated electors should incline toward more liberal and cosmopolitan voting options, and the poorly educated toward illiberal options.
- Occupation: manual workers ought to be staunchly oppositionist, and managers and professionals more reform-minded.
- Religion: Orthodox believers should be partial toward nationalist parties and candidates, the ones that overtly celebrate traditional symbols and values.
- Ethnicity: all things being equal, ethnic Russians should favor nationalist politicians more than non-Russians would.
- CPSU membership: former members of the hegemonic party should turn out more than others for its heir, the KPRF.

- Income: financial haves should prefer the government and other reformers, and have-nots should prefer the hard opposition.
- The new economy: active participants in the marketizing economy (through employment and home ownership) ought to support the government.
- Age: the young should be attracted to reformist candidates, and the old and set in their ways to anti-reform candidates.
- Gender: aside from the LDPR and Women of Russia (which we are not analyzing in detail), there will be few gender effects on the vote, as most contestants ignore family issues and relations between the sexes.
- Geography: voting preference may be affected by area of residence per se, over and above demographic characteristics. If that is indeed the case, residency in the Russian north should be conducive to pro-government and liberal voting sympathies, in the south to socialist sympathies, and in the east to nationalist sympathies.[29]

To pursue these leads, let us begin by selecting a few social characteristics of theoretical interest and arraying them one at a time against electoral behavior. Figures 3.1 and 3.2 do that visually. They plot minimum

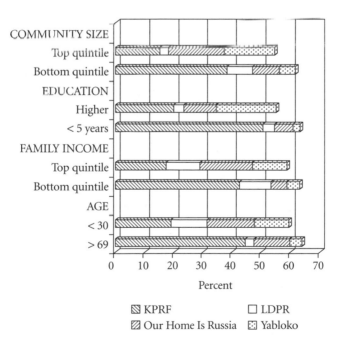

Figure 3.1. Social Characteristics and the Party-List Vote, 1995

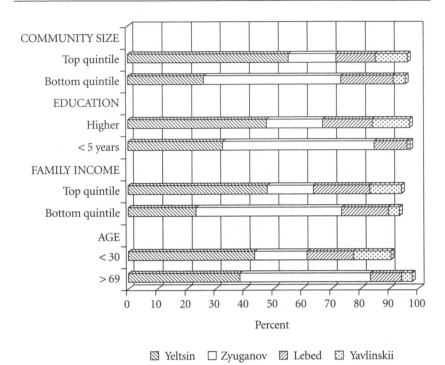

COMMUNITY SIZE
Top quintile
Bottom quintile

EDUCATION
Higher
< 5 years

FAMILY INCOME
Top quintile
Bottom quintile

AGE
< 30
> 69

0   10   20   30   40   50   60   70   80   90   100

Percent

⊠ Yeltsin   □ Zyuganov   ▨ Lebed   ⊡ Yavlinskii

Figure 3.2. Social Characteristics and the First-Round Presidential Vote, 1996

and maximum values of four cardinal social attributes—urbanization and education (modernization-related variables) and family income and age (transition-related variables)—against the vote for the largest parties in the 1995 State Duma election and for the leading presidential aspirants in the first round in 1996.

The eye immediately picks up the congruency of many of the relationships. Most blatant are those for backers of the KPRF, the intransigent foe of the Yeltsin administration. Its support is concentrated in the very places we have conjectured it would be: it decreases with urbanization, educational level, and family income and increases with the voter's age. The proportion of the electorate backing the party's slate in 1995 was 23 percentage points lower in the top quintile by community size than in the bottom quintile; 31 points lower among persons with a higher education than among those with fewer than five years in school; 24 percent lower in the richest fifth than in the poorest; and 26 percent lower among voters eighteen to twenty-nine years old than at age seventy and over. For the 1996 presidential candidacy of the KPRF's leader, Gennadii Zyuganov, the commensurate gaps in the first round of the voting are 31 percentage points for urbanization, 33 points for education, 34 for family income, and 27 percentage points for age group. For all of these four indicators, the chances of the most pro-Communist social subgroup voting for the KPRF or its nominee are more than double the chances of the least well-inclined subgroup doing so.[30]

Nor are preferences for other parties and candidates strewn at random across our four designated social categories. In the 1995 proportional-representation ballot, the vote for Yabloko (and the liberal opposition as a whole) is a weak mirror image of the KPRF's, cresting in the metropolitan areas and among educated, well-heeled, and youthful voters.[31] The appeal of the government's Our Home Is Russia is not dissimilar, except that it tapers off among the best-educated and overtakes Yabloko in the highest-income bracket. The nationalist LDPR has the most allure in 1995 among residents of middle-sized cities and persons with a vocational education (neither of these points is evident from the abridged information in Figure 3.1) and among the young.

In the presidential election of 1996, Yeltsin's constituency has some commonalities with Our Home Is Russia in 1995 and some with the liberal opposition. First-round votes for the incumbent president are most voluminous among urbanized, well-educated, and high-income voters; in generational terms, the results are best at both ends of the age scale, young and old.[32] Group support for Grigorii Yavlinskii echoes support for his political movement, Yabloko, the year before, with the difference that the gradients between the most and the least hospitable subgroups are shallower. And the nationalist Aleksandr Lebed, not unlike Zhirinovskii and the LDPR in 1995, gets his best support from younger voters, the technically trained,[33] and persons not in the largest cities.

Our stripped-down charts vouch for what seem to be meaningful associations between social factors and voting behavior in transitional Russia. But they should also caution us against jumping to the false conclusion that social divisions translate automatically into electoral divisions.

For one thing, the fraction of Russians in most social categories who support the parties and candidates in question is quite low. Yabloko's 20 percent among voters with a higher education puts to shame its 2 percent share among individuals with zero to four years in the classroom, but it also leaves other parties to rack up 80 percent of the ballots of the college-educated—not exactly a big show of solidarity for Yabloko.[34] Almost never is a party or candidate patronized by the numerical majority of a social grouping; when this does happen, it is not by much.[35] If we applied the 1995–96 data to one widely used touchstone of sociopolitical division—the so-called Alford Class Voting Index—the result would suggest that Russia is not much polarized in these terms.[36]

Likewise, Figures 3.1 and 3.2 point up a congenital problem with socially based theories of voting—their clumsiness in coping with changes in preferences. If the same electorate renders different verdicts in more than one election, social structure alone cannot explain its choices.[37] Consider several relationships glimpsed in the charts. Nineteen percent of our respondents in the most urbanized communities vote for Our Home Is Russia in December 1995; 55 percent of these same urbanites prefer President Yeltsin in June 1996. The party that has the most support among citizens with a higher education in 1995 is Yabloko, with 20 percent; Yavlinskii gets 13 percent of the votes in this same group in 1996, outscored by Yeltsin, Zyuganov, and Lebed. Seventeen percent of high-income voters throw in their lot with Our Home Is Russia in 1995, but 48 percent with President Yeltsin, whose economic platform is a carbon copy of Our Home's, in 1996.[38] And Our Home Is Russia wins the endorsement of 16 percent of voters under the age of thirty in 1995, to 43 percent for Yeltsin in 1996.[39]

A further stumbling block is the existence of overlaps among sociological variables—the four we have highlighted and many others.[40] Examination of interlinked variables in isolation from one another will ascribe spurious effects to them. The remedy for this defect is to graduate from bivariate to multivariate analysis of the influence of underlying social characteristics.

This we can do on the basis of the simulation laid down in Tables 3.1 and 3.2. They are in the form that tables like them will follow in the rest of the book. The parameters listed give the difference in the predicted probability of a Russian voter choosing the party or candidate when the explanatory variable shifts from its minimum to its maximum value, holding other terms in the equation constant at their medians. Values are computed from a multinomial logit regression. By design, all predicted probabilities in the model sum to unity and differences in predicted probabilities sum to zero. To economize on the presentation, I give only the "total-effect" estimates for our fourteen social variables here. Fuller versions of the estimates (giving bivariate, total, and residual effects) are available as Tables D.1 and D.2 in Appendix D; Appendix B contains information about the regression technique and tests.

Table 3.1 Total Effects of Social Characteristics on the Party-List Vote, 1995 (Differences in Predicted Probabilities)[a]

Social characteristic	KPRF	LDPR	Our Home	Yabloko
Urbanization[b]	−.17**	−.01	.07**	.06**
Education[c]	−.07	−.01	−.04	.10**
Occupation				
Worker[d]	.05*	.01	−.06**	−.00
Managerial/professional[d]	.01	−.06**	−.02	.01
Orthodox[e]	−.05*	.00	.00	−.02
Ethnic Russian[d]	−.01	.02	−.01	.02
Former member CPSU[d]	.16**	−.03	−.02	−.01
Family income[f]	−.11**	.03	.06*	.01
New economy				
Private or foreign employer[d]	−.05	.01	.04	.00
Privatized housing[d]	−.04	−.04**	.00	.01
Age[g]	.28**	−.08**	−.02	−.06**
Woman[d]	.04	−.09**	−.02	−.02
Geography				
North[h]	−.24**	.01	.03	.05*
East[i]	−.01	.21**	−.07**	−.02

**p ≤ .01

*p ≤ .05

a. Sample N = 2,143.

b. Five-point index, by quintile within the survey sample.

c. Five-point index (values for zero to four years of school, five years through incomplete secondary education, secondary, secondary specialized or incomplete higher, and higher education).

d. Binary measure.

e. Binary measure, coded as positive for individuals who were religious believers or leaned toward belief and gave their faith as Russian Orthodox.

f. Five-point index, by quintile within the survey sample. Missing values coded in middle category.

g. Six-point index (values for eighteen to twenty-nine years, thirties, forties, fifties, sixties, and seventies and older).

h. Continuous measure of latitude of the capital of the voter's region of residence.

i. Continuous measure of longitude of the capital of the voter's region of residence.

The total-effect statistics adduced in this volume control for the effects of other explanatory variables that are causally antecedent to or collateral with the variable under review. For Russian citizens' social characteristics, which, we presume, shape their voting preferences early in the progression, the control variables assimilated are the other social indicators. Intro-

Table 3.2 Total Effects of Social Characteristics on the Presidential Vote, 1996 (Differences in Predicted Probabilities)

Social characteristic[a]	First round[b]				Runoff[c]	
	Yel.	Zyug.	Leb.	Yav.	Yel.	Zyug.
Urbanization	.21**	−.21**	−.04	.04*	.25**	−.27**
Education	.04	−.09*	.03	.06	.07	−.12*
Occupation						
Worker	.00	.03	−.01	−.03	−.05	.06
Managerial/professional	.01	.06	−.03	−.02	−.05	.07
Orthodox	.06*	−.05*	−.02	.02	.02	−.03
Ethnic Russian	−.04	−.02	.03	.01	−.09*	.07*
Former member CPSU	−.06	.10**	−.00	.01	−.12**	.11*
Family income	.14**	−.21**	.05	.02	.24**	−.24**
New economy						
Private or foreign employer	.06	−.06	−.02	−.02	.11*	−.11*
Privatized housing	.04	−.05**	.02	.02	.07**	−.07**
Age	−.05	.28**	−.08**	−.07**	−.18**	.27**
Woman	.03	−.00	.00	−.03	.02	−.02
Geography						
North	.10*	−.09*	−.09*	.03	.09	−.10
East	−.11	.05	−.05	.01	−.14**	.07

** $p \leq .01$
* $p \leq .05$
a. Coded as in Table 3.1.
b. Sample N = 1,990.
c. Sample N = 1,937.

ducing them into the analysis in a bloc weeds out confounding effects from other social attributes correlated with the indicator under scrutiny.

It is abundantly clear from Tables 3.1 and 3.2 that there are *some* orderly connections between social structure and voting choice in Russia's young democracy. This finding flies in the face of protestations of the complete irrelevance of social structure to mass politics after Communism. For example, controlling statistically for the effects of other social characteristics, the probability that a resident of one of the largest urban communities would vote for Zyuganov in 1996 was .21 (21 percentage points) less than if that person hailed from a town or village in the lowest quintile by community size; .09 less if the citizen had a higher education than if he or she had fewer than five years in school; .21 less if the family's income was in the top fifth of the population than if it were in the lowermost fifth; and .28 higher if the voter was over sixty-nine years of age than if he was aged eighteen to twenty-nine. For two of these explanatory variables (community size and family income), the total effects are somewhat smaller than the differences in revealed support for Zyuganov in the raw data, as summarized in Figure 3.2—which takes no account of encroachments among the variables. For age group the effects are the same as in the raw data. Only for education is the statistical total effect on the Zyuganov vote ($-.09$) much smaller than the difference given in the raw data (.33, or 33 percentage points).

Multivariate analysis does not lend itself (any more than the simpler analysis condensed in the figures) to the claim that social divisions have transcendent power in transitional mass politics. With cognate variables taken into the reckoning, we are left with assorted effects which are of small to middling magnitude and which for some Russian parties and candidates are of no consequence, or virtually none. Even the larger of them are inferior to the effects of quite a few of the explanatory factors to be perused later in the book.

The KPRF/Zyuganov vote has the largest number of social coordinates whose total effects clear the conventional threshold for statistical significance of a relationship ($p \leq .05$). Seven out of fourteen social indicators qualify as significant predictors of support for the KPRF in 1995, five for the LDPR, four for Our Home Is Russia, and four for Yabloko. In the presidential first round in 1996, sixteen of the fifty-six associations are above the significance threshold (eight for Zyuganov, four for Yeltsin, and two each for Lebed and Yavlinskii); in the Yeltsin-Zyuganov runoff, sixteen associations (out of twenty-eight possibilities) are of statistical significance.

Statistical significance, or a high degree of certainty that the measure of the relationship differs from zero for some reason other than random chance, is not the same as *substantive importance.* For that, I will adopt a rule of thumb whereby any statistically significant total effect with a magnitude of .10 or more (representing a shift in the predicted probability of voting for a party or candidate of at least 10 percentage points up or down) is considered to be a *major* effect. Any time the relationship, while statistically significant, is associated with a probability change in the voting outcome smaller than .10, I will designate it a *minor* effect.

By that rule of thumb, a mere five social indicators (for a low score on urbanization, CPSU membership, a low income bracket, older age, and southern residence) qualify as major influences on the KPRF vote in 1995. A worse problem for the theory of socially determined voting is that a grand total of two characteristics produce major effects for all three of the other large parties put together (eastern location for the LDPR and higher educational attainment for Yabloko—and none for Our Home Is Russia). In the opening round of the presidential election in 1996, seven of the statistically significant total effects are major effects (four for the Zyuganov vote and three for Yeltsin, with none for either Lebed and Yavlinskii); in the runoff round, there are eleven major effects.

Our suppositions about discrete social traits check out as below:

- At least one significant effect on voting behavior can be uncovered for all fourteen of our social indicators, most of them in the predicted direction.
- Major total effects (statistically significant and with a magnitude of .10) are observed for but eight indicators: three that grow out of modernization or Soviet development (urbanization, education, and CPSU membership), three related to the transition (family income, age, and employment in the new economy), and two geographic indicators (north-south and east-west location). Sex has a minor total effect on the LDPR vote in 1995 (-.09 for female gender), yet has no major effects.[41]
- Orthodoxy and Russian ethnicity, flouting expectations about an upsurge in their import after Communism, produce minor electoral effects. So do our two occupational indicators and residence in privatized housing.
- Rather than always form conspicuous "cleavages," sociological effects often resolve into more complicated and more muted configurations. The dominant effect differs by party, presidential candidate, and election: it is age for the KPRF in 1995 and for Zyuganov and Yavlinskii in the first round of 1996, easterly location for the LDPR, urbanization for Our Home Is Russia and Yeltsin, education for Yabloko, and southerly location for Lebed.
- The heaviest sociological impact in both 1995 and 1996—linking *age* with the KPRF and its leader—is transition-related, not modernization-related.[42] Generational differences, rooted in the ebb and flow of Russian history, are of more moment to post-Soviet electoral politics than any other element of social structure, bar none.

Assuming that we are entitled to speak of a modest correspondence between aspects of social structure and electoral choice in Russia, nothing so far explains how the influence of these social attributes will be conveyed. Lack of insight into mediating mechanisms, a shortcoming of the sociological school of U.S. voting behavior,[43] would hobble any bid to link social factors to voting in a new democracy like Russia.

The linkages between social background and electoral choice, when all is said and done, are attitudinal. A postwar British worker did not vote Labour "because" he or she was a worker. Rather, the behavior was informed by beliefs, cognitions, and mores endemic to the working class of the time. In Russia, too, pathways to the voting decision lie through attitudes— which begs the question, through *which* attitudes?

The multistage analysis encapsulated in Table 3.3 affords a window on the process. To keep the discussion manageable, the first-difference estimations are strictly for the probability of voting for the KPRF in 1995 and for Zyuganov in 1996, and they deal with only the four social variables from Figures 3.1 and 3.2. Bivariate relationships with the vote, considering only the association between the particular social characteristic and electoral choice, take up the first row of each panel. The statistics in the gray-toned second row give total effects. The statistics beneath them estimate the social variable's effect as variables causally downstream from social traits enter the analysis one bloc at a time. Residual effects, measuring the direct impact of each sociological variable once all other variables in the model are internalized, are in the bottom row.[44]

Look carefully at row-wise changes in the parameters in Table 3.3. The larger the difference in the probability of voting for the KPRF or Zyuganov from one row to the next, the more we can link differences in voting behavior between persons in different categories of the explanatory variable to divisions on the bloc of variables that have been incorporated into the analysis at that stage. Voters' age is a good example. Taking only this into account, the logit-based model predicts that the oldest Russians would have been .36 (36 percentage points) more likely to vote for the KPRF in 1995 than the youngest. Controlling for the other social variables cuts this difference to .28—the "total effect" of the age variable. The predicted probability of voting KPRF hardly quivers when voters' perceptions of current conditions in Russia are factored in, but inclusion in the estimation of their partisanship (a theme we will take up in Chapter 4) reduces it substantially (by .10) and the inclusion of their issue opinions reduces it by a bit more than that (by .13); no other bloc of variables puts a noticeable

Table 3.3 Elaboration of Consequences of Four Social Characteristics for Vote for KPRF in 1995 and Vote for Zyuganov in 1996 (Differences in Predicted Probabilities)

Variables progressively incorporated in regression	Urbanization	Education	Family income	Age
1995 parliamentary election (KPRF)[a]				
Given social characteristic only	−.24**	−.28**	−.26**	.36**
Also other social characteristics[b]	−.17**	−.07	−.11**	.28**
Also perceptions of current conditions	−.15**	−.06	−.06*	.26**
Also partisanship (but not issue opinions)	−.16**	−.03	−.06	.18**
Also issue opinions (but not partisanship)	−.12**	−.02	−.04	.15**
Also partisanship and issue opinions	−.14**	.03	−.05	.10
Also retrospective evaluations of incumbents	−.15**	.03	−.06	.13*
Also party leaders	−.13**	.04	−.07	.12*
Also prospective evaluations of parties	−.10*	.05	−.07	.09
1996 presidential election (Zyuganov), first round[c]				
Given social characteristic only	−.32**	−.32**	−.35**	.36**
Also other social characteristics[b]	−.21**	−.09*	−.21**	.28**
Also perceptions of current conditions	−.18**	−.13*	−.14**	.27**
Also partisanship (but not issue opinions)	−.11**	−.11*	−.13**	.13**
Also issue opinions (but not partisanship)	−.08**	−.05	−.11**	.07
Also partisanship and issue opinions	−.06*	−.06	−.09**	.03
Also retrospective evaluations of incumbents	−.05*	−.06	−.07**	.03
Also leadership qualities	−.02	−.04	−.07**	.03
Also prospective evaluations of candidates	−.04	−.02	−.05*	.04

dent in the observed effect of age. We can thus deduce that approximately one-half (.15/.28) of the influence of age on the likelihood of voting for the KPRF is owing to differences in normative opinions between young and old and approximately one-third (.10/.28) is owing to differences in partisan loyalties. In the presidential election, the pattern is similar but more pronounced. Assimilation of issue opinions into the first-round estimation

Table 3.3 (continued)

Variables progressively incorporated in regression	Urbanization	Education	Family income	Age
1996 presidential election (Zyuganov), runoff[d]				
Given social characteristic only	−.36**	−.35**	−.38**	.34**
Also other social characteristics[b]	−.27**	−.12*	−.24**	.27**
Also perceptions of current conditions	−.23**	−.20**	−.12**	.24**
Also partisanship (but not issue opinions)	−.16**	−.22**	−.10*	.08
Also issue opinions (but not partisanship)	−.10**	−.06*	−.07*	.00
Also partisanship and issue opinions	−.07*	−.11*	−.05	−.04
Also retrospective evaluations of incumbents	−.07**	−.07*	−.03	−.01
Also leadership qualities[e]	−.05	−.03	−.05*	−.00
Also prospective evaluations of candidates[e]	−.05*	−.00	−.04	.01

**p ≤ .01
*p ≤ .05
a. Sample N = 2,143.
b. Gray-toned rows give the total effect of the given social characteristic, as discussed in the text.
c. Sample N = 1,990.
d. Sample N = 1,937.
e. Two finalists only.

pulls down the parameter for age effects on the Zyuganov vote by three quarters (.21/.28) in the first round, and by 100 percent (.27/.27, in our calculations) in the runoff.

Inspection of the rest of Table 3.3 yields the general conclusion that the intermediary variable through which social differences typically exert the greatest impact on the vote in transitional Russia (the neo-Communist vote, in any case) is indeed voters' issue opinions, with partisanship also playing a considerable role. For urbanization, education, and age in 1995 and in both rounds of the 1996 election, more of the influence of the social factor on the KPRF/Zyuganov vote runs through normative opinions than through any other mediating variable. For the fourth social variable examined, things are quite different. As makes good intuitive sense, the main intermediary for the electoral influence of family income is people's perceptions of current conditions in the country.[45]

Current Conditions

A second corpus of scholarly work concerning societal conditions and elections also has intriguing implications for transitional voting. Its kernel is the proposition that voters snatch cues from trends in the social environment: when things are going badly, citizens lash out at the "ins" and lavish favor on the "outs"; when they are going well, it is the reverse.

The staple version of the theory dwells on economic conditions. Behind the motto tacked on the wall of Bill Clinton's 1992 campaign headquarters—"It's the Economy, Stupid!"—is a learned literature so vast "that one needs a review by now to keep up with reviews of the literature."[46] It posits two main forms of economic voting. In "pocketbook voting," individuals react to the everyday economic conditions at the personal and family level, prime among them fluctuations in standard of living and employment security. "Citizens preoccupied with their pocketbooks support candidates and parties that have advanced their own economic interests and oppose candidates and parties that appear to threaten them." The second form, usually described as "sociotropic voting," is fueled by visions of the health of the entire economy. "In reaching political preferences, the prototypic sociotropic voter is influenced most of all by the nation's economic condition. Purely sociotropic citizens vote according to the country's pocketbook, not their own."[47] The regnant conclusion in the older democracies is that both pocketbook and sociotropic voting take place, yet the sociotropic variant is preponderant.[48]

These formulaic categories make a laboratory-produced impression and may mislead if not used with discernment. They should not connote equivalence of content from country to country. In the political economy of a transitional society the ante is immensely higher than in the Atlantic democracies because governments wrestle, not with the run-of-the-mill peaks and valleys of the business cycle, but with the awesome task of instituting capitalism ex nihilo. For many of the participants, the stay in the "economic emergency room"[49] is so excruciating that one has to wonder if it is endurable—all the more so when democratic rules authorize the mangled patient to pick the medical team in periodic elections. To quote Adam Przeworski's glum prognosis:

> Market-oriented reforms . . . necessarily cause a temporary fall in aggregate consumption. They are socially costly and politically risky . . . They hurt large social groups and evoke opposition from important political forces. And if that happens, democracy may be undermined or reforms abandoned, or both . . . Under democratic conditions, where the discontent can find political expression at the polls, even the most promising reform strategies may be abandoned. Either politicians are concerned about electoral support and reverse policies that will cause them to lose elections, or they lose to competitors more attuned to the political consequences of structural transformation. And in some cases, egalitarian ideologies with strong populist and nationalistic overtones can be mobilized against both democracy and reforms.[50]

For Russia and its former satellites, much scholarly energy has gone into tracking public assessments of economic conditions and relating them to preferences about economic change. In the twilight of Soviet rule, analysts found that a burst of outrage at the performance of the planned economy stimulated enthusiasm at the mass level for a breakthrough to the market, previously despised as antediluvian and "bourgeois."[51] With the unveiling of sweeping reforms by successor governments, economic discontent quickly resurfaced, refocused on the post-Communist elite, and, more or less as Przeworski predicted, fomented anguish over and in some instances outright rejection of the Westernizing transformation of the economic system.[52]

Little is understood about whether, how much, and through what paths these citizen perceptions of economic trends affect post-Soviet electoral conduct.[53] The prospect that events will be propelled by calculations of economic advancement and decline must be checked against the data. But it would be myopic not to ask in the same breath about the *political* component of current conditions. The overhaul of the Soviet-type societies was not initiated solely for economic reasons and has not been limited to the economic sphere. Political authority and freedom have been key stakes since the process caught fire in the 1980s. The transitional electorate should be no less willing to pass sentence on the success of political reform than on bread-and-butter economics.

Emerging or Submerging?

There may soon come a day when Russians and their families will bask in prosperity and security within a blossoming market economy. The 1990s, alas, was no such time. True, the reforms pursued under Boris Yeltsin's aegis did bear some fruit: a price liberalization which eliminated most queues in retail trade; stabilization and internal convertibility of the ruble from 1994 to 1998; membership in the International Monetary Fund; a spike in foreign investment; the gutting of the USSR's planning bureaucracy and the extrusion of many facilities from state control; and the startup of thousands of businesses, banks, a stock exchange, and a bond market.[54] That said, the reform ledger also overflows with mishap and mismanagement. The bankers and industrialists at the heart of Russia's "crony capitalism" excelled at asset stripping and currency speculation, not at investment and growth. National output fell every year in the decade but 1997 and 1999, and the ruble devaluation and stock-market crash that hit in 1998 were to be a devastating reminder of the fine line between an emerging and a submerging market.

As the first campaign leaflets went to press in 1995, the worst misery lay ahead, but signs of distress were impossible to miss. The Russian economy, by the available measures, had subsided to around half of its 1990 size, unemployment was creeping up, and millions of workers were on reduced wages in semi-idle enterprises. Millions more received their pay envelopes or their government pensions and transfer payments months in arrears.

Against such a backdrop it is understandable that economic woes have preyed on the thoughts of Russian voters. More than 60 percent of survey respondents in 1995 and 1996, when asked in an open-ended question to name the most serious problems the motherland "has faced in recent times," listed an economic malady first. Most often cited were the economic crisis in general, unemployment, and issues relating to living standards, inflation, and payment of back wages. Political and constitutional controversies, headed by the misadventure in Chechnya, ranked well back, followed by law and order, social issues, and the "nationality" problem, with foreign policy and national security a distant last.[55]

At the pocketbook level, about three-fifths of Russians believed in 1995 that their household finances had worsened in the preceding twelve months; they were a trifle less irascible the next summer (see Table 3.4).[56] Among the rigors of market reform, joblessness has stayed in the single

Table 3.4 Assessments of Current Economic Conditions, 1995 and 1996
(Percentages)

Measure	1995[a]	1996[b]
Trend in family finances over past twelve months		
Much worse	36	25
Slightly worse	25	25
No change	28	36
Slightly better	9	12
Much better	1	1
Don't know	2	1
Experience of unemployment		
Yes	15	—
No	85	—
Arrears in wages, pensions, or social allowances in past six months		
Some, and worse than previous six months	—	46
Some, and same as previous six months	—	18
Some, but better than previous six months	—	5
None	—	31
Trend in national economy over past twelve months		
Much worse	42	25
Slightly worse	25	23
No change	18	32
Slightly better	9	12
Much better	0.1	0.1
Don't know	5	8

a. N = 2,841 weighted cases.
b. N = 2,472 weighted cases.

digits in Russia, yet is an ominous specter as firms lay off workers and the federal government chops public spending and credits to balance its budget. Fifteen percent of our survey panel in late 1995 were seeking work, had an unemployed spouse, or had been sent on unpaid leave in the past year. This group was twice as likely to rate unemployment as Russia's worst problem than were people who had had no experience of it.[57] In 1996, instead of reproducing the unemployment questions, we asked in detail in our election survey about the nagging hardship of arrears in wages and social security payments, which the government attempted to allay during

Yeltsin's reelection run. Its social scope is broader than the dread of unemployment. About 70 percent of citizens said they suffered payment delays in the first half of 1996, and most of them said arrears were worse in 1996 than in the second half of 1995.[58]

Alarmed as they are about their private fate, Russians are more mortified by what has happened to the national economy. Two-thirds felt in 1995 that it had slid downhill in the preceding twelve months, and fewer than 10 percent sensed an improvement (see the bottom entry in Table 3.4). The mood lightened up some by 1996, but the pessimists were still four times more numerous than the optimists, and most of the change was toward neutrality. In any established democracy these numbers, compounding the concern about family welfare, would spell trouble for incumbents in an election campaign.[59]

We have said that current conditions in the political domain may also be of electoral relevance to transitional citizens. Politics does not display the hard measures of crisis and recovery the economy provides, but there is no reason to doubt that Russians keep mental scorecards as best they can. We asked our survey panel after both the parliamentary and the presidential elections how satisfied they were "in general . . . with how democracy is developing in Russia" *(v tselom . . . razvitiyem demokratii v Rossii).* The query, unlike the economic questions posed, makes no distinction between macro and micro levels, specifies no time frame, and has no neutral response. The distribution of views (see Table 3.5) has, as with the economy, a dour hue overall, but attitudes range from utter condemnation to praise. As with the economy, satisfaction with political conditions rises some in the span between the 1995 and 1996 elections.

Table 3.5 Satisfaction with Democratization in Russia, 1995 and 1996 (Percentages)

Assessment	1995[a]	1996[b]
Completely dissatisfied	19	15
Dissatisfied	46	42
Satisfied	15	25
Completely satisfied	1	1
Don't know	20	17

a. N = 2,774 weighted cases. Some respondents were interviewed in January 1996.
b. N = 2,472 weighted cases.

Current Conditions and the Vote

Do assessments of the state of their society have any relation to how Russians vote? The data tell us they most assuredly do. As theories of economic voting—extended for our purposes into politics—would predict, citizens pleased with current conditions were more likely to prefer pro-government and pro-reform candidates in 1995 and 1996. The displeased took their votes elsewhere and were much more likely to endorse the KPRF in 1995 and Zyuganov in 1996.[60]

The zero-order association holds for egocentric and sociotropic economic assessments and for political assessments alike, as Figures 3.3 and 3.4 attest. (The two positive response categories for family finances, the economy, and democratization are fused in the figures since the topmost ones contain such a paucity of respondents.) The graphs are consonant in basic respects, most obviously in the incidence of KPRF/Zyuganov support. In 1995 turnout for the KPRF was 26 percentage points higher among the voters unhappiest about their household finances than among the most contented. For assessments of the national economy in 1995, the

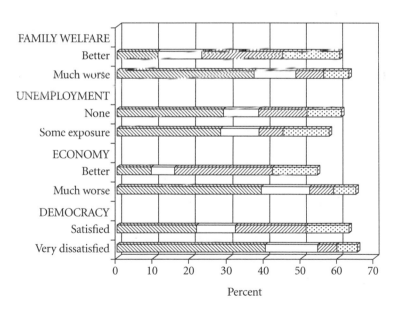

Figure 3.3. Perceptions of Current Conditions and the Party-List Vote, 1995

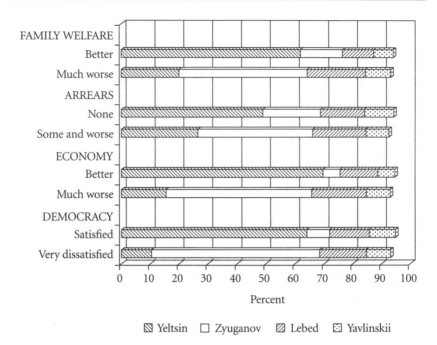

FAMILY WELFARE
- Better
- Much worse

ARREARS
- None
- Some and worse

ECONOMY
- Better
- Much worse

DEMOCRACY
- Satisfied
- Very dissatisfied

Percent

⊠ Yeltsin   ☐ Zyuganov   ▨ Lebed   ⊡ Yavlinskii

Figure 3.4. Perceptions of Current Conditions and the First-Round Presidential Vote, 1996

KPRF's edge among the disgruntled was 30 percent, and for democratization it was 18 percent.

But the figures cannot tell the whole story. Inasmuch as each of the triad of summary measures of conditions—and experiences with unemployment and arrears—is associated with voting behavior and with one another,[61] bilateral associations do not say which one of them has the most punch. We are left wondering which other variables, if any, confound the apparent effects of perceptions of current conditions, and which relay them down the causal chain. And we are in the dark about why the two elections appear to differ so much. How is it that Zyuganov locked up the votes of about 50 percent of the citizens angriest about the national economy and 60 percent of those most perturbed by the course of democratization in 1996, when his KPRF drew around 40 percent in each group in 1995? Why did Our Home Is Russia's 19 percent of voters satisfied with the progress of democracy become Yeltsin's 64 percent? Why on one score after the other did optimists dissipate their votes among rival parties in 1995 but go to Yeltsin, like iron filings to a magnet, in 1996?

Multivariate analysis dispels some of these mysteries. The total-effect estimates in Tables 3.6 and 3.7 permit us to plot systematically the electoral influence of Russians' assessments of current conditions. The total effects, this time around, control for the influence on the vote of the citizen's social attributes (which are at the prior causal stage in our model) and for other perceptions of current conditions (which are at the same causal stage).

In the economic realm, pocketbook assessments and personal traumas do have measurable, independent effects, and in the predicted direction, on voting outcomes. The state-initiated metamorphosis of the Russian economy is actively *creating* interests that in turn feed back into the political domain. These interests are quite apparent even though the new, capitalist economic system is nowhere near complete.

The citizen most sanguine about his or her family's welfare in 1995 was .13 (13 percentage points) less likely to vote for the KPRF than the most alienated citizen and also a statistically insignificant .03 more likely to vote for Our Home Is Russia, holding the control variables constant. In the first round of the presidential election, the citizens' contentment with their lot would have increased the probability of voting for Yeltsin by .17 and decreased the probability of voting for Zyuganov by .07 ($p > .05$) and of voting for General Lebed by .11. Personal experience of unemployment in

Table 3.6 Total Effects of Assessments of Current Conditions on the Party-List Vote, 1995 (Differences in Predicted Probabilities)[a]

Variable	KPRF	LDPR	Our Home	Yabloko
Pocketbook economic assessments[b]	−.13**	.01	.03	.04
Experience of unemployment[c]	−.01	.01	.06**	−.02
Sociotropic economic assessments[d]	−.21**	−.09**	.16**	.04
Assessments of democratization[e]	−.10*	−.03	.14**	.03

**p ≤ .01

*p ≤ .05

a. Sample N = 2,143.

b. Five-point index (much worse, slightly worse, no change, slightly better, much better). Missing values (55 unweighted cases) coded at mean of distribution.

c. Binary measure, with some experience of unemployment as lower value.

d. Five-point index (much worse, slightly worse, no change, slightly better, much better). Missing values (157 unweighted cases) coded at mean of distribution.

e. Four-point index (completely dissatisfied, dissatisfied, satisfied, completely satisfied). Missing values (576 unweighted cases) coded at mean of distribution.

Table 3.7 Total Effects of Assessments of Current Conditions on the Presidential Vote, 1996 (Differences in Predicted Probabilities)

Variable	First round[a]				Runoff[b]	
	Yel.	Zyug.	Leb.	Yav.	Yel.	Zyug.
Pocketbook economic assessments[c]	.17**	−.07	−.11*	−.03	.14*	−.10
Experience with arrears in wages and social allowances[d]	.11**	−.06*	−.02	.01	.13**	−.14**
Sociotropic economic assessments[e]	.35**	−.28**	−.03	−.02	.49**	−.43**
Assessments of democratization[f]	.65**	−.39**	−.14**	−.04	.70**	−.60**

**p ≤ .01

*p ≤ .05

a. Sample N = 1,990.

b. Sample N = 1,937.

c. Five-point index (much worse, slightly worse, no change, slightly better, much better). Missing values (24 unweighted cases) coded at mean of distribution.

d. Four-point index (some and worse than previous six months, some and same as previous six months, some but better than previous six months, none reported).

e. Five-point index (much worse, slightly worse, no change, slightly better, much better). Missing values (203 unweighted cases) coded at mean of distribution.

f. Four-point index (completely dissatisfied, dissatisfied, satisfied, completely satisfied). Missing values (436 unweighted cases) coded at mean of distribution.

1995 and of pay arrears in 1996 had a statistically robust if not always substantively major effect on voting decisions, with arrears being the better predictor of the two.[62] Public-regarding assessments of the economy as a whole also have an impact on the vote and, as in most democracies, these opinions have the upper hand over self-regarding assessments. Post-Soviet voters, it is fair to say, are more animated by Russia's pocketbook than by their own. For the KPRF vote in 1995, for example, the reduced-form estimate for sociotropic assessments comes close to doubling that for pocketbook assessments; for the first-round vote for Yeltsin in 1996, it is about exactly double.

There is a crude symmetry in the impact of current economic conditions on the probability of voting for pro-government and liberal parties and candidates, on the one hand, and for the stridently anti-government socialist opposition, on the other: satisfied citizens lean one way, the dissatisfied the other. Electoral players with other points of view are affected in less obvious combinations. Nationalist candidates, who have drawn about one-fifth of the votes in Russian elections, fare erratically under current discontents. In the 1995 parliamentary election, LDPR supporters were on average dissatisfied with the economy as a whole but not with their personal economic plight. In the 1996 presidential election, it was the other way around for the leading nationalist candidate, Aleksandr Lebed, who profited from pocketbook but not sociotropic discontent.

The other moral of Tables 3.6 and 3.7 is about citizen appraisals of the *political* side of regime change. These would be immaterial to electoral choice in a consolidated democracy; they are highly material in Russia's protodemocracy. In the 1995 Duma election, favorable opinions about the course of democratization had a major positive effect (.14) on the likelihood of voting for Our Home Is Russia and a negative effect (−.10) on the likelihood of voting for the KPRF; both parameters are less than those for sociotropic economic considerations. In the presidential election, political appraisals *dwarf* the economic variables in impact: compare the total-effect statistic for the preliminary-round Yeltsin vote (.65) to those for pocketbook economic assessments (.17), arrears (.11), and sociotropic economic assessments (.35).

Tables 3.8 through 3.11 elaborate multistage estimates for the two most important kinds of perceptions of current conditions—assessments of the national economy and of democratization— estimates which let us make inferences about the factors that mediate between these perceptions and Russians' voting choices. Several patterns are visible, with a number of intermediary variables playing at least some part in the transmission. For the political forces of the post-Soviet status quo (Our Home Is Russia and Yeltsin) and the vanguard of the opposition to it (the KPRF and Zyuganov), issue opinions and citizens' evaluations of Yeltsin and his administration play the principal roles.[63]

The contrast in how current conditions play out in the parliamentary and presidential electoral formats merits emphasis. They are of moment in both contests, but more so in 1996 than in 1995. And the explanatory ability of specific assessments varies in several respects: sociotropic economic assessments are more important in the presidential than in the parliamentary setting and acquire greater salience relative to pocketbook assessments; and political appraisals become more influential and gain massively vis-à-vis both genres of economic assessment.

Why the fork in the road? A large literature in comparative politics

Table 3.8 Elaboration of the Impact of Sociotropic Economic Assessments on the Party-List Vote, 1995 (Differences in Predicted Probabilities)[a]

Variables progressively incorporated in regression	KPRF	LDPR	Our Home	Yabloko
Sociotropic assessments only	−.33**	−.09**	.22**	.13**
Also social characteristics	−.23**	−.08**	.17**	.05*
Also other current conditions[b]	−.21**	−.09**	.16**	.04
Also partisanship (but not issue opinions)	−.17**	−.04*	.13**	.01
Also issue opinions (but not partisanship)	−.16**	−.06**	.14**	.01
Also partisanship and issue opinions	−.13**	−.03*	.12**	−.02
Also retrospective evaluations of incumbents	−.09	−.02	.08	−.01
Also party leaders	−.11	−.01	.05	−.01
Also prospective evaluations of parties	−.10	−.01	.05	−.01

**p ≤ .01
*p ≤ .05
a. Sample N = 2,143.
b. Gray-toned row gives the total effect of sociotropic assessments.

points to electoral rules. Winner-take-all presidential elections tend to bifurcate electorates; parliamentary elections fought under proportional-representation rules multiply citizens' options and scatter their votes, especially if the hurdle for seating in the legislature is low.[64] A complementary approach would bring in a more compendious set of institutional factors that shape what G. Bingham Powell and Guy D. Whitten call "clarity of responsibility" for governments' economic actions. For voters to turn their wrath on the sitting government, they must see signs that it exercises "unified control of policymaking." "Both positive and negative effects of economic performance will be diminished in countries where responsibility is widely diffused," say Powell and Whitten—a situation that may result from disunity within the dominant party, coalition government, a profusion of parties, or a committee system that splinters legislative authority among many parties and factions.[65] In the United States, where decision powers are split between legislative and executive branches but the latter calls the shots on the economy, scholars have found business conditions to matter less in congressional than in presidential elections.[66]

Both Russia's cross-bred electoral system and the lopsided distribution

Table 3.9 Elaboration of the Impact of Sociotropic Economic Assessments on the Presidential Vote, 1996 (Differences in Predicted Probabilities)

Variables progressively incorporated in regression	First round[a]				Runoff[b]	
	Yel.	Zyug.	Leb.	Yav.	Yel.	Zyug.
Sociotropic assessments only	.60**	−.47**	−.07*	−.02	.67**	−.60**
Also social characteristics	.57**	−.36**	−.11**	−.04*	.61**	−.53**
Also other current conditions[c]	.35**	−.28**	−.03	−.02	.49**	−.43**
Also partisanship (but not issue opinions)	.34**	−.25**	−.04	−.03	.48**	−.42**
Also issue opinions (but not partisanship)	.25**	−.13**	−.04	−.04	.32**	−.24**
Also partisanship and issue opinions	.26**	−.16**	−.04	−.04	.34**	−.25**
Also retrospective evaluations of incumbents	.08	−.09**	.00	−.02	.13**	−.11**
Also leadership qualities	−.01	−.06*	.03	.00	.09*[d]	−.08*[d]
Also prospective evaluations of candidates	−.04	−.05	−.03	−.00	.07[d]	−.06[d]

$**p \leq .01$

$*p \leq .05$

a. Sample N = 1,990.

b. Sample N = 1,937.

c. Gray-toned row gives the total effect of sociotropic assessments.

d. Two finalists only.

of power under its "superpresidential" constitution help explain the different potency of current conditions in parliamentary and presidential elections. Not only did the structure of the 1996 presidential contest draw voters' eyes to candidates with a realistic chance of winning a majority, but what was at issue was ascendancy over an executive branch whose say in public policy, budgets, and rule enforcement far outstrips the Duma's. It was eminently sensible for self-interested citizens to link their concerns about economic and political conditions more snugly to their voting choices in 1996 than in 1995.

None of this decisively explains why political assessments would come to the fore so rousingly in 1996 as to trump economics. The magic ingredi-

Table 3.10 Elaboration of the Impact of Assessments of Democratization on the Party-List Vote, 1995 (Differences in Predicted Probabilities)[a]

Variables progressively incorporated in regression	KPRF	LDPR	Our Home	Yabloko
Assessments of democratization only	−.23**	−.06**	.19**	.08*
Also social characteristics	−.16**	−.05*	.16**	.04
Also other current conditions[b]	−.10*	−.03	.14**	.03
Also partisanship (but not issue opinions)	−.02*	−.03	.12**	−.00
Also issue opinions (but not partisanship)	−.02	−.02	.13**	.01
Also partisanship and issue opinions	.04	−.02	.12*	−.02
Also retrospective evaluations of incumbents	.15*	−.02	.05	−.03
Also party leaders	.15	−.00	.02	−.02
Also prospective evaluations of parties	.12	−.01	.05	−.01

**p ≤ .01
*p ≤ .05

a. Sample N = 2,143.

b. Gray-toned row gives the total effect of assessments of democratization.

ent is the distinct character of *transitional* mass politics. Russians rate economic ills as the most pressing problems on the national agenda. But their behavior in 1996 bares the crucial premise of this judgment—namely, agreement that there will be no rollback of the political reforms which millions take as rightfully theirs. President Yeltsin's brilliant campaign to equate a vote for Zyuganov with a vote for restoration of Soviet tyranny shows how excitable the transitional citizenry is about the issue. Such an equivalence would have been unconvincing in 1995, when voters were electing a weak parliament; in 1996, when the prize was the apparatus of the state, it struck a bull's-eye. Place the total-effect statistics for democratization in the two elections side by side—+.14 for Our Home Is Russia and −.10 for the KPRF in 1995, +.65 for Yeltsin and −.39 for Zyuganov in the first round in 1996—and they make a stunning corroboration of the point.

Conclusions

The data at our disposal refute prophesies that politics and electoral choice after Communism will be entirely divorced from the architecture of soci-

Table 3.11 Elaboration of the Impact of Assessments of Democratization on the Presidential Vote, 1996 (Differences in Predicted Probabilities)

Variables progressively incorporated in regression	First round[a]				Runoff[b]	
	Yel.	Zyug.	Leb.	Yav.	Yel.	Zyug.
Assessments of democratization only	.76**	−.58**	−.10**	−.03	.81**	−.72**
Also social characteristics	.74**	−.46**	−.15**	−.05**	.77**	−.67**
Also other current conditions[c]	.65**	−.39**	−.14**	−.04	.70**	−.60**
Also partisanship (but not issue opinions)	.59**	−.25**	−.19**	−.07**	.61**	−.47**
Also issue opinions (but not partisanship)	.55**	−.18**	−.19**	−.08**	.48**	−.34**
Also partisanship and issue opinions	.53**	−.13**	−.21**	−.09**	.45**	−.30**
Also retrospective evaluations of incumbents	.26**	−.04	−.13*	−.05	.15**	−.09*
Also leadership qualities	.20*	−.02	−.14	−.02	.13*[d]	−.06[d]
Also prospective evaluations of candidates	.07	.01	−.08	−.01	.07[d]	−.02[d]

**p ≤ .01
*p ≤ .05
a. Sample N = 1,990.
b. Sample N = 1,937.
c. Gray-toned row gives the total effect of assessments of democratization.
d. Two finalists only.

ety or ineluctably will depend on ethnic and religious identities. In transitional Russia, we have seen, there are definite, measurable linkages between social divisions and the vote. And it is not ethnicity or confession that stands out as a source of political conflict but rather the citizen's age, urbanism and geographic location, income, educational level, prior membership in the Communist Party of the Soviet Union, and ties to the profit-seeking sector of the economy. Of all these, it is age and generation that counts the most.

This is far from an excuse to swing to the opposite extreme in interpretation. Paul F. Lazarsfeld's adage about the postwar United States—that "a person thinks, politically, as he is, socially"—would be as misleadingly reductionist a claim about Russian voters today as it would be about contemporary American voters. To conceive of Russians in the polling booth as acting out geometrically neat social alignments and nothing else would be to oversimplify group contradictions and to embellish their effects. Better to speak of regularities in the social distribution of electoral preferences, some (but not all) of which are substantively important, and none of which should be omitted from the analysis of other causal factors.

Current conditions within society are more mutable in the short term than social morphology, and less remote from the voting decision. Economically, Russians' perceptions of how they and the nation are or are not making ends meet have unambiguous consequences for where they decide to place their voting support. There is an uncanny resemblance of form here to economic voting in the West. The main differences from a well-buffered regime are two. The first is that sensations of pain and gain ensue expressly from the Promethean project of trying to substitute one economic system for another, and the backlash against that endeavor, rather than from the routine ups and downs of an installed system. The second is the amount of weight that appraisals of change of the political regime carry in the transitional electorate's deliberations; there is no equal for this in the workings of a stable democracy. Given that departure from the accepted electoral script, the credo of an up-and-coming Russian politician could just as well be "It's the Polity, Stupid!" as "It's the Economy, Stupid!"

Partisanship in Formation

From background factors, mainly nonpolitical ones, we move to the electoral impact of an explicitly political variable: the public's response to the parties and quasi-party groupings which have arisen in the course of Russia's democratization. It is a maxim of political science that parties and democratic governance go hand in hand. "The development of parties," Maurice Duverger wrote years ago in one of the jewels of the discipline, is "bound up with that of democracy."[1] In the same vein, Leon D. Epstein said it is a waste of time to ask metaphysically whether democracies can get by without parties: "At the level of empirical analysis, one can rest content with the view that, so far, parties have developed in every democratic nation" as mediators between societal interests and the state.[2] And Otto Kirchheimer, in another classic study, depicted parties as "permanently organized transmission belts between population and government" without which policies responsive to the people would be unimaginable.[3]

Encomiums to parties should not distract us from the gritty task at their core. While parties may play other consequential roles, such as coordinating legislative assemblies and socializing citizens, their reason for being is to contest and control elections. So it is in Russia and the ex-Soviet bloc.

This is not to say all Russian parties acquit themselves well at this pivotal electoral function. Many patently do not, and they pay the supreme penalty for failure: obliteration. Even most of those which have notched a victory or two are organizational tadpoles no discriminating scientist will mistake for the mature species. Far from offering grounds for banishing them from electoral analysis, the immaturity of the parties is a compelling theoretical reason for dealing them in. Turbulent Russia is an exquisite laboratory for observing parties and party sentiment in their initial phases of formation.

Our scrutiny here begins with a brief description of the inceptive party system and of Russian attitudes toward it, which typically are disapproving. This will not be our primary mission, though. Wherever elections are structured wholly or partly by political parties, as is the norm in democracies, citizens mark their ballots for individual parties and the candidates they endorse, not for the party system as a whole. It is binding on us, therefore, to probe how Russians relate to specific parties. Research into this question in the Western world turns on a seminal concept—popular "identification" with parties—and on the controversy over its validity.[4] To look for fully ripened, stable partisan identification in Russia at so early a date would be pointless. I focus here on a more contingent and more ambiguous mindset, which I dub *transitional partisanship*. We will explore the evidence for its existence, its extent within Russian society, the objects of its affection, and, as much as information allows, its temporal dialectic. The payoff comes in linking partisanship to voting choice, which we shall do in the parliamentary and presidential settings, using the data from 1995–96.

Parties and People

A party is an organization that aspires to get candidates elected to public office under a given label. The almighty Communist Party of the Soviet Union by that touchstone was not a party at all, in that choreographing the country's pseudo-elections was not its chief purpose. Nonmonopolistic political parties popped up in the USSR during Mikhail Gorbachev's reign and acquired legal protection when the Soviet constitution was amended in March 1990 to do away with the CPSU's hegemony. They grew into going concerns only after the Soviet regime fell apart in 1991.[5]

In the new Russia, parties in the aggregate have been a roaring success—several hundred have been accredited at any one moment—but the vast majority of individual parties have been duds. So minuscule, so ephemeral, and so bumbling are many of them that they are all but invisible and all but irrelevant to the voter and the scholar. Of the armada of forty-three parties that cruised into the 1995 parliamentary election, twenty-eight received fewer than 1 million votes, and sixteen fewer than the 200,000 registration signatures they collected before the campaign.[6] Eleven got fewer than 100,000 votes.

The shipwreck of political parties by the dozen has not soured Russian leaders on building them. Parties in general are for them inseparable from political modernity. From a selfish standpoint, they, like so many ambitious politicos, encounter "more or less continual incentives . . . to consider party organizations as means to achieve their goals," starting with winning elective office and sharing out the spoils.[7] They have enacted laws and regulations that indulge the apprentice parties and their executives, without going so far as to cede them a hammerlock on nominations and electioneering. Every second seat in the State Duma has been staked out since 1993 for national party lists, which explains the willingness of even the shrillest enemies of the government to take part in the electoral game as soon as Boris Yeltsin set it up by presidential decree.[8] In the 225 territorial districts, party nominees fight for their spots with independents. Election of the president is closer in spirit to the cross-bred district races than to the war of the party lists—this at the insistence of Yeltsin, stealing a leaf from Charles de Gaulle, that as father and guardian of the state he ought to stay above the partisan fracas.[9] Nonetheless, all the larger parties took part in the 1996 presidential election, and the head of the most imposing of them, the KPRF's Gennadii Zyuganov, gave the incumbent the stiffest fight.

Duverger distinguished "mass parties," their feet planted on a bedrock of individual members, from "cadre parties," "grouping[s] of notabilities for the preparation of elections, conducting campaigns and maintaining contacts with the candidates."[10] With the borderline exception of the KPRF, Russia's parties are cadre parties. The KPRF purports to have a membership of 600,000; this is a respectable base, yet only a fraction of what the great West European parties commanded in their prime. All other political parties and movements in the federation add up to a few hundred thousand members.[11] The internal organization of most Russian parties is haphazard. Moscow leadership cliques are often so out of touch with local cadres that the parties "combine organizational hypercentralization with operational decentralization."[12] Lax internal discipline, sectarianism toward abutting parties, and a predilection for personality fads and vendettas all make for a fragmented partisan mosaic. Many Western parties, it has been said, are becoming "catch-all parties" which "value electoral victory over ideological or sociological purity."[13] Most Russian parties are best captioned "catch-some" parties, organized by opportunists for whom finding and sheltering an electoral niche—victory be damned—outweighs the wish to pump up their public constituency or forge external alliances and carry out an ideological program. For some—the tongue-in-cheek Beer

Lovers' Party, whose national list pulled in 428,727 votes in December 1995, is a blatant example—the coveted niche is so tiny and eccentric that Russian commentators accurately speak of them as "political humorists" who are in the game for a laugh as much as for seats in the Duma.[14]

Were democracy to rise or fall on the public's devotion to political parties, it would be doomed in Russia. The plain truth is that Russians think poorly of their parties in ensemble. On the same confidence scale we have employed for governments, three citizens voice distrust of the neophyte parties for every one who trusts them (see Table 4.1, for 1996). This is stin-

Table 4.1 Citizen Assessments of Russian Political Parties

Assessment	Percentage
Trust in parties[a]	
Complete distrust	10
Distrust	44
Trust	15
Complete trust	2
Don't know	29
Agreement with statement, "Competition among various political parties makes our system stronger"[b]	
Strongly disagree	5
Disagree	24
Unsure	15
Agree	29
Strongly agree	7
Don't know	20
Attitude toward number of parties Russia currently has[a]	
Too few	1
Too many	75
About right	10
Don't know	14
Optimal number of parties in Russia[c]	
None	3
1	33
2–5	59
More than 5	5

a. 1996 survey (N = 2,472 weighted cases).

b. 1995 pre-election survey (N = 2,841 weighted cases).

c. 1996 survey, among respondents who gave a number (N = 1,535 weighted cases).

gier than the low grades the population awards to state institutions. Almost 30 percent of survey respondents shrug their shoulders and give no evaluation.[15]

Nor is there much gusto for the interparty competition which bloomed in Russia in the 1990s. Asked if sparring among various political parties strengthens the political system, almost as many citizens disagree with as concur in the statement; another third cannot say (Table 4.1 again, from 1995 data). The outstanding irritant is the numerical proliferation of parties. Barely anyone believes the country does not have enough political parties; three-quarters believe it has too many. Most Russians would prefer a political system with several parties seeking their votes: the mean number of parties survey respondents saw as optimal in 1996 was 2.8. It is troubling, though, that many Russians are still in the grip of Soviet-era attitudes, in which competition is an evil to be avoided. The modal response to our question in 1996 about the optimal number of parties, returned by a third of those willing to answer, was that *one* party would suffice.[16]

Tolerance of many rival parties, and perforce of multiparty politics, flows deeper in some quarters than in others. Historical experience has left its scars, as the desired size of the party system varies by generation (see Figure 4.1). Up to approximately the age of seventy, the older Russians are, and hence the more likely their outlooks are to have cohered in Soviet times, the more they yearn for simplicity and often for the one-party system; the younger they are, the more at ease they are apt to be with the pro-

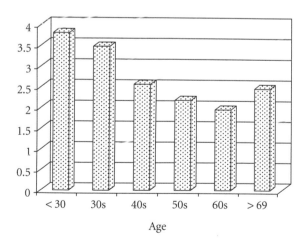

Figure 4.1. Number of Parties Desired for Russia by Age Group, 1996

fusion of parties. The oldest citizens, inexplicably, condone almost as many parties as persons in their forties. The differences are steeper and more monotonic by education group than by age (see Figure 4.2). The optimal number of parties climbs from 1.5 among those with fewer than five years in an elementary school (most of whom are also elderly) to 4.1 among graduates of higher education.[17]

Whether Russian voters esteem or scorn the number of parties and the whole party system, electoral politics normally confronts them with a different set of choices. They have to decode information about, and beamed in their direction by, particular parties or party-affiliated candidates pursuing their support. To digest information of this kind costs time and effort in any society.[18] In older democracies, the moderate or small quantity of parties and the familiarity that comes with time make that toll manageable. In a protodemocracy abuzz with tyro parties, information costs for prospective voters will be higher than normal.

How many political aficionados, let alone others, could possibly have sorted out the pack of parties running for the Russian State Duma in 1995? The problem bedevils the citizen and also the researcher trying to find out who knows what: no survey respondent would sit still for prying questions about forty-odd political organizations. In our 1995 pre-election poll, we used a more down-to-earth test. We requested that interviewees evaluate on a feeling thermometer a subset of ten of the more prominent Russian

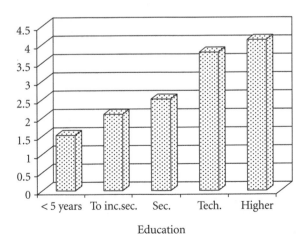

Figure 4.2. Number of Parties Desired for Russia by Education Level, 1996

parties, which, it transpired, finished first through fifth, seventh, and ninth through twelfth in the proportional-representation vote. Figure 4.3 shows how many informants recognized and were able to assign numerical scores to each of the ten. For name recognition, the range is from the 89 percent conversant with the KPRF to the 67 percent conversant with the national- istic KRO; for recognition and ability to evaluate, it goes from the KPRF's 75 percent to KRO's 44 percent.

In light of the plethora of partisan options and the breathtaking new- ness of the entire exercise, these are salutary results. Eighty-six percent of Russians in 1995 could recognize and evaluate at least one party; 26 per- cent did this for all ten. The mean number of parties recognized was 7.8, and 5.8 out of ten were recognized and evaluated.[19]

Acquaintance with the parties is not evenly distributed in the transi- tional electorate. How much Russians know about the parties depends on the degree of their political engagement, as calibrated by any indicator of interest, involvement, and competence. The awareness scale used exten- sively in this book is as stout a predictor as any (see Figure 4.4). Citizens in the politically least attuned fifth of the populace could evaluate an average of 2.6 parties in 1995; for those in the top fifth it was 8.0 parties, three

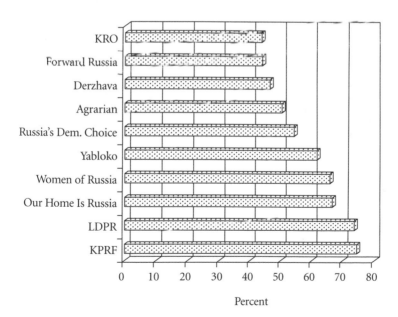

Figure 4.3. Ability to Recognize and Evaluate Ten Main Parties, 1995

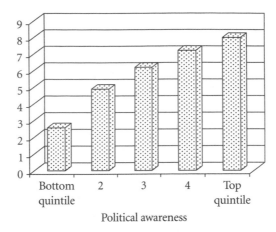

Figure 4.4. Number of Parties Recognized and Evaluated by Level of Political Awareness, 1995 (Maximum = 10)

times as many.[20] The data also reveal a clean break between knowing the parties and approving them or the multiparty competition in general. Citizens who felt that competition among the parties is bad for Russia's political system knew virtually as much as proponents of competition did about individual parties in 1995.[21]

Transitional Partisanship

The theory of party identification has been at or near the center of electoral research in the West since the 1950s. The locus classicus of the theory, *The American Voter,* defined partisan identification as the citizen's "psychological identification" with or "affective attachment" to a political party. It found this inclination to be well-nigh ubiquitous in the U.S. electorate, sturdy over time, and more prescriptive of voting choice than any other variable. For the Michigan School, as it came to be known, identification affected the vote straight-away or, more often, obliquely, through other attitudes: "Identification with a party raises a perceptual screen through which the individual tends to see what is favorable to his partisan orientation. The stronger the party bond, the more exaggerated the process of selection and perceptual distortion will be."[22]

Four decades of fact-finding and refinement of the notion have not dislodged it from the mainstream of the American and comparative literature on public opinion and electoral conduct. Warren E. Miller (one of the authors of *The American Voter*, published in 1960) and J. Merrill Shanks typify party identification in their *The New American Voter* (1996) as "the most enduring of political attitudes, responsible for shaping a wide variety of values and perceptions," and hence the launch point for any inquiry into national elections.[23] Other scholars trenchantly argue its relevance to electoral behavior overseas.[24]

For analysts of new democracies, the debate over party identification in the established democratic systems provides food for thought on several counts. If there is a point of unison, it is how finicky one must be about measurement techniques—the wording and ordering of survey items among them—if the empirical claims about attitudes toward parties are to be cogent for the society concerned and comparable to other nations.[25] This caution is as imperative in Russia as in the United States or France.

Substantively, scholars differ on the balance between emotional and instrumental content in partisan identities. Some continue to underline the affective properties. Others, harking back to the work of Anthony Downs, play up the utility of partisanship in the near term as an "information shortcut" and emitter of cues that assist citizens in handling baffling surroundings.[26]

Disagreement over content has stoked revisionism and debate concerning the temporal aspect of partisan affiliation. *The American Voter* asserted that identification for most persons was imprinted during childhood and adolescent socialization and continued ticking on undisturbed in adult life. In contrast, Morris P. Fiorina has alleged on the basis of U.S. panel data that identification "waxes and wanes in accord with a citizen's evaluations of the recent performance of the party in power." He prefers to conceptualize it as a "running tally of retrospective evaluations" rather than as "something learned at mommy's knee and never questioned thereafter."[27] Quite similar conclusions have been drawn about Britain, Western Europe, and Canada.[28]

Other scholars, while standing by partisan continuity, have done longitudinal research documenting the weaning of maturing adults away from parental loyalties. In a remarkable project on American political attitudes, a team of scholars led by M. Kent Jennings interviewed high school seniors and their parents in 1965, then reinterviewed the offspring in 1973 and 1982. Some stuck by their parents' party and political interests; others adopted an apolitical posture; and still others switched parties: "These patterns of partisan change demonstrate how the traditional influence of parent socialization can be modified in face of a powerful competing *Zeitgeist* at a critical point in the life cycle. They attest to striking intergenerational discontinuities in even the most stable of political systems."[29] Party identification, Jennings and his colleagues say, does not change randomly or only in reaction to the performance of the party in government, as Fiorina stressed, but in conformity with individuals' evolving ideas and policy preferences.[30] Even some latter-day champions of party identification, Miller and Shanks among them, are agnostic about its origins and molding forces. Again, the repercussions for transitional Russia are worth pondering.

Partisanship in Russia

Might party identification be at work in Russia's protoplasmic political system? If the benchmark is the rock-ribbed Republicans and Democrats celebrated in *The American Voter,* a second's rumination will yield a resounding No. Political parties have not been on the Russian scene long enough to beget the abiding allegiances and aversions that are the nucleus of mature partisan identification, to say nothing of the notion of malleable youngsters absorbing them at mommy's or daddy's knee. Party identification as "the most enduring of political attitudes" will not jell until the parties themselves harden into standing features of Russia's civic landscape.

But this injunction does not nearly exhaust the topic. Some proponents of identification in the United States, we have noted, put emphasis on its pliability and its utility as an information sieve, not on its learned or indoctrinated quality. So why could such a rationale not have a bearing on Russia right now? Partisan identification in the entrenched democracies did not descend like manna from heaven. It evolved among ordinary men and women impelled by contemporaneous considerations who, in their own way, survived transitional times. In the United States, the cradle of the modern political party a century and a half ago, social scientists were not around to witness the harbingers and nascent forms of identification. In Russia we have the good fortune to be present at the creation.

A sizable section of the post-Soviet population exhibits what I call, for want of a more elegant phrase, "transitional partisanship." Like full-fledged partisan identification, transitional partisanship is a visceral sense of kinship with a political party. Unlike identification of the sort normally envisioned in the West, in Russia, where democratic freedoms and parties are of such recent vintage, it crystallizes in the short to medium term rather than during a protracted political education. And, unlike the prototypical identification bond, it is vulnerable to other short-run forces and hence abnormally volatile.

Early probes of partisan feeling in Russia, done through a variety of optics, have arrived at a variety of conclusions. In *How Russia Votes,* Stephen White, Richard Rose, and Ian McAllister note an "absence of party identification" there. They adduce a 1993 survey to this effect—in which 22 percent of respondents did in fact appear to signal identification—and say, "The result is that Russian elections do not register popular commitment to the parties that are elected."[31] In an article based on another data set from 1993, William Miller, Stephen White, and Paul Heywood state that only about 20 percent of Russians and 14 percent of Ukrainians questioned around the same time had party attachments. This fact they attribute to the lengthy dominance of the CPSU, which "left voters in the former Soviet Union peculiarly allergic to the idea of committing themselves to any party."[32] Geoffrey Evans and Stephen Whitefield report on surveys conducted in 1993–94 in Russia and seven ex-Communist countries nearby. Thirteen percent of their Russian respondents interviewed in the summer of 1993 gave answers indicating "party identification" or "party attachment." This was the least of any of the countries; Lithuania led with 50 percent.[33] Arthur H. Miller and his associates from the University of Iowa come to a much more upbeat assessment. They found that about half of Russians, 60 percent of Lithuanians, and 30 percent of Ukrainians had a party identification in the spring of 1995. By the beginning of 1997, the proportion in those three countries was up to 61 percent, signifying a "rapid rise in partisanship."[34]

Timing and question crafting must be reckoned with in interpreting these results. Russians might well have reacted to an interrogation about parties in 1993, prior to the first multiparty election, differently from how they would respond only a few years later, when organized opposition to the government was a less outlandish idea and particular parties had logged some time in the limelight. White, Rose, and McAllister's question was rendered as, "Do you identify with any particular political party or movement?"—wording which is cumbersome in Russian and probes more than would have been advisable at the time for fixity in the relationship. The question fielded by Evans and Whitefield and by the Iowa team—"Do you think of yourself as a supporter of any particular party?"—is soft and might conflate psychic attachment with voting intention, with past voting practice, or with a utilitarian appraisal of a party's platform more blood-less than any that would smack of "identification." The decision of both groups to show respondents a card listing the parties might also have had the unwitting effect of "leading the witness" and elevating the proportion of affirmative responses. In many meticulous surveys in Western democra-cies, party ID questions are modified by words such as "generally speaking" or "usually." In Russia in the early post-Soviet years, such nomenclature would have tended to mystify, inasmuch as it couches as recurrent a situa-tion which for the bulk of the citizenry is still a novelty. Miller, White, and Heywood's lead question was worded, "Generally speaking, do you think of yourself as a supporter of any political party?", a formulation which might suffer from this flaw.

Our election surveys in 1995 and 1996 included a battery of questions which I would defend as better suited to bring out evidence of such mental affinities with parties and near-parties as may tenably form in the crucible of transitional politics soon after the initial appearance of a party system. The 1995 sequence, fielded in the pre-election interview, is the most thor-oughgoing of any surveys done in Russia, to the best of my knowledge. It led off with the question, "Please tell me, is there any one among the pres-ent parties, movements, and associations about which you would say, 'This is my party [*moya partiya*], my movement, my association'?" The posses-sive "my" translates into the Russian vernacular the intensity and exclusiv-ity at the heart of partisanship without endowing it with a false perma-nency. Persons who gave a Yes to the opening question were requested to name the organization (unprompted—no list was given) and, as a check on comprehension, to name one or several of its leaders. That done, the interviewer asked whether the designated party "reflects your interests, views, and concerns" completely or partially. Finally, respondents who had replied in the negative to the first question or were unable to answer were asked if any party, movement, or association "reflects your interests, views, and concerns more than the others?" Those who said so were invited to name the party and its leaders.

The series allows construction of an ordinal scale of strength of parti-sanship. Post-Communist *strong partisans,* as I shall christen them, say they have "[their] party," recall its name, and say it fully embodies their concerns. *Moderate partisans* come up with a party of their own but say it meets their needs only partially. *Weak partisans,* though negative on the "my party" question, later finger a party which "more than the others" corresponds to their needs. *Nonpartisans* either give straight negative responses or cannot answer.[35]

The pie wedges in Figure 4.5 represent the distribution of strength of partisanship in the Russian electorate in 1995. As befits a country where parties are just now sinking roots, more people match the nonpartisan profile than the partisan. The number of political independents is extremely high by comparison with the United States (less so by comparison with Western Europe). Yet the margin of nonpartisans over partisans is wafer-thin. Forty-nine percent of our respondents, and 55 percent of those who turned out to vote for the State Duma, can be described as partisans of some ilk during the 1995 campaign, with weak partisans being the largest subgroup. Russian political parties, perishable and ungainly as they are—and obnoxious as they may be in the plural to citizens—do seem to strike a chord with the public.

The direction of partisanship is harder to map than its strength, since Russia lacks a universally acknowledged, unidimensional ruler for classifying political ideas and programs, such as the left-right continuum put to use in multiparty systems in Western Europe.[36] Figure 4.6 sorts partisans in 1995 categorically by individual party and party family preferred. Twenty-eight percent of partisans (or 14 percent of all citizens) can be counted as being in the KPRF's camp in 1995, as many as the second-ranking party (the LDPR), the third (Our Home Is Russia), and the fourth (Yabloko) combined. Behind the big four, followed by the centrist Women of Russia, the nationalist KRO, and the socialist Agrarians, ten other parties had won the hearts of 1 to 4 percent of the partisan-minded apiece, epitomizing the balkanization of Russian mass politics.[37] By programmatic family, more than one-third of all Russian partisans were committed as of 1995 to a so-

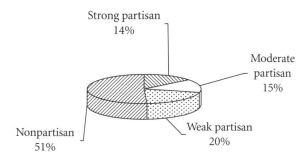

Figure 4.5. Strength of Partisanship, 1995

(a)

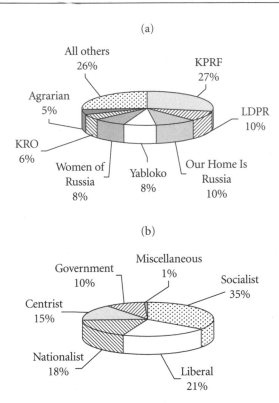

(b)

Figure 4.6. Distribution of Partisans, 1995
a. By Party
b. By Party Family

cialist party. Parties in the liberal, nationalist, and centrist oppositions and Prime Minister Chernomyrdin's government party came behind the so-cialists. The miscellaneous groups on the fringes of politics brought up the rear with 1 percent in total.

There is an exquisite irony here: the KPRF and its socialist brethren, in ideas the most backward-looking of Russia's political parties, are the most avant-garde in their ability to captivate a popular following for the organization.

Correlates of Partisanship

Where does partisanship come from? The accepted approach in the West would be to excavate for clues in the citizen's biography, beginning with family and parents. This approach does not suit the former Soviet Union, where political socialization under the CPSU was the job of the single-party state, not the family. There is no evident connection between parental values and post-Soviet partisan identity, although subsequent research may tell us more. We asked Russians in the post-presidential election survey in 1996 about frequency of discussion of political topics at home in their childhood years. Forty-eight percent said politics was never discussed in their households, 38 percent said it was discussed a little, and 5 percent said there were frequent discussions. Relating this indicator to current-day partisan feelings, we find that individuals who had no conversations about political affairs in the family kitchen are no more or less partisan on average than individuals who had them occasionally or often.[38]

The officially sanctioned hub of political discussion and action in the Soviet period was the Communist Party of the Soviet Union, which had 11 million dues-paying members in Russia, and 20 million in the USSR, before its dissolution. Erstwhile CPSU membership, unlike the family connection, is somewhat predictive of the acquisition of partisanship in the post-Soviet system. Ex-CPSU members were 15 percentage points more likely to be transitional partisans in 1995 than persons who had never been party members.[39] They were about twice as likely as others to be socialist (mainly KPRF) partisans, as we see in Figure 4.7. As the figure also shows, a

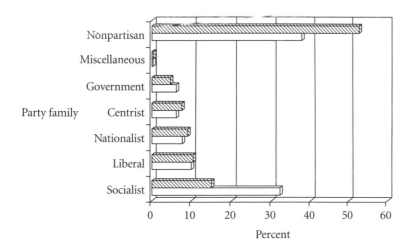

□ Former members of CPSU   ▨ Never members of CPSU

Figure 4.7. Past Membership in the CPSU and Partisanship: Percentage of Former CPSU Members and Others Who Are Nonpartisan and in Party Families, 1995

CPSU past does not alter the chances of having liberal, nationalist, or centrist partisanship and it but slightly raises the likelihood of sympathies with the government party. Russians' transitional partisanship is not a simple offshoot of membership in the extinct CPSU. Eighty-three percent of all partisans at the time of our 1995 interview—including 73 percent of all partisans of the KPRF itself—had never carried a CPSU party card.

In terms of demographic correlates, post-Soviet partisanship resembles the modes of political participation discussed in Chapter 2. Partisanship (strong, moderate, or weak) was about 20 percentage points more prevalent in 1995 among persons in their forties, fifties, and sixties than among those under the age of thirty, and about 10 points greater than among persons in their thirties and over sixty-nine (see Figure 4.8).[40] Under the age of forty, the liberal and nationalist party families each have more partisans than the socialist parties; over the age of fifty-nine, socialist affiliations, those most congruent with the Soviet way of life, exceed all others combined.

Susceptibility to partisanship also varies with educational attainment; it is about 20 percentage points more widespread among Russians with a college-level education than among the least educated (see Figure 4.9).[41] Once again the socialist parties part company with the rest. Among the least-educated voters, the worst equipped to cope with a pluralistic democ-

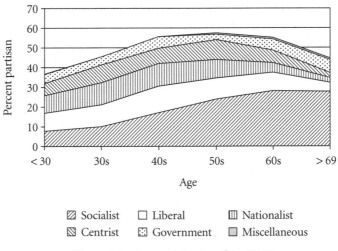

Figure 4.8. Age and Partisanship, 1995

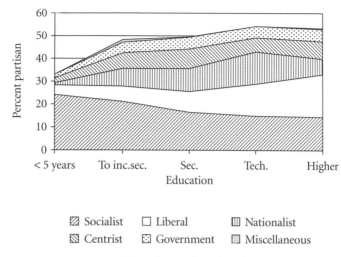

Figure 4.9. Education and Partisanship, 1995

racy, socialist partisans are far and away the most plentiful. Among voters with a higher education, liberal parties outstrip all other groups. The acme of nationalist partisanship is among Russians with a technical education. Our Home Is Russia and the centrist parties show no particular pattern.[42]

What, then, impels some individuals in the course of a political transition to turn partisan when the rest are happy to remain unattached? The middle-aged, the better educated, and former members of the CPSU show a greater tendency to latch onto a party. But that tendency must be activated in any sociological group by a trigger or triggers in the present political environment. Just what the exact stimuli are is not known with certainty, but several possibilities are intuitively convincing and consistent with the Russian data:

- For many citizens in a transitional polity, partisanship is a spontaneous accommodation to interparty electoral competition and to the pressure to clarify one's position in advance of the voting decision.
- Partisanship is midwifed by mass communications. Showered with messages from partisan entrepreneurs—many of them handsomely wrapped in the razzle-dazzle of television commercials—individuals yield to one that appeals to them and internalize it.
- The initiative comes from local or sectoral elites. The tractor driver on

a collective farm, say, is urged by his chairman to look kindly on the Agrarian party. The Moscow banker or trader who subsists on government contracts hears only the best news about Our Home Is Russia. The university undergraduate is impressed that her professor is running for Yabloko.

• Consciously or subconsciously, individuals may fear being left out or appearing antisocial or gauche if they do not have a favorite party—a bit like youngsters who must have a sports team to root for.

• Partisanship in a weakly institutionalized democracy may feed on repulsion as much as attraction, with transitional citizens gravitating to a party they see as the opposite of a party or parties they despise. Sixty-three percent of respondents in our 1995 post-election survey agreed there was one or several parties they "would never vote for." Fifty-seven percent of those individuals would be classified as partisans by our separate questions on that score; many fewer, 37 percent of them, were nonpartisans, suggesting some tie between the two phenomena.[43]

• Partisanship is a convenient filter and sorter of information. Even in the United States, with its tidy two-party system, some scholars conceive of party identification as an economizing device that helps people process political information at low cost in time and energy.[44] In Russia and Eastern Europe, where party systems are fluid, uncertainty is high, and electoral seasoning is slight, I suspect that pseudo-identification has a similar cognitive payoff for a good many electors.[45]

Do Russian partisans think and behave any differently from their compatriots? If not, we need not really seek to determine how extensive partisanship is or what is its wellspring. In one sense—faith in the overall party system—partisanship at this time makes little difference. The proportion of citizens who voice distrust in political parties in general is exactly the same among partisans as among nonpartisans.[46]

On the positive side, the data tell us loud and clear that transitional partisanship correlates with a magnified subjective involvement in public and electoral affairs. Figure 4.10 graphs five measures of political interest and attentiveness in 1995 against our four-point partisanship index. Every plot line dangles higher values for strong partisanship. Strong partisans are 33 percentage points more likely than nonpartisans to keep abreast of political events all the time; 24 points more likely to evaluate a large number of the parties in the Duma campaign; 22 points more likely to be highly inter-

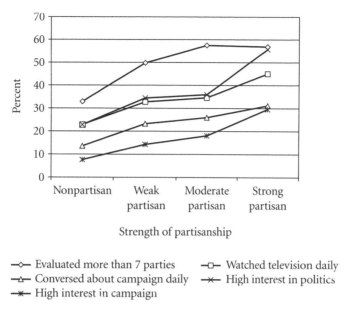

Figure 4.10. Partisanship and Political Involvement, 1995

ested in the election; 22 points more likely to watch election news on television daily; and 18 percentage points more likely to chat daily with family and friends about the election. Partisanship is good grease for the wheels of democracy in Russia.[47]

Causality here surely is reciprocal much of the time. Zealous partisans, in step with a party and solicitous of its fate, will have more of an incentive to care about politics than the nonaligned; but interest in public events will in its own right be conducive to psychological involvement with a party. Helped by cognitive shortcuts to make sense of uncertainty-soaked events, Russian partisans might well know more than independents about the protagonists in an electoral campaign; but knowledge of the party panorama could spur an attachment to one of the parties. Whichever direction the causal arrows point, we can say with assurance that partisans are more absorbed in the political and electoral game, better informed about it, and better plugged into the general communication grid.

When it comes to perceptions of the political parties, studies of democracies with well-developed party systems have found that "allegiance to a party means that it becomes a positive reference group," and that the partisan citizen also engages in "prejudicial rejection of leaders, positions, and actions associated with competing parties."[48] The same two-pronged effect pertains in protodemocratic Russia: partisanship elevates opinion of the party of one's choice and, to a lesser extent, depresses opinions of other parties. The ratings afforded the ten Russian parties on our 1995 questionnaire catch this admirably. On a thermometer scale of 0 to 100 degrees, the average rating assigned by partisans to their own parties is invariably in the 80s and 90s (see Table 4.2). This soars above the mean given by persons who are not partisans of the party—by a minimum of 36 points (for Women of Russia) and a maximum of 68 points (for the LDPR). Partisans of other parties, meanwhile, give these same parties much lower scores; six times out of nine,[49] partisans whose preferred party falls within the fold of another programmatic family are more censorious of the party than partisans from the same family. Nonpartisans chiefly give ratings within a few points of the average for all respondents.

Table 4.2 Mean Feeling-Thermometer Ratings of Ten Main Parties by Partisans and Nonpartisans, 1995 (0 to 100)[a]

| Party | Partisans of the party | Other partisans | | Non-partisans | All not partisans of the party | All respondents |
		Own party family	Other party families			
Agrarian (socialist)	86	50	32	36	37	39
Derzhava (nationalist)	91	23	24	24	24	25
Forward Russia (liberal)	85	37	30	33	32	34
KPRF (socialist)	87	59	28	37	34	44
KRO (nationalist)	86	30	35	36	35	38
LDPR (nationalist)	84	17	14	19	16	21
Our Home Is Russia (government)	84	—	32	34	33	36
Russia's Democratic Choice (liberal)	81	33	21	28	25	27
Women of Russia (centrist)	82	42	45	48	46	48
Yabloko (liberal)	84	46	32	39	36	40
Average	85	37	26	30	30	28

a. Pre-election interview (N = 2,841 weighted cases).

Dynamics of Partisanship

The scholarly exchange about party identification in the United States is as much about how this identification changes over the life cycle as about how it first comes into the young person's head. The question of stability of the attitude is provocative for students of transitional citizenship. Russia specialists have not until now had panel data that might allow study of the dynamics of partisanship at the individual level. Our 1995–96 data, although compiled over a short interval, allow us to make a first pass at the issue. The effort is sobering.

In the summer of 1996, in the several weeks after the runoff to the presidential election, we replicated with our national panel of respondents the main part of the skein of partisanship questions administered to them in the first survey wave, on the eve of the parliamentary election.[50] The third-wave responses disclose two perplexing deviations from the previous winter. First, the gross share of committed partisans in the electorate plummets from 49 percent in late 1995 to 31 percent of citizens (and 34 percent of first-round presidential voters) in mid-1996 (see Figure 4.11). The decline is most abrupt among moderate partisans (down 9 points to 6 percent of the population) and weak partisans (down 6 points to 14 percent) and not as pronounced among strong partisans (down 3 points to 11 percent).

The second big change is in the apportionment of partisans across parties and party families. Four of the seven parties with partisan followings of 5 percent and more of the total in 1995—the nationalist LDPR and KRO, the centrist Women of Russia, and the socialist Agrarians—lose

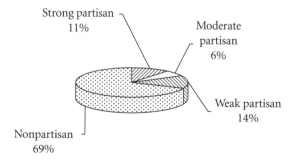

Figure 4.11. Strength of Partisanship, 1996

ground by a combined 18 percentage points (see Figure 4.12). Two leading parties—the socialist KPRF and the liberal Yabloko—buck the trend, augmenting their shares by 21 and 5 percentage points; Our Home Is Russia holds its own. The 26 percent of the sworn partisans of the smaller parties in 1995 dwindles to 18 percent by 1996. Agglomerating the partisans into party families, we find the socialists and liberals waxing by 18 percent and 3 percent of the partisan total, respectively. The government party maintains its share; the nationalist and centrist party groupings wane by 21 percentage points between them.[51]

Figure 4.13 sums up continuity and change in our 1995–96 panel. Taken singly, only 20 percent of voting-age Russians pass our partisanship test (as strong, moderate, or weak partisans) in both years.[52] Forty percent come

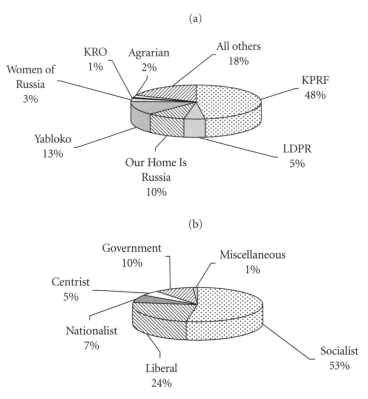

Figure 4.12. Distribution of Partisans, 1996
a. By Party
b. By Party Family

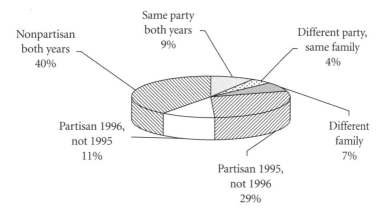

Figure 4.13. Stability of Partisanship, 1995–96

across as transient or peripatetic, partisans one time but nonpartisans the other. And 40 percent are invariantly nonpartisan. Of the 20 percent of citizens who do rate as partisans on consecutive occasions, those who defect from one party to another between interviews outnumber those who hold fast with their original attachment—by 11 percent to 9 percent. Switches in partisanship appear less frantic if we locate citizens by party family rather than by specific party: 13 percent out of the two-time partisans, or about two-thirds of them, stand pat; 7 percent, or about one-third, change party family.

As can be seen in more detail in the top and bottom panels of Table 4.3, changing over to a party radically different in program is quite rare in Russia, as much as we can tell from the 1995–96 data. Notice that the proportion of 1995 partisans who stick with the party the next year is no higher than 35 percent (for the KPRF) and goes as low as an abysmal 12 percent (for the LDPR). Notice also the important point, previewed in Figure 4.13, that the chameleons usually switch not from one party to another or from one party family to another, but from partisanship to nonpartisan neutrality or from nonpartisanship to partisanship. Anywhere from 46 percent (for the KPRF) to 74 percent (for the LDPR) of the 1995 adherents of the four big parties turned nonpartisan in 1996.

What could flag more expressively than these data the fluidity of transitional citizenship? The fickleness voters exhibited in but two or three seasons of the calendar in 1995–96 makes the motility that prompted the

Table 4.3 Individual-Level Shifts in Partisanship, 1995–96 (Percentages)[a]

Partisanship 1996 By party family Family	Partisanship 1995						
	Socialist	Liberal	Nationalist	Centrist	Government	Miscellaneous	Nonpartisan
Socialist	47	7	11	13	6	38	10
Liberal	3	24	5	6	9	0	7
Nationalist	0	3	10	2	0	0	2
Centrist	0	3	0	7	0	0	1
Government	1	4	3	5	20	0	2
Miscellaneous	0	0	0	0	0	13	0
Nonpartisan	48	60	70	67	65	50	78

By major party Party and party family	KPRF	LDPR	Our Home Is Russia	Yabloko
Same party	35	12	20	26
Other party	19	15	15	21
Same family	50	12	20	37
Other family	4	15	15	10
Nonpartisan	46	74	65	53

a. Among respondents interviewed in both first and third waves of panel survey (N = 2,472 weighted cases).

wave of revisionist scholarship on the American voter look torpid by comparison.[53]

The most general explanation of these vicissitudes is the semi-organized uncertainty that, fog-like, shrouds transitional politics. For those adrift in it, the genesis of a democratic party system is a juncture of great creativity but also of monumental consternation, indecision, and mutability.

It is necessary to realize, though, that not everything in popular assessments of the parties changes with such celerity, and that individual citizens do not succumb to the flux uniformly. Table 4.4 contains important information in both these connections. It describes attitudes toward those seven Russian parties for which we re-administered the feeling-thermometer items, along with the partisanship series, in the 1996 presidential survey.

As is evident, citizens' ratings of the parties on the thermometer, which gauges like or dislike of the given organizations one at a time, betray far less variation between 1995 and 1996 than do the partisanship measures, which entail more hard-edged, either/or judgments. The four parties that hurdled the 5 percent limit for seating in the Duma in 1995 (the KPRF, LDPR, Our Home Is Russia, and Yabloko) evince moderate continuity in individuals' thermometer assessments, with correlation coefficients ranging between .34 and .50. Partisanship, rendered here as a four-point index

Table 4.4 Intertemporal Correlations for Partisanship and Thermometer Scores for Seven Parties, 1995–96, by Level of Political Awareness (Pearson's r)[a]

Party	Partisanship			Thermometer scores		
	Low awareness	High awareness	All	Low awareness	High awareness	All
Agrarian	.09**	.14**	.13**	.36**	.41**	.40**
KPRF	.25**	.43**	.34**	.39**	.55**	.50**
KRO	−.03	.14**	.13**	.26**	.25**	.26**
LDPR	.23**	.12**	.18**	.45**	.39**	.41**
Our Home Is Russia	.19**	.25**	.24**	.31**	.36**	.34**
Russia's Democratic Choice	−.01	.42**	.34**	.20**	.42**	.36**
Yabloko	.14**	.24**	.24*	.28**	.43**	.39**

**$p \leq .01$ (two-tailed test). Missing values deleted pairwise.

a. Among respondents interviewed in both first and third waves of panel survey (N = 2,472 weighted cases).

for each party,[54] throws off coefficients of between .18 and .34 for the same party foursome. Equally illuminating is the stabilizing effect of political sophistication, as defined in our knowledge-based awareness index. Saw the Russian electorate in two, and you find persons in the high-awareness half manifesting greater temporal stability than those in the low-awareness half for six of seven parties on partisanship and five of seven on the thermometer.

Of the other regularities in the 1995–96 data on Russian citizens and their parties, the most disconcerting is the systematic downturn in partisanship from 1995 to 1996. I attribute it principally to electoral context and rules. Parliamentary campaigns in Russia are waged nationally and to a large degree locally by political parties. Parties have their names and logos inscribed on the proportional-representation ballot, and in 1995 nominated 60 percent of the district candidates. Admen pitch partisan labels, partisan images, and partisan slogans and jingles. Media coverage dwells on the election's partisan angle. It is natural for such a milieu to evoke and reinforce partisanship—which it did for half of the electorate in 1995.

How different things are in a Russian presidential campaign. The 1996 election was a battle among politicians, not all of whom had been formally nominated by parties. Four of the parties and quasi-parties that had stood for the Duma (the KPRF through a front organization, the LDPR, Yabloko, and the centrist Employees' Self-Management Party) nominated candidates in 1996; the thirty-nine parties that stayed on the sidelines, participating indirectly or eschewing any involvement, had claimed 55 percent of the votes in December 1995. The star nonpartisan entrant was the eventual winner, Boris Yeltsin. In so personalized an environment, partisan attractions and antipathies persist under the surface and can still be manipulated by office seekers, but they do not have the focal quality they have in a party-list election for the legislature. It is not accidental that the political grouping most resistant to the hemorrhaging of partisanship in 1996 was the socialist opposition, the set of players best represented in the Duma—who closed ranks early on and delivered a third of the votes to Zyuganov in the first round of the presidential election.[55]

Besides the voter's prior partisanship, several other factors influence the contemporary partisanship of a citizen in a transitional polity. The greatest potential resides in personal assessments of how things are going in the country.[56] The conditions that move the members of a transforming society will include economic realities (of individual and national scope) and political realities. A Russian whose assessment of current conditions is negative may, we surmise, be tugged toward an opposition party hostile to the authorities; a more favorable assessment may deflect partisanship in the opposite direction, toward the government party or a liberal opposition party amenable to its overall course.

The statistics in Table 4.5, drawing on the 1995–96 panel surveys, furnish a crude trial of these possibilities for the KPRF, the LDPR, Our Home Is Russia, and Yabloko. The values, as with our tests for influences on the vote, are derived from probabilities predicted by a multinomial logit regression. The regression has as its dependent variable 1996 partisanship (measured as a five-way categorical variable, with values for the four parties and for all other partisan possibilities), and as its independent variables 1995 partisanship (expressed as four dummy variables), 1996 assessments of family finances and of trends in the national economy, individual experience with arrears in the payment of wages and social allowances, and satisfaction with the course of political democratization (with "how democracy is developing" in Russia). Each entry in the table is the difference between the fitted probability of a citizen's expression of a given partisanship in 1996 if the explanatory variable in question is set at its minimum value, and the fitted probability if the explanatory variable is set at its maximum value, all other terms in the equation being held constant at their median.

The top row in Table 4.5 confirms that an individual's 1995 partisanship exerted a significant influence on his or her 1996 partisanship for all four

Table 4.5 Influences on 1996 Partisanship (Differences in Predicted Probabilities)[a]

Explanatory variable	KPRF	LDPR	Our Home	Yabloko
Partisanship for given party, 1995	.22**	.43**	.24**	.35**
Assessment of family welfare, 1996	−.14	−.02	.14**	.03
Arrears in wages and social allowances, 1996	−.13**	−.02	.00	.07**
Assessment of national economy, 1996	−.22**	−.00	.09*	.04
Satisfaction with democratization, 1996	−.45**	−.01	.18**	.20**

$**p \leq .01$

$*p \leq .05$

a. Sample N = 749.

parties, albeit more tenuously than would be the case in a stable party system.[57] But the most arresting result of the analysis is the independent influence on partisanship of current conditions. *Ceteris paribus*, the person whose wages or social benefits were up to date was .13 (13 percentage points) less likely to have an affiliation with the vociferously anti-government KPRF in 1996 than someone whose payments were the most in arrears. Variation in the family finances variable produced an effect on KPRF affiliation of roughly the same magnitude (though it just fails to attain significance at the .05 level), assessments of the condition of the national economy a rather larger effect, and assessments of political change in Russia a much larger effect (.45, or 45 percentage points). The opposite effects are apparent on 1996 partisanship in favor of the government's Our Home Is Russia for three of the four current conditions (all except arrears), and in favor of the liberal Yabloko party for all four. For the nationalistic LDPR, the effects on partisanship point in the same direction as for the KPRF, although none rises to statistical significance.

Partisanship and Electoral Choice

The proof of the pudding for the electoral analyst is to ascertain whether transitional partisanship is meaningfully connected with Russians' voting behavior. The changeability of current partisanship rules it out as a motivating force of long horizon. But the time frame of any variable in mass politics should not be confused with its weight in decisions or its theoretical import. Causal elements liable to fluctuation in the short haul may have an appreciable impact on voting, even in consolidated democracies where other factors are steady. The literature on the granddaddy of them all, the United States, takes such variable elements very seriously.[58]

The Party-List Vote

When they go to the polls in a parliamentary election, Russia's declared partisans do very much side with the party with which they feel that camaraderie. Seventy percent of partisans voted for "their" parties on the proportional-representation ballot for the State Duma in December 1995. These consistent partisans comprised almost 40 percent of the participating electorate in 1995, only 5 percent less than the nonpartisan plurality; inconsistent partisans, who vote for a party other than the one they count

as their own, constituted 16 percent. Partisan consistency in voting increases with the strength of partisanship: it was 66 percent for weak partisans in 1995, but 69 percent for moderate partisans and 77 percent for
strong partisans.[59] A vote consistent with partisan self-image is also more
common among partisans of the larger Russian parties than of the smaller
parties. In 1995, 84 percent of KPRF partisans voted for their chosen
party, as did 89 percent of LDPR partisans, 67 percent of Our Home Is
Russia partisans, and 81 percent of Yabloko partisans. Consistency was 54
percent for devotees of the organizational midgets that missed the 5 percent barrier.

For any useful explanatory variable, the trick is to understand how it enters into the voting decision in conjunction with other causal factors. Table
4.6 elaborates the impact of partisanship on Russians' voting choices in
1995. The statistics again take the form of logit-based estimates of the difference in the probability of the voting outcome occurring that is associated with a shift in the explanatory variable from its minimum to its maximum value. The values in the top row restate in a different metric the

Table 4.6 Elaboration of the Impact of Partisanship on the Party-List Vote, 1995 (Differences in Predicted Probabilities)[a]

Variables progressively incorporated in regression	KPRF	LDPR	Our Home	Yabloko
Partisanship for given party only	.64**	.84**	.58**	.72**
Also social characteristics	.61**	.80**	.54**	.68**
Also current conditions	.60**	.80**	.53**	.68**
Also other partisanship (but not issue opinions)	.53**	.78**	.48**	.66**
Also issue opinions (but not other partisanship)	.58**	.77**	.57**	.68**
Also issue opinions and other partisanship[b]	.50**	.76**	.51**	.66**
Also retrospective evaluations of incumbents	.48**	.77**	.49**	.66**
Also party leaders	.36**	.28**	.32**	.40**
Also prospective evaluations of parties	.29**	.24**	.19**	.34**

**p ≤ .01
a. Sample N = 2,143.
b. Gray-toned row gives the total effect of partisanship.

bivariate relationship between the main explanatory variable (an indicator of partisanship for the KPRF, the LDPR, Our Home Is Russia, and Yabloko, in turn, all coded as dummy variables)[60] and the vote. The relationship is a powerful one. Being a KPRF partisan, for example, hoists the probability of voting for the KPRF by .64 (64 percentage points), blind for the moment to all other potential influences on the vote.

In all four columns of Table 4.6, the second-row values may be read as an index of the influence of partisanship on the vote for the party in question, this time also gauging the effect on voting preference of variation in the citizen's social characteristics, which are at the beginning of the causal chain in our presumptive model of transitional citizenship. In lower rows of the table, the parameters still estimate the electoral effect of partisanship, but measure it as other explanatory variables—voter perceptions of current conditions, partisanship along other dimensions,[61] issue opinions, evaluations of incumbents, judgments of party leaders, and prospective evaluations of the parties in government—are incorporated in blocs into a multivariate analysis. The iterations assume that social characteristics and assessments of current conditions are causally prior to partisanship; that issue opinions are causally at the same stage as partisanship; and that evaluations of incumbents, leaders, and parties are causally posterior to partisanship.

The key row in Table 4.6 is the sixth row down, shaded in gray. The total-effect estimates show that, holding constant the influence of causally prior and equivalent variables, the probability that a partisan of one of the four parties in 1995 would vote for that party's national list went up by .50 (50 percentage points) in the case of the KPRF, about that in the case of Our Home Is Russia, about .70 in the case of Yabloko, and almost .80 in the case of the LDPR. Only small minorities within the electorate qualify as partisans of any one of these organizations, but those who do are far more likely to vote for it than other citizens are. The estimates of total effect pass with flying colors our double-edged test for major substantive importance (a magnitude of .10 or more) and statistical significance (at the .05 level).

For all four of the larger Russian parties in 1995, we see a marked abatement in the apparent electoral consequences of partisanship as causally posterior variables, notably those at the penultimate and final stages, are assimilated into the equation. What this suggests is that much of the effect of partisanship on voting decisions is shunted through Russians' assessments of leaders and party capabilities, although the coefficients that linger in the lowermost row speak to unmediated effects from partisanship as well. For the KPRF, if we take the predicted-probability ratios literally, about one-quarter (.12/.50) of the effect of partisanship is transmitted by leadership evaluations, and rather less (.07/.50) by assessments of the parties' capacity to govern, leaving about one-half as a leftover direct effect. For the LDPR, two-thirds (.49/.76) of the influence of partisanship goes through the reputation of its leader (Vladimir Zhirinovskii) and of other party leaders. Our Home Is Russia and Yabloko fall nearer to the LDPR prototype than to the KPRF.

A methodologist might spot an endogeneity problem here. Maybe transitional partisanship, as clocked during or immediately after an election campaign, is nothing more than a restatement of the citizen's voting intention or latest voting decision. At our present stage of knowledge of post-Communist politics, it cannot be conclusively disproved that the categories are garbled in the minds of some and perhaps many of the voters. My own judgment is that feedback from voting choice does not fatally compromise measures of transitional partisanship. The question wording we followed in Russia in 1995–96 drew no overt line between the profession of attachment to a political party and the act of voting, anticipated or accomplished. And more than one scholar, including me in another research project, has found indications of partisan sentiment in the Russian and post-Soviet electorates at times other than during or right after an election campaign.[62]

Another trap to guard against is that partisanship may be closely linked to a causal factor quite distant from the vote, in which case an ostensible association between partisanship and electoral choice would be spurious, and the root cause of voting preference would be the distal variable. Russian data from 1995 do not lend credence to this hypothesis (see Table 4.6). Estimates of the electoral impact of partisanship in the Duma election are highly robust, retaining their value with an invariance unusual by Western criteria as other variables are piled layer by layer into the analysis. Only for the KPRF does the internalization into the model of causally prior and equivalent variables in 1995 make more than a trivial dent in the original value (.14 out of .64).[63] Partisanship, while influenced some by other factors, does not seem to come into the determination of electoral preferences as an epiphenomenon of other variables. Were it to be a mere extension of social traits, the voter's perceptions of current conditions, or normative issue opinions, its statistical effect on electoral choice would plunge when that confounding variable was entered into the model. No such drop is evident for any of the parties.

The Presidential Vote

The question of the effect on partisanship on presidential voting in Russia deserves to be posed in spite of the sharp difference in rules between the presidential and parliamentary contests and the cooling off of self-avowed partisanship in the months separating the 1995 and 1996 election extravaganzas. In fact, seven of the ten presidential candidates in the 1996 campaign—including the runner-up, Zyuganov—were nominated by parties or quasi-parties, and under the election law the parties' names were on the ballot next to the candidates'.[64] The seven overtly partisan entrants in 1996 bagged 36.5 million of the valid votes in the first round, or 48.97 percent of those cast. Even the victorious Yeltsin, his formal papers filed by a shadowy alliance of 250 pro-Kremlin associations, informally had his own sponsoring party: Our Home Is Russia, the government tribune founded on his personal instructions and led since its inception by his prime minister, Chernomyrdin. At the mass level, partisanship was less prevalent in 1996 than in 1995, but a not negligible one-third of the electorate did qualify as strong, moderate, or weak partisans.

Table 4.7 sets forth the results of a multivariate analysis aimed at isolating the effect of transitional partisanship on the presidential vote. Partisanship is taken as articulated in the post-presidential survey interview.[65] The KPRF's Zyuganov and Grigorii Yavlinskii, the nominee of his Yabloko party, present no classification problems. I take some liberties with Yeltsin, who was not nominated de jure by Our Home Is Russia, in treating him de facto as the potential recipient of sentiment for that party. Likewise, for the third-running Aleksandr Lebed, the partisan feelings attach to the nationalistic party, KRO, which he did not legally represent in 1996. But General Lebed had been co-head of KRO's campaign for the Duma in 1995 and was still connected to it in some media coverage; if there were to be any home-team effect on his presidential candidacy, it would have to come from the diminutive pool of KRO partisans.[66]

The top row of Table 4.7 again displays considerable partisanship effects on the vote in both rounds of the presidential election.[67] Like the KPRF and Our Home Is Russia in the Duma contest, the relationship between partisanship and the first-lap vote for the heavyweight candidates, Yeltsin

Table 4.7 Elaboration of the Impact of Partisanship on the Presidential Vote, 1996 (Differences in Predicted Probabilities)

Variables progressively incorporated in regression	First round[a]				Runoff[b]	
	Yel.	Zyug.	Leb.	Yav.	Yel.	Zyug.
Partisanship for candidate's party only	.53**	.65**	.51**	.54**	.45**	.63**
Also social characteristics	.48**	.67**	.53**	.49**	.41**	.64**
Also current conditions	.49**	.64**	.59**	.58**	.41**	.61**
Also other partisanship (but not issue opinions)	.39**	.65**	.53**	.55**	.34**	.63**
Also issue opinions (but not other partisanship)	.38**	.51**	.53*	.58**	.27**	.59**
Also issue opinions and other partisanship[c]	.34**	.54**	.53**	.56**	.23*	.62**
Also retrospective evaluations of incumbents	.29**	.46**	.48**	.47**	.11	.51**
Also leadership qualities	.27**	.26**	.47**	.23**	.11[d]	.31*[d]
Also prospective evaluations of candidates	.10	.11*	.15	.08	.04[d]	.12*[d]

**p ≤ .01
*p ≤ .05
a. Sample N = 1,990.
b. Sample N = 1,937.
c. Gray-toned row gives the total effect of partisanship.
d. Two finalists only.

and Zyuganov, softens somewhat when social characteristics, perceptions of current conditions, and issue opinions merge into the analysis. For Lebed and Yavlinskii, this does not occur. In the first presidential round, the total-effect statistics in the gray-toned row are close to those observed in the State Duma election for Zyuganov (comparing Zyuganov in 1996 with the KPRF in 1995) but are quite a bit smaller for Yeltsin (as compared to Our Home Is Russia in 1995), Lebed (as compared to the nationalistic LDPR in 1995), and Yavlinskii (as compared to the Yabloko ticket in 1995). Except for the KPRF, we can say that partisanship plays a smaller (though still very substantial) role in shaping citizen decisions in the presidential arena than in the parliamentary arena.

Observe also that for three of the four presidential candidates the estimated effects of partisanship sag as variables that we posit to lie causally downstream from partisanship join the analysis. And they descend rowwise in Table 4.7 to magnitudes lower than those obtained in the voting for parliament. The reduction happens because later-stage variables at a lesser remove from the vote—evaluations of the sitting president and Russian government, assessments of the leadership qualities of the presidential candidates, and evaluations of them as prospective rulers—intercede between partisanship and the voting decision more efficiently than they do in the parliamentary framework.

In the presidential runoff (see columns 5 and 6 of Table 4.7), the same general sequence of effects is observed for Yeltsin and Zyuganov as was seen in the first round. Of the two, it is Zyuganov, the leader of Russia's largest political party, whose partisan coattails hold up against wear and tear: witness his three-to-one advantage over Yeltsin in total-effect statistics, about double the ratio in the opening round.

Conclusions

Moisei Ostrogorski wrote in his famous treatise on political parties at the turn of the last century that in almost every European country "the organization of parties working regularly outside Parliament is still but little developed," and the parties' voters "often present only floating masses."[68] Much of what he said would apply to the Russian Federation today. Parties and party graffiti abound. But the organizations behind the facade are often primitive in comparison to their namesakes in the West, the most venerable of which are comparable in longevity and solidity to authoritative state institutions. All in all, Russia's newly empowered citizens take a dim view of the parties. They distrust them more than they distrust state institutions, believe they are far too numerous, and are nearly as likely to see the competition among them as harmful to the country as beneficial to it. And many do indeed float like driftwood from one party to another or into and out of political agnosticism.

At the same time, survey data show that Russians, regardless of their attitude toward the party system, recognize and have formed opinions, favorable or unfavorable, about a number of specific parties. The more engaged they are in political affairs, the more they are likely to know and have a feel for particular parties. The most important development in relations between the electorate and the parties is that a fair number of individuals, perhaps one-half of eligible voters in 1995, cultivate provisional attachments to a political party. Whatever they make of the multitude of parties as a whole, many Russians feel attracted to one face in the crowd. These elective affinities generally have little to do with their past life: transitional Russia's partisans are made, not born. Nor are these sentiments necessarily long-lived: some resemble a passing fling more than a durable romance or marriage. But when Russians shift partisan fealty, as many do, we have found that there is usually some reason for it beyond serendipity and happenstance.

Only time will tell whether and how quickly these tentative impulses will evolve into the steadfast identifications discovered in so many studies of Western polities, and whether the catch-some parties, bolstered by such sensations, will fill out into the "permanently organized transmission belts between population and government" celebrated in democratic theory.

In the meantime, the labile, restive partisanship of the transition period has major demonstrable effects on political consciousness and behavior. These fresh partisan proclivities do influence the vote, if unevenly, across parties and party families and across electoral settings.

5

Opinions, Opinions . . .

Elections in modern democratic theory have no function more vital than to induce officials to abide by the will of the majority. We normally speak of that popular will as residing in opinions—mental images people have "of themselves, of others, of their needs, purposes, and relationships," in the words of Walter Lippmann.[1] The most germane to mass political behavior are normative opinions, those that go beyond identifying and diagnosing a collective problem to stipulating a remedy for it.

Voting studies in the West for some time in the past downplayed issue preferences to the advantage of such tried and true sources of behavior as social cleavages and party loyalties. Academic fashion has shifted with a vengeance: lately analysts of elections dwell more on issues than on any other class of explanatory variable. Arousing their curiosity is the prospect that, as Anthony Downs posits, rational individuals in a democracy will reward with their votes the politicians whose policy programs dovetail with their "conception of the good society."[2] The assumption is that candidates bid for support partly by propounding rival programs for the provision of public goods. About voters, it is assumed that they possess values and beliefs, selfish or altruistic,[3] appertaining to the issues of the day; that they construe government as an instrument for realizing those objectives; and that they view elected representatives as agents who will see to it that government does right by them. It is a more ennobling vision of the citizen in action than one hanging on social background, household budgets, assessments of economic and political trends, or partisan habit.

In this chapter I put this picture of citizenship to the test in the laboratory of democratizing Russia. In so doing it is necessary to face a tangle of practical questions about common people's prescriptive opinions, which must be dealt with in order to gauge the influence of opinions on the vote. These caveats exist in any country, but the unsettled circumstances of a transitional polity make us doubly vigilant. The most essential question, about the very existence of value-laden inclinations toward governmental goals and policy, will be the simplest to answer: citizens of the Russian Federation are nothing if not opinionated. Some other prefatory questions are not so easily disposed of. One involves the quality, not the quantity, of opinions; information about their stability over time will offer us tips in this respect. Another point concerns interrelatedness among political opinions. Do Russians today have convictions we can properly label ideological? If they harbor opinions at multiple conceptual levels that do not amalgamate into a formal ideology, do broader views take precedence over ones of narrow scope? We further want to understand what Russian voters know about the positions political parties and candidates espouse on the issues. Citizen familiarity with them—at a bare minimum, with the position of the party or candidate they vote for—would facilitate opinion-based voting.

With these facts on the record, we can go on to plumb Russians' opinions on a series of contested issues and to relate them to parliamentary and presidential voting, using the same estimation tools as for other theories of the vote.

Opinions in a Transitional Polity

There is no need to wonder whether Russian voters hold politically relevant opinions: they do. Indigenous and foreign scholars have by now conducted dozens of sample surveys in the Russian Federation and the former USSR.[4] They invariably discover that the typical adult is ready to venture responses to queries about all manner of public issues, from the loftiest to the pettiest. The election polls on which the present volume rests are no different.

Our pre-election questionnaire during the 1995 campaign for the State Duma, for example, contained a generous assortment of closed-ended questions and question items about societal problems and their solutions—thirty-six in total.[5] One might have guessed from the recency of political freedom in Russia and the wrenching difficulty of the issues besetting the country that the panel would be intimidated and would fail to answer many questions. This thunderously was not the case. The mean number of questions answered was thirty-three, or 91 percent of the quota; 33 percent of respondents had the acuity to reply to every question asked.

Transitional voters are not equally blessed with normative opinions. Their stock of issue opinions, like a great many participatory assets, tends to go up with their global political awareness, though at a less steep rate than certain other skills do. The more attentive Russians were to political affairs in 1995, the more opinions they enunciated in the pre-election interview (see Figure 5.1). But the gap between the best and the least prepared quintile of the electorate—about 5.5 opinions proffered out of the 36—was not large, and most of it was due to the poor score realized by the bottom quintile.[6]

Quality and Stability

Can such data mislead? Opinion researchers in the United States have long worried that proficiency at batting back answers to survey questions may for many individuals cloak a root ignorance of the issues in play. "Asking uninformed people to state opinions on topics to which they have given little if any previous thought," warns the political psychologist John R. Zaller, summons up opinion statements that "give every indication of be-

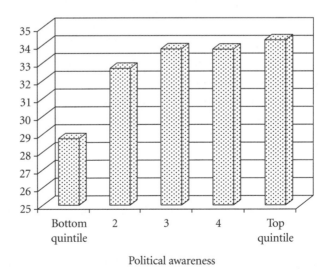

Political awareness

Figure 5.1. Number of Normative Opinions Held in the 1995 Campaign by Level of Political Awareness (Maximum = 36)

ing rough and superficial."[7] In Russia, the same caution applies. We cannot accept unreflectingly that a few words exchanged in a survey interview express piercing insight into an issue or a deeply held idea of what to do about it. If anything, we should tread more gingerly than in the West, given a society where the state has always lorded it over a politically disengaged populace.

But neither can we presume that Russians' impromptu responses to issue questions are vacant of meaning. Well-constructed questionnaires on topics applicable to local conditions, and professionalism in the training and supervision of interviewers, should rule out sloppy results that distort informants' sentiments or misrepresent them as firmer than they are. In appraising the solidity of issue opinions, we can avail ourselves of the oft-observed fact that when opinions are glib and lack any underlying foundation of belief, they will tend to oscillate over time. The declared opinions of policy dilettantes, as Zaller says, "vacillate randomly across repeated interviews of the same people."[8]

The panel design of our 1995–96 electoral surveys permits a reading of the stability of opinion, and obliquely of its quality, under post-Communist conditions. Table 5.1 pulls together Russians' responses to six isomorphic questions about economic and social policy, asked in the pre-parliamentary election survey in November–December 1995 and repeated word for word and in the same order in the post-presidential election survey in July–September 1996. All were administered by reading a statement aloud and calling on the subject to voice strong agreement, agreement, indifference, disagreement, or strong disagreement with it. The assertions made were about full employment, protection of Russian industry from imports, control of food prices, foreign investment, privatization of land, and income inequalities.

Many on the panel flip-flopped on the half-dozen national issues. On five items, more than half of the informants responded differently to the same questions in 1996 than they had in 1995. The interrogatory about foreign investment called forth the most flux (63 percent) and that about guaranteed employment the least (46 percent).

But the gross rate of change is qualified considerably by breaking down the shifts of opinion into categories according to the totality of the change. Only a fraction of the panelists—from 4 percent of two-time responders (for full employment) to 18 percent (for foreign investment and land ownership)—reversed the direction of their answers from agreement to

Table 5.1 Comparison of Panel Responses to Six Statements about Economic and Social Policy, 1995 and 1996 (Percentages)[a]

Statement	Same response 1996 as 1995	Changed direction	Changed intensity	Into or out of indifference
The government ought to guarantee a job to everyone who needs one[b]	54	4	37	4
We must protect our industry against competition from foreign firms that are out to seize the Russian market[c]	41	12	28	18
The state should set food prices[d]	43	12	28	18
Russia should attract foreign investment in its economy[e]	37	18	14	30
Private property in land should exist in our country[f]	38	18	18	26
The state should limit the incomes of the rich[g]	39	16	23	22

a. Only for respondents who answered question in both 1995 pre-election survey and 1996 post-election survey, excluding "Don't know" responses.
b. N = 2,398 weighted cases.
c. N = 2,206 weighted cases.
d. N = 2,341 weighted cases.
e. N = 1,923 weighted cases.
f. N = 2,046 weighted cases.
g. N = 2,182 weighted cases.

disagreement with one of the statements or vice versa. Obviously, opinions that seesaw so frivolously as these over less than a year are rough and superficial. The verdict cannot be so stinging, though, for the much more numerous respondents who amended their thinking in less erratic ways (see the third and fourth columns of Table 5.1). Fourteen to 37 percent modified their responses in intensity and not in direction (this was the mode for four of the six questions), while 4 to 30 percent cycled into or out of the indifferent slot (the mode on two questions). Individuals who changed intensity or pleaded neutrality in one or both interviews were anywhere from two-and-a-half times to ten times as many, depending on the question, as persons who changed their mind altogether from 1995 to 1996. If these snippets are any barometer, issue preferences do *not* necessarily fluctuate more in latter-day Russia than in settled democracies, in spite of the uncertainty plaguing its transitional political environment.[9]

Russia is also in the company of the older democracies in manifesting the nexus between opinion stability and knowledge. As Zaller substantiates, Americans who are more attuned to political news and issues manifest less chance variability in their opinions from one time to the next than do the unengaged.[10] So it proves to be with Russians in the period of transition. With regard to the six economic and social questions posed in 1995 and replicated the following year, persons who rated high for political awareness were more apt to respond on the two occasions than the politically less aware.[11] As for the content of opinions, we see the same kind of differentiation. Dividing the Russian survey sample into halves by political awareness, we find that for every one of these same six questions the 1995 survey responses are significantly more predictive of 1996 responses for the more knowledgeable person than for the less knowledgeable one (see Table 5.2). The intertemporal correlation coefficients for high-awareness citizens are on average about one-third again as high as for low-awareness citizens.

Table 5.2 Intertemporal Correlations for Responses to Statements about Economic and Social Policy, 1995–96, by Level of Political Awareness (Pearson's r)[a]

Issue	Low awareness	High awareness	All
Guarantee jobs	.23**	.30**	.29**
Protect industry	.32**	.39**	.37**
Set food prices	.24**	.40**	.36**
Attract foreign investment	.24**	.29**	.28**
Allow private land	.22**	.35**	.30**
Limit incomes	.35**	.40**	.38**

**p ≤ .01 (two-tailed test). Missing values deleted pairwise.

a. Only for respondents who answered question in both 1995 pre-election survey and 1996 post-election survey, excluding "Don't know" responses. N's same as in Table 5.1.

Formal Ideology

Political opinions come in sundry sizes, shapes, and formulations. Social scientists argue that people frequently cope with their civic choices by filtering them through a peculiar set of opinions—an ideology, an omnibus belief system that wraps together an extended range of ideas and attitudes and guides political action. A crucial role of ideology is to define a "fixed firmament" of meanings against which political objects may be located.[12] The vocabulary used to plot that firmament varies from country to country. The accepted metric in the United States is a continuum from liberal to conservative; in Western Europe and Latin America, it runs from left to right.[13]

In Russia, the words "conservative" and "liberal" are fresh imports into the language that seldom infiltrate political debate, except in rarefied intellectual circles.[14] "Left" *(levyi)* and "right" *(pravyi)* are more propitious markers. Referring in everyday speech to human anatomy and the organization of space and motion, they figured metaphorically in orthodox Soviet discourse about politics, which portrayed the ruling CPSU as a party of the left. The party's stranglehold on power rendered the niceties of location somewhat bogus in internal politics, but there is no denying the compatibility in goals with Marxists and other social radicals in the West and the Third World. In an ironic twist, participants and observers depicted the anti-Communist movement of the late 1980s in the USSR as originating on the left, in the strategic sense of rupturing the status quo after decades of stagnation, and equated the right with resistance to change.[15] The fit was uncomfortable, because the free-enterprise economics of most Russian democrats was at odds with the allure that state ownership and planning held for traditional European and Soviet-bloc leftists.

The lunge into marketizing reform by Boris Yeltsin's post-Soviet cabinets, and the conspicuousness of the neo-Communist KPRF in the opposition to it, paved the way for emergence of a conventional left-right political spectrum. "Russian political commentators," an American research team wrote on the eve of the 1996 presidential election, "have begun to move toward western nomenclature by using the terms *Left* and *Right* in their western meanings. The Communists and those close to them are the Left (or, pejoratively, the Reds), while the strong pro-market forces are the Right."[16] Seconding the newspaper columnists and academics, Russian politicians have started to pepper their rhetoric with left-right jargon.

The parlance of left and right, whatever its cachet among elites, will not explain voting decisions unless it seeps into mass consciousness. Feeling other matters to be more urgent, we did not make ideology a priority in the 1995–96 Russian surveys, but some questions were written into the 1996 interview. The following question was delivered to all respondents: "Sometimes, in describing other persons, people say, 'This is a person of left political views' or, 'This is a person of right political views.' Imagine a scale from 1 to 7, where 1 denotes persons with views on the far left and 7 persons with views on the far right. Where on this scale are you?" Next came requests to locate the five leading presidential candidates (Yeltsin, Zyuganov, Lebed, Yavlinskii, and Zhirinovskii) and seven national political parties on the scale. The battery concluded with an open-ended question about "the most important differences between left and right."

A slight majority, 56 percent of our respondents, could site themselves on the seven-point scale, a response ratio far inferior to the 80 or 90 percent for like questions in Western Europe. The ability to conduct an ideological self-analysis is highly dependent on people's overall political awareness and finesse. More than 70 percent of Russians in the most attentive quintile of the population knew their place on the left-right axis in 1996, as against one-third in the lowest quintile (see Figure 5.2).[17] Apart from the slew of nonresponses, the dominant feature of the self-placements on the left-right scale is the prevalence of its midpoint, category 4 (see Figure 5.3).

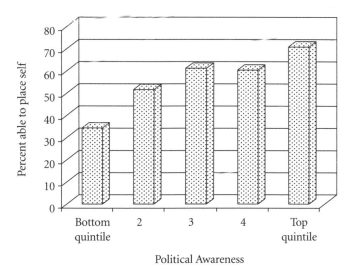

Figure 5.2. Ability to Place Self on Left-Right Scale by Level of Political Awareness, 1996

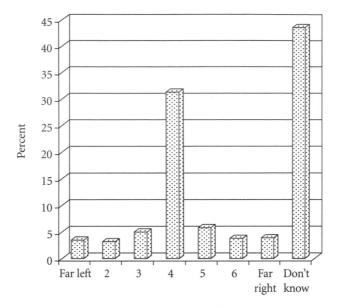

Figure 5.3. Self-Locations on Left-Right Scale, 1996

It was selected by 31 percent of those interviewed, or 6 percent more than all other actual responses combined. The average score was 4.1.[18]

Most of our survey respondents who categorized themselves on the left-right axis followed suit for classifying the leading presidential candidates in 1996.[19] The ideological locations imputed (see Table 5.3) testify in part to popular shrewdness. Gennadii Zyuganov, with a mean score of 3.1, comes out as the most left-wing candidate and Yeltsin, at 4.7, as firmly to the right of center. Among the most knowledgeable voters, the spread between the two antagonists was wider still.[20] But, dismayingly, almost equal numbers held Vladimir Zhirinovskii, the ranting leader of the LDPR, to be an extreme rightist, a centrist, and a rabid leftist, and his average score falls a hair to the left of center. In a well-ordered European polity, he surely would be reckoned a mainstay of the fascistic far right, in the mold of a Jean-Marie Le Pen in France or a Jörg Haider in Austria.

Also to be swallowed with a grain of salt are many qualitative remarks about the connotations of left and right. Sixty percent of our Russian sample—and 40 percent of informants who located themselves on the left-right scale—were not up to supplying any answer about the differences be-

Table 5.3 Placement of Five Presidential Candidates on Left-Right Scale, 1996[a]

Candidate	Position on scale (percentages)							Don't know	Mean score[b]
	1 (far left)	2	3	4	5	6	7 (far right)		
Boris Yeltsin	6	3	4	13	6	6	16	46	4.7
Gennadii Zyuganov	24	5	3	5	4	3	9	46	3.1
Aleksandr Lebed	2	3	6	18	8	7	8	48	4.5
Grigorii Yavlinskii	2	3	6	17	7	7	5	53	4.3
Vladimir Zhirinovskii	9	6	6	9	5	6	9	50	3.9

a. N = 2,472 weighted cases.

b. Among respondents who assigned the candidate a position.

tween left and right (see Figure 5.4). This is way in excess of the perplexity citizens of the advanced democracies evince on the same sort of question.[21] Many of the 60 percent gave up without comment; others said to the interviewer they cared nothing about such esoterica or that, the political world having been rocked to its foundations, they had lost track of left and right.[22] The 14 percent who either saw no difference between left and right or gave indecipherable answers lifted the total proportion of those who were ignorant on the subject to three-quarters of all respondents. Less than one-fifth of the sample hitched left-right differences to abstract axioms of government, history, or social organization. Disproportionately of above-average political awareness,[23] such individuals mostly allied a leftist approach with Communism and the Soviet regime and rightism with the transformation of Russia into a democracy and market economy—but some, ludicrously, saw it the other way around. A smattering of respondents tethered the definitions of left and right to social groups, to positions politicians take on distinct issues, and to political leaders and their styles.

All told, the analytical value of holistic ideology, as encoded in the international terminology of left and right, is polluted in Russia by the low state of public consciousness about it.[24] A bare majority of the electorate can spot themselves on a left-right scale. Fewer still can impute left-right positions to politicians, and much guesswork goes into it for those who do. Only four Russians in ten in 1996 could articulate a left-right distinction; half or more of them were confused or defined it counter to customary usage.

Overt ideology does deserve to be watched in Russia and may gain in

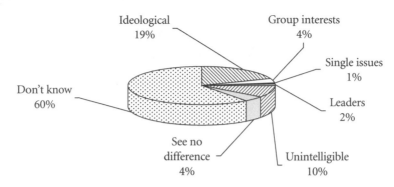

Figure 5.4. Meanings Attributed to Differences between Left and Right, 1996

importance in future elections. It cannot yet assume a prominent place in interpretations of the mass politics of the Russian transition.

Principles and Preferences

The Russian electorate's debility of formal ideological reasoning after Marxism-Leninism does not necessarily mean that the public is devoid of beliefs that are less comprehensive than an elaborate, creedal ideology but more broad-ranging than opinions about isolated issues. In the United States, in addition to investigating the liberal-conservative schema, political scientists have found it useful to examine the electoral impact of beliefs of intermediate generality relating to questions such as social equality, the size of government, and traditional morality. Warren E. Miller and J. Merrill Shanks, in the best treatment of the topic, find middle-range "policy-related predispositions" to affect voting directly and through bridging variables, including citizen opinions on more concrete and time-bound controversies. Examples of the latter might be taxation, gun control, and abortion.[25]

The foremost reason for surmising that predispositions are causally prior to issue-specific preferences is, for Miller and Shanks, a claim about chronology. "Policy-related predispositions," they say, "represent 'long-term' influences on the vote in the sense that they are acquired well before the current campaign" and are "less malleable and more persistent" than other opinions; preferences on discrete issues are "more volatile and changeable" than predispositions.[26]

Does this distinction, made about the developed West, hold for semi-developed Russia? The panel format of our 1995–96 surveys affords some clues. In the sphere of economic and social policy, besides asking the delimited questions about unemployment, tariffs, and so forth, we posed several questions of a more philosophical bent. Three of them were laid before respondents in both the first-wave survey (in late 1995) and the third-wave survey (in mid-1996). The first wide-bore question was directed to the citizen's "view of the transition to a market economy in Russia." The answer options were threefold: (1) "You are for a market economy and believe the transition to the market should be quick"; (2) "You are for a market economy and believe the transition to the market should be gradual"; and (3) "You are against the transition to a market economy." The second question was about control of economic property. The respondent was asked to pick one of five eventualities for Russia: (1) exclusively private ownership, (2) mostly private ownership, (3) an equal blend of private and state ownership, (4) mostly state ownership, and (5) exclusively state ownership. The third question, subsuming cultural as much as economic values, took aim at foreign social models. The informant could flag one of three choices: (1) "Russia should entirely follow the path of the West, using its experience"; (2) "Russia should borrow from the West only what suits it"; and (3) "Russia should have its own unique path of development and has no need of the West's experience."

Were Miller and Shanks' long-term/short term calculus to prevail in protodemocratic Russia, the responses to questions about sweeping tenets of economic and social transformation should show greater continuity in the interim than responses to more circumscribed questions. But that is not what the longitudinal correlations in Table 5.4 reveal. Set them side by side with the coefficients in Table 5.2, and you uncover no greater persistence in principled attitudes toward the transition to the market, property, and emulation of the West than in the less far-reaching preferences. Indeed, for all respondents, the average of the three coefficients in Table 5.4 (.30) is marginally lower than the average of the six coefficients in Table 5.2 (.33). Attitudes toward Russia and the West are the most frangible of the nine opinions, and this is the sole question on which high-awareness respondents are less steadfast in their opinions than low-awareness respondents.

In modeling the Russian electorate's decision making, we thus have no empirical basis for privileging any one subset of opinions over others and assigning it to a prior causal stage. This homogenization is a logical by-

Table 5.4 Intertemporal Correlations for Responses to Questions about Principles of Economic and Social Policy, 1995–96, by Level of Political Awareness (Pearson's r)[a]

Issue	Low awareness	High awareness	All
Transition to market[b]	.33**	.34**	.35**
Property[c]	.27**	.37**	.34**
Emulation of West[d]	.27**	.23**	.27**

**p ≤ .01 (two-tailed test). Missing values deleted pairwise.

a. Only for respondents who answered question in both 1995 pre-election survey and 1996 post-election survey, excluding "Don't know" responses.

b. N = 1,852 weighted cases.

c. N = 2,064 weighted cases.

d. N = 2,175 weighted cases.

product of the transitional political milieu. In an institutionalized democracy moored in a sound social and economic system, short-term conflicts pose little threat to the continuance and structure of the polity and of the basal arrangements of society. In a crisis-ridden democracy-in-the-making, by contrast, there is no firewall between issue types. Disagreement over specifics is of a piece with disagreement over the basics, and elections are fought over a medley of issues ranging from the most parochial and acute to the most universal and chronic. In a protodemocracy, everything is up for grabs at election time.

Opinions and Electoral Choice

Before getting to the influence of opinions on the electoral choices of Russian voters, we need to ascertain what citizens believe are the issue stands of the parties and candidates suing for their votes and the gist of their moralizing opinions.

The discussion presupposes that parties and candidates *take* stands on the issues in Russia. That is not a chimerical claim. The campaign manifestos of Russian politicos, it has correctly been noted, sometimes have a "fuzzy focus."[27] But that indefiniteness should not be exaggerated. Analysts have had little trouble parsing the field of parties into programmatic groups (such as the government, liberal, centrist, nationalist, and socialist families detailed in this book). Most political parties in the 1993 and 1993 Duma campaigns "did produce documents that were fairly recognizable as party platforms."[28] In the most salient policy area, the economy, the government and liberal parties, on the one hand, and their bitter adversaries in the socialist opposition, on the other hand, "differ fundamentally on the course, direction, and pace of economic change, and they present the electorate . . . with disparate policy choices and visions of the future."[29] The nationalist movements, their positions on economic issues a populist hodge-podge,[30] save their firepower for law-and-order issues and foreign policy, calling for draconian punishment of criminals and venal officials, a strong presidency, and an assertive policy in the "Near Abroad," the post-Soviet space outside the federation. In the 1996 presidential election, the two finalists, Yeltsin and Zyuganov, blazoned sharply different programs on economic reform, social policy, and foreign relations. The third-running candidate, the nationalist Lebed, was "deliberately vague" on the economy but emphatic about social control, promising "to crack down on crime on the streets and corruption in the government."[31]

What Citizens Know

How cognizant are Russians of the postures parties and candidates strike on the campaign trail? In the survey interview before the 1995 parliamentary vote, we selected for experiment a couple of opinion questions—about economic privatization and battling crime and corruption "at all costs, even if the rights of citizens are violated." After asking respondents to state their own positions on these neuralgic issues, we invited them to locate the corresponding platforms of each of the ten main political parties in the race. Five-point scales printed on cards were used for both issues. We reran the questions in the 1996 post-election survey for the five leading presidential candidates.[32]

Our subjects, true to form, were unabashed about airing their preferences on privatization and the policy of the iron hand: upwards of 90 percent, question by question, had a point of view. Far fewer, though, could say where the parties stood on the two issues in 1995 (see Table 5.5), volunteering an average of 31 percent (6.2 out of 20) of the possible party locations. In 1996, while the respondents were again less confident of the contenders' positions than of their own, they felt a lot more certain about the presidential candidates than about the parties in 1995. Mean success

Table 5.5 Ability to Give Positions on Two Issues for Ten Political Parties, 1995, and Five Presidential Candidates, 1996 (Percentages)

Party or candidate	Among all respondents		Among respondents who recognize and evaluate party or candidate	
	Property	Crime and corruption	Property	Crime and corruption
1995 parliamentary election[a]				
Agrarian	25	29	52	58
Derzhava	20	30	43	65
Forward Russia	19	27	43	61
KPRF	40	46	53	62
KRO	19	29	44	67
LDPR	27	51	37	69
Our Home Is Russia	31	39	47	58
Russia's Democratic Choice	25	32	47	60
Women of Russia	24	40	36	60
Yabloko	27	36	44	59
Average	26	36	45	62
1996 presidential election[b]				
Yeltsin	74	76	78	80
Zyuganov	71	73	77	79
Lebed	55	77	60	84
Yavlinskii	56	61	70	78
Zhirinovskii	53	75	59	83
Average	62	72	69	81

a. Total N = 2,841 weighted cases. Proportion of respondents who recognize and evaluate party varies from party to party.

b. Total N = 2,472 weighted cases. Proportion of respondents who recognize and evaluate candidate varies from candidate to candidate.

was 67 percent (6.7 out of 10 candidate-issue pairings). The 1996 response rates were moderately lower than in established democracies; the 1995 rates were much lower.[33]

The ability to discern the issue positions of parties and politicians is, as one would anticipate, tied to Russians' political awareness. But the disjunction between the parliamentary and the presidential settings stays intact even when we control for personal sophistication. Figure 5.5 traces cit-

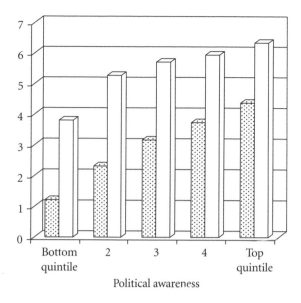

⊡ Four parties 1995   □ Four candidates 1996

Figure 5.5. Positions on Property and Crime and Corruption Imputed to Parties and Presidential Candidates: Number by Level of Political Awareness, 1995 and 1996

izens' avowed understanding of issue positions in 1995 and 1996 on the same two questions (property and crime and corruption) and for the same quantity of electoral actors (the four top parties in 1995 and the four top presidential nominees in 1996). In both campaigns mastery of the information ascends monotonically with political awareness. And yet, at all plateaus of awareness, acquaintance with where the players stand on the issues is more complete in the presidential election than in the parliamentary.[34]

Without doubt, then, systemic and not only individual-level factors shape transitional citizens' competence on the issues. Most likely, two institutional realities were at work in 1996. First, the ten-man field of presidential candidates, headed by Russia's first head of state, was more legible to the rank-and-file citizen than the milling crowd of forty-three parties in the parliamentary election. Another way to put it is that the information costs of tying the electoral combatants to issues and policy stakes are lower in the presidential than in the parliamentary arena. Notice in Table 5.5 that the issue positions of Zyuganov, the leader of the KPRF, were more accessible to voters in 1996 than the KPRF's interchangeable positions on these issues were the preceding year. The second contributing factor is the allotment by Russia's constitution of the lion's share of power after election day to the president and his appointees in the executive branch. The State Duma is but one wing of a bicameral Federal Assembly, and anyway half of its deputies are elected in territorial districts, not by party list. Voters have more incentive to bone up on the policy positions of presidential hopefuls than of the parties fighting to be seated in the weak and fractious Duma.[35]

As Table 5.6 shows, approximately 80 percent of those presidential voters who voted for one of the five pacesetting candidates did say they rec-

Table 5.6 Ability to Give Positions on Two Issues for Parties and Candidates, by Party or Candidate Voted for, 1995 and 1996

	Percent who located that party or candidate		Total positions recognized	
Party or candidate voted for	Property	Crime and corruption	Property	Crime and corruption
1995 parliamentary election[a]				
Agrarian	51	57	3.1	4.1
Derzhava	52	62	3.0	4.0
Forward Russia	40	53	3.8	4.9
KPRF	51	56	2.7	3.4
KRO	42	59	3.5	4.8
LDPR	45	65	2.8	3.7
Our Home Is Russia	45	61	3.3	4.7
Russia's Democratic Choice	57	62	4.0	5.2
Women of Russia	27	50	1.6	2.9
Yabloko	47	61	3.4	4.7
All 10 parties	46	58	2.9	4.0
1996 presidential election (first round)[b]				
Yeltsin	80	87	3.3	3.9
Zyuganov	76	80	3.0	3.6
Lebed	69	84	3.4	3.8
Yavlinskii	72	82	3.4	4.1
Zhirinovskii	71	88	3.3	3.9
All 5 candidates	76	84	3.3	3.9

a. Total N = 1,657 weighted cases.
b. Total N = 1,952 weighted cases.

ognized his position on the property and iron-hand questions, and the average voter knew the positions of three or four candidates on the two issues. There was more uncertainty about where the parties stood in 1995, but even here it would be hyperbole to say all Russian voters flew blind. Forty-six percent of supporters of the ten parties about which we made inquiries could pigeonhole their favored party on the property issue, and 58 percent could do so on the crime-and-corruption issue.[36] Of those unable to vocalize where the party belonged on these issue scales, chances are that more than a few had an intuition of it. And these same voters might have situated the party on other issues, had we asked the question.

Not to know about a party's or candidate's issue position is one thing; to have a biased perception is another. A nagging suspicion in the literature on voting in the United States is that citizens, anxious to reduce cognitive dissonance and rationalize the vote choice, may project onto their electoral favorites positions falsely akin to their own. Conversely, they may impute to parties or candidates they disfavor positions that err in the contrary direction.[37]

In Russia too such wishful thinking does occur, as Table 5.7 certifies. On the property issue, first-round supporters of Yeltsin in 1996 judged his position to be almost one full point less anti-state ownership (or pro-privatization) than did supporters of other candidates. On clamping down on crime and corruption, projection seems to be at work for three of the four top parties in 1995 (all except Yabloko), and for four of the five leading presidential candidates in 1996 (all except Yavlinskii). Over and over, persons who cast a ballot for a party or candidate believed it or him to be more solicitous of individual rights than other voters did. For one party (the KPRF) and three presidential candidates (Yeltsin, Zyuganov, and Lebed), supporters and nonsupporters planted the party or candidate on opposite sides of the mean of the scale (value 3.00).[38]

The projection problem, the limited capacity of the members of a new democracy for comparing issue positions, particularly in a parliamentary campaign, and the surfeit of parties and politicians bring me to a simplifying assumption about the method for verifying opinion effects on the vote. All considerations militate against use of the "issue proximity" indicators—measures of the distance between preferences and perceptions of where contestants stand on the issue—which were once the vogue in U.S. electoral studies.[39] Russians possess issue opinions, and have some signposts to where some politicians stand on the issues, but the best way to

Table 5.7 Imputed Issue Positions of Parties and Candidates, 1995 and 1996 (Mean Scores, Scales of 1 to 5)

Party or candidate	Property (favor state ownership)		Crime and corruption (favor iron hand)	
	Voted for	Voted against	Voted for	Voted against
1995 parliamentary election[a]				
Agrarian	3.53	3.36	1.90	2.35
Derzhava	3.24	3.38	2.58	3.10
Forward Russia	3.10	2.60	1.57	2.44
KPRF	4.33	4.36	2.05	3.01
KRO	3.54	3.34	2.51	2.88
LDPR	3.56	3.09	3.67	4.47
Our Home Is Russia	2.88	2.54	1.87	2.30
Russia's Democratic Choice	2.41	2.32	1.39	2.36
Women of Russia	3.58	3.34	1.35	1.83
Yabloko	2.53	2.61	2.10	2.10
1996 presidential election (first round)[b]				
Yeltsin	2.58	2.05	2.41	3.05
Zyuganov	4.11	4.28	2.07	3.39
Lebed	3.14	2.98	2.71	3.15
Yavlinskii	2.73	2.58	1.79	2.27
Zhirinovskii	3.03	2.63	4.01	4.45

a. Total N = 2,166 weighted cases. Proportion of respondents who impute a position to party varies from party to party.

b. Total N = 2,013 weighted cases. Proportion of respondents who impute a position to candidate varies from candidate to candidate .

get at the interface between prescriptive opinions and voting behavior is the least complicated one: to enlist unmodified measures of the opinions themselves as explanatory variables.

What Citizens Want

A word is in order about the substance of Russians' normative opinions. I work here only with attitudes distilled from the parliamentary and presidential election surveys of 1995–96. All were sought out on account of their relevance to contemporary political debate in Russia and the former Soviet Union, and are included in the analysis because they exhibit some statistical relationship to the vote.[40] Ten opinion variables from the data set qualify in each of the two elections. Seven derive from matching questions administered on both occasions; three variables join the analysis for the State Duma election only, and three for the presidential election only. Question wording and the distribution of responses are given in Appendix C.

ECONOMIC AND SOCIAL POLICY.   Five out of the seven repeat items speak to Russia's economic crisis, to the quantum leap from socialism toward capitalism, and to the social consequences thereof. I alluded above to the questions about the velocity of the transition to the market, privatization, trade protectionism, and foreign investment. Responses to three other aforementioned questions concerning government redistributive and regulatory activity—about full employment policy, controls over the price of food, and caps on incomes—are so organically related that I fuse them into an additive "welfarism" index.[41]

The data show Russians as of the mid-1990s to be sympathetic toward transiting to a market economy—only about every fifth person condemned it outright—but deadly cautious about ways and means. While 61 percent of survey respondents in 1996 were for a gradual transition to the market, and 8 percent for a speedy transition, only 10 percent wished property in Russia to be wholly or mostly in private hands; 42 percent foresaw ownership lying entirely or mostly with the state. Just under 50 percent got the maximum score on welfarism, simultaneously demanding a state guarantee of a job to all workers, setting of food prices by government edict, and curbs on the incomes of the rich; another 28 percent acceded to two of the three. Forty-five percent of our informants in 1996 were very or somewhat welcoming of foreign investment, a sign of receptivity to the world economy—even as 67 percent wanted domestic industry shielded against imports.

POLITICAL AND CONSTITUTIONAL ISSUES.   We invested less survey time in political and constitutional controversies, partly in deference to the consensus among Russians that their most crushing problems are economic. Two questions tapping diffuse liberal and democratic values were asked in 1995 and duplicated in 1996: the first, the query about wielding an iron hand against crime and corruption (see Tables 5.5 through 5.7); the second, asking whether "It is better to live in a society with strict order than to give people so much freedom that they may destroy society." Two questions of narrower compass, addressing the institutional balance between the federal government and the regions and between the president and the parliament, yield significant results in 1995.[42] In 1996 we did not reiterate the constitutional questions, around which there was nowhere near as much verbal swordplay as during the 1995 Duma campaign. In the polarized presidential election—in which the incumbent, Yeltsin, fulminated that Zyuganov and the KPRF were planning to reinstate the Soviet dictatorship and Zyuganov accused Yeltsin of pandering to the West—we drew respondents out on "what kind of political system" Russia ought to have. The alternatives cited were the pre-Gorbachev Soviet system, the current regime, and "democracy of the Western type."

The responses on citizen rights and order versus freedom suggest a profound ambivalence within the transitional Russian electorate on core political values. Fewer than 10 percent in our survey sample said crime and corruption should be assailed at all costs, about two-thirds sanctioning the pro-civil rights positions on the scale. Still, two respondents in three in both 1995 and 1996 believed that it would be better for society to have strict order than unlimited liberty. On the explicit constitutional questions bruited in 1995, pluralities took a compromise position commending an equal sharing of powers between Moscow and the regions and between president and parliament. On federalism, decentralizers outnumbered centralizers; on the division of central powers, pro-parliamentary and pro-presidential attitudes were voiced almost equally. And on the recipe for Russia's political system in 1996, opinion was badly split, with one in every three citizens selecting the Soviet order, nearly 40 percent endorsing either the status quo or a Western democracy, and the remainder offering an ad lib response or refraining from any.

FOREIGN POLICY.   Barely anyone in the mid-1990s thought foreign policy after the Cold War was the most grievous problem on the nation's agenda. One problem about which we made inquiries is relations with the fourteen adjacent states descended from the USSR. The 1995 question was phrased in terms of attitude toward the second most populous successor country, Ukraine. Half of respondents felt that Russia and Ukraine should be reunited; approval of Ukrainian independence was confined to about 15 percent of the electorate. The 1996 item asked more broadly if Russia was well advised to strive for economic and political integration with all the ex-Soviet republics, "regardless of the cost." Almost two-thirds of respondents answered to some extent in the affirmative. In 1996 we also probed the eastward expansion of the NATO military alliance. Opinion on whether

Russia should do "everything possible" to bar accession of former Soviet satellites in Eastern Europe was fragmented and unsure. About one-quarter of citizens went along with such a stance, about 20 percent did not, and the rest were indifferent or could not answer.

CORRELATIONS AMONG OPINIONS. All of these and other opinions of transitional citizens are not unrelated: indeed, they commingle in an intricate web. A few of the associations among them are summarized in the correlation matrix in Appendix Table C.1 (for 1995) and Table C.2 (for 1996). The opinion indicators are all coded as they appear in the multivariate analysis of voting behavior that ensues—so that larger values go with a greater likelihood of voting for the KPRF in 1995 or Zyuganov in 1996.

The cross-attitudinal associations are in many instances quite substantial, especially among Russians' various economic opinions. With one arresting exception, the threads joining political, constitutional, and foreign-policy preferences to one another and to economic opinions are looser. The exception is preference for political system in 1996, which is moderately associated with other political opinions and highly correlated with preferences on the economy. Associations between opinions are very stable over the time lapsed, especially if one recalls the variability in the attitudes as such. The seven questions asked in 1995 and recapitulated in 1996 yield twenty-one opinion dyads per campaign. Comparing 1995 with 1996, we see a difference in coefficients between the two years, pairing by pairing, of no more than .05 for sixteen of the twenty-one correlations; four of the five outliers are occasioned by one variable ("Order over liberty").[43] All in all, as scholars of post-Soviet public opinion have shown at greater length, pro-market and pro-democratic attitudes are mutually reinforcing in transitional Russia.[44] Although voters' views might be combined into multi-item scales or principal components for other analytical purposes, I shall stick with discrete opinions and estimate their effects on electoral choice as straightforwardly as possible.

The Party-List Vote

Correspondence between normative opinions and Russian electoral behavior is not hard to confirm. Let us lead off with issue cleavages in parliamentary voting.

Figures 5.6 and 5.7 cross votes for the lists of the four biggest parties in the 1995 State Duma election with two issue opinions, one economic and one political: the first about property relations, for which we also know popular assessments of the parties' stands; the second about the tradeoff between order and liberty, which has a more consistent relationship to voting than the extravagantly worded iron-hand item. On both of these grand dilemmas, the main Russian parties broadcast intelligible if not always impeccably lucid positions in 1995. Faithful to its Marxist and Soviet bloodline, the KPRF championed a state-managed and chiefly state-owned economy and the supremacy of collective goals over individual liberties. The government's Our Home Is Russia and Yabloko, the pillar of the liberal opposition, stood for building a capitalist economy and a democratic political system. The nationalist LDPR was incoherent on economics and followed the Communist authoritarian line on many points of political process and civil rights.

Concordance between opinions on property and the vote is as plain as could be in 1995 (Figure 5.6). Support for the KPRF is three-and-one-half times as widespread among diehard defenders of state ownership (where it stands at 46 percent) as among the most ardent privatizers (13 percent). For the pro-market Our Home Is Russia and Yabloko, it is the inverse. No regularity is detectable for the waffling LDPR. On the conflict between order and liberty (Figure 5.7), Communist electors again march to a different drum than Our Home Is Russia and Yabloko. The KPRF slate outperforms the two pro-reform parties 37 percent to 17 percent among citizens who fully agree with the need for strict order in society, while it is thoroughly

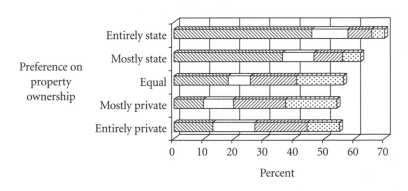

Figure 5.6. Opinions about Property and the Party-List Vote, 1995

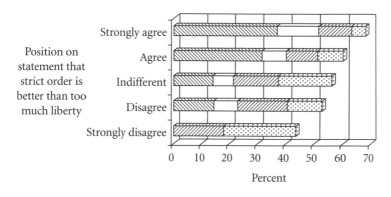

Position on
statement that
strict order is
better than too
much liberty

☒ KPRF   ☐ LDPR   ▨ Our Home Is Russia   ⊡ Yabloko

Figure 5.7. Opinions about Social Order and the Party-List Vote, 1995

ruled out by those who strongly disagree (as compared to a 44 percent share for Our Home and Yabloko). The LDPR, meantime, is also shunned by voters who put freedom first and gets 15 percent of the votes of persons who exalt order at the expense of liberty.

This attitude-by-attitude exploration can be extended to the eight remaining normative opinions encompassed in the analysis. The top section of Table D.3 in Appendix D may be consulted for zero-order measures of the electoral influence of all ten opinion variables in 1995. The measures, first differences in predicted probabilities, are simulated from a multinomial logit regression with a single independent variable only. They reveal supporters of the KPRF to be not only relatively hostile to privatization but wary of the market in general, protectionist, against foreign investment, and enthusiastic about government welfarism. On the political dimension, these voters' subordination of personal liberty to social order is complemented by a mailed-fist approach to crime and corruption. On matters constitutional, they are inclined to uphold central power over the regions and the legislative over the executive branch (which had been under Yeltsin's thumb continuously since 1991), while in foreign policy they lean toward unification with the Russians' fellow Slavs in Ukraine. On most scores, the balance of preferences in the Our Home Is Russia and Yabloko camps is the other way—pro-market, pro-privatization, anti-welfare, and so on. LDPR voters share some of the KPRF's disciplinarian leanings, but on the constitutional front are pro-region and pro-president; in economics, they show weak mixed signs.

As with social and partisanship factors in Chapters 3 and 4, we cannot rest content with scanning these bilateral associations. None of the attitudes tapped here comes within hailing distance of accounting for all the variation in the parliamentary vote. And the real question is not whether normative opinions are omnipotent but how, comparatively speaking, they figure in the multicausal analysis pursued in the book as a whole.

The total-effect estimates in Table 5.8 push the analysis forward. They differ from the bivariate estimates in the key respect that they take into account the role of causally prior influences on the vote (that is, voters' social characteristics and perceptions of current conditions) and simultaneous influences (other opinion measures and partisanship). Holding the effects of these other components of our explanation constant, and thereby subtracting their statistical contribution to the vote from the estimates of the effects of the issue preferences, we get a much truer picture of the electoral consequences of normative opinions than we would from looking at detached opinions only.

The consistent result of moving to total-effect estimates is to thin out the apparent electoral impact of our opinion measures. Knowing only the Russian voter's opinion about the transition to the market economy, for example, we would estimate statistically that a shift in that opinion

Table 5.8 Total Effects of Normative Opinions on the Party-List Vote, 1995 (Differences in Predicted Probabilities)[a]

Opinion	KPRF	LDPR	Our Home	Yabloko
Oppose market	.18**	−.00	−.05	−.08*
State ownership	.13*	−.01	.02	−.04
Welfarism	.08*	−.00	.03	−.05
Protectionism	.09	.02	−.03	−.03
No foreign capital	.01	−.04**	−.09*	.01
Order over liberty	.17**	.01	−.05	−.05
Iron hand	.10*	.04**	−.05	−.01
Centralization	.02	−.04	.02	−.00
Strong parliament	.12**	−.04**	−.05	.00
Reunite with Ukraine	.09*	−.01	.03	.02

**p ≤ .01
*p ≤ .05
a. Sample N = 2,143.

from its most zealously pro-market to its most recalcitrantly anti-market value would heighten the probability of voting for the KPRF by .44, or 44 percentage points. Once we discount for the confounding influence of that voter's social characteristics, reading of current conditions, partisanship, and preferences on other public issues, the effect of attitude toward marketization becomes .18—a not negligible value, but considerably less than estimated in the bivariate procedure.

Taken as a whole, the total-effect estimates summarized in Table 5.8 bespeak appreciable opinion effects on Russians' voting behavior, but not as weighty as some we have encountered in Chapters 3 and 4 or will encounter in Chapter 6. Eleven opinion/voting linkages out of a possible forty (ten opinions X four parties) are of statistical significance ($p \leq .05$) and a mere five rate as being of major substantive importance by our rule of thumb (magnitude of the total effect $\geq .10$).

So far as particular parties are concerned:

- The most opinion-sensitive voters by far are the KPRF's. Six of the eleven significant associations and *all* five of them with a significant total effect of .10 or more in 1995 are for the KPRF vote. The largest effects are exerted by opposition to marketization and partiality toward order over liberty. Rather smaller effects on the probability of an individual's voting for the KPRF stem from preferences for state over private ownership of property, parliamentary over presidential power, and the iron hand; minor effects in the predicted direction are for reunification with Ukraine and welfarism.
- For the nationalist LDPR, the runner-up in the 1995 election and the top finisher in the proportional-representation voting in 1993, three opinion effects (for attitudes toward foreign investment, the iron hand, and parliament versus president) attain statistical significance, but are of minor magnitude, well below .10.
- The only significant opinion effects on the vote for Our Home Is Russia or the liberal Yabloko movement are minor and are discernible for one issue preference apiece—fondness for foreign investment in the case of Our Home Is Russia and for rapid construction of a market economy in the case of Yabloko. For all other relationships, most signs for the effect measures are in the expected direction, but the parameters are not reliably different from zero.

Tables 5.9 and 5.10 augment the analysis by presenting the full hierarchical elaboration of the impact of two selected opinion indicators—about

Table 5.9 Elaboration of the Impact of Opinions about Property on the Party-List Vote, 1995 (Differences in Predicted Probabilities)[a]

Variables progressively incorporated in regression	KPRF	LDPR	Our Home	Yabloko
Opinions about property only	.43**	.01	−.12**	−.20**
Also social characteristics	.29**	.03	−.08*	−.08**
Also current conditions	.25**	.02	−.04	−.07**
Also partisanship (but not other issue opinions)	.24**	−.02	−.01	−.08**
Also other issue opinions (but not partisanship)	.13**	.00	−.01	−.03
Also partisanship and other issue opinions[b]	.13**	−.01	.02	−.04
Also retrospective evaluations of incumbents	.14**	−.01	.01	−.04
Also party leaders	.10	−.00	.03	−.01
Also prospective evaluations of parties	.08	−.00	.02	−.01

**p ≤ .01
*p ≤ .05
a. Sample N = 2,143.
b. Gray-toned row gives the total effect of opinions about property.

property and social order—on the party-list vote. As before, the statistics in successive rows of the tables estimate the impact of the same explanatory variable as other variables are shoehorned into the analysis in blocs. Although bivariate effects on the vote have a value of .10 or more seven times out of eight (the exception being property and the LDPR vote), only two of the associations, as was seen in Table 5.8, survive as significant and important total effects (in the gray-toned rows of tables 5.9 and 5.10) once causally anterior and concurrent variables have been annexed. Both effects are for the KPRF vote. Also evident is the progressive attenuation of the estimates as social characteristics, current conditions, partisanship, and the individual's other issue opinions enter the picture. These variables confound the effects of our two issue opinions in differing ways, as can be seen through row-wise comparisons. For votes in favor of the KPRF, the main beneficiary of issue-centered voting, social characteristics (age, in particular) and the individual's other issue opinions are about equally important, with current conditions also playing a role. The effects of those blocs pass "through" the pair of issue opinions, in a sense, leaving the total effect as

Table 5.10 Elaboration of the Impact of Opinions about Social Order on the Party-List Vote, 1995 (Differences in Predicted Probabilities)[a]

Variables progressively incorporated in regression	KPRF	LDPR	Our Home	Yabloko
Opinions about social order only	.33**	.08**	−.11**	−.16**
Also social characteristics	.24**	.09**	−.08**	−.07**
Also current conditions	.21**	.09**	−.06*	−.06**
Also partisanship (but not other issue opinions)	.22**	.03	−.05	−.07*
Also other issue opinions (but not partisanship)	.15**	.05*	−.05	−.04
Also partisanship and other issue opinions[b]	.17**	.01	−.05	−.05
Also retrospective evaluations of incumbents	.17**	.01	−.04	−.06
Also party leaders	.16*	.01	−.04	−.03
Also prospective evaluations of parties	.14*	.01	−.04	−.03

$**p \le .01$

$*p \le .05$

a. Sample N = 2,143.

b. Gray-toned row gives the total effect of opinions about social order.

the best measure of the size of that influence on the vote which originates with the normative opinion itself.

Monitoring the causal minutiae as we forge analytically from the two issue opinions forward to the electoral decision reveals little of interest. In only one case (order over liberty for the KPRF) does a statistically significant residual effect greater than .10 materialize in the bottom row of the column.

The Presidential Vote

Figures 5.8 and 5.9 revisit the terrain at President Yeltsin's re-election in 1996. The opinions graphed are responses to the same two hot-button questions—about property and social order—already posted for 1995. Both figures convey strong direct associations between opinions on these issues and the first-round presidential vote. Zyuganov has a surplus of 44 percentage points over Yeltsin among the voters most opposed to privatization but a 64-point deficit among the most fervent supporters of privat-

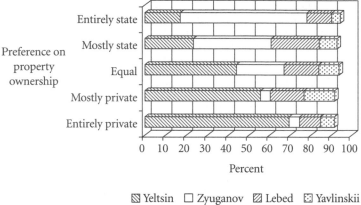

Figure 5.8. Opinions about Property and the First-Round Presidential Vote, 1996

ization. On the tension between order and personal freedom, Zyuganov outstrips the president 45 percent to 21 percent among the most pro-order citizens, while Yeltsin turns the tables on him by 67 percent to 7 percent among the most pro-liberty citizens.

The total-effect measures reported in Table 5.11 provide more systematic evidence. The reader again can supplement them with fuller information from Appendix D (Table D.4). Since Russians in 1996 were more conversant with the issue positions of the presidential candidates than they were in 1995 with the parties' views, we might expect them to be more open to persuasion by the candidates' issue stands. Looking at discrete opinions (see Chapter 7 for combined opinions) we see some backing for the prediction. Of the forty first-round entries in Table 5.11, the issue opinion in question is estimated to have a statistically significant total effect on the probability of voting for the presidential candidate in seven pairings—three for Yeltsin, two for Zyuganov, and one for Lebed and Yavlinskii. Six of the seven are major effects. In the parliamentary election, there were five major pairings, all of them for the KPRF vote. In the presidential runoff, five of the twenty pairings show a significant effect, in every case of .10 or more—two for the Yeltsin vote and three for the Zyuganov vote. Moreover, some of the first differences of interest are larger than their counterparts in the analysis of the Duma vote. Two total effects in the first-round estimation are higher than .20; one in the runoff analysis is above .20 and two are higher than .40.

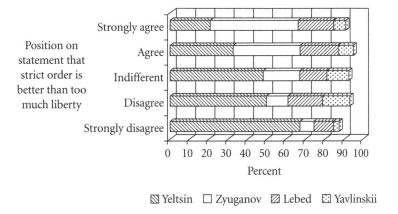

Figure 5.9. Opinions about Social Order and the First-Round Presidential Vote, 1996

Table 5.11 brings out both similarities and differences with voter choice in the parliamentary election:

- Preferences for the way things were under the Soviet regime fuel the Zyuganov vote, as they did the KPRF vote in 1995.
- But Boris Yeltsin offers an alternative to these retrograde opinions much more efficaciously than did Our Home Is Russia or any other pro-reform party in the campaign for the Duma. Unlike in 1995, the non-Communist or anti-Communist vote is not dissipated in 1996.
- General Lebed's main appeal is in one opinion niche—among supporters of a strict social order who do not want to reinstate the one-party Soviet political system.[45] He gets no lift out of favoring reintegration of the USSR and condemning NATO enlargement, issues that strike one as ready-made for a nationalist politician.
- The liberal Yavlinskii, blocked by Yeltsin, has minor issue appeal on one issue only, opposition to a Soviet-like political system.

The signal difference between the presidential and the parliamentary elections in the issue realm[46] has to do with the accumulation by one specific normative opinion of an unusual quotient of explanatory power. That opinion is no garden-variety attitude but a preference of the sort that can surface only in a transitional or revolutionary situation—the opinion relating to the type of political system (Soviet, current, or Western) Russia needs. Regrettably, we did not ask survey respondents this bald question in

Table 5.11 Total Effects of Normative Opinions on the Presidential Vote, 1996 (Differences in Predicted Probabilities)

Opinion	First round[a]				Runoff[b]	
	Yel.	Zyug.	Leb.	Yav.	Yel.	Zyug.
Oppose market	−.10	.13**	−.04	−.00	−.22*	.17**
State ownership	−.07	.07	.04	−.03	−.12	.12*
Welfarism	−.02	.05	−.05	.02	−.03	.08
Protectionism	−.07	.02	.00	.02	−.07	.05
No foreign capital	−.16*	−.02	.10	.06	−.04	−.02
Order over liberty	−.16*	.03	.13*	.01	−.09	.03
Iron hand	−.03	.00	.00	.03	−.07	.04
Soviet political system	−.22**	.23**	.00	−.06*	−.47**	.41**
Reintegrate USSR	.12	.01	−.02	−.05	.12	−.04
Resist NATO	−.05	.05	.02	−.01	.01	−.01

**p ≤ .01
*p ≤ .05
a. Sample N = 1,990.
b. Sample N = 1,937.

1995, though it is not likely that the answer would have formed a compelling nexus with the vote: no mainline politician advocated terminating the existing regime in 1995, and the legislative veto, military and police powers, and other prerogatives of the federal president would have precluded any threat to do so through the Duma. The balance of hopes and fears was different in 1996. The imperial Russian presidency, not the Duma, was the prize in dispute. Zyuganov, laying Russia's travails squarely at the door of post-Soviet institutions and elites, agitated openly for a new constitution—or, in some materials, an extraconstitutional "government of national trust"—and for restoration forthwith of "the soviets," the thronging assemblies that in the Soviet period were at the beck and call of the CPSU apparatus. Yeltsin for his part pledged to cement the new system and contended self-righteously that a victory for Zyuganov would turn back the clock to Stalinist despotism.

The question for us is not whether the prognostications of either principal candidate were factually true, let alone whether they were sincerely motivated, but whether the polemic influenced votes and the electoral outcome. Here the survey data fairly shout confirmation. In the qualifying round of the election in June 1996, the total-effect statistics for attitudes toward the political system outrank all other opinions in impact on votes for Yeltsin and Zyuganov. They are also larger than any opinion-based influence measures for the parliamentary election of December 1995. In the climactic runoff in July 1996, as the electorate regroups—and as first-round supporters of Lebed and Yavlinskii swing to the president—the political-regime opinion dominates the field. Controlling for corollary factors, the change in a voter's mind from a preference for a Western democracy to a wish for reinstatement of the Soviet system would have been associated with a .41 increase in the chances of voting for Zyuganov and a .47 decrease in the chances of voting for Yeltsin.[47]

The multistage analysis in Tables 5.12, 5.13, and 5.14 shows the path-

Table 5.12 Elaboration of the Impact of Opinions about Property on the Presidential Vote, 1996 (Differences in Predicted Probabilities)

Variables progressively incorporated in regression	First round[a]				Runoff[b]	
	Yel.	Zyug.	Leb.	Yav.	Yel.	Zyug.
Opinions about property only	−.50**	.58**	.02	−.09**	−.68**	.69**
Also social characteristics	−.48**	.39**	.08*	−.02	−.59**	56**
Also current conditions	.29**	.34**	.02	−.07	−.49**	.49**
Also partisanship (but not other issue opinions)	−.24**	.20**	.04	−.02	−.39**	.36**
Also other issue opinions (but not partisanship)	−.08	.09*	.04	−.04	−.16*	.17**
Also partisanship and other issue opinions[c]	−.07	.07	.04	−.03	−.12	.12*
Also retrospective evaluations of incumbents	−.03	.05	.02	−.03	−.05	.06
Also leadership qualities	−.02	.02	.03	−.02	−.02[d]	.03[d]
Also prospective evaluations of candidates	−.01	.02	.11	−.01	.02[d]	.03[d]

**p ≤ .01
*p ≤ .05
a. Sample N = 1,990.
b. Sample N = 1,937.
c. Gray-toned row gives the total effect of opinions about property.
d. Two finalists only.

Table 5.13 Elaboration of the Impact of Opinions about Social Order on the Presidential Vote, 1996 (Differences in Predicted Probabilities)

Variables progressively incorporated in regression	First round[a]				Runoff[b]	
	Yel.	Zyug.	Leb.	Yav.	Yel.	Zyug.
Opinions about social order only	−.42**	.42**	.06	−.07*	−.50**	.47**
Also social characteristics	−.41**	.28**	.11**	−.01	−.43**	.38**
Also current conditions	−.27**	.22**	.08	−.04	−.31**	.27**
Also partisanship (but not other issue opinions)	−.24**	.12**	.11*	.01	−.23**	.17**
Also other issue opinions (but not partisanship)	−.15**	.04	.12**	−.02	−.09	.03
Also partisanship and other issue opinions[c]	−.16*	.03	.13*	.01	−.09	.03
Also retrospective evaluations of incumbents	−.17*	.03	.14**	.01	−.05	.01
Also leadership qualities	−.16*	.01	.14*	.00	−.01[d]	−.03[d]
Also prospective evaluations of candidates	−.14	.04	.08	.01	−.03[d]	−.02[d]

**p ≤ .01
*p ≤ .05
a. Sample N = 1,990.
b. Sample N = 1,937.
c. Gray-toned row gives the total effect of opinions about social order.
d. Two finalists only.

ways to the vote leading through and away from three normative opinions in 1996—those concerning property, social order, and the choice of political system. As in the parliamentary election, inserting causally prior and coincident terms into the analysis lessens the magnitude of the estimates of electoral effect from their bivariate levels, sometimes dramatically. For the two center-court candidates, Yeltsin and Zyuganov, other issue opinions generally have the biggest depressing effect, although social traits, perceptions of current conditions, and partisanship also figure prominently. Any failure to analyze the electoral consequences of these and other opinions in tandem with the appropriate control variables would result in wildly inac-

Table 5.14 Elaboration of the Impact of Opinions about the Political System on the Presidential Vote, 1996 (Differences in Predicted Probabilities)

Variables progressively incorporated in regression	First round[a]				Runoff[b]	
	Yel.	Zyug.	Leb.	Yav.	Yel.	Zyug.
Opinions about political system only	−.49**	.64**	−.03	−.12**	−.78**	.76**
Also social characteristics	−.48**	.46**	.04	−.05	−.72**	.67**
Also current conditions	−.35**	.42**	−.01	−.08**	−.67**	.64**
Also partisanship (but not other issue opinions)	−.30**	.27**	.02	−.04	−.57**	.50**
Also other issue opinions (but not partisanship)	−.27**	.35**	−.01	−.07**	−.54**	.49**
Also partisanship and other issue opinions[c]	−.22**	.23**	.00	−.01*	−.47**	.41**
Also retrospective evaluations of incumbents	−.15*	.16**	−.00	−.05	−.29**	.24**
Also leadership qualities	−.11	.10**	−.00	−.02	−.23**[d]	.17**[d]
Also prospective evaluations of candidates	−.08	.07*	.02	−.02*	−.19**[d]	.11**[d]

**p ≤ .01
*p ≤ .05
a. Sample N = 1,990.
b. Sample N = 1,937.
c. Gray-toned row gives the total effect of opinions about the political system.
d. Two finalists only.

curate estimates. For Zyuganov in the first round, as an example, merging of the control indicators into the logit analysis reduces the apparent impact of opinions about privatization from .58 to .07, of opinions about order over liberty from .42 to .03, and of a preference for the Soviet political system from .62 to .23.

The downstream effects of the trio of normative opinions are mediated in 1996 by several intervening clusters of variables. While no one category predominates, Russian voters' evaluations of the performance of incumbents—of their sitting president and the government which serves at his pleasure—appear to be the prime conduit. As differences between the sixth and seventh rows of Table 5.14 show, of the total effect of preference about the political system on the presidential vote, roughly one-third (.07/.22 for

Yeltsin and .07/.23 for Zyuganov) is transmitted through citizen evaluations of incumbents. In the second round, that proportion rises to roughly two-fifths (.18/.47 for Yeltsin and .17/.41 for Zyuganov).

Conclusions

The editors of an anthology on voting in the United States write that there are now no grounds for controversy, if ever there were, about whether issues and issue opinions count in elections in the world's most ancient democracy: "Particular campaigns may be more or less issue-oriented, and some candidates and some voters stress issues more than others. But there is no doubt that issues often play an important part in elections, especially in salient campaigns, such as for the presidency."[48] In one of the world's youngest and most flawed democracies, we can responsibly come to a similar soft conclusion.

Without attributing to them more sagacity and high-mindedness than they have, the data allow us to say that Russia's subjects-turned-citizens nurture a wealth of prescriptive political opinions. They do not have them in equal measure: the politically more attentive have them in greater abundance than the less attentive, and their opinions are better grounded and less likely to alter over time. Nor do most Russians have the benefit of an ideological umbrella to shelter their separate opinions. And they are not terribly good at saying where office seekers stand on the issues, especially in parliamentary campaigns.

Inexperienced, unsystematic, and imperfectly tutored though Russia's transitional voters may be, their didactic opinions are reflected in their voting behavior: so far, they have been most strongly related to the likelihood of casting a vote for socialist parties and candidates and, in 1996, for the incumbent president. The opinion tally can predict far less on the electoral chances of nationalists, as represented by the LDPR and Aleksandr Lebed, and liberals, as exemplified by Yabloko and Grigorii Yavlinskii.

There are probably many reasons why policy opinions have so uneven an impact on the fortunes of different parties and presidential hopefuls. A primary reason, though, is surely the behavior of the politicians themselves. The Communists have waged issue-based campaigns, and Yeltsin in his own fashion aped their strategy in seeking to energize mass support for his re-election. Transitional citizens respond in kind to issue-rich campaigns and give their normative opinions much less play in coming to closure about leaders who wage issue-deprived campaigns. They are also best at sizing up issue platforms that resonate with their upbringing and life experiences. From this perspective, it was easier for a Russian voter in 1996 to relate his ballot options to whether the Soviet dictatorship should be restored or privatization should be continued than to decide who had most to offer on tariffs, welfare payments, or the expansion of NATO.

Although political scientists have rightly been summoned to analyze the electoral ramifications of voters' conceptions of the good society, it is the rare election in a consolidated democratic system that grapples with anything like the rallying themes in post-Soviet Russian campaigns. In the West, politicians traffic in issues of greater or lesser consequence, but elections are hardly ever the court for rendering fateful decisions on the irreducibles of the political, economic, and social setup. Market or plan, government control or freedom, and above all authoritarian or liberalized state institutions—in Russia and countries like it, the stakes are incalculably higher. National elections in a protodemocracy deliberate no less than the question of whether and how the country is to continue reinventing itself.

Performance, Personality, and Promise

The three variables named in the chapter title comprise the last set of generic theories of electoral behavior that we will use to gain comprehension of how Russians vote. Diverse in their particulars, they converge on a preoccupation with citizens' first-hand evaluations of the elite political actors seeking their endorsement in a campaign. The variables stressed—appraisals of governments, of governing and opposition parties, and of would-be presidents—are conceptually and temporally proximate to the voting decision. Electors must make most of the calculations that count, or at a minimum bring them up to date, in the short run.

The first of the three paradigms makes an election, be it in transitional Russia or elsewhere, into a figurative whip for enforcing governmental accountability to the people: citizens vote their assessments of the recent past, spurred by the "performance ratings" they mete out to the present occupants of public office.[1] The next approach locks on the personalities and styles of the leaders who seek electoral mandates, solo or as nominees of political parties. The third explanation is about the future: the voters' expectation of what candidates will do with power when the ballots have been toted.

The second of the three interpretations, geared to individual politicians, their characters, and their mystiques, has prompted the most commentary in the early research on post-Soviet politics. "Personalistic" political parties, Jerry F. Hough writes, abound on the Russian political stage and are "a typical phenomenon in democratization of developing nations."[2] It is standard practice in Russia for the founder who initiated a party on a shoestring to remain years later its leader and incarnation, and the party is then colloquially seen as the fief "of" that leader—as in "the party of

Zhirinovskii" or "the party of Yavlinskii."[3] The LDPR, in thrall to its lifetime leader, Vladimir Zhirinovskii, is a case in point: "it remains unclear whether this organization is a cult movement or a political party, as the organization would collapse almost instantaneously without Zhirinovskii."[4] Party machines with more of a corporate ethos, such as the KPRF, also rely heavily on their principal leaders in campaign season[5] and in their interelection publicity, fund-raising, and rituals. A Russian scholar, Susaina Pshizova, noting that personalism is growing in the mature democracies, puts her country's situation this way: "It is understandable that, given the absence in the post-socialist countries of old parties with firm reputations, the leadership factor is strengthened many times over. In Russia only the KPRF has a more or less firm reputation . . . so that a voter can orient himself mainly to the party and not to the leader. In all other cases the authority, charisma, or reputation of concrete leaders defines not only the success but the very existence of the organization."[6]

Russian presidential elections, where individual politicos rather than party organizations compete, and their faces smile out at voters from countless billboards and television screens, would seem to afford even greater latitude to personalism and charisma. Not all those faces are equal in stature. Of the Russian presidential personalities on our radar screen, Yeltsin is a rare bird, the patriarch whose name—like Charles de Gaulle's in France, Nelson Mandela's in South Africa, or Lech Wałęsa's in Poland—is indelibly linked with epoch-making events and with the laying of the foundations of the political system.

Assertions about charisma's bearing on the vote in Russia are plausible, and could be padded out by invoking the strongmen of the Soviet regime and perhaps the legend of the benevolent tsar, but attempts to authenticate them in painstaking empirical research have been scanty.[7] Equally good arguments could be spun for the primacy of the first and third mechanisms in transitional voting. The inhabitants of a protodemocracy, deprived of the information sources and political cues that imbue a vested democratic system, might be uncommonly reliant on their retrospective appreciations of sitting governments. Or, alternatively, the uncertainty of the transition and the policy failures of post-Communist governments might lead voters to forget charisma and past performance and stake everything on the putative benefits electoral contestants are to dispense to them and to society in future.

Investigation in any one of these veins must grant the possibility that statements about candidates or parties imparted in an opinion survey may be compromised by endogeneity—feedback from the impending or consummated act of voting. As in a mature democracy, the researcher takes the chance that "that which we are attempting to explain, the voter's choice between candidates, becomes the cause" of the interview response, which simultaneously serves as grist for analysis of the vote.[8] The methodological risk is well worth taking. If due caution is exercised, there is much to be gained from combing the Russian data about performance, personality, and promise and much to be accomplished by way of honing questions for further work.

What Have You Done for Me Lately?

The sine qua non of performance-oriented voting is that rank-and-file citizens make judgments about the job incumbents have been doing. While these attitudes may be tinted by their perceptions of current national conditions—as well as by partisanship and normative opinions—they are not synonymous with any of these things. Performance appraisals, unlike current assessments, explicitly allot credit or culpability for the status quo to governmental personnel. Discretion is woven into the attributive process. A worker in Moscow, say, might believe that Russia is in a shambles and hold the prime minister or minister of finance responsible; his brother in Murmansk might paint no rosier a picture but pin the blame on the neo-Communists in parliament who have obstructed economic reform; his cousin in Magnitogorsk might cast aspersions on the International Monetary Fund or on a world Zionist conspiracy.[9]

Post-Soviet Russians fairly burst with summary judgments of rulers and their deeds, beginning with the giant persona of the federal president. When they were asked in the first (preparliamentary) wave of our 1995–96 election surveys to what degree they "approve of [odobryayete] Yeltsin's activity in the post of president," 97 percent of respondents did not flinch at expressing an opinion; the exact same percentage answered in the third wave, following the presidential ballot (see Table 6.1). Evaluations of the president on the five-point scale displayed considerable variation for the two years. Disapproval of Yeltsin's record since 1991 was voiced much more often than approval, though by a thinner margin in 1996 than in 1995; the modal response in each outing was the ambivalent "Approve some, disapprove some."

Table 6.1 Evaluations of Russian Governmental Executives, 1995 and 1996 (Percentages)

Evaluation	1995[a]	1996[b]
Approval of Boris Yeltsin's performance as president		
Completely disapprove	31	12
Disapprove	28	21
Approve some, disapprove some	33	50
Approve	4	11
Completely approve	1	2
Don't know	3	3
Trust in the Russian government		
Completely distrust	9	5
Distrust	42	45
Trust	37	34
Completely trust	2	6
Don't know	9	10

a. N = 2,774 weighted cases for trust in the Russian government (post-election interview) and 2,841 weighted cases for approval of Yeltsin (pre-election interview). Some respondents in the post-election survey were interviewed in January 1996.

b. N = 2,472 weighted cases.

Allocation of policy responsibility in the Russian parliamentary framework is not so cut and dried. The 1993 constitution establishes a dual executive, similar in outline to that of the French Fifth Republic. Besides the elected president, who has his own staff and is authorized under Article 90 of the constitution to issue binding decrees with few limitations, there is a federal "government" *(pravitel'stvo)* headed by a prime minister who is nominated by the president and confirmed by the State Duma. He and the several dozen agency heads from whom the bureaucracy takes routine instructions (they do not need to be approved in their positions by the Duma) comprise a Council of Ministers, which seldom meets as a body and does not answer collectively to the legislature. Deputies pass laws, adopt the annual budget, and ratify treaties, yet exert little oversight over executives; if they turn mutinous, they can usually be quelled or bypassed by presidential or ministerial edict.

In this nebulous configuration, there is no foolproof measure of public approval of the two-legged executive. The representatives voters install on the Duma benches have meager influence over policy and its administration. The insiders' party skippered by Prime Minister Chernomyrdin, Our Home Is Russia, was rejected by nine-tenths of the electorate in 1995, only to have Chernomyrdin linger in office and not be sent packing by Yeltsin until the spring of 1998, more than halfway through the Duma's term; five months later, Yeltsin had an unsuccessful try at reinstating him. The best indicator we have of the grassroots view of Chernomyrdin's cabinet in 1995–96 is the response to a question about trust or confidence in the government of Russia. The distribution of attitudes is tabulated in Table 6.1. Distrust wins out both years, but somewhat less lopsidedly in the 1996 interview.

Government Performance and the Vote

Performance ratings have something to do with how Russians vote, as Figures 6.1 and 6.2 should telegraph to anyone's satisfaction. In the 1995 parliamentary election (see Figure 6.1) high levels of approval of the president's conduct and trust in the central government comport with a preference for Our Home Is Russia, and disapproval accompanies a preference

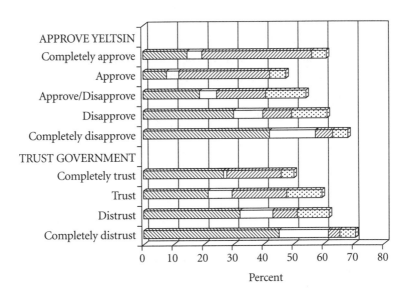

Figure 6.1. Approval of Yeltsin's Record, Trust in the Russian Government, and the Party-List Vote, 1995

for either the socialistic KPRF or the nationalistic LDPR, with Yabloko support going with lukewarm scores. In the 1996 presidential derby (see Figure 6.2), the data speak most eloquently about the main antagonists, Yeltsin and Gennadii Zyuganov. Voters with no confidence at all in the government split for Zyuganov 57 percent to 3 percent in the first round; those who find the government completely trustworthy opt 65 percent for the president and 16 percent for his arch rival. Ninety-five percent of the unvarnished boosters of Yeltsin's actions as president vote for his re-election in June 1996, and a negligible 1 percent of them for Zyuganov; among those most sour on his record, 4 percent support Yeltsin and 66 percent support Zyuganov.[10]

In addition to gross associations in the direction dictated by common sense, the graphs point up several differences:

- Performance grades and electoral choice are more tightly aligned in the presidential than in the parliamentary setting. This is true for evaluations of both the government and the president.

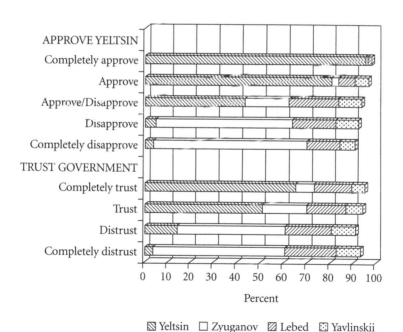

Figure 6.2. Approval of Yeltsin's Record, Trust in the Russian Government, and the First-Round Presidential Vote, 1996

- Of the two kinds of citizen evaluation, those of the president seem on the whole to be more closely fastened to voting outcomes than are appraisals of government activity. Opinions of the Yeltsin record were almost as good predictors of the vote as were appraisals of the government in 1995—when the parliament, not the president, was up for election.[11]

The simulated probabilities in Tables 6.2, 6.3, 6.4, and 6.5 unpack performance-driven voting. Evaluations of incumbents are modeled, as they are consistently in this book, at the fourth stage of the multistage process climaxing in the vote. With all precursor and concurrent variables taken into account, trust in the Russian government has major total effects on the vote for the KPRF in 1995 (−.20, or minus 20 percentage points) and Our Home Is Russia (+.12, or plus 12 percentage points). Approval ratings for President Yeltsin have a slightly smaller effect on support for the KPRF and an insignificant effect on preference for Our Home Is Russia. In the presidential election of 1996, the concordance for key players is similar in thrust but different in some details and more pronounced than in 1995.

Table 6.2 Elaboration of the Impact of Trust in the Russian Government on the Party-List Vote, 1995 (Differences in Predicted Probabilities)[a]

Variables progressively incorporated in regression	KPRF	LDPR	Our Home	Yabloko
Trust in Russian government only	−.30**	−.11**	.24**	.04
Also social characteristics	−.29**	−.09**	.21**	.03
Also current conditions	−.23**	−.07*	.16**	.02
Also partisanship (but not issue opinions)	−.23**	−.03	.12**	.03
Also issue opinions (but not partisanship)	−.19**	−.05*	.17**	.01
Also partisanship and issue opinions	−.22**	−.02	.14**	.02
Also approval of President Yeltsin[b]	−.20**	−.02	.12*	.02
Also party leaders	−.22**	−.00	.10*	.02
Also prospective evaluations of parties	−.18**	−.00	.10	.02

**p ≤ .01

*p ≤ .05

a. Sample N = 2,143.

b. Gray-toned row gives the total effect of trust in the Russian government.

Table 6.3 Elaboration of the Impact of Approval of President Yeltsin on the Party-List Vote, 1995 (Differences in Predicted Probabilities)[a]

Variables progressively incorporated in regression	KPRF	LDPR	Our Home	Yabloko
Approval of President Yeltsin only	−.38**	−.12**	.27**	.08*
Also social characteristics	−.31**	−.11**	.22**	.04
Also current conditions	−.25**	−.10**	.15**	.02
Also partisanship (but not issue opinions)	−.26**	−.03	.10*	.03
Also issue opinions (but not partisanship)	−.17**	−.08**	.13**	.01
Also partisanship and issue opinions	−.19**	−.03	.09	.01
Also trust in Russian government[b]	−.18**	−.03	.07	.01
Also party leaders	−.15*	−.01	−.02	.02
Also prospective evaluations of parties	−.12	−.01	−.04	.02

**p ≤ .01

*p ≤ .05

a. Sample N = 2,143.

b. Gray-toned row gives the total effect of approval of President Yeltsin.

Positive scores on trust in the government in Moscow impact positively on the vote for President Yeltsin (the total-effect parameter in the first round is .37, almost quadruple the measure for impact on the Our Home Is Russia vote in 1995), and negatively on the vote for all three of Yeltsin's main challengers in the first round and for Zyuganov in the second round. Approval of the president's past feats, meantime, has a huge stimulating effect on the vote for Yeltsin (.82, or 82 percentage points, in the first round, and .76 in the runoff, or 76 percentage points) and large dampening effects on the likelihood of voting for his opponents. If the KPRF is the chief beneficiary of anti-government and anti-Yeltsin ire in the Duma election, in the presidential vote it is the KPRF's Zyuganov and the nationalist Aleksandr Lebed who profit equally, once statistical controls for confounding variables have been imposed.

There may be some overestimation of causal effect here, due to subliminal echoes of voting choice. A person who days before had ticked off a ballot slip for Yeltsin in 1996, for instance, might have been leery of criticizing Yeltsin's record in a survey interview; someone fresh from voting for Zyuganov might have had the opposite reaction. But this backwash cannot be all the interview picks up. If it were, the relationships disclosed should

Table 6.4 Elaboration of the Impact of Trust in the Russian Government on the Presidential Vote, 1996 (Differences in Predicted Probabilities)[a]

Variables progressively incorporated in regression	First round[a]				Runoff[b]	
	Yel.	Zyug.	Leb.	Yav.	Yel.	Zyug.
Trust in Russian government only	.76**	−.56**	−.09**	−.07**	.86**	−.74**
Also social characteristics	.78**	−.50**	−.13**	−.08**	.88**	−.74**
Also current conditions	.60**	−.35**	−.10**	−.08**	.75**	−.62**
Also partisanship (but not issue opinions)	.55**	−.21**	−.17**	−.09**	.69**	−.51**
Also issue opinions (but not partisanship)	.61**	−.22**	−.16**	−.13**	.71**	−.51**
Also partisanship and issue opinions	.56**	−.15**	−.20**	−.12**	.64**	−.40**
Also approval of President Yeltsin[c]	.37**	−.07	−.16*	−.11**	.40**	−.23**
Also leadership qualities	.26*	−.04	−.20*	−.04	.30**[d]	−.16**[d]
Also prospective evaluations of candidates	.23*	−.07	−.10	−.05	.34**[d]	−.15**[d]

**p ≤ .01
*p ≤ .05
a. Sample N = 1,990.
b. Sample N = 1,937.
c. Gray-toned row gives the total effect of trust in the Russian government.
d. Two finalists only.

be uniform and uniformly exaggerated—and they are not.[12] Nor should there be interference across institutional borders, as when evaluations of the president shade the parliamentary vote in 1995 and evaluations of the prime minister and government shade the presidential vote in 1996. The statistical compatibilities exposed, in other words, seem to reflect a legitimate relationship in the minds of the Russian electorate.

The bottom three rows of Tables 6.2 through 6.5 let us trace the transmission of the electoral influence of evaluations of the government and president. In both electoral environments, and especially the parliamentary, the statistical measures of total effect are quite robust. Row-by-row changes are rather greater in absolute magnitude in the tables for 1996, but

Table 6.5 Elaboration of the Impact of Approval of President Yeltsin on the Presidential Vote, 1996 (Differences in Predicted Probabilities)

Variables progressively incorporated in regression	First round[a]				Runoff[b]	
	Yel.	Zyug.	Leb.	Yav.	Yel.	Zyug.
Approval of President Yeltsin only	.94**	−.72**	−.10**	−.05**	.97**	−.87**
Also social characteristics	.94**	−.60**	−.15**	−.07**	.97**	−.84**
Also current conditions	.90**	−.53**	−.14**	−.07**	.95**	−.81**
Also partisanship (but not issue opinions)	.87**	−.39**	−.23**	−.08**	.92**	−.74**
Also issue opinions (but not partisanship)	.88**	−.34**	−.22**	−.13**	.88**	−.66**
Also partisanship and issue opinions	.85**	−.27**	−.28**	−.11**	.85**	−.59**
Also trust in Russian government[c]	.82**	−.26**	−.26**	−.08**	.76**	−.55**
Also leadership qualities	.69**	−.17**	−.28**	−.03	.58**[d]	−.34**[d]
Also prospective evaluations of candidates	.64**	−.13**	−.11	−.02	.56**[d]	−.27**[d]

**p ≤ .01
*p ≤ .05
a. Sample N = 1,990.
b. Sample N = 1,937.
c. Gray-toned row gives the total effect of approval of President Yeltsin.
d. Two finalists only.

the residual effects listed in the lowermost rows remain large. For the verdict on Boris Yeltsin's five years in the Kremlin, a minimum-to-maximum change (from complete disapproval to complete approval) would hike the predicted probability of a citizen voting for his re-election in the first round by a staggering 64 percentage points, even when the effects of every other variable in the fully specified model are internalized.

Tables 6.2 through 6.5 divulge as much about influences *on* performance ratings in Russian politics as about the influence *of* popular performance ratings on the vote. Although trust in the government and approval of the president's work have their own authentic content, their impact on voting choice diminishes as other factors return, thus confirming that performance evaluations interpenetrate with and are shaped by these other realities.

True as this is in general, the role of these prior and collateral factors in Russian elections fluctuates from party to party, candidate to candidate, and election to election. Absorption into the statistical model of the variation among voters in their social traits, perceptions of current conditions, partisanship, issue opinions, and other evaluations of incumbents' performance has the effect in most iterations of reducing the apparent effect on the vote of sentiments of trust in the central government and of approval of the president.

There are two interesting deviations from this more or less predictable gestalt. One concerns the most pronounced relationship visible in Tables 6.2 through 6.5: the influence of presidential approval on the vote for Yeltsin's re-election. The riveting thing here (see Table 6.5) is how little difference it makes to the electoral effect to blend all causally antecedent and equivalent variables into the analysis. Net of any and all other influences, Russians' judgments of how good or bad a job the president has been doing have a colossal impact on their use of the democratic franchise. Those judgments cannot be reduced to derivatives of other attitudes.

The second anomaly is the behavior of the parameters estimating the impact on the Lebed vote in 1996. Trust in the government in Moscow and approval of Yeltsin's performance have much larger total effects on support for General Lebed—effects, that is, that hold all causally antecedent and equivalent variables constant—than they have as bivariate effects, or effects of that explanatory variable alone. For the presidential approval measure, for example, the bivariate estimate for Zyuganov, $-.72$, fades to a total effect of $-.26$; for Lebed, a bivariate effect of $-.10$ swells to a total effect of $-.26$, equal to that for the Zyuganov vote. This counterintuitive result has an explanation: the nationalist Lebed wins the hearts of citizens who are disgruntled with governmental performance but would not otherwise (by reason of their social position, view of current economic conditions, and so forth) be inclined to be so malcontent. The neo-Communist Zyuganov appeals much more to citizens whose antipathy to the prime minister and president is grounded in other causes, so that the observed statistical clout of performance evaluations diminishes as those other causes come into the estimation.

Leadership

Analysts of post-Soviet affairs, we have said, have conjectured that, owing to the crudity of party organization and the weakness of other social and institutional supports, electoral politics will be intensely personalized and, by insinuation, trivialized. One need not accept that the formerly Communist countries are congenitally prone to personalization in order to be inquisitive about leadership effects on voting. The theme has, in fact, come into its own in research on mass attitudes and behavior in the older democracies.

It was not always so. Scholars for years were snobs about leaders, consigning them and their electoral influence to the nether realms of journalism. Even in presidential systems where chief executives are popularly elected, and even with larger-than-life characters, the presumption was that little could be generalized about the subject. An early exception to this neglect, an essay by Philip E. Converse and Georges Dupeux on the political careers of the "victorious generals" Charles de Gaulle and Dwight Eisenhower, treated them as one-of-a-kind characters and claimed neither would leave a lasting mark on his country. Political personalities, they said, "like broad historical conditions, impress us with their infinite variety, and the interaction of the commanding personality with his unique times seems thereby to lie at a double remove from orderly analysis."[13]

While political personalities always held the interest of the media, popular commentators, and political consultants who perennially give the topic play,[14] academic interest in the subject caught fire in the 1970s. Many specialists on American politics argue that changes in the political environment—reforms in presidential nominating procedures (replacing conventions with primary elections) and the explosion of political advertising on television—magnify the electoral role of the personality factor. The sample surveys of the U.S. National Election Studies have contained a module of detailed questions about the presidential candidates since 1980. With these and other data in hand, political scientists and psychologists have adumbrated blanket categories for classifying politicians' traits and images, maintaining that "when thinking about political candidates, people tend to rely on the same information processing capabilities that guide their thinking and actions in other, nonpolitical domains."[15] The emphasis has thus shifted from the unique gifts and foibles of the candidate to his or her fit with public expectations of what a good person and leader ought to be like.

Attention to candidate effects has also grown apace in parliamentary systems, where scholars and pundits used to disparage prime ministers and opposition leaders as ciphers for their party organizations and platforms. Not only do many analysts concede that leadership figures have all along been important in rallying support, but they also point to a "presidentialization" of campaign tactics and citizen awareness in country after country.[16] Margaret Thatcher's personal eminence, for example, is said to have augmented the Conservatives' margin of victory in Britain's 1983 general election, shortly after the Falklands war, by 4 to 7 percentage points.[17] Typologies of leadership characteristics in parliamentary democracies differ little from those employed in the analysis of American presidential politics.

Leadership Images

What of the post-Soviet scene? One thing we know for sure is that Russians have a better sense of their politicians than they do of political parties. Whereas the average number of parties citizens recognized and were able to rate on a feeling thermometer at the time of the 1995 Duma campaign was 5.8 out of 10, the typical respondent did the same for 7.0 of the 10 leaders of those parties.[18] In 1996 the mean tally of presidential hopefuls descried was 7.6 out of 10, or approximately 2 more than the parties sized up in 1995.[19]

For Russians, cognizance of parties, party leaders, and presidential candidates runs in tandem with political awareness. But the sophistication gap between the least and the most knowledgeable voters is less on the subject of party leaders than on the parties they captain, and less still when it comes to presidential candidates. The average citizen in the worst-informed quintile of the electorate could evaluate 4.7 fewer party leaders than someone in the most aware quintile in 1995, while rating 5.4 fewer out of the 10 parties (see Figure 6.3).[20] In 1996 people in the politically least aware stratum could evaluate only 3.1 presidential nominees fewer than the most proficient citizens were able to rate.

Tables 6.6 and 6.7 lay out recognition-and-evaluation levels and mean thermometer scores for the ten party heads in 1995 and the ten presidential candidates in 1996. The thermometer scores in 1995 fluctuate from a

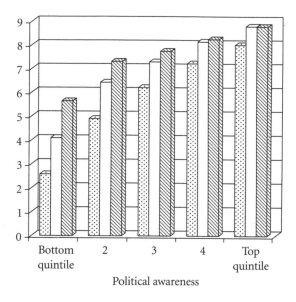

Legend: ⊡ Parties 1995   ☐ Party leaders 1995   ◫ Presidential candidates 1996

Figure 6.3. Parties, Party Leaders, and Presidential Candidates Recognized and Evaluated: Numbers by Level of Political Awareness, 1995 and 1996 (Maximum = 10)

low of 20 points out of 100 (the average for Vladimir Zhirinovskii) to a high of 44 points (for Aleksandr Lebed), and in 1996 from 7 points (for the pharmaceuticals mogul Vladimir Bryntsalov) to 56 (for Lebed). The dispersion of these scores tells us that leaders incite as much disagreement within the Russian body politic as parties do. Mean ratings in the thirties and the inability of all but one statesman—the telegenic Lebed in 1996— to rise above the 50-point benchmark of indifference are unsubtle hints that politicians as a group are not held in any great reverence.

The other message of Tables 6.6 and 6.7 is how interlaced the personal standing of most Russian elective politicians is with the party they lead or have struck an alliance with.[21] Declared partisans of the ten parties on which we have ratings in 1995 awarded the leaders of their chosen party an average of forty-five thermometer points more than other respondents did.[22] For presidential candidates in 1996 the premium was forty-four points, despite the fact that two of the six candidates at issue—Yeltsin and Lebed—were unofficial champions of their parties and not legally their

Table 6.6 Recognition and Evaluation of Leaders of Ten Main Parties, 1995[a]

Leader	Party	Recognize and evaluate leader (percentage)	Feeling-thermometer rating (0 to 100)		
			Mean	Mean among partisans of party	Correlation (r) with party rating
Gennadii Zyuganov	KPRF	76	41	82	.78**
Vladimir Zhirinovskii	LDPR	88	20	80	.84**
Viktor Chernomyrdin	Our Home Is Russia	88	35	72	.66**
Grigorii Yavlinskii	Yabloko	79	38	81	.75**
Mikhail Lapshin	Agrarian	40	33	80	.69**
Yegor Gaidar	Russia's Democratic Choice	83	25	82	.73**
Aleksandr Lebed	KRO	66	44	78	.64**
Yekaterina Lakhova	Women of Russia	54	42	73	.70**
Boris Fedorov	Forward Russia	59	37	84	.68**
Aleksandr Rutskoi	Derzhava	76	30	89	.67**
Average		71	35	80	.71

**$p \leq .01$ (two-tailed test). Missing values deleted pairwise.

a. Total N = 2,841 weighted cases.

nominees. Correlation coefficients between the temperatures for the parties and for their flag bearers averaged .71 in 1995 and .64 in 1996.

Contrived though it is to relegate Russian leaders and their organizations to watertight compartments, it would be a mistake to misread one for the other. Careful survey questions allow separation of personal qualities from the properties of political entities, leaving it to subsequent statistical analysis to pick apart their electoral effects. In the 1995 parliamentary election, our project mounted only the all-purpose feeling-thermometer question. In 1996, however, we supplemented the thermometer with a battery of items about the top five candidates for president. Interviewers enumerated five desirable personal attributes, all of them prominent in the literature, and asked how Yeltsin, Zyuganov, Lebed, Yavlinskii, and Zhirinovskii shaped up in terms of them:

- Intelligence—can the candidate be said to be "an intelligent and knowledgeable person"?
- Strength—is he "a strong leader"?
- Integrity—would you call the candidate "a decent and trustworthy person"?
- Vision—does he have "his own vision of the country's future"?
- Empathy—does he "really care about people like you"?

Table 6.7 Recognition and Evaluation of Ten Presidential Candidates, 1996[a]

Candidate	Party with which affiliated	Recognize and evaluate candidate (percentage)	Feeling-thermometer rating (0 to 100)		
			Mean	Mean among partisans of the party	Correlation (r) with party rating
Boris Yeltsin	Our Home Is Russia	95	47	79	.55**
Gennadii Zyuganov	KPRF	93	44	84	.86**
Aleksandr Lebed	KRO	91	56	88	.39**
Grigorii Yavlinskii	Yabloko	79	41	69	.70**
Vladimir Zhirinovskii	LDPR	90	21	74	.68**
Svyatoslav Fedorov	Employees' Self-Management Party	71	37	51	ND[b]
Mikhail Gorbachev	None	90	13	NA[c]	NA[c]
Martin Shakkum	Party of Socio-economic Reform	41	14	NP[d]	ND[b]
Yurii Vlasov	National Patriotic Party	43	17	NP[d]	ND[b]
Vladimir Bryntsalov	Russian Socialist Party	64	7	NP[d]	ND[b]
Average		76	30	74	.64

**p ≤ .01 (two-tailed test). Missing values deleted pairwise.

a. Total N = 2,472 weighted cases.

b. ND = No data (thermometer rating for party not asked in the interview).

c. NA = Not applicable.

d. NP = No partisans (no partisans of that party in the survey sample).

The allowable responses were "Yes," "Probably yes," "Probably no," and "No."[23]

American national politicians, as a cutting-edge researcher put it some while ago, "elicit distinctive and intelligible profiles" among voters.[24] So we discover it to be in democratizing Russia, with the cavil that a sizable number of electors have no opinion on some of the leaders.

What Russians saw in the five presidential candidates in 1996, trait by trait, is docketed in Table D.5 in Appendix D. Nonresponses to the character questions run from an average of 13 percent for the veteran Yeltsin to 34 percent for Grigorii Yavlinskii. The palette of characteristics ascribed has a friendly coloration, with affirmative signals topping pejorative ones in eighteen of the twenty-five candidate/trait dyads. Most laudatory are the assessments of the leaders' intelligence, with a large surplus of positive over negative answers for all five men. On but one of the attributes—empathy, caring for ordinary people—do negatives eclipse positives for every nominee.

Candidate by candidate, there is a kernel of discerning realism to these street-level representations. Receiving the most kudos on every character trait is Lebed—the stiff-necked, avowedly incorruptible professional soldier, who as the commanding officer in one of the army's infrequent battle successes in recent times is the closest thing Russia has to a contemporary military hero.[25] Lebed is graded much less charitably on empathy than elsewhere, though even here he bests his rivals. The rambunctious and at times clownish Zhirinovskii has the most dismal ratio of positive to negative responses four times out of five (for intelligence, integrity, vision, and empathy). The Moscow intellectual Yavlinskii, trailing only Lebed in the sphere where his career path gives him the edge (intelligence), fares dead last on the yardstick where his egghead style does him the most damage (strength). Zyuganov, the earnest if drab secretary-general of the KPRF, finishes second on strength, vision of the future, and empathy, and third by the remaining two standards. And President Yeltsin, physically infirm and scarred politically by a half-decade as maestro of stop-and-go economic reforms, rates third on strength of leadership and a desultory fourth on intelligence, integrity, vision, and empathy—by which last measuring rod his defenders outnumber detractors two to one.

Evaluations of the particular traits of Russian leaders plug convincingly into their holistic thermometer ratings (see the regression coefficients in Table 6.8). Only two of twenty-five pairings in 1996 (vision for

Table 6.8 Influence of Evaluations of Presidential Candidates' Character Traits on 101-Point Feeling-Thermometer Scores, 1996 (Unstandardized Regression Coefficients)

Trait[a]	Yeltsin[b]	Zyuganov[c]	Lebed[d]	Yavlinskii[e]	Zhirinovskii[f]
Intelligence	5.08**	2.48**	5.67**	3.98**	3.59**
Strength	2.58**	2.50**	.50	4.49**	1.79**
Integrity	9.30**	7.96**	7.38**	6.88**	7.22**
Vision	4.40**	.80	3.05**	2.21**	1.71**
Empathy	5.37**	14.96**	5.59**	5.34**	5.55**
Adjusted R²	.490	.504	.234	.259	.288

**$p \le .01$

a. All evaluations of character traits are four-point indices, with missing values coded at the sample mean.

b. Sample N = 2,336.

c. Sample N = 2,273.

d. Sample N = 2,207.

e. Sample N = 1,910.

f. Sample N = 2,188.

Zyuganov and strength for Lebed) lack a significant statistical relationship between assessments of the characteristic and the leader's thermometer score. Of the qualities calibrated, it is perceived integrity that (for four of the five men) has the strongest impact on synoptic judgments. The outlier is Zyuganov, for whom empathy is the main drawing card—consonant, maybe, with his and his party's socialistic philosophy.

Global assessments of leaders, I said earlier in the chapter, are correlated with partisanship. When we scrutinize the ingredients of politicians' reputations, we also find correlations with a host of other variables. As an illustration, let us relate the aspect of character of priority to most voters—integrity—to three factors we know are tied up with the ultimate voting decision. Figure 6.4 plots the integrity scores for the four poll-leading candidates in 1996 against polar values of citizen attitudes toward the trend in the national economy, private versus state property, and Yeltsin's record as president.

Russians who feel their economy is on the mend, unreservedly prefer private to state enterprise, and admire Boris Yeltsin's first term in the Kremlin are much more amenable than others to saying he is a man of honor. For Gennadii Zyuganov, the main pretender to the throne, it is the reverse: the less favorable the appraisal of the economy, the more dis-

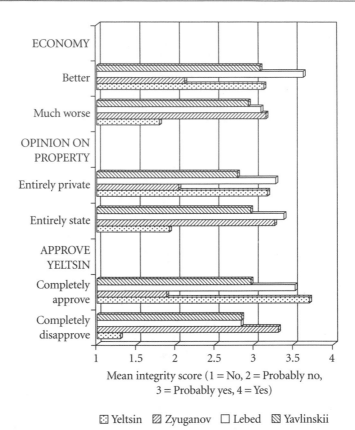

Figure 6.4. Some Influences on Assessments of Integrity of Four Presidential Candidates, 1996

paraging the view of private property, and the more scathing the take on the incumbent's record, the better the odds that the citizen's opinion of Zyuganov's integrity will be high. Although the criss-crossing assessments of the two finalists' personal decency must have some intrinsic value, and are affected by the barrage of daily television news and political conversation, they also carry strong connotations of other opinions and values. Assuming that connections with economic perceptions, issue opinions, and retrospective grade sheets reflect a causal relationship of some sort,[26] the arrows of causality surely fly at character assessments from the other variables. It strains credulity to imagine Russians first arriving at a valuation of Yeltsin's or Zyuganov's personality and then deriving *from* it inferences about the economic crisis, economic and social reform, and presidential performance.[27]

Consider now Lebed and Yavlinskii, the politicians who crossed the finishing line third and fourth in 1996. Character assessments of them are not affected as powerfully as Yeltsin's and Zyuganov's by the antecedent variables. One searches in vain for any clear relationships for Grigorii Yavlinskii in the grouped data in Figure 6.4. His integrity score is but faintly influenced by citizen attitudes toward the state of the economy, paths to reform, and Yeltsin's record. For Lebed, there are tepid relationships with economic optimism and approbation of the Yeltsin presidency and a barely detectable loop to opinions on privatization.[28] The moral is that other political attitudes bias the transitional electorate's assessments of politicians some and even much of the time but not all the time. One size does not fit all.

The Party-List Vote

As mentioned, the data about Russian party leaders do not go beyond the generalized affect (feeling-thermometer) scores in 1995. Their shortcomings conceded, these indicators give us some basis for mating leadership with voting behavior in a party-list election.[29]

Figure 6.5 arrays the vote for the four largest parties in the State Duma election against the mean thermometer scores for their leaders, partitioned into twenty-point segments. Banking upward to the right, the plot lines demonstrate an egregiously positive association between rating of the leader and the likelihood of casting a vote for the party. Even if we knew nothing else about their thinking, we would have a good chance of auguring how Russians will vote in a parliamentary election from their opinions of particular party leaders.

Again, the juxtaposition of a single explanatory variable with electoral choice raises as many questions as it answers. While the lines in Figure 6.5 all slope up to the right, they do so at visibly different pitches. Support for the KPRF is 66 percentage points more among persons who give Zyuganov a thermometer score of 80 or higher than for voters who put him below 20 on the scale. For assessment of Zhirinovskii and vote for the LDPR, the gap is 58 percentage points. For the third- and fourth-finishing parties, the difference is quite a bit less—44 points for Chernomyrdin and Our Home Is Russia and 37 points for Yavlinskii and his Yabloko party. Why the asym-

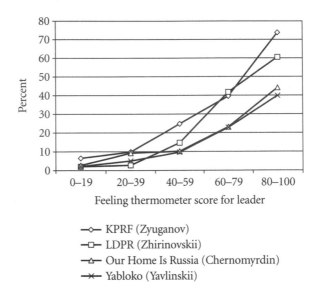

Figure 6.5. Evaluations of Party Leaders and the Party-List Vote, 1995

metry? And how much of the bilateral relationship portrayed in the figure describes the workings of leadership variables in their own right and how much the relaying of other, more deep-seated influences on the vote?

The multivariate analysis reported in Table 6.9 confirms that leadership assessments do have an important independent influence on how Russia's transitional electorate behaves in the parliamentary voting environment. The total effects are all major and range from .30 (for Zhirinovskii and the LDPR, Chernomyrdin and Our Home Is Russia, and Yavlinskii and Yabloko) to almost .50 (for Zyuganov and the KPRF).[30]

Two points need explaining. One is that, contrary to all predictions, the Communist party leader's personality rating is most formative of the vote for his party. The other is that the influence of the leadership factor is by no means off the charts when compared to some of the other explanatory variables examined in this book. The assertion that in the post-Communist systems the role of the individual leader "is strengthened many times over" its base-line level in an established democracy would seem to be mistaken, or at least unproven. Of most interest to us is the comparison between leadership effects and partisanship effects. For the KPRF, the LDPR, Our Home Is Russia, and Yabloko, the total-effect parameters for evaluations of leaders are smaller than those for attachments to the parties they head (cf. Table 4.6 in Chapter 4).[31]

Table 6.9 Elaboration of the Impact of Evaluations of Party Leaders on the Party-List Vote, 1995 (Differences in Predicted Probabilities)[a]

Variables progressively incorporated in regression	KPRF	LDPR	Our Home	Yabloko
Evaluation of given party's leader only	.66**	.60**	.38**	.40**
Also social characteristics	.61**	.59**	.33**	.31**
Also current conditions	.59**	.59**	.32**	.31**
Also partisanship (but not issue opinions)	.48**	.27**	.25**	.25**
Also issue opinions (but not partisanship)	.54**	.60**	.36**	.31**
Also partisanship and issue opinions	.42**	.26**	.29**	.24**
Also retrospective evaluations of incumbents	.44**	.28**	.26**	.23**
Also other party leaders[b]	.47**	.30**	.30**	.30**
Also prospective evaluations of parties	.36**	.16**	.24**	.19**

**p ≤ .01
a. Sample N = 2,143.
b. Gray-toned row gives the total effect of evaluations of party leaders.

Row-wise comparisons within Table 6.9 are informative about where citizen appreciations of party leaders fit into the causal stream leading to the party-list vote. Disparities between the estimates of bivariate and total effect—from a difference of .30 out of .66 for Zyuganov and the KPRF to .08 out of .38 for Chernomyrdin and Our Home Is Russia—give us a sense of how assessments of the leaders mediate between other variables and Russians' voting decisions. Regardless of party, the drop in the estimated effect of leadership appraisals is most precipitous when partisanship enters into the equation. By implication, leadership evaluations mediate more on behalf of partisanship than of any other bundle of antecedent variables. A goodly portion of the observed correlation between attitude toward Zyuganov and a vote for his KPRF, for example, seems to be the result of displacement onto the leader's personality of popular sentiments toward the party and other players in Russia's political system. At the final causal stage, leadership assessments are partially funneled into voting choice via prospective evaluations of the parties.

The Presidential Vote

There is a richer seam of information about leadership for presidential than for parliamentary voting. We can be grateful for that, for Russia's first post-Soviet presidential ballot accosts us with a paradox: the most revered candidate did *not* walk away with the election of 1996. Aleksandr Lebed, already the best liked party leader in 1995, burnished his image in the intervening half-year as the brainiest, toughest, most trustworthy, most visionary, and most compassionate of the aspirants to the presidency. But that enviable personal aura did not deter Russians from voting en masse for a raft of other candidates. Lebed finished in third place in votes received, behind an incumbent who was inferior to him in thumbnail character assessments and ranked a dreary third or fourth on the components of leadership.

Figures 6.6 and 6.7 relate leadership assessments to voting choice in the opening round of the 1996 election.[32] That those assessments are linked to the vote at some level of abstraction is incontestable. Scanning the five leadership traits one by one (Figure 6.6), we see between 55 percent and 70 percent of the voters who situate any one candidate cleanly ahead of all the others casting a ballot for that favorite candidate; of voters who rank a candidate below a rival, the proportion who vote for the candidate never exceeds 10 percent. When we break down the data by candidate, though (Figure 6.7), the waters muddy. Summing across character traits, 90 percent of citizens who place Zyuganov first for a particular trait vote for him; for

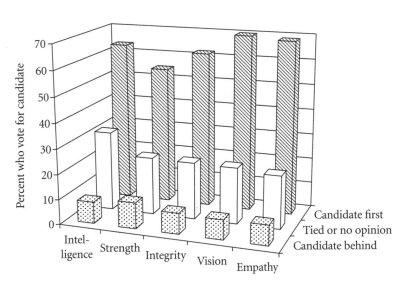

Figure 6.6. Assessments of Candidate Traits and the First-Round Presidential Vote by Trait, 1996

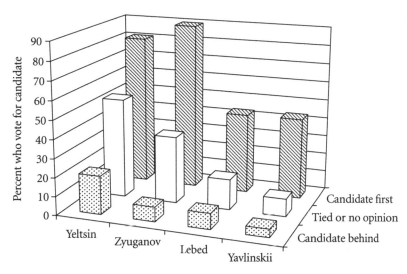

Figure 6.7. Assessments of Candidate Traits and the First-Round Presidential Vote by Candidate, 1996

Yeltsin the ratio is 81 percent. For Lebed and Yavlinskii, the proportion of voters ranking them first on any given attribute and going on to vote for them—43 percent for both—is about half what it is for the two titans. Indeed, among persons who rank either Lebed or Yavlinskii first for a leadership trait, the percentage who vote for them is 10 points less than the proportion of citizens who merely *tie* Boris Yeltsin for the lead with some other nominee or nominees and still support the incumbent.

The statistics in Table 6.10 verify the relevance of leadership evaluations to presidential voting. The candidates' personal qualities are coded as the mean of the grades assigned for intelligence, strength, integrity, vision, and empathy, rounded off to the nearest integer. They enter the estimation at the second-to-last stage of the statistical model, the fifth. The influence on voting choice is there to behold for all four of the principal candidates, as it was for the leaders of all the principal parties in 1995. Its magnitude, as approximated in the total-effect statistics, is comparable to that observed in parliamentary voting.

Notice that evaluations of the leadership qualities of the golden boy, Aleksandr Lebed, do work in favor of his candidacy, but that the total effect on voting choice, assimilating the electoral consequences of other causal variables up to and including evaluations of rival candidates, is largest for

Table 6.10 Elaboration of the Impact of Evaluations of the Leadership Qualities of the Candidates on the Presidential Vote, 1996 (Differences in Predicted Probabilities)

Variables progressively incorporated in regression	First round[a]				Runoff[b]	
	Yel.	Zyug.	Leb.	Yav.	Yel.	Zyug.
Qualities of the candidate only	.69**	.69**	.20**	.26**	.82**	.78**
Also social characteristics	.73**	.58**	.21**	.23**	.83**	.74**
Also current conditions	.62**	.61**	.25**	.26**	.76**	.78**
Also partisanship (but not issue opinions)	.60**	.45**	.28**	.23**	.71**	.68**
Also issue opinions (but not partisanship)	.60**	.46**	.26**	.28**	.66**	.58**
Also partisanship and issue opinions	.58**	.35**	.28**	.24**	.62**	.50**
Also retrospective evaluations of incumbents	.43**	.27**	.25**	.20**	.30**	.33**
Also qualities of other candidates[c]	.49**	.28**	.28**	.19**	.36**[d]	.32**[d]
Also prospective evaluations of candidates	.38**	.21**	.16**	.10*	.22**[d]	.24**[d]

**p ≤ .01
*p ≤ .05
a. Sample N = 1,990.
b. Sample N = 1,937.
c. Gray-toned row gives the total effect of leadership qualities.
d. Two finalists only.

the decidedly *un*charismatic Yeltsin. Of the four top-tier candidates, personal traits wield the least influence for Yavlinskii; Zyuganov and Lebed occupy the middle ground. Evaluations of Yeltsin's character have less effect on the outcome in the winner-take-all election runoff than in the first round. Cognate factors all held constant, citizens with the most favorable construction of Boris Yeltsin personally were 36 percentage points more likely to vote for his re-election in the second round than citizens with the most unfavorable image of him; the advantage was 49 percentage points in the first round. The influence on the Zyuganov vote of evaluations of Gennadii Zyuganov's personality goes up slightly between rounds.

As the bottom two rows of Table 6.10 show, personality considerations affect the presidential vote directly and indirectly through forward-looking evaluations of the candidates' likely performance in office. More important is what higher rows in the table say about the transmission of the effects of other, causally antecedent variables through evaluations of leadership qualities. For Yavlinskii and Zyuganov, a bevy of prior variables are potent in this regard. For Yeltsin in both rounds of the election, though, assessments of current conditions in Russia and, above all, citizen evaluations of the government and of Yeltsin's presidential record predominate. For the Yeltsin vote in the qualifying round, the apparent impact of evaluations of his character dwindles from .69 in the bivariate estimation to .49 in the total-effect estimation; almost all of this decline is associated with factoring into the analysis current conditions and evaluations of incumbents. The proportionate reduction for incorporation of these same factors is comparably large for the Yeltsin vote in the runoff.

Lebed is the odd-man-out in the charisma race in 1996, in that the estimated effect of evaluations of his leadership qualities actually rises as additional variables are taken into account. Lebed's character generates the lowest bivariate effect on the vote (.20) but an average total effect (.28). His personality ratings are not mediators between other causes and the vote but gain in influence as other factors are incorporated into the analysis.

The Politics of Anticipation

We take aim now at transitional citizens' pictures of the future. Aside from what they make of the past performance of incumbent governments and of the personal qualities of candidates and leaders, Russian voters are as free as American or French voters to rack their brains over how the contestants in an election campaign will govern after the campaign is over. Consciously or unconsciously, they may base their electoral decisions on such expectations. It is human nature for people to anticipate the consequences tomorrow of their actions today. Forward-looking speculation seems apropos in electoral politics, since parties and candidates must trade to some extent in promises and proffered cures for society's ills. Anticipations of ensuing events may be extensions of other political attitudes—of assessments of current national conditions, for example, or of partisanship, views of the past performance of incumbents, or normative opinions. But they are not coterminous with any of these factors. It is appropriate, therefore, that in the analysis of voting in any country, providing that campaigning has an effect, "prospective evaluations may . . . add a consideration that is missing from all of the other queries on which we [can] base our reconstruction of the voting decision."[33]

Prepared to Govern

Prospective evaluations can electrify voters only if they have information with which they can envisage future performance. The high uncertainty of the transition makes this information harder to come by in Russia than in established democracies. We might further predict that the store of pertinent information will be scarcer about political parties than about presidential candidates, since we have seen that Russians know less overall about the parties and have formed assessments of fewer of them than of presidential nominees. In a Russian parliamentary election, another impediment to prospective voting is that, as we have observed with relation to other explanatory factors, the national legislature since 1993 has had far less leverage over public policy than do the president and the executive branch. Even citizens who know much about the parties may therefore feel less incentive to link their voting choices to their opinions of the parties' governing capacity than they would for the candidates for president.

Our evidence about the Russian electorate's prospective evaluations of political parties is limited. In interviews before and after the 1995 election to the State Duma, we did not solicit assessments of how the parties might perform in distinct policy domains. We eschewed them because questionnaire piloting suggested that policy-specific questions about so crowded a field of parties would draw a blank with many respondents. As a substitute, we asked in the pre-election interview for comments on "positive and negative characteristics" of the ten main parties, which we hoped would flush out perceptions of their capacity to make good policy choices. The question items were broached only for those parties the respondent had been able, in the preceding question, to evaluate on a feeling thermometer.[34] Four criteria were used:

- Preparation: were the party and its leadership "well prepared for governing the country and capable of taking correct political decisions"?
- Trustworthiness: could the party be trusted?
- Responsiveness: "the degree to which [the] party reflects the interests of the people, its needs and hopes, that is . . . how close it is to the people."

• Conflict resolution: "whether [the] party is capable of bringing about accord and civil peace in society."

Each time the respondent gauged the party on a five-point scale. The scale's top and bottom values, along with tick marks for intermediate values, were printed on a card handed out by the interviewer.

Table 6.11 provides a summary of attitudes about the capabilities of the KPRF, LDPR, Our Home Is Russia, and Yabloko. Popular ignorance and disinterest are in bountiful evidence. From 32 to 49 percent of the sample, depending on the question item and the party, were unable to give an evaluation of the party or say whether it was well-prepared, trustworthy, responsive to the population, or good at conflict resolution. Russians conferred the most positive ratings in all four categories on the KPRF, which was to lead at the polls in December 1995, with Our Home Is Russia and Yabloko neck and neck in second place and the LDPR a remote fourth. As the correlation coefficients in the last row of Table 6.11 convey, appraisals of the parties' qualifications for governing were closely interconnected. So high was the correlation between the scores assigned on the four scales—.80, on average, party by party—that there was little texture to mass perceptions. A citizen who thought well of a party on one dimension would in all probability have a favorable opinion about it on the next.

To explain electoral choice among presidential candidates in Russia, we have better data about envisaged performance. Just after grilling respondents in the 1996 post-election survey about the personal characteristics of the candidates, interviewers asked them to volunteer which presidential nominee "could handle better than the others" (*smog by luchshe drugikh spravit'syas*) an assortment of six policy problems:

• Economic recovery;
• Unemployment;
• Crime and corruption;
• Foreign policy;
• Developing democracy in Russia;
• Guaranteeing Russia's "stability and social tranquility."[35]

Respondents were explicitly given the option of indicating "no particular difference between the candidates" on each issue.

The results of these questions are reported in Table 6.12. As they did when evaluating the competence of the political parties in 1995, significant

Table 6.11 Expectations of Four Parties in Government, 1995 Pre-Election Interview (Percentages)[a]

Criterion	KPRF	LDPR	Our Home Is Russia	Yabloko
Competence				
Positive	29	11	22	21
Neutral	13	10	15	13
Negative	23	44	21	19
Don't know[b]	35	36	42	47
Trustworthiness				
Positive	28	10	20	21
Neutral	14	9	17	14
Negative	26	48	24	20
Don't know[b]	32	32	39	45
Responsiveness				
Positive	31	12	19	18
Neutral	14	10	17	16
Negative	22	43	23	19
Don't know[b]	33	35	41	46
Conflict resolution				
Positive	27	10	19	19
Neutral	13	9	17	14
Negative	23	43	20	18
Don't know[b]	37	38	44	49
Average correlation (r) among 5-point scales for all 4 items[c]	.82	.81	.77	.80

a. N = 2,841 weighted cases.

b. Includes respondents to whom the question was not given because they were not able to evaluate the party on a feeling thermometer.

c. Missing values deleted pairwise.

numbers of Russians—from 19 percent (for crime and corruption) to 49 percent (for democratic development)—articulated no opinion. But the opinions they did vent in 1996 were highly variegated, differentiating among the candidates for president in ways that a detached observer of the campaign will find shrewd.[36] A plurality of respondents thought Yeltsin would do the best job of sustaining democracy (for better or for worse, the

Table 6.12 Assessments of Presidential Candidates Who Would Best Handle Specific Problems, 1996 Post-Election Interview (Percentages)[a]

Candidate	Economic recovery	Unemployment	Crime and corruption	Foreign policy	Developing democracy	Social stability
Yeltsin	16	10	3	21	25	12
Zyuganov	20	27	8	12	8	18
Lebed	6	7	59	6	3	23
Yavlinskii	17	6	0.4	5	8	3
Another candidate	11	11	11	10	7	7
Makes no difference or Don't know	30	37	19	47	49	37

a. N = 2,472 weighted cases.

Russian public associates him with its advent) and of managing foreign policy (over which he had presided since 1991); a mere 3 percent felt him to be the best bet for taming crime and corruption, which, as every school-child knows, mushroomed during his first term in office. Zyuganov, the Communist and proponent of a strong state hand in the economy, got top grades for ability to foster economic recovery and curb unemployment. The stern army general, Lebed, was by an overwhelming margin vouched most likely to rein in crime and corruption and also came out ahead on buttressing social stability. And Yavlinskii, the professional economist who had figured in the national debate over economic reform since Gorbachev's reign, was barely nosed out by Zyuganov on the economy but won few points in any other domain—on the crime-and-corruption issue he was vanquished by Lebed by a ratio of 132 to 1!

Like the retrospective evaluations of incumbents and character measures analyzed in the first two sections of Chapter 6, forecasts of how a Russian political party or presidential candidate will do after election day are apt to be affected by other variables in the causal flow. So too will estimates of the electoral impact of prospective performance be affected.

The Party-List Vote

Do Russians' prospective evaluations of political parties affect their electoral behavior? Figure 6.8 steers us toward some kind of correspondence in the 1995 proportional-representation voting. The average expectations graphed for the KPRF, LDPR, Our Home Is Russia, and Yabloko are means derived from the responses to the four items about party capacity (preparedness, trustworthiness, responsiveness, and conflict resolution). Respondents are classified as rating the party the best of all ten parties asked about in the survey item, tied in merit with another party or parties, or inferior to one or more parties; persons with no opinion are coded in the middle category. The tall columns in the background show relatively high proportions of citizens voting for any party they score ahead of all the others on a particular scale (the gamut is from 56 percent for Our Home Is Russia to 82 percent for the KPRF); the stubs in the foreground show tiny numbers (from 3 percent for the LDPR to 9 percent for the KPRF) voting for parties they rate below others in governing capacity; and the columns in the center band show outcomes in between.

As always, enticing evidence of one-to-one correspondence between a

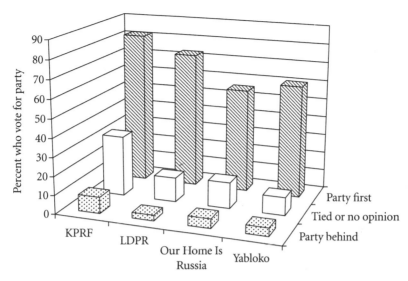

Figure 6.8. Summary Expectations of the Parties in Government and the Party-List Vote, 1995

causative factor and voting choice must be thrown into perspective through multivariate testing. Table 6.13 presents such an analysis, adhering to the hierarchical logic we have pursued for all explanatory variables and placing prospective evaluations at the sixth and last stage of the model. The evaluations of the Russian parties are measured for purpose of the logit regression as averages of the five-point scores for the four dimensions of capacity, rounded off to integers; missing values are coded in the middle, third category. As we have found repeatedly, the apparent impact of the explanatory variable at hand is much smaller in the total-effect estimation, where causally precedent and concurrent variables are absorbed, than in the bivariate estimation, which excludes all other indicators.[37]

The range of the quantitative estimates of effect is very wide—from a low of .06 for the LDPR to a high of .42 for the KPRF—and is congruous with the qualitative evidence. It is no accident that the large Russian party for which prospective evaluations have the least total effect on the vote, the LDPR, is the most disorganized and has the most erratic policies. Nor is it likely to be idle chance that future-regarding evaluations have the largest net effect on the vote for the relatively coherent and goal-directed KPRF, followed by Our Home Is Russia, the advocate of the government. It is con-

Table 6.13 Elaboration of the Impact of Prospective Evaluations of the Parties on the Party-List Vote, 1995 (Differences in Predicted Probabilities)[a]

Variables progressively incorporated in regression	KPRF	LDPR	Our Home	Yabloko
Prospective evaluation of the party only	.67**	.66**	.36**	.38**
Also social characteristics	.61**	.62**	.30**	.26**
Also current conditions	.59**	.63**	.29**	.25**
Also partisanship (but not issue opinions)	.46**	.27**	.22**	.18**
Also issue opinions (but not partisanship)	.55**	.59**	.33**	.25**
Also partisanship and issue opinions	.42**	.23**	.27**	.17**
Also retrospective evaluations of incumbents	.43**	.25**	.23**	.17**
Also party leaders	.32**	.05**	.16**	.07**
Also prospective evaluations of other parties[b]	.33**	.06**	.24**	.12**

**p ≤ .01

a. Sample N = 2,143.

b. Gray-toned row gives the total effect of prospective evaluations of parties.

sistently the case that the apparent effects of future-oriented evaluations of the parties slump the most when the two antecedent variables most connected to the parties as organizations—partisanship and evaluations of the party leaders—are brought into the equation.

The Presidential Vote

As for presidential voting, the data tell us without doubt that Russians prefer the candidates whom they reckon to be the most dexterous at handling the country's problems after the election. In 1996 more than 60 percent of voters who considered a nominee the best suited to deal with the economy, unemployment, foreign policy, democratic development, and social tranquility cast a vote for that person in the first round of the election (see Figure 6.9). Only for crime and corruption, where 38 percent voted for the most capable candidate but 62 percent supported someone else, did less than a majority side with the best problem-solver.

Figure 6.10 parades the cumulative effect of prospective evaluations of presidential candidates in 1996. The more policy domains in which any of our four spotlighted candidates was held to be superior, the more likely the voter was to prefer him as president. A Russian who expected a politician

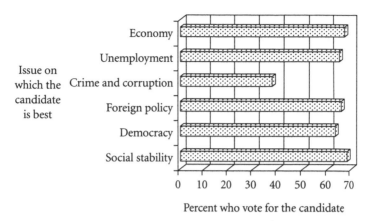

Figure 6.9. Prospective Job Performance and the First-Round Presidential Vote by Policy Domain, 1996

to be the most skillful manager of more than three national issues was virtually certain to vote for him in the first round of the election if that candidate were Yeltsin (96 percent) or Zyuganov (97 percent), and very likely to do so if it were Lebed (70 percent) or Yavlinskii (77 percent). The discordance between the two finalists and the two also-rans, which was also plain in the matter of personal qualities, continues to puzzle. A citizen who believed Zyuganov or Yeltsin to be the most capable on two or three issues had a greater chance in 1996 of voting for that contestant than someone who put Lebed ahead on more than three issues did of voting for Lebed, while someone who gave Yeltsin the nod on a single issue had a greater chance of voting to re-elect him than the person who gave Lebed the advantage on two or three issues had of voting for Lebed.

The statistics from multistage logit analysis in Table 6.14 inject the needed dose of realism by folding other relevant variables into the computation. Not unlike prospective evaluations of the parties in 1995, expectations of the presidential candidates' performance in office have a significant and substantively important influence on electoral behavior. As we have seen so many times in this volume, the magnitude of the apparent influence tends to diminish as it is qualified by larding other presumed causes into the analysis. The total effects that survive in the table's bottom row are larger than those evinced for the parties in the parliamentary election, but the measures in the two settings are so disparate that not much can be concluded about the comparison.

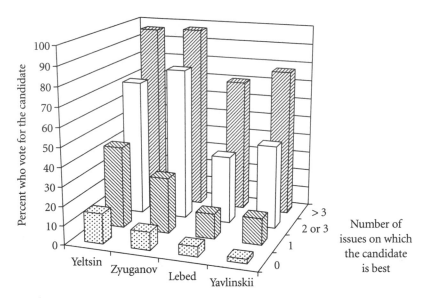

Figure 6.10. Prospective Job Performance and the First-Round Presidential Vote by Candidate, 1996

Another point to come out of Table 6.14 is that there are again sizeable differences among the candidates in the ways other variables join the causal progression. For Yeltsin, retrospective evaluations of his and the government's record are responsible for the largest row-by-row disturbance in the parameters. For Zyuganov and especially Yavlinskii, the personal qualities of the candidates are most important. For Lebed, though, the amazing thing is how little the introduction of other variables changes the observed effect of prospective evaluations of him as president: they are almost perfectly autonomous of other opinions. Lebed from this vantage point is a "personalist" candidate with a difference: voters were mobilized, not by his charm and charisma, but by his promise as a fixer of what ails Russia.

The final observation to take from Table 6.14 is the contrast between the two finalists, Yeltsin and Zyuganov, from one round of the presidential election to the next. Whereas the effect of prospective evaluations of Zyuganov on the Zyuganov vote increases, prospective evaluations of Yeltsin affect the Yeltsin vote less in the runoff than in the opening round. A reason for this, one guesses, is that many voters believed some other can-

Table 6.14 Elaboration of the Impact of Prospective Evaluations of the Candidates on the Presidential Vote, 1996 (Differences in Predicted Probabilities)

Variables progressively incorporated in regression	First round[a]				Runoff[b]	
	Yel.	Zyug.	Leb.	Yav.	Yel.	Zyug.
Prospective evaluation of the candidate only	.81**	.89**	.81**	.94**	.67**	.85**
Also social characteristics	.74**	.91**	.81**	.93**	.61**	.84**
Also current conditions	.73**	.90**	.82**	.93**	.61**	.81**
Also partisanship (but not issue opinions)	.69**	.87**	.81**	.88**	.54**	.82**
Also issue opinions (but not partisanship)	.68**	.90**	.82**	.94**	.45**	.88**
Also partisanship and issue opinions	.65**	.84**	.81**	.90**	.41**	.88**
Also retrospective evaluations of incumbents	.54**	.84**	.79**	.88**	.23**	.92**
Also leadership qualities	.48**	.67**	.75**	.60**	.20**c	.85**c
Also prospective evaluations of other candidates[d]	.37**	.52**	.80**	.58**	.15**c	.83**c

**p ≤ .01
a. Sample N = 1,990.
b. Sample N = 1,937
c. Two finalists only.
d. Gray-toned row gives the total effect of prospective evaluations of the candidates.

didate—Lebed or Yavlinskii, primarily—was the best man for the job, but were willing to accede to Yeltsin as second best.[38]

Conclusions

The three approaches to electoral behavior reviewed in this chapter differ in their fine points but share a common interest in citizens' short-run assessments of the organizations and politicians competing for their votes. All three paradigms pay off plentifully in analyzing Russia's transitional polity.

First, Russian citizens almost invariably form judgments of how their government has been performing, and these judgments are decidedly important influences on their electoral choice. They are more puissant in the presidential than in the parliamentary arena, and more for popular assessments of the president than of the other half of Russia's dual executive, the cabinet headed by the prime minister. Second, it is equally indisputable that Russians develop evaluations of party leaders and presidential characteristics and respond to them in the polling booth. These personalized images, though, come up shorter of being the decisive element in political reasoning and choice than some of the literature on the former Soviet Union and the politics of regime change would lead us to expect. The data also testify, third, to the presence and the electoral effect of prospective evaluations of how parties and would-be presidents will cope with the country's problems, from reviving the economy to directing its foreign relations.

Add these three sets of associations to those accumulated in preceding chapters, and we face an analytical embarrassment of riches. So many factors seem to be associated with voting behavior in protodemocratic Russia. Sorting out their relative significance in any one analytical category is a complex enough business, we have found over and over again. What about conclusions concerning the overall importance of whole categories of causes? To this question, the last chapter of the book turns.

Tying the Strands Together

My goal in this book has been to lay bare the microfoundations of voting in the semi-organized uncertainty of Russian politics after the Soviet Union. Having framed the problem in Chapter 1 and described turnout and grassroots campaign involvement in Chapter 2, I edged toward this objective in Chapters 3 through 6 by scanning a series of factors that my reading of transitional dynamics and theories of mass politics suggested might account for how Russians make electoral choices. In this chapter I will pull the strands of the argument together, spell out conclusions about Russian electoral behavior, and prognosticate briefly about the future of voting in a protodemocratic community.

Highly Patterned Behavior

A regime change plunges elections and the whole political process into uncertainty. Distracted by their private woes and apathetic about public affairs, a large minority of the members of a transitional polity do not bother to exercise their newfound suffrage rights. Those who do can be capricious, suspicious of trickery, fearful they will be ambushed by economic or political catastrophe, and hesitant. Subjects-become-citizens set sail on the electoral waters without some of the navigational aids Westerners nonchalantly take for granted: prolonged familiarity with the players and the issue agenda, socialized identification with established political parties, holistic ideologies, transcripts of achievement against which to check the promises of incumbents and oppositionists, antennae for picking out charlatans and crooks. In a late-democratizing society, the institutional infrastructure of participation is rough-hewn and the signals that parties and candidates emit are thin and static-filled. The legislators Russians send to the Duma to represent them have limited sway over governmental policy. And questions arise about executive positions, too: an astute voter might wonder what difference the declarative policies of a corrupt and battered state make for life outside Moscow's ring road.

This litany of impediments to normalcy notwithstanding, electoral decisions in post-Communist Russia clearly are a far cry from the impetuosity, accident, and drift we would foresee if uncertainty conquered all. Instead, Russian voting is quite highly patterned behavior. Its components and attitudinal underpinnings interrelate in lawful ways that submit to rigorous analysis.

We hypothesized at the outset that Russians' voting choices could originate in any of a number of clusters of causes:

- Social structure and group loyalties;
- Citizens' assessments of current conditions in the country;
- Partisan sentiments;
- Normative opinions on burning national issues;
- Retrospective evaluations of incumbents;
- Appraisals of the personal qualities of leaders; and
- Prospective evaluations of the services victorious parties and candidates would provide after the election.

According to our analysis, variables in *all* of these groups have some systematic bearing on how Russians vote and on the corresponding cleavages within the electorate. The scholarly literature characterizes post-Communism as muddled and combustible, and not without reason. What Russians' voting patterns hint at even at this early juncture is the existence of tangible, offsetting pressures toward order and determinacy.

Not a Tabula Rasa

Where do these incipient regularities come from? Why is mass politics in the aftermath of dictatorship not the empire of pure, unadulterated chaos?

Up to a point, civic behavior reflects the inherent logic and workings of elections. In the nonviolent tussle between political rivals that is a democratic election, who wins is decided through a collective choice of sovereign individuals.[1] Think of it as a boxing or wrestling match—in Russia, a free-for-all with a multitude of athletes in the ring—in which the audience, not a referee or panel of judges, fills out the scorecard. Circling one another warily, the up-and-coming gladiators have every incentive to try to seduce the crowd, or a portion of it, to their side. In a modern society—and Russia, for all its torments, is one—technologies of electronic communication and suasion whisk their images into almost every family's living room, along with their promises to restore justice and bring on happy days. Leaders of the sitting government, anxious to cling to democratic legitimacy and power, vie to boost the electoral chances of their clients and allies.

Citizens themselves, and not only the logic of the contest and the blandishments of the contestants, are entitled to credit for the orderliness of electoral behavior. One lesson of Russian and post-Soviet practice is that humble people are not at a loss when thrust into an electoral situation. They tend to have an inkling of what to do, in the sense of recognizing that the ballot is theirs to cast in response to felt needs. Those for whom the act is empty or distasteful can always abstain. The rapidity with which transitional voting takes shape implies that, so long as the environment is permissive, there is an innate and reflexive quality to electoral behavior. Voting and voting sensibly is easier than building a flourishing stock exchange or bond market, as Russians have found out to their dismay.

In Chapter 1 I quoted Valerie Bunce and Maria Csanádi's assertion that in post-Soviet Europe and Eurasia, "The usual bases for political identity and for political activity are missing." Although it is fair enough to say that some of the rudiments of individual behavior evinced in a mature liberal democracy are absent or assume a different flavor in a country like transitional Russia, it does not pay to overdraw the point. The emergent electorate is not a tabula rasa on which politicos or media wizards can inscribe any message they wish. The old and the middle-aged bring their baggage with them into democratizing politics: the knowledge, beliefs, wants, and prejudices they acquired before the era of reform as well as their reactions to the reforms undertaken. Different circumstances and shocks have molded the young, not least of them the implosion of the Soviet civilization their elders regarded as immutable. Voters of all generations and persuasions learn from shared and parochial experiences. They change their minds. Nearly everyone talks politics with kin and friends, and one Russian adult in three or four, we documented in Chapter 2, attempts in an election campaign to instruct a peer how to vote. I will not pretend to have mastered the labyrinthine routes through which information and values are transferred and assimilated, yet every chapter of this volume displays their results.

The General and the Particular

I pegged my inquiry on universal categories adapted from the study of mass political behavior in the older democracies. I have found Russian voters to be impelled by local versions of, or variations on, many of the same kinds of generic variables that steer electoral choice in countries democratically governed for decades. We will attend in a moment to the ones that seem most important, and to the question of time horizon, but first it is worth restating the caution flagged at the start of the book about not mistaking scientifically detectable symmetry of form for factual or moral parity of content.

To overlook this caveat is to overlook the drama and pathos of politics in the ex-USSR. It was observed in Chapter 3, for example, that Russians, like Americans, react at the polls to their perceptions of how things are going in the national economy. That equation would be incomplete if we omitted Russians' gut feelings about trends in the political sphere, and especially if we did not acknowledge the out-of-the-ordinary quality of the particular manifestations of these general phenomena. In the realm of economics, Russia has for a decade been mired in a crisis compared to which the interwar Great Depression looks tame. In politics, the only episode in the American past to approach the seismic transformation spearheaded by Boris Yeltsin would be the emancipation of the slaves in the 1860s.

Likewise with the issue preferences encountered in Chapter 5. In outer form, issue-driven voting in Russia echoes issue-driven voting in the West. The difference is in the subject matter of the issues. Voters in the advanced liberal democracies are confined nowadays to conflicts about problems that are at the margins of healthy and wealthy social systems. The uproar in Russia is about systems per se and about their design and survivability. The opinion that had far and away the greatest concordance with the 1996 presidential vote was about what sort of political system—a recycled Soviet regime or a more democratic one—the Russian Federation ought to have. Civil wars have been waged over less.

The Bottom Line: What Matters Most?

Discovering that Russian voters are sensitive in some degree to roughly the same variables that Western voters respond to does not slake curiosity about transitional citizens' conduct. To round out the inquiry, we need to know which of these variables contribute *most* to the vote. This question is endlessly complicated by the intricacy of electoral options and outcomes in Russia's rowdy politics, which parse into multiple nonordered categories by party or presidential candidate.[2] But face up to it we can if we employ statistical tools that fit the task. The first differences in predicted probabilities used in preceding chapters, extracted from multinomial logit regressions, are such a tool, and they have already told us plenty about how Russians vote.

Chapters 3 to 6 proceeded in sequence through bundles of explanatory variables. This tactic permitted us to ascertain whether any one potential cause is systematically linked to electoral choice in Russia. The statistical measure of association on which we have placed the most reliance is the "total-effect" estimate for that variable, a parameter which controls for the effects of variables that precede and coincide with the variable in the multistage causal ordering stipulated by our presumptive model of the voting decision. Inspection of the magnitude and significance level of this term allowed us in Chapter 3, for example, to disqualify ethnicity and religious affiliation as the weighty influences on Russian voters in some academic forecasts. In Chapter 6 we were able to show that evaluations of the personal qualities of political leaders have some impact on voting, but nothing like the paramountcy certain scholars have imputed to them.

Another virtue of working bloc by bloc is that it facilitates comparison of the electoral effects of variables within the respective blocs. These effects must by their nature be trained on discrete parties and candidates. A variable may have a large apparent impact on the odds of voting for party A, but be immaterial to choosing party B. The permutations and combinations are kaleidoscopic in their variety.[3] We were able to make out in Chapter 3, among other things, that age is more of an influence on Russian voting behavior than education, income, or any other social attribute. We saw in the same chapter that sociotropic economic evaluations were more strongly associated than pocketbook economic evaluations with a vote for the opposition KPRF in 1995 and for Zyuganov in 1996, whereas citizen assessments of the course of political democratization trumped both classes of economic assessment in the presidential showdown. In the same fashion, we determined in Chapter 5 that normative preferences about the speed of the transition to a market economy and the tradeoff between order and personal liberty had the largest effects of any issue opinions on the likelihood of voting for the KPRF in 1995, but in 1996 the issue of the desirability of reinstating the Soviet political system was most influential in the Zyuganov vote. Chapter 6 showed popular ratings of the record of the president to be more germane to voting than assessments of the government cabinet led by the prime minister.

A final advantage of the mode of analysis and presentation followed here is that it equips us to retrace the pathways that transmit the electoral influence of variables of interest to us. For some causal variables, the parameters gauging impact on the vote are very robust, not much budged when other terms are absorbed into the analysis; this implies mostly unmediated influence. Other effects are severely altered—almost invariably downward—by the entry of additional variables into the estimation. We have interpreted this diminution as indicating indirect, brokered effects on the vote, and have panned the statistical record for clues about the structure of the mediation.

The numerous advantages of targeting separate independent variables in the analysis do not redeem its glaring disadvantage: failure to pin down which broad types of variables harmonize best with transitional citizens' electoral choices. For example, we have demonstrated that sociotropic economic assessments tell more on Russian voters than pocketbook assessments, and that assessments of the fortunes of democratizing political change surge in importance in the presidential election of 1996 as compared with the State Duma election of 1995. But what are the combined electoral implications of all perceptions of prevailing conditions, economic and political? How do they stand up against other blocs of variables? Are they in their totality more or less important guides to behavior than issue opinions or partisanship or evaluations of the performance of incumbents? Are evaluations of politicians' personal qualities more or less significant than what a Russian thinks about their aptitudes as problem-solvers and binders of the nation's wounds?

In their comprehensive study of the 1992 presidential election in the United States, Warren E. Miller and J. Merrill Shanks conclude that identification with the Democratic party, normative predispositions, and evaluations of George Bush's performance as president sealed Bush's fate and did the most to open the door of the White House to Bill Clinton. Prospective performance evaluations, current policy preferences, perceptions of current conditions, and evaluations of the personal qualities of the two men had smaller if still perceptible effects.[4]

To carry out a bottom-line analysis of Russian voting, it is necessary to extend our statistical procedures, again gleaning inferences from statistical simulations grounded in the 1995–96 survey data. In Chapters 3, 4, 5, and 6 the resulting counterfactuals—careful speculations about states of the world that would have obtained had selected conditions differed from what they were in the cases studied—engender successive predictions of the results of changes in the values of *single* variables in the model. With a pragmatic revision of technique, I shall now adduce the counterfactuals stemming from tests simultaneously involving entire *blocs* of causal factors.

Earlier renditions set forth the differences in predicted probabilities associated with extreme changes, from minimum to maximum, in the value of the variable under scrutiny. If we followed this precedent in pinning down the electoral consequences of groups of explanatory variables, it would lead us to conjecture about coordinated shifts in attitudes and behavior that for the most part would be hard to imagine coming to pass in the real world. We learned in Chapter 5, for instance, that a shift in preference on economic reform from the most profoundly pro-market position to the most profoundly anti-market position (when proper controls are instituted) would raise a citizen's probability of voting for the KPRF in 1995 by .18 (18 percentage points). That is helpful information for the analyst to have at his fingertips. But how helpful would it be to measure the impact of polar shifts in someone's opinions on every last one of the ten issues for which we have attitudinal data—everything from grocery prices to Russian-Ukrainian diplomacy? Similarly, how much would we benefit from pitting the predicted behavior of a Russian who had the most pessimistic perception of trends in his or her family's welfare, in the national economy, and in the course of democratization, and who recently had a brush with joblessness to boot, against a notional voter who had diametrically opposite, upbeat convictions on all current conditions and no contact with unemployment?

To circumvent the artificiality of such antipodal comparisons, I will report tests done for less outlandish eventualities: concurrent, comparable, and moderately large conjoint changes in the values of all terms within a bloc of variables. The value shifts which I define as "moderately large" are described in Table B.1 in Appendix B. They rest on my considered and fallible judgment of what such a change would consist of in Russian politics. I decline to do the test for values of the social characteristics of the populace, since I feel it would be contrived, and since social structure and the demographic traits of individuals, unlike their mental states, cannot change sharply in the short run. Social characteristics will, of course, be retained in the analysis as control variables.[5] One of our other analytical categories—transitional partisanship—also poses difficulties, because the indicators we have utilized in the voting analysis are binary and because partisanship scores for different political parties are constrained by the concept of partisanship as an exclusive attachment to a single party.[6] I arbitrarily define a moderately large change in partisanship in favor of any one party as constituting a shift from nonpartisanship or partisan sentiment for another political party to professed allegiance to said party.

The Party-List Vote

Table 7.1 lists the products of the statistical analysis of the electoral effects of blocs of variables in the State Duma election of 1995. The modified total effects are not unlike the total effect parameters adduced earlier in the book, except that they are for clumps of explanatory factors, not one factor, and for moderately large shifts in them, not minimum-to-maximum shifts. As before, the electoral effects of antecedent and synchronous variables are incorporated, and their values kept constant at their medians. There is no exact statistical index to summarize the relative roles of our six blocs of causal variables across all four parties. For descriptive purposes, the weighted average of the absolute values of the modified total effects, in the bottom line of the table, is as handy as any.

It turns out that transitional partisanship has more explanatory potency than any of the other blocs of variables. Partisan affinity in favor of the socialistic KPRF, the nationalistic LDPR, the government's Our Home Is Russia, or the liberal Yabloko increases the likelihood of voting for that party in 1995 by .50 to .76, discounting for other applicable causal factors.[7] Our inability to devise an indicator of a moderate shift in partisanship truly analogous to the treatment of other blocs of variables makes it likely that Table 7.1 overstates the role of partisanship. Even at that, there cannot be much doubt that partisanship, as defined in Chapter 4, has considerable electoral clout in transitional Russia.

As Table 7.1 shows, the second most important effect on party-list voting in 1995 is attitude toward the individual leaders of the parties (Gennadii Zyuganov, Vladimir Zhirinovskii, Viktor Chernomyrdin, and Grigorii Yavlinskii).[8] Thwarting some scholarly predictions about the

Table 7.1 Modified Total Effects of Blocs of Explanatory Variables on the Party-List Vote, 1995 (Differences in Predicted Probabilities for Simultaneous, Moderately Large Changes in All Variables in Bloc)[a]

Party	Current conditions	Partisanship	Issue opinions	Retrospective evaluations of incumbents	Party leaders	Prospective evaluations of parties
KPRF	−.17**	.50**	.41**	−.15**	.34**	.28**
LDPR	−.05**	.76**	−.04	−.02*	.19**	.06**
Our Home Is Russia	.22**	.51**	−.06	.08**	.23**	.23**
Yabloko	.02	.66*°	−.11**	.01	.18**	.12**
Weighted average of absolute values	.13[b]	.57	.22[b]	.09[b]	.27	.21

**$p \leq .01$

*$p \leq .05$

a. Sample N = 2,143. Estimates control for effects of all causally antecedent and simultaneous variables.

b. Counting effects where $p > .05$ as 0.

"charismatic" essence of post-Soviet politics, though, the parameter in every case falls short of the electoral effect of partisan feeling oriented toward the party as a whole, and the weighted average of the values by party is less than half the average for partisanship. Issue opinions and prospective evaluations of the parties come next in order of causal importance. And perceptions of current conditions and their retrospective evaluations of the incumbents exert the least effect over voter behavior in 1995.

It will be noticed that Table 7.1 has a quilt-like character. As in the analysis of the effects of individual variables, the particular parties present quite distinct configurations. The weighted means in the bottom row tell us about average tendency only. Row-wise and column-wise comparisons speak to enormous variability around the average. The sources of the vote for the KPRF, the winner of the largest number of Duma seats, are the most thickly structured. All the group effects are larger than .10 and statistically significant at the .05 level, the three biggest influences being partisanship, issue opinions, and evaluations of party leaders. For the LDPR, partisanship and leadership are the only two blocs of variables that have a joint effect of .10 or more, and issue opinions have no significant effect whatever. For Our Home Is Russia, prospective evaluations of the parties, leadership, and current conditions are in a dead heat for influence after partisanship. For Yabloko, current conditions are irrelevant, but leadership evaluations, prospective evaluations, and issue opinions weigh in after partisanship.

Partisanship is a common thread for all four parties, but the relative place of the other factors mirrors the public face each party presents. It is not surprising, as was observed in Chapter 5, that voting for the KPRF, the party with the most self-conscious and cohesive program, would be most congruent with issue opinions. Nor should it surprise many that leadership would play a disproportionate role for Vladimir Zhirinovskii's LDPR; that perceptions of current conditions most affect the likelihood of voting for the party of the Russian establishment, Our Home Is Russia; or that Yabloko, the most liberal of the large parties and the only one headed by an intellectual, would have the second highest parameter for influence of issue opinions, after the KPRF.

The Presidential Vote

The estimates in Table 7.2 use the same agglutinative method to get to the bottom of the 1996 presidential vote. Table 7.3, giving the rank orderings

Table 7.2 Modified Total Effects of Blocs of Explanatory Variables on the Presidential Vote, 1996 (Differences in Predicted Probabilities for Simultaneous, Moderately Large Changes in All Variables in Bloc)[a]

Candidate	Current conditions	Partisanship	Issue opinions	Retrospective evaluations of incumbents	Leadership qualities	Prospective evaluations of candidates
First round[b]						
Yeltsin	.33**	.34**	−.37**	.61**	.33**	.25**
Zyuganov	−.14**	.54**	.38**	−.17**	.19**	.17**
Lebed	−.12**	.53**	.03	−.22**	.15**	.25**
Yavlinskii	−.04*	.56**	−.01	−.09**	.08**	.14**
Weighted average of absolute values	.22	.46	.27[c]	.34	.23	.21
Runoff[d]						
Yeltsin	.27**	.23**	−.60**	.60**	.19**[e]	.22**[e]
Zyuganov	−.22**	.62**	.55**	−.40**	.17**[e]	.16**[e]
Weighted average of absolute values	.27	.41	.58	.51	.18	.19

** $p \le .01$

* $p \le .05$

a. Estimates control for effects of all causally antecedent and simultaneous variables.

b. Sample N = 1,990.

c. Counting effects where $p > .05$ as 0.

d. Sample N = 1,937.

e. Two finalists only.

Table 7.3 Rank Ordering of Weighted Averages of Absolute Values of Modified Total Effects, 1995 and 1996

Rank	Party-list vote, 1995	Presidential vote, 1996, first round	Presidential vote, 1996, runoff
1	Partisanship	Partisanship	Issue opinions
2	Party leaders	Retrospective evaluations of incumbents	Retrospective evaluations of incumbents
3	Issue opinions	Issue opinions	Partisanship
4	Prospective evaluations of parties	Leadership qualities	Current conditions
5	Current conditions	Current conditions	Prospective evaluations of candidates
6	Retrospective evaluations of incumbents	Prospective evaluations of candidates	Leadership qualities

of the weighted means from Tables 7.1 and 7.2, affords leverage on the comparison between elections.

Major differences are apparent between presidential and parliamentary voting. Partisanship still, on average, wields the most influence on behavior in the presidential first round in 1996, but its margin over the other blocs of explanatory factors is more slender than in 1995. Retrospective evaluations of Yeltsin and the government, last on the overall list in 1995, move up to second place, and prospective evaluations of the candidates move down two notches from where prospective evaluations of the parties stood in 1996.

The second round of the presidential election brings still more changes. The biggest is that citizens' issue opinions—capped by their outlook on Russia's political system—shoot to the head of the queue of causal factors. Retrospective evaluations of the incumbents, in second place, are also much more consequential in absolute terms than in the qualifying round, while partisanship slips to third place. The bloc of perceptions of current conditions in the country gains some in stature. The variables measuring assessments of the personal qualities of the candidates, on the other hand, drop to the very bottom of the rank order.

Again, there are substantial discrepancies among the players, permitting us to make out very different profiles of the relationship with the electorate (see Table 7.2). The first-round Yeltsin vote is most tied to evaluations of incumbents' performance—aptly enough for the occupant of the Kremlin for the preceding five years—followed by issue opinions. For Zyuganov, like the KPRF, the two cardinal influences are partisanship and issue opinions, with all others far behind. For Aleksandr Lebed, whose rhetoric emphasized Yeltsin's failings as president and the job he would do in his place, prospective evaluations of the candidates and assessments of incumbents turn out to matter the most after partisanship. For Yavlinskii, partisanship and prospective evaluations are the only blocs to have a group influence of more than .10. Outflanked by Yeltsin, Yavlinskii loses the attraction for liberal-minded Russians that his party, Yabloko, had in the Duma race. In the presidential runoff, issue opinions become more important determinants of the vote for both Yeltsin and Zyuganov. The array of group influences on the two finalists is quite similar, the main differences being Zyuganov's greater dependence on partisanship and Yeltsin's greater dependence on retrospective evaluations.

Good for Democracy?

Is all of this good news or bad news for democracy in Russia? There is no unequivocal answer to the question, given what we know about the differences among parties and candidates and across elections. In Chapter 2 I took the position that Russians' level of engagement with the electoral process, while less than ideal, is on balance a hopeful sign. When it comes to voting behavior, I would also accentuate the positive.

On the one hand, a philosophical approach to democracy would lead us to say it functions at its public-spirited best when individuals' principled "conceptions of the good society" impel their electoral choices. Issue opinions do affect how Russians vote, but it would be a stretch to say they are dominant. The heartening exception is the runoff round of the presidential election, when normative opinions leap to the top of the list of desiderata.

On the other hand, we can take solace from noting that elections in the 1990s avoided two syndromes that arguably are injurious to responsible democratic choice: voting chiefly on the basis of selfish pocketbook concerns, and infatuation with charismatic leaders. On the first point, Chapter 3 showed Russians to be more motivated by the nation's pocketbook than their own, and also found attitudes toward political trends to be as pertinent to voting as both types of economic voting. And leadership qualities, while not without impact, had more effect on the party-list vote than on the presidential vote—though one would have thought a priori that the presidential election would be the more susceptible of the two to personalistic appeals. Assessments of the character of the presidential nominees finished in effect in a last-place tie in influence in both rounds of the presidential election.

The Importance of Context

Snapshots of mass behavior and its determinants in any one Russian election are revealing in and of themselves. The longitudinal *contrasts* between elections remind us of one other point about transitional citizenship on which the text has commented from time to time. That point, in a nutshell, is the significance of institutional and political context in shaping the electoral result.[9]

Many Western scholars have been justifiably critical of the exaggerated presidentialism of Russia's post-Soviet political system. They have faulted the relegation of parliament to a junior constitutional position, the president's excessive power to issue decrees, and the feebleness of legislative oversight of the state bureaucracy and presidential apparatus. Institutional asymmetry has had a negative influence on the transparency, responsiveness, and effectiveness of Russian government. But the information condensed in the tables says, perversely enough, that it has subtly *positive* effects on the quality of electoral politics in the presidential arena.

In a Russian presidential election, the top executive office in the land is on the line, not seats in a legislative debating society. The format of the campaign generates cues and incentives that induce citizens to act rather differently than they would in a parliamentary election. The magnitudes of the effect statistics in Tables 7.1 and 7.2 indicate that voting for Russia's president was a more highly structured act than the vote for the State Duma. In both the first round and the runoff in 1996, the weighted averages of the group effects are larger than the averages from the 1995 parliamentary election for three of six blocs of variables (current conditions, issue opinions, and retrospective evaluations of incumbents). All represent what I would defend as benign adjustments in citizens' demeanor. The greater salience of assessments of the status quo introduces a note of accountability for governmental actions which is in short supply in the looser parliamentary context. And the greater relevance of issue opinions gives more scope to ideals and moral concerns—to the very sweep of human experience in whose name systemic reforms were launched in the Soviet Union and which has too often slipped from sight since.

Contingencies for Transitional Citizenship

Anyone who studies Russia and the former Soviet Union knows full well the danger of making ironclad prognoses. The country repeatedly astonished us in the twentieth century with its sudden swings of course. I would be amazed if other bombshells did not await us in the twenty-first century.

Our inventory of paradigms of voting behavior in Chapter 1 distinguished between factors of long duration, such as social makeup and party identification, and short-term factors such as the current state of the economy and the personalities of candidates. Multicausal theories of voting in the West use a time frame to order causal factors from long-acting, slow-changing factors to the most recent, volatile, and short-term factors. Miller and Shanks do this in their opus on *The New American Voter*. The classic of an earlier time to which they pay homage, *The American Voter*, summed up its model of the vote in the celebrated metaphor of the "funnel of causality." "We can range freely in time back through the funnel," wrote the authors. "Each cross section contains all the elements that will successfully predict the next, and so on, until we have arrived at the final political act."[10]

It is precisely assurance about the temporal ordering of causal forces, theoretically coherent and consistent with empirical evidence, that is in deficit in sizing up the future of Russian electoral politics. In investigating a transitional citizenry still a newcomer to the stage, I have necessarily stressed short-term influences. In a country where almost everything seems to be in motion, short-term measures are often the best the analyst can get.

To be sure, certain of our blocs of variables do refer to continuous realities: social and socioeconomic characteristics, some of which change glacially if at all; and attitudes toward Boris Yeltsin, the founding father of the post-Soviet polity. But parts of Russia's social foundation are in flux, and Yeltsin is about to depart the scene. For Russians' issue opinions, we saw no difference in stability between fundamental predispositions and stances on contemporary controversies, and so are in no position to say how durable those beliefs might be. And elsewhere our analysis has emphasized attitudinal origins of electoral behavior which are subject to fluctuation over months and years, not decades or generations. Even partisanship—which as ingrained party identification is held by scholars to be the solidest of all political attitudes in the United States—wavers in the short run in Russia, as our 1995–96 survey panel brought out.

Little is to be gained from brooding about where Russian democracy will be fifteen or twenty years—three, four, or five presidents—down the road. The banal truth is that it mostly depends on what happens between now and then. Russians have been presented with a historic opportunity to construct a democratic polity whose citizens earn their daily bread in a market economy. As the grim headlines on the economic front drive home, there are no money-back guarantees about living in the transition period. Opportunities can be seized or squandered. The post-Soviet zone in 2000 offers a wide spectrum of interim outcomes, everything from a swiftly Europeanizing Poland or Lithuania to seedy stagnation, economic basket cases, oil sheikdoms, ethnic war zones, and neo-Soviet autocracies. Nothing in the transitional story thus far presages convergence on a unified model of success any day soon.

The most profitable musings are about contingencies over the next five to ten years that will affect the long-run prospects of Russian electoral politics. Here we should focus not so much on the anticipated results of impending electoral clashes—intriguing as they may be—as on *how* those results come about and create institutional legacies. There are two strategic domains in which events immediately ahead deserve the closest monitoring.

One is the area of *economic reform and recovery*. Yeltsin's dismissal of Prime Minister Chernomyrdin in March 1998 and the financial crash of that August mark the end of the formative period of Russia's post-Communist economic system that commenced with the shock therapy and the opening toward privatization of 1991–92. The crash was a blow to the banks, the most conspicuous beneficiaries of an artificially high exchange rate, but a boon to commodity exporters and to consumer-sector producers, for whom the cheap ruble is an effective tariff wall. For most ordinary people, bank failures and inflation have made hard times harder. If Russia tips into yet another downward economic spiral because of a cutoff of foreign credit or some domestic seizure, we cannot exclude that electoral competition will be overtaken by a Weimar-like mood of despair and extremism, in which fierce accusations about national degradation and betrayal crowd out all other modes of discourse. If state breakdown ever became an imminent possibility, I would not rule out an elite and popular reconsideration of the democratizing bargain of a decade ago.

The other and not so menacing realm where major developments are or may be afoot is that of *political leadership and organization*. Three political contingencies warrant special attention.

The first is the exit of Boris Yeltsin, by no later than the expiry of his second term in 2000, and with it the end of the founder's era in Russian politics. It should not be forgotten that evaluations of Yeltsin and his record played a huge role in the presidential election of 1996, and a lesser but still considerable part in the parliamentary election of 1995. Yeltsin has been a stabilizing presence—achieving stabilization through polarization—and now that steadying fact is about to disappear. The vacuum may be filled in various ways, be it through a strong personality or a compelling idea. It is hard to tell in advance which is the most likely to succeed.

The second contingency to watch concerns the Russian constitution and relations between the legislative and executive branches of government. There is growing discussion within the Russian elite about amending the 1993 constitution to the disadvantage of the imperial presidency and the advantage of the Federal Assembly. The regional leaders who fill the upper house, the Federation Council, envisage a greater role for themselves and see the council as an agent of federal-regional condominium. But many elective politicians at the national level want the State Duma, the lower house, to gain in any reshuffling of powers. Yevgenii Primakov's eight months as prime minister, from September 1998 to May 1999, may conceivably show the way to greater respect and fuller legal prerogatives for the Duma. Were this to happen, we can expect repercussions on citizenship and voting behavior, since the different style and tone of parliamentary as opposed to presidential campaigning and voting hinges on the weakness and perforce the irresponsibility of the Duma. Enhancement of the Duma's authority would lessen the disparity between parliamentary and presidential elections, and that would be a good thing.

In a third area, partisanship, fluidity in the years ahead can have positive or negative ramifications. The next several rounds of national elections will tell whether there is a trend toward institutionalization and normalization of the electoral and governing role of Russia's parties. The KPRF, the strongest party organization with the staunchest partisan supporters, is not likely to show the way, because of the aging of its corps of loyalists and because of its increasing vulnerability to schism between radicals and moderates. Of the other older parties, the LDPR is floundering, while Yabloko may be entering a modest growth phase. Our Home Is Russia, burdened by its association with failed economic policies, is probably doomed, although it may simply give way to a new "party of power," with no program save perpetuation of the status quo. A straw in the wind was the 1998 decision by Mayor Yurii Luzhkov of Moscow, who has avidly wanted to succeed Yeltsin as president, to establish a political movement, Otechestvo (Fatherland), rather than march into electoral battle as a solitary warrior. An important milestone will be the presidential election of 2000. The more it is fought out on a partisan basis, the more we can say that Russian political parties are moving toward center stage in mass politics.

In all these ways and more, transitional citizenship can be expected to live up to its name. It refers to a time-bound condition, not an end state. It is marked by high yet not boundless uncertainty. It lacks many of the organizational and psychological buffers against destabilizing change that a consolidated liberal democracy has. But, as this study has demonstrated, it does not lack regularities and patterns. Post-Soviet voters make the choices they do for reasons that are susceptible to analysis and understanding. Let us hope that they transit to something better, not worse, and that our modes of studying them and their fellows in Eastern Europe and Eurasia keep up with them.

APPENDIXES

NOTES

ACKNOWLEDGMENTS

INDEX

Post-Soviet Election Results, 1993–1996

Table A.1. Voting for Party Lists for State Duma, December 12, 1993

Party or quasi-party	Formal status of organization	Party family[a]	Percentage of valid votes[b]
LDPR (Liberal-Democratic Party of Russia)	Party	Nationalist	22.92
Russia's Choice	Movement	Government	15.51
KPRF (Communist Party of the Russian Federation)	Party	Socialist	12.40
Women of Russia	Movement	Centrist	8.13
Agrarian Party of Russia	Party	Socialist	7.99
Yabloko	Bloc	Liberal	7.86
PRES (Party of Russian Unity and Accord)	Party	Liberal	6.73
Democratic Party of Russia	Party	Centrist	5.52
Russian Movement for Democratic Reform	Movement	Liberal	4.08
Civic Union	Movement	Centrist	1.93
Future of Russia/New Names	Bloc	Centrist	1.25
KEDR (Constructive Ecological Movement of Russia)	Movement	Centrist	0.76
Dignity and Compassion	Bloc	Centrist	0.70
Voted against all parties	NA[c]	NA[c]	4.22

a. Author's classification.

b. Omits invalid ballots. Total valid ballots cast 53,751,696.

c. NA = Not applicable.

Source: Byulleten' Tsentral'noi izbiratel'noi komissii Rossiskoi Federatsii, no. 12 (1994), pp. 38, 67.

Table A.2. Voting for Party Lists for State Duma, December 17, 1995

Party or quasi-party	Formal status of organization	Party family[a]	Percentage of valid votes[b]
KPRF (Communist Party of the Russian Federation)	Party	Socialist	22.73
LDPR (Liberal-Democratic Party of Russia)	Party	Nationalist	11.40
Our Home Is Russia	Movement	Government	10.33
Yabloko	Association	Liberal	7.02
Women of Russia	Movement	Centrist	4.70
Communists for the Soviet Union	Bloc	Socialist	4.62
KRO (Congress of Russian Communities)	Movement	Nationalist	4.39
Employees' Self-Management Party	Party	Centrist	4.06
Russia's Democratic Choice	Bloc	Liberal	3.94
Agrarian Party of Russia	Party	Socialist	3.85
Derzhava	Movement	Nationalist	2.62
Forward Russia	Movement	Liberal	1.98
Power to the People	Bloc	Socialist	1.64
Pamfilova-Gurov-Lysenko Bloc	Bloc	Liberal	1.63
Union of Labor	Bloc	Centrist	1.59
KEDR (Ecological Party of Russia)	Party	Centrist	1.42
Rybkin Bloc	Bloc	Centrist	1.13
Govorukhin Bloc	Bloc	Nationalist	1.01
My Fatherland	Movement	Centrist	0.73
Common Cause	Bloc	Liberal	0.70
Beer Lovers' Party	Party	Liberal	0.63
NUR Moslem Movement	Movement	Misc.	0.58
Transformation of the Fatherland	Bloc	Centrist	0.50
National-Republican Party	Party	Nationalist	0.49
Bloc for Defense of Pensioners and Veterans (with other groups)	Bloc	Misc.	0.48

Table A.2 (continued)

Party or quasi-party	Formal status of organization	Party family[a]	Percentage of valid votes[b]
PRES (Party of Russian Unity and Accord)	Party	Liberal	0.36
Association of Lawyers	Association	Misc.	0.36
For the Motherland	Bloc	Centrist	0.29
Christian-Democratic Union	Party	Misc.	0.28
Bloc for Defense of Children (with other groups)	Bloc	Misc.	0.21
People's Union	Party	Misc.	0.19
Tikhonov-Tupolev-Tikhonov Bloc	Bloc	Misc.	0.15
Union of Housing and Municipal Workers	Union	Misc.	0.14
Social Democrats	Bloc	Liberal	0.13
Party of Economic Freedom	Party	Liberal	0.13
Russian All-People's Movement	Movement	Nationalist	0.13
Bloc of Independents	Bloc	Liberal	0.12
Federal-Democratic Movement	Movement	Liberal	0.12
Stable Russia	Movement	Centrist	0.12
Duma-96	Movement	Misc.	0.08
Generation of the Frontier	Bloc	Misc.	0.65
Eighty-nine Regions	Bloc	Liberal	0.06
Inter-ethnic Union	Bloc	Centrist	0.06
Voted against all parties	NA[c]	NA[c]	2.83

a. Author's classification.

b. Omits invalid ballots. Total valid ballots cast 67,884,200.

c. NA = Not applicable.

Source: Tsentral'naya izbiratel'naya komissiya Rossiiskoi Federatsii, *Vybory deputatov gosudarstvennoi dumy 1995: Elektoral'naya statistika* (Moscow: Ves' Mir, 1996), pp. 90–91.

Table A.3. Percentage of Valid Party-List Votes by Party Family, 1993 and 1995 Elections

Party family	1993	1995
Government	15.51	10.33
Liberal	18.67	16.83
Centrist	18.29	14.59
Nationalist	22.29	20.04
Socialist	20.39	32.84
Miscellaneous	0	2.54
Voted against all parties	4.22	2.83

Table A.4. Voting for President, First Round, June 16, 1996

Candidate	Nominated by	Percentage of valid votes[a]
Boris Yeltsin	Independent	35.79
Gennadii Zyuganov	Bloc of Popular-Patriotic Forces of Russia (dominated by the KPRF)	32.49
Aleksandr Lebed	Independent	14.73
Grigorii Yavlinskii	Yabloko	7.45
Vladimir Zhirinovskii	LDPR	5.79
Svyatoslav Fedorov	Employees' Self-Management Party	0.94
Mikhail Gorbachev	Independent	0.52
Martin Shakkum	Party of Socioeconomic Reform	0.37
Yurii Vlasov	National Patriotic Party	0.20
Vladimir Bryntsalov	Russian Socialist Party	0.17
Voted against all candidates	NA[b]	1.56

a. Omits invalid ballots. Total valid ballots cast 74,515,019. The 308 write-in votes for Aman-Geldy Tuleyev, who officially withdrew the week before the election, are counted in the vote total.

b. NA = Not applicable.

Source: Tsentral'naya izbiratel'naya komissiya Rossiiskoi Federatsii, *Vybory Prezidenta Rossiiskoi Federatsii 1996: Elektoral'naya statistika* (Moscow: Ves' Mir, 1996), p. 128.

Table A.5. Voting for President, Second Round, July 3, 1996

Candidate	Nominated by	Percentage of valid votes[a]
Boris Yeltsin	Independent	54.40
Gennadii Zyuganov	Bloc of Popular-Patriotic Forces	40.73
Voted against both candidates	NA[b]	4.88

a. Omits invalid ballots. Total valid ballots cast 73,910,698.

b. NA = Not applicable.

Source: Tsentral'naya izbiratel'naya komissiya Rossiiskoi Federatsii, *Vybory Prezidenta Rossiiskoi Federatsii 1996*, pp. 128, 130.

Survey Data, Methods, and Models

The purpose of this appendix is to describe important technical aspects of the data collection and analysis undergirding the book which I was not able to treat in detail in the body of the text.

Survey Sample and Methods

The information backbone for *Transitional Citizens* is data from three panel surveys of the Russian electorate undertaken in 1995 and 1996. Although survey research has developed rapidly in Russia and the former Soviet Union since the liberalization of political restraints on it in the late 1980s, many pitfalls remain.[1] The surveys reported here were done with an eye to avoiding those pitfalls and assembling a data base that meets international standards for opinion and electoral research. The work was carried out by the Demoscope group at the Institute of Sociology of the Russian Academy of Sciences, headed by Polina Kozyreva and Mikhail Kosolapov, with the methodological and logistical assistance of Michael Swafford of Paragon Research International. William Zimmerman of the University of Michigan was my co-principal investigator and took a hand in every aspect of the work. The questionnaire was jointly drafted in Russian by Russian and American collaborators. Demoscope managed field operations and coded, entered, and cleaned all data in-house, utilizing double-entry verification of closed-ended questions.

The sample for the linked surveys was a multistage area probability sample of the Russian Federation's voting-age population as of December 1995. We deliberately excluded persons institutionalized in prisons, hospitals, and the military. We also excluded residents of the republic of Chechnya, which was undergoing armed conflict at the time; of

Kaliningrad oblast (which is separated from the rest of Russia by Lithuania); of the island of Sakhalin; and of territories in the north and east of the Russian mainland with very low population density, severe weather, or transportation difficulties. Altogether, areas with about 4.4 percent of the population were left out of the sample, producing a sample frame with approximately 140.4 million people in 1,850 administrative districts and towns. Moscow, Moscow oblast, and St. Petersburg were included in the sample with certainty. Elsewhere, ten geographical regions were delineated; twenty-nine strata were apportioned within them according to each region's measure of population size; and one primary sampling unit per stratum was chosen randomly using probability proportional to size.[2] Within the primary sampling units, the population was further divided into rural and urban substrata, and villages (in the rural areas) or microcensus enumeration districts (in the towns and cities) were selected systematically as second-stage units.[3] The final stage was a random selection of households, working in the villages from official lists of households and in the urban areas from an enumeration of dwellings compiled by Demoscope. Interviewers then used the Kish procedure to select one eligible adult from each household.[4]

The sample was large because of the complexity of the political choices we wanted to study and because the rarity of panel studies in Russia created great uncertainty about response rates. Interviewers were required to contact each potential respondent three times and could make no substitutions. The first survey was done during the campaign for the election of the State Duma held December 17, 1995; interviews were done between November 19 and December 16. The second wave of interviews came after the Duma election, between December 18, 1995, and January 20, 1996. Eighty-six percent of these interviews were done by December 31. The third wave followed the runoff vote in the presidential election, which was held July 3, 1996. There was some trouble locating respondents in the summer season, so these reinterviews, three-quarters of which did occur in the three weeks after the runoff, were not completed until September 13, 1996.

The total number of citizens drawn into the sample was 3,559, of whom 2,841, or 79.8 percent, were questioned in the first wave. Almost exactly half of those sampled who were not interviewed in the first wave (360 out of 718) refused the interviewer's request to be interviewed, either with a specific reason or with none offered. In most of the remaining cases, no one was at home during three visits or the respondent selected was away. Resistance to a follow-up interview was less than we anticipated; 2,776 individuals, or 97.7 percent of our first-wave informants, were quizzed the second time. For the third-wave survey, interviewers attempted to arrange interviews of all first-wave respondents. Some 2,456 individuals were interviewed in the third wave, or 86.4 percent of the initial group. The great majority of them had already been interviewed in both the first and the second wave, but 29 respondents had previously been interviewed in the first wave only. Outright refusals to be interviewed were relatively rare in the summer of 1996 (they were given by 125 out of 385 persons not interviewed, or 32.5 percent), while absence of the respondent or other members of the household was more common (it was the reason for the failure to conduct the interview in 180 cases, or 46.8 percent).[5]

All interviews were conducted face-to-face in the Russian language. Average length of the session was sixty-four minutes in the first wave, fifty-nine minutes in the second wave, and seventy-four minutes in the third wave. All interviewers were personally briefed by local field supervisors and required to watch a video tape acquainting them with the specific character of the election project, to rehearse the interview in triads, and to do written exercises on the questionnaire. Interviewers who had not previously worked with Demoscope also watched a longer tape reviewing interview techniques. Inspectors from Moscow verified the quality of about 10 percent of the interviews.

Assuring confidentiality of the interviews, an especially important consideration in a country with an authoritarian heritage, was complicated by the panel design of the surveys. Identification codes assigned to each respondent in the first wave were retained in the second and third waves, allowing the survey data to be linked across surveys. Respondents were promised that "All information obtained in the project will be used only in generalized form." Interviewers and supervisors recorded the first names and patronymics of the respondents, so as to help in locating them later, but last names were not recorded. As a further protection, information about names and addresses was kept out of the data set distributed to the investigators, and this information was stored by the contractor in files separate from the main data files.

Sample Weights

Multistage sampling procedures which culminate in selection of one individual within a dwelling unit over-represent individuals who live alone or in small households, such as young, single persons or widows. To correct this bias, sample weights based on the number of eligible adults in each household were devised for the Russian survey data. I have applied those weights in generating all descriptive statistics in the book, in all bivariate analysis (including cross-tabulations and correlations), and in all figures based on univariate or bivariate statistics. Application of the sample weights produces 2,841 weighted cases for the first-wave survey (the same number as in the unweighted data), 2,774 weighed cases for the second wave (versus 2,776 in the raw data), and 2,472 cases for the third wave (versus 2,456 in the raw data). For the multivariate analyses reported in the book, however, the sample weights were not applied, since household size is not correlated with the political behavior under examination.

Missing Data

Nonresponses, as is normal in such research, create some missing data on most of our attitudinal measures. Nonresponses were indicated by our interviewers on the questionnaire form and took two forms: "Finds it hard to say" (*Zatrudnyayetsya otvetit'*) and "Refuses to answer" (*Otkaz*). In tables, I combine these two into a single "Don't know" category. "Don't know" cases are always included in the denominator in calculating proportions.

The multivariate analysis on which the book relies heavily includes several dozen explanatory variables. Listwise deletion of all cases with missing values was thus highly undesirable, as it would have drastically reduced the number of observations available for analysis. I therefore resorted to substitution of the weighted mean of the distribution for missing values on the attitudinal variables. This procedure biases estimates of the parameters in the logit regressions downward, but I accepted that as the lesser evil.

Regression Model and Tests

I have estimated relationships between explanatory variables and voting choice by means of multinomial logit regression, the functional form most appropriate to analysis of a dependent variable comprising discrete nonordered categories.[6] Alternative forms, including linear regression, will yield biased and potentially misleading or even absurd results.[7] Multinomial logit estimates parameters through successive iterations that maximize the likelihood of a given set of parameters obtaining in the population. It simultaneously yields estimates of the association between the independent variables and each category of the dependent variable, net of the effects of other independent variables in the model. Plots of predicted probabilities of any category of the outcome obtaining follow an S-shaped curve bounded at zero and one, not the straight line of ordinary least squares regression.

The parameters computed directly—logit coefficients, which give the proportional change in the log odds of an outcome occurring that is associated with a one-unit change in the independent variable—are not themselves of substantive interest. They are also very sensitive to the selection of the base or excluded category of the dependent variable. To arrive at clearer and more reader-friendly measures of association, I supplemented the regressions with Monte Carlo statistical simulations, following an approach and a statistical package developed by Gary King, Michael Tomz, and Jason Wittenberg,[8] which in turn yielded predicted probabilities of the voting outcome occurring under counterfactual conditions which I specified. The predicted probabilities are constrained to sum to one across all categories of the dependent variable, and in no case can the predicted probability be less than zero or more than one.

The measure of effect on voting choice employed in Chapters 3 through 6, as discussed briefly in the text, is the first difference between the probability predicted when the explanatory variable in question is set at its minimum value and that predicted when the variable takes its maximum value, all other independent variables in the estimation being held at their medians. The first differences are expressed in the tables as point estimates, which are approximately the means of their probability distributions. The estimates would be more informative if they were rendered as confidence intervals around the point estimate, but space considerations prevented me from including this information. As a compromise, I have accompanied the point estimates with two asterisks if there is a 99 percent chance that they differ from zero ($p \leq .01$) or with one asterisk if there is a 95 percent chance that they differ from zero ($p \leq .05$). By fiat, I describe parameters which are significant at the .05 level and have a magnitude of .10 or higher as indicating major effects; significant parameters of lesser magnitude indicate minor effects.

"Moderately Large Differences" in the Explanatory Variables

In Chapter 7 I use this approach to estimate influences on voting choice, but compute first differences for combinations of "moderately large differences" within whole blocs of explanatory variables. Table B.1 shows the

Table B.1. "Moderately Large Differences" in Explanatory Variables, 1995 and 1996

Blocs and Variables	1995	1996	Lower value	Higher value
Current conditions				
Pocketbook assessment of economy	√	√	Slightly worse	Slightly better
Exposure to unemployment	√		None	Some
Experience with arrears in wages and social allowances		√	Some and same as previous 6 months	None
Sociotropic assessment of economy	√	√	Slightly worse	Slightly better
Assessment of democratization	√	√	Dissatisfied	Satisfied
Partisanship				
Partisanship for given party	√	√	Nonpartisan	Partisan of that party
Issue opinions				
Oppose market	√	√	Gradual transition to market	Against transition to market
State ownership	√	√	Property mostly private	Property mostly state
Welfarism	√	√	Agree with 1 welfare measure	Agree with all 3 welfare measures
Protectionism	√	√	Disagree	Agree
No foreign capital	√	√	Disagree	Agree
Order over liberty	√	√	Disagree	Agree
Iron hand	√	√	Disagree	Agree
Centralization	√		Disagree	Agree
Strong parliament	√		Disagree	Agree
Reunite with Ukraine	√		Disagree	Agree
Soviet political system		√	Prefer current political system	Prefer Soviet political system
Reintegrate USSR		√	Disagree	Agree
Resist NATO		√	Disagree	Agree

Table B.1 (continued)

Blocs and Variables	1995	1996	Lower value	Higher value
Retrospective evaluations of incumbents				
Trust in Russian government	√	√	Disapprove	Approve
Approval of President Yeltsin	√	√	Disapprove	Approve
Party leaders				
Thermometer evaluations	√		Evaluation of party's own leader 20 to 39 points; evaluations of other 3 parties' leaders 60 to 79 points.	Evaluation of party's own leader 60 to 79 points; evaluations of other 3 parties' leaders 20 to 39 points.
Leadership qualities				
Mean of 4-point scores for intelligence, strength, integrity, vision, and empathy, rounded off to nearest integer		√	Quality probably does not apply to given candidate; quality probably applies to other candidates (presidential first round) or candidate (presidential runoff).	Quality probably applies to given candidate; quality probably does not apply to other candidates or candidate.

lower and higher values of the variables that the moderately large differences cover.

My general principle was to describe changes that stand for a shift in direction but fall short of swinging from one polar value to another. Most of the choices are self-explanatory. Partisanship, as I mention in Chapter 7, poses a unique difficulty, in that it I express it as a dichotomous indicator, leaving no intermediate categories for a moderately large difference. I arbi-

Table B.1 (continued)

Blocs and Variables	1995	1996	Lower value	Higher value
Prospective evaluations of parties				
Mean of 5-point scores for preparation, trustworthiness, responsiveness, and conflict resolution, rounded off to nearest integer	√		Given party scored at 2 of 5; other 3 parties scored at 4.	Given party scored at 4 of 5; other 3 parties scored at 2.
Prospective evaluations of candidates				
Number of policy domains (economic recovery, unemployment, crime and corruption, foreign policy, developing democracy, and guaranteeing social stability) which candidate could handle best		√	Given candidate can handle no domain best; other candidate or candidates can handle 1.27 domains each best.	Given candidate can handle 2 domains best; other candidate or candidates can handle 0.6 domains each best.

trarily define a moderate difference in partisanship as equivalent to an immoderate difference, that is, as marking a shift from nonpartisanship or partisanship for another political party to professed partisanship for the given party. The measures for prospective evaluations of the presidential candidates also created difficulties. My reasoning for the minimum/maximum values is as follows: the mean number of positive responses to the questions (which were about policy domains this or that candidate could best handle) was 3.8 out of a maximum of 6. If a given candidate is supposed counterfactually to be best at dealing with none of the 3.8 problems, I apportion all 3.8 problems solved equally among the remaining three candidates, for an average score of 1.27. If 2 domains out of 3.8 best handled constitutes a moderately large difference from 0 problems solved, this leaves 1.8 problems to be apportioned among the remaining three candidates, giving an average score of 0.6. The same values were used for Yeltsin and Zyuganov in both rounds, but the variables constructed for Lebed and Yavlinskii were not included in the second-round estimations.[9]

Political Awareness Scale

In discussing citizen involvement in the electoral process, I repeatedly utilize a scale of political awareness. I base it on factual knowledge, following John R. Zaller, *The Nature and Origins of Mass Opinion* (Cambridge: Cambridge University Press, 1992). The index is a simple additive scale with values from zero to sixteen. It was constructed from fourteen items. One, giving the survey interviewer's evaluation of the respondent's comprehension in the interview preceding the Duma election, has three values. All other items have one value derived from questions put in the second-wave interview. These ask what are the positions occupied at the time by five national leaders (Viktor Chernomyrdin, Russian prime minister; Anatolii Chubais, first deputy prime minister; Pavel Grachev, defense minister; Ivan Rybkin, speaker of the State Duma; and Vladimir Shumeiko, chairman of the Federation Council); they request evaluations of four lesser-ranking politicians (Yurii Luzhkov, mayor of Moscow; Sergei Kovalev, a parliamentarian and human rights advocate; Boris Nemtsov, governor of the Nizhnii Novgorod region; and Anatolii Sobchak, mayor of St. Petersburg); they ask what countries are led by Jacques Chirac and John Major; and ask what is the International Monetary Fund and about Russia's membership in it. One point was for correct answers to the questions about Chirac, Major, and the IMF, and one point for ability to answer each of the other items. *Alpha* reliability for the scale is .86. It has a mean of 8.67 and a standard deviation of 4.01.

Summary of Issue Opinions

The 1995a tag refers to questions asked of survey respondents in the interview prior to the election to the State Duma in 1995 (N = 2,841 weighted cases). Questions 1995b were administered after the Duma election (N = 2,774 weighted cases). The 1996 questions were asked after the presidential election of 1996 (N = 2,472 weighted cases).

Responses are coded as ordered categorical variables. In the multivariate analysis, "Don't know" and "Indifferent"[1] responses are coded at the sample mean (weighted) of the distribution of answers to the given question.

Oppose market (1995a and 1996)

"What is your view of the transition to a market economy in Russia? Which of the opinions I shall now read out is closest to your opinion?"

Response[a]	Percentage 1995	Percentage 1996
You are for a market economy and believe the transition to the market should be quick	6	8
You are for a market economy and believe the transition to the market should be gradual	58	61
You are against the transition to a market economy	21	16
Don't know	16	15

a. Values of "Oppose market" as utilized in the multivariate analysis are coded in the order given here.

State ownership (1995a and 1996)

"What do you think about the privatization of state property in Russia? Please look at the card and say which alternative best corresponds to your opinion."

Response[b]	Percentage 1995	Percentage 1996
All property in the economy should be in private hands	2	1
Economic property should for the most part be in private hands	9	9
The shares of private and state property in the economy should be equal	35	41
Economic property should for the most part belong to the state	24	27
All property in the economy should belong to the state	20	15
Don't know	11	8

b. Values of "State ownership" as utilized in the multivariate analysis are coded in the order given here.

Welfarism (1995a and 1996)

Sums "Strongly agree" and "Agree" responses to three statements: (1) "The government ought to guarantee a job to everyone who needs one"; (2) "The state should set food prices"; and (3) "The state should limit the incomes of the rich."

Number of positive responses[c]	Percentage 1995	Percentage 1996
0	4	6
1	15	18
2	32	28
3	49	48

c. Values of "Welfarism" as utilized in the multivariate analysis are coded in the order given here.

Protectionism (1995a and 1996)

"We must protect our industry against competition from foreign firms that are out to seize the Russian market."

Response[d]	Percentage 1995	Percentage 1996
Strongly agree	43	29
Agree	28	38
Indifferent	10	14
Disagree	12	12
Strongly disagree	2	1
Don't know	6	7

d. Values of "Protectionism" as utilized in the multivariate analysis are coded in reverse of the order given here.

No foreign capital (1995a and 1996)

"Russia should attract foreign investment in its economy."

Response[e]	Percentage 1995	Percentage 1996
Strongly agree	10	9
Agree	32	36
Indifferent	19	21
Disagree	21	17
Strongly disagree	5	3
Don't know	13	14

e. Values of "No foreign capital" as utilized in the multivariate analysis are coded in the order given here.

Order over liberty (1995b and 1996)

"It is better to live in a society with strict order than to give people so much freedom that they may destroy society."

Response[f]	Percentage 1995	Percentage 1996
Strongly agree	21	17
Agree	47	46
Indifferent	14	15
Disagree	9	11
Strongly disagree	1	1
Don't know	7	9

f. Values of "Order over liberty" as utilized in the multivariate analysis are coded in reverse of the order given here.

Iron hand (1995a and 1996)

"There is a lot of discussion today about matters of legality, law and order, corruption, and crime in Russia. Various points of view exist about how order should be brought about in our country. So what do you think about this? Use a scale where 1 denotes that order should be introduced at all costs, even if the rights of citizens are violated, and 5 denotes that in introducing order the rights of citizens must not under any circumstances be violated."

Response[g]	Percentage 1995	Percentage 1996
1—Order at all costs	13	10
2	4	5
3	11	12
4	11	13
5—Order without violating rights	55	55
Don't know	5	4

g. Values of "Iron hand" as utilized in the multivariate analysis are coded in reverse of the order given here.

Centralization (1995a)

"Some people think that in Russia everything should be decided by the top organs of government in Moscow, that the center should be strongest. Others think that everything should be decided in the regions, that the regional authorities should be strongest. What do you think about this?"

Response[h]	Percentage
Everything should be decided in Moscow	5
Most questions should be decided in Moscow	7
Some questions should be decided in Moscow and some in the regions	45
Most questions should be decided in the regions	27
Everything should be decided in the regions	11
Don't know	6

h. Values of "Centralization" as utilized in the multivariate analysis are coded in reverse of the order given here.

Strong parliament (1995a)

"Some people believe that the President of Russia should have more powers than the Parliament. Others want the Parliament to have more powers than the President. What is your point of view? Please use a scale from 1 to 5, where 1 denotes that the President should have much more power than Parliament and 5 denotes that Parliament should have much more power than the President."

Response[i]	Percentage
1—President much stronger	18
2	7
3—President and parliament equal	40
4	6
5—Parliament much stronger	17
Don't know	13

i. Values of "Strong parliament" as utilized in the multivariate analysis are coded in the order given here.

Reunite with Ukraine (1995b)

"There exist various views about relations between Russia and Ukraine. Some say that Russia and Ukraine should be completely separate countries. This would correspond to position 1 on a five-point scale. Others think that Russia and Ukraine should be one country, which on the scale would correspond to position 5. Which position on the scale corresponds to your point of view?"

Response[j]	Percentage
1—Russia and Ukraine should be completely separate countries	11
2	4
3	16
4	11
5—Russia and Ukraine should be one country	50
Don't know	9

j. Values of "Reunite with Ukraine" as utilized in the multivariate analysis are coded in the order given here.

Soviet political system (1996)

"What kind of political system, in your opinion, would be most appropriate for Russia?"

Response[k]	Percentage
The Soviet system we had in our country before *perestroika*	33
The political system that exists today	26
Democracy of the Western type	13
Other	10
Don't know	18

k. Values of "Soviet political system" as utilized in the multivariate analysis are coded in reverse of the order given here, except that "Other," like "Don't know," is coded at the mean of the distribution.

Reintegrate USSR (1996)

"Russia should strive for economic and political integration with the former republics of the Soviet Union regardless of the cost."

Response[l]	Percentage
Strongly agree	18
Agree	45
Indifferent	15
Disagree	6
Strongly disagree	1
Don't know	15

l. Values of "Reintegrate USSR" as utilized in the multivariate analysis are coded in reverse of the order given here.

Resist NATO (1996)

"Russia should do everything possible to prevent the former socialist countries of Eastern Europe from entering NATO."

Response[m]	Percentage
Strongly agree	6
Agree	20
Indifferent	21
Disagree	15
Strongly disagree	3
Don't know	35

m. Values of "Resist NATO" as utilized in the multivariate analysis are coded in reverse of the order given here.

Table C.1 Correlation Matrix (Pearson's *r*) for Opinion Variables, 1995[a]

	State ownership	Welfarism	Protectionism	No foreign capital	Order over liberty	Iron hand	Centralization	Strong parliament	Reunite with Ukraine
Oppose market	.41**	.32**	.29**	.37**	.16**	.13**	.04	.09**	.12**
State ownership		.41**	.32**	.32**	.18**	.15**	.06**	.12**	.16**
Welfarism			.44**	.30**	.24**	.13**	.03	.08*	.20**
Protectionism				.28**	.25*	.07**	.01	.08**	.17**
No foreign capital					.11**	.13**	.03	.08**	.05*
Order over liberty						.10**	.03	.01	.17**
Iron hand							.07**	.01	.04*
Centralization								.05**	.04*
Strong parliament									.08**

*p ≤ .05 (two-tailed test)
**p ≤ .01 (two-tailed test)
a. N = 2,774 weighted cases.

Table C.2 Correlation Matrix (Pearson's r) for Opinion Variables, 1996[a]

	State ownership	Welfarism	Protectionism	No foreign capital	Order over liberty	Iron hand	Soviet political system	Reintegrate USSR	Resist NATO
Oppose market	.42**	.38**	.31**	.33**	.20**	.17**	.50**	.09**	.20**
State ownership		.42**	.33**	.31**	.29**	.14**	.46**	.13**	.21**
Welfarism			.41**	.27**	.39**	.12**	.44**	.18**	.27**
Protectionism				.30**	.34**	.11**	.35**	.20**	.32**
No foreign capital					.17**	.13**	.39**	.00	.16**
Order over liberty						.15**	.29**	.21**	.25**
Iron hand							.15**	.04	.09**
Soviet political system								.14**	.22**
Reintegrate USSR									.23**

**$p \leq .01$ (two-tailed test)
a. N = 2,472 weighted cases.

Supplementary Tables

Table D.1. Social Characteristics and the Party-List Vote, 1995 (Differences in Predicted Probabilities)[a]

Analysis and explanatory variables[b]	KPRF	LDPR	Our Home	Yabloko
Bivariate regression				
Urbanization	−.24**	−.02	.10**	.11**
Education	−.28**	−.03	.04	.18**
Occupation				
Worker	.09**	.06**	−.05**	−.05**
Managerial/professional	−.08**	−.08**	.01	.09**
Orthodox	−.02	−.02	.01	−.04**
Ethnic Russian	−.02	.02	−.01	.02
Former member CPSU	.15**	−.04*	−.01	.01
Family income	−.26**	.03	.10**	.08**
New economy				
Private or foreign employer	−.17**	.02	.08**	.07**
Privatized housing	−.02	−.04	.00	.01
Age	.36**	−.11**	−.04	−.09**
Woman	.02	−.07**	−.00	−.03*
Geography				
North	−.31**	−.02	.08**	.09**
East	.02	.20**	−.09**	.03
Incorporating other social characteristics (total effects)				
Urbanization	−.17**	−.01	.07**	.06**
Education	−.07	−.01	−.04	.10**
Occupation				
Worker	.05*	.01	−.06**	−.00
Managerial/professional	.01	−.06**	−.02	.01
Orthodox	−.05*	.00	.00	−.02

Table D.1 (continued)

Analysis and explanatory variables[b]	KPRF	LDPR	Our Home	Yabloko
Ethnic Russian	−.01	.02	−.01	.02
Former member CPSU	.16**	−.03	−.02	−.01
Family income	−.11**	.03	.06*	.01
New economy				
Private or foreign employer	−.05	.01	.04	.00
Privatized housing	−.04	−.04**	.00	.01
Age	.28**	−.08**	−.02	−.06**
Woman	.04	−.09**	−.02	−.02
Geography				
North	−.24**	.01	.03	.05*
East	−.01	.21**	−.07**	−.02
Incorporating all explanatory variables				
Urbanization	−.10**	−.01	.07**	.03
Education	.05	−.00	−.08	.06*
Occupation				
Worker	.06	.00	−.07*	.01
Managerial/professional	−.01	−.01*	−.02	−.01
Orthodox	−.01	.00	−.03	−.02
Ethnic Russian	−.03	.00	−.00	.03*
Former member CPSU	.06	−.00	−.00	−.00
Family income	−.07	−.00	.06*	.00
New economy				
Private or foreign employer	−.01	.00	.04	−.02
Privatized housing	−.06	−.01	−.01	.03*
Age	.09	−.01	−.05	−.03
Woman	.06	−.02*	−.04	−.03
Geography				
North	−.25**	.01	.04	.03
East	.03	.02	−.02	−.02

**p ≤ .01

*p ≤ .05

a. Sample N = 2,143.

b. Explanatory variables coded as in Table 3.1, Chapter 3.

Table D.2. Social Characteristics and the Presidential Vote, 1996 (Differences in Predicted Probabilities)

Analysis and explanatory variables[a]	First round[b]				Runoff[c]	
	Yel.	Zyug.	Leb.	Yav.	Yel.	Zyug.
Bivariate regression						
Urbanization	.26**	−.32**	−.01	.07**	.34**	−.36**
Education	.16**	−.32**	.06*	.11**	.29**	−.35**
Occupation						
Worker	−.06**	.10**	−.01	−.04**	−.11**	.13**
Manag./prof.	.07**	−.06*	−.01	.03	.09**	−.09**
Orthodox	.04*	−.02	−.02	.00	.00	−.00
Ethnic Russian	−.01	−.03	.02	.01	−.06	.04
Former member CPSU	−.06	.10**	−.01	−.01	−.10**	.09**
Family income	.22**	−.35**	.05	.08**	.36**	−.38**
New economy						
Private or foreign empl.	.13**	−.18**	.01	.01	.21**	−.23**
Privatized hous.	.04	−.04*	.02	.02	.06*	−.06*
Age	−.09*	.36**	−.11**	−.10**	−.25**	.34**
Woman	.02	.01	−.00	−.02	.01	−.01
Geography						
North	.18**	−.21**	−.06	.06*	.21**	−.21**
East	−.13**	.10*	−.03	.00	−.18**	.11*
Incorporating other social characteristics (total effects)						
Urbanization	.21**	−.21**	−.04	.04*	.25**	−.27**
Education	.04	−.09*	.03	.06	.07	−.12*
Occupation						
Worker	.00	.03	−.01	−.03	−.05	.06
Manag./prof.	.01	.06	−.03	−.02	−.05	.07
Orthodox	.06*	−.05*	−.02	.02	.02	−.03
Ethnic Russian	−.04	−.02	.03	.01	−.09*	.07*
Former member CPSU	−.06	.10**	−.00	.01	−.12**	.11*
Family income	.14**	−.21**	.05	.02	.24**	−.24**

Table D.2 (continued)

Analysis and explanatory variables[a]	First round[b]				Runoff[c]	
	Yel.	Zyug.	Leb.	Yav.	Yel.	Zyug.
New economy						
Private or foreign empl.	.06	−.06	−.02	−.02	.11*	−.11*
Privatized hous.	.04	−.05**	.02	.02	.07**	−.07**
Age	−.05	.28**	−.08**	−.07**	−.18**	.27**
Woman	.03	−.00	.00	−.03	.02	−.02
Geography						
North	.10*	−.09*	−.09*	.03	.09	−.10
East	−.11	.05	−.05	.01	−.14**	.07
Incorporating all explanatory variables						
Urbanization	.16**	−.04	−.04	.01	.06	−.05*
Education	.03	−.02	−.05	.01	−.01	−.00
Occupation						
Worker	.04	−.04	.01	−.02	.00	−.00
Manag./prof.	−.03	.05	.05	−.00	−.07	.05
Orthodox	.05	−.01	−.00	.00	−.00	.00
Ethnic Russian	.08	−.07	.02	.00	−.04	.03
Former member CPSU	.07	−.01	.03	.01	−.01	−.01
Family income	−.09	−.05*	.13**	.01	.02	−.04
New economy						
Private or foreign empl.	−.00	−.02	−.10*	−.01	.02	−.02
Privatized housing	.01	−.02	.06	.01	.02	−.03
Age	.12	.04	−.07	−.00	−.07	.01
Woman	.07	−.03	.04	−.01	.03	−.04
Geography						
North	.11	−.07*	−.15**	.01	.03	−.02
East	−.19*	.03	−.03	.02	−.19*	.07

**p ≤ .01
*p ≤ .05
a. Explanatory variables coded as in Table 3.1, Chapter 3.
b. Sample N = 1,990.
c. Sample N = 1,937.

Table D.3. Normative Opinions and the Party-List Vote, 1995 (Differences in Predicted Probabilities)[a]

Analysis and explanatory variables	KPRF	LDPR	Our Home	Yabloko
Bivariate regression				
Oppose market	.44**	.04	−.14**	−.20**
State ownership	.43**	.01	−.12**	−.20**
Welfarism	.34**	.04	−.08**	−.22**
Protectionism	.33**	.05**	−.09**	−.19**
No foreign capital	.37**	−.05*	−.13**	−.12**
Order over liberty	.33**	.08**	−.11**	−.16**
Iron hand	.13**	.08**	−.05*	−.05**
Centralization	.10*	−.07*	.02	−.03
Strong parliament	.23**	−.08**	−.08**	.00
Reunite with Ukraine	.23**	−.01	−.02	−.05*
Incorporating social characteristics, current conditions, partisanship, & other opinions (total effects)				
Oppose market	.18**	−.00	−.05	−.08*
State ownership	.13*	−.01	.02	−.04
Welfarism	.08*	−.00	.03	−.05
Protectionism	.09	.02	−.03	−.03
No foreign capital	.01	−.04**	−.09*	.01
Order over liberty	.17**	.01	−.05	−.05
Iron hand	.10*	.04**	−.05	−.01
Centralization	.02	−.04	.02	−.00
Strong parliament	.12**	−.04**	−.05	.00
Reunite with Ukraine	.09*	−.01	.03	.02
Incorporating all explanatory variables				
Oppose market	.18**	−.00	−.06	−.04
State ownership	.08	−.00	.02	−.01
Welfarism	.03	−.00	.04	−.03
Protectionism	.04	.01	−.01	−.01
No foreign capital	−.04	−.03	−.06	.02
Order over liberty	.14*	.01	−.04	−.03
Iron hand	.12**	.01	−.05*	.01
Centralization	.01	−.03*	.02	.02
Strong parliament	.07	−.04**	−.03	.01
Reunite with Ukraine	.11*	−.02	.03	.01

**p ≤ .01; *p ≤ .05

a. Sample N = 2,143.

Table D.4. Normative Opinions and the Presidential Vote, 1996 (Differences in Predicted Probabilities)

Analysis and explanatory variables	First round[a]				Runoff[b]	
	Yel.	Zyug.	Leb.	Yav.	Yel.	Zyug.
Bivariate regression						
Oppose market	−.50**	.68**	−.08*	−.08**	−.77**	.76**
State ownership	−.50**	.58**	.01	−.09**	−.68**	.69**
Welfarism	−.34**	.42**	−.03	−.06	−.47**	.50**
Protectionism	−.37**	.40**	.01	−.04	−.47**	.46**
No foreign capital	−.38**	.43**	−.00	−.03	−.53**	.50**
Order over liberty	−.42**	.42**	.06	−.07*	−.50**	.47**
Iron hand	−.13**	.13**	−.01	−.01	−.19**	.18**
Soviet political system	−.49**	.64**	−.03	−.12**	−.78**	.76**
Reintegrate USSR	−.10	.29**	−.05	−.11**	−.18**	.26**
Resist NATO	−.25**	.35**	−.03	−.06	−.32**	.33**
Incorporating social characteristics, current conditions, partisanship, and other opinions (total effects)						
Oppose market	−.10	.13**	−.04	−.00	−.22*	.17**
State ownership	−.07	.07	.04	−.03	−.12	.12*
Welfarism	−.02	.05	−.05	.02	−.03	.08
Protectionism	−.07	.02	.00	.02	−.07	.05
No foreign capital	−.16*	−.02	.10	.06	−.04	−.02
Order over liberty	−.16*	.03	.13*	.01	−.09	.03
Iron hand	−.03	.00	.00	.03	−.07	.04
Soviet political system	−.22**	.23**	.00	−.06*	−.47**	.41**
Reintegrate USSR	.12	.01	−.02	−.05	.12	−.04
Resist NATO	−.05	.05	.02	−.01	.01	−.01
Incorporating all explanatory variables						
Oppose market	.02	.05	.02	.01	−.07	.03
State ownership	−.01	.02	.11	−.02	.02	.02
Welfarism	.05	.04	−.18**	.01	−.02	.05
Protectionism	−.06	−.04	−.01	.01	.04	−.05
No foreign capital	−.14	.03	.10	.03	−.09	.03
Order over liberty	−.13	.04	.08	.01	−.05	−.00
Iron hand	−.03	.01	−.09*	.02	−.06	.04
Soviet political system	−.08	.06*	.02	−.02*	−.17**	.10**
Reintegrate USSR	.14	.01	−.05	−.01	.07	−.01
Resist NATO	−.06	.06	.09	.01	.00	−.02

**p ≤ .01; *p ≤ .05
a. Sample N = 1,990.
b. Sample N = 1,937.

Table D.5. Assessments of Personal Traits of Five Presidential Candidates, 1996 (Percentages)[a]

Trait and assessment	Yeltsin	Zyuganov	Lebed	Yavlinskii	Zhirinovskii
Knowledge					
Yes or probably yes	64	71	83	71	44
No or probably no	27	15	6	6	4
Don't know	9	14	11	23	15
Strength					
Yes or probably yes	45	47	79	29	32
No or probably no	45	28	7	35	48
Don't know	9	25	15	36	21
Integrity					
Yes or probably yes	39	47	72	49	13
No or probably no	41	26	10	13	59
Don't know	20	27	18	38	28
Vision					
Yes or probably yes	55	59	66	56	39
No or probably no	33	22	15	15	41
Don't know	13	19	19	30	20
Empathy					
Yes or probably yes	28	39	52	31	11
No or probably no	58	34	19	27	64
Don't know	14	27	30	42	24

a. N = 2,472 weighted cases.

Notes

Preface

1. There were 108,589,050 registered voters in Russia at the time of the presidential runoff election in July 1996. The number has probably declined by several million since then. The Russian electorate currently ranks fourth behind the Indian, U.S., and Brazilian electorates. China, the most populous country in the world, has not had democratic national elections. Indonesia also has more people than Russia; it remains to be seen whether its competitive parliamentary election in 1999 will be a harbinger of systematic democratization.

2. Yu. M. Luzhkov, "Otkrytoye pis'mo moskvicham" (Open Letter to Muscovites), handbill in the possession of the author.

3. This term is used in Yu. A. Levada, "'Chelovek politicheskii': Stsena i roli perekhodnogo perioda," in VTsIOM, *Ekonomicheskiye i sotsial'nyye peremeny: Monitoring obshchestvennogo mneniya,* July–August 1996, p. 8.

4. Zyuganov interview in *Pravda Moskvy,* no. 32 (June 1996), p. 1; Luzhkov, "Otkrytoye pis'mo moskvicham."

5. Stephen White, Richard Rose, and Ian McAllister, *How Russia Votes* (Chatham, N.J.: Chatham House, 1997). White is a senior specialist on Russian politics. Rose and McAllister wrote multicountry studies and books on British, American, and Australian politics before becoming interested in the post-Communist transition.

6. Timothy J. Colton and Jerry F. Hough, eds., *Growing Pains: Russian Democracy and the Election of 1993* (Washington, D.C.: Brookings Institution, 1998).

7. Michael Urban, "December 1993 as a Replication of Late-Soviet Electoral Practices," *Post-Soviet Affairs,* 10 (April–June 1994), pp. 127–158; Darrell Slider, Vladimir Gimpel'son, and Sergei Chugrov, "Political Tendencies in Russia's Regions: Evidence from the 1993 Parliamentary Elections," *Slavic Review,* 53 (Fall 1994), pp. 711–732; Richard Sakwa, "The Russian Elections of December 1993," *Europe-Asia Studies,* 47 (March 1995), pp. 195–228; Ralph S. Clem

and Peter R. Craumer, "A Rayon-Level Analysis of the Russian Election and Constitutional Plebiscite of December 1993," *Post-Soviet Geography*, 36 (August 1995), pp. 459–475; Matthew Wyman, Bill Miller, Stephen White, and Paul Heywood, "Parties and Voters in the Elections," in Peter Lentini, ed., *Elections and Political Order in Russia: The Implications of the 1993 Elections to the Federal Assembly* (Budapest: Central European University Press, 1995), pp. 124–142; Michael McFaul, *Russia between Elections: What the December 1995 Results Really Mean* (Washington, D.C.: Carnegie Endowment for International Peace, 1996); Jerry F. Hough, Evelyn Davidheiser, and Susan Goodrich Lehmann, *The 1996 Russian Presidential Election*, Brookings Occasional Papers (Washington, D.C.: Brookings Institution Press, 1996); Daniel Treisman, "Why Yeltsin Won," *Foreign Affairs*, 75 (September–October 1996), pp. 64–77; Erik Depoy, "Boris Yeltsin and the 1996 Russian Presidential Election," *Presidential Studies Quarterly*, 26 (Fall 1996), pp. 1140–1163; Timothy J. Colton, "Economics and Voting in Russia," *Post-Soviet Affairs*, 12 (October–December 1996), pp. 289–317; Richard Rose and Evgeny Tikhomirov, "Russia's Forced-Choice Presidential Election," ibid., pp. 351–379; M. Steven Fish, "The Predicament of Russian Liberalism: Evidence from the December 1995 Parliamentary Elections," *Europe-Asia Studies*, 49 (March 1997), pp. 191–220; Mikhail Myagkov, Peter Ordeshook, and Alexander Sobyanin, "The Russian Electorate, 1991–1996," *Post-Soviet Affairs*, 13 (April–June 1997), pp. 134–166; Stephen White, Matthew Wyman, and Sarah Oates, "Parties and Voters in the 1995 Russian Duma Election," *Europe-Asia Studies*, 49 (July 1997), pp. 767–798; Richard Rose, Evgeny Tikhomirov, and William Mishler, "Understanding Multi-Party Choice: The 1995 Duma Election," ibid., pp. 799–824; Laura Belin and Robert W. Orttung, *The Russian Parliamentary Elections of 1995: The Battle for the Duma* (Armonk, N.Y.: M. E. Sharpe, 1997); Michael McFaul, *Russia's 1996 Presidential Election: The End of Polarized Politics* (Stanford: Hoover Institution Press, 1997); Yitzhak M. Brudny, "In Pursuit of the Russian Presidency: Why and How Yeltsin Won the 1996 Presidential Election," *Communist and Post-Communist Studies*, 30 (1997), pp. 255–275; and David S. Mason and Svetlana Sidorenko-Stephenson, "Public Opinion and the 1996 Elections in Russia: Nostalgic and Statist, Yet Pro-Market and Pro-Yeltsin," *Slavic Review*, 56 (Winter 1997), pp. 698–717.

8. As with election studies, the authors include both scholars of Russia and Eastern Europe and newcomers who made their careers in comparative and American politics. See Ada W. Finifter and Ellen Mickiewicz, "Redefining the Political System of the USSR: Mass Support for Political Change," *American Political Science Review*, 86 (December 1992), pp. 857–874; James L. Gibson, Raymond M. Duch, and Kent L. Tedin, "Democratic Values and the Transformation of the Soviet Union," *Journal of Politics*, 54 (May 1992), pp. 329–371; Raymond

M. Duch, "Tolerating Economic Reform: Popular Support for Transition to a Free Market in the Former Soviet Union," *American Political Science Review,* 87 (September 1993), pp. 590–608; Arthur H. Miller, William M. Reisinger, and Vicki L. Hesli, eds., *Public Opinion and Regime Change: The New Politics of Post-Soviet Societies* (Boulder, Co.: Westview, 1993); William M. Reisinger, Arthur H. Miller, Vicki L. Hesli, and Kristen Maher, "Political Values in Russia, Ukraine and Lithuania: Sources and Implications for Democracy," *British Journal of Political Science,* 24 (April 1994), pp. 183–223; Arthur H. Miller, Vicki L. Hesli, and William M. Reisinger, "Reassessing Mass Support for Political and Economic Change in the Former USSR," *American Political Science Review,* 88 (June 1994), pp. 399–411; William Zimmerman, "Markets, Democracy, and Russian Foreign Policy," *Post-Soviet Affairs,* 10 (April–June 1994), pp. 103–126; Arthur H. Miller, Vicki L. Hesli, and William M. Reisinger, "Comparing Citizen and Elite Belief Systems in Post-Soviet Russia and Ukraine," *Public Opinion Quarterly,* 59 (Spring 1995), pp. 1–40; Geoffrey Evans and Stephen Whitefield, "The Politics and Economics of Democratic Commitment: Support for Democracy in Transition Societies," *British Journal of Political Science,* 25 (October 1995), pp. 485–514; Arthur H. Miller, William M. Reisinger, and Vicki L. Hesli, "Understanding Political Change in Post-Soviet Societies," *American Political Science Review,* 90 (March 1996), pp. 153–166; James L. Gibson, "A Mile Wide But an Inch Deep (?): The Structure of Democratic Commitments in the Former USSR," *American Journal of Political Science,* 40 (May 1996), pp. 396–420; Robert J. Brym, "Re-evaluating Mass Support for Political and Economic Change in Russia," *Europe-Asia Studies,* 48 (July 1996), pp. 751–766; James L. Gibson, "Political and Economic Markets: Changes in the Connection Between Attitudes Toward Political Democracy and a Market Economy Within the Mass Culture of Russia and Ukraine," *Journal of Politics,* 58 (November 1996), pp. 954–984; Matthew Wyman, *Public Opinion in Postcommunist Russia* (New York: St. Martin's, 1997); Arthur H. Miller, Thomas F. Klobucar, William M. Reisinger, and Vicki L. Hesli, "Social Identities in Russia, Ukraine, and Lithuania," *Post-Soviet Affairs,* 14 (July–September 1998), pp. 248–286; the New Russia Barometer reports by Richard Rose and his associates at the University of Strathclyde (used by White, Rose, and McAllister, *How Russia Votes);* and William L. Miller, Stephen White, and Paul Heywood, *Values and Political Change in Postcommunist Europe* (London: Macmillan, 1998).

9. A welcome exception is Matthew Wyman, Stephen White, and Sarah Oates, eds., *Elections and Voters in Post-communist Russia* (Cheltenham, U.K.: Edward Elgar, 1998), which contains papers given at a conference on Russian political parties held at the University of Glasgow in 1997. A companion volume is John Löwenhardt, ed., *Party Politics in Post-Communist Russia* (London: Cass, 1998).

10. As the authors say, the series of New Russia Barometer surveys on which *How Russia Votes* relies is "in no sense . . . a conventional voting study." Its purpose is to "to concentrate on activities of concern to ordinary people in their everyday lives" and to look at elections as part of that undertaking (p. 273). Their election-related surveys were done after the elections (for the 1993 parliamentary election, three to four months afterward); this procedure limits what can be learned about citizen participation and decision making in the campaign. Other scholars have dredged data gathered well in advance of a Russian election for clues about voting. For example, Stephen Whitefield and Geoffrey Evans, in the mistitled "The Russian Election of 1993: Public Opinion in the Transition Experience," *Post-Soviet Affairs,* 10 (January–March 1994), pp. 38–60, rely on a survey carried out in June–August 1993—well before the parliamentary election of that December had been scheduled and before a number of the parties that ran in it had even been formed.

11. I cannot exempt my own published papers from this criticism. See in particular "Economics and Voting in Russia" and "Determinants of the Party Vote," in Colton and Hough, *Growing Pains,* pp. 75–114.

12. Warren E. Miller and J. Merrill Shanks, *The New American Voter* (Cambridge, Mass.: Harvard University Press, 1996). See also J. Merrill Shanks, "Unresolved Issues in Electoral Decisions: Alternative Perspectives on the Explanation of Individual Choice," in M. Kent Jennings and Thomas E. Mann, eds., *Elections at Home and Abroad: Essays in Honor of Warren E. Miller* (Ann Arbor: University of Michigan Press, 1994), pp. 17–38. Miller and Shanks acknowledge a debt to Paul F. Lazarsfeld, Morris Rosenberg, and James Davis on the "logic of causal analysis." They unveiled early versions of the argument in articles in the *British Journal of Political Science* in the 1980s and early 1990s.

1. Subjects into Citizens

1. It is not hyperbole to call the tide of events in Russia and Eastern Europe revolutionary. As David S. Landes reminds us (*The Wealth and Poverty of Nations: Why Some Are So Rich and Some So Poor* [New York: Norton, 1998], p. 187), most of history's great revolutions are "deep rather than fast."

2. Arend Lijphart, *Democracies: Patterns of Majoritarian and Consensus Government in Twenty-One Countries* (New Haven: Yale University Press, 1984), p. 2.

3. *Rossiiskaya gazeta,* March 7, 1997, p. 3.

4. The question was asked in the survey done after the second round of the presidential election (weighted $N = 2,472$). Russians are no more charitable toward their political system on this point than Haitians are. See *The People Have Spoken: Global Views of Democracy* (Washington, D.C.: U.S. Information Agency, Office of Research and Media Reaction, January 1998), p. 42.

5. The awareness scale is based on citizens' knowledge of political facts, taking inspiration from John R. Zaller, *The Nature and Origins of Mass Opinion* (Cambridge: Cambridge University Press, 1992).

6. For the association between political awareness and agreement that Russia is a democracy, omitting "Don't know" responses, $r = -.14$ and $p \leq 01$.

7. Yeltsin took 59.72 percent of the popular vote. The second-ranked candidate, Nikolai Ryzhkov, received a mere 17.56 percent.

8. On the election rules, see Thomas F. Remington and Steven S. Smith, "Political Goals, Institutional Context, and the Choice of an Electoral System: The Russian Parliamentary Election Law," *American Journal of Political Science*, 40 (November 1996), pp. 1253–1279, and Jerry F. Hough, "Institutional Rules and Party Formation," in Timothy J. Colton and Jerry F. Hough, eds., *Growing Pains: Russian Democracy and the Election of 1993* (Washington, D.C.: Brookings Institution, 1998), pp. 37–74.

9. This was a change from the first State Duma election in 1993, when 62 percent of the deputies elected in the districts were independents. See Tsentral'naya izbiratel'naya komissiya Rossiiskoi Federatsii, *Vybory deputatov Gosudarstvennoi Dumy 1995: Elektoral'naya statistika* (Moscow: Ves' Mir, 1996), pp. 145–198.

10. Firsthand analysis of ten regions from 1993 can be found in chaps. 11–20 of Colton and Hough, *Growing Pains.*

11. Since 1995 the council has consisted ex officio of the chief executive and the council chairman of each Russian region.

12. A recent review of fifty-five democracies found twenty-six to elect their presidents directly or through an electoral college bound by popular vote. Of the older Western democracies, the only ones where the people elect the president are the United States, France, Finland, and Ireland. André Blais and Louis Massicotte, "Electoral Systems," in Lawrence LeDuc, Richard G. Niemi, and Pippa Norris, eds., *Comparing Democracies: Elections and Voting in Comparative Perspective* (Thousand Oaks, Calif.: Sage, 1996), pp. 49–81.

13. Timothy J. Colton, "Introduction: The 1993 Election and the New Russian Politics," in Colton and Hough, *Growing Pains,* pp. 1–36.

14. Russia's Choice in fact elected one more deputy overall, on the strength of its superior performance in the single-member districts. Sixty-four LDPR candidates were elected, fifty-nine of them on the party list and five in districts. The number of Russia's Choice nominees elected was sixty-five—forty on its party list and twenty-five in districts.

15. Leon D. Epstein, *Political Parties in Western Democracies* (New York: Praeger, 1967), p. 9.

16. In the first post-Soviet election in 1993, there was no prior date by which electoral associations had to have registered. In 1995 registration had to be com-

pleted by six months before the election. Subsequent legislation has extended the waiting time to one year and tightened up the eligibility criteria somewhat.

17. One hundred thousand signatures were required for the party-list portion of the first State Duma election in 1993, 200,000 for the analogous election in 1995, and 1 million for the 1996 presidential election. In the two Duma elections, no more than 15 percent of the signatures could be collected in any one unit of the Russian Federation; for presidential nominees in 1996, no more than 7 percent could be collected in one unit. A new law in 1999 allowed parties and Duma candidates to substitute a cash deposit for signatures.

18. Eight would-be participants in 1993 were disqualified for irregularities in signatures and documentation. Several of them complained loudly of mistreatment. See Colton, "Introduction," pp. 16–17.

19. Tsentral'naya izbiratel'naya komissiya Rossiiskoi Federatsii, *Vybory deputatov Gosudarstvennoi Dumy 1995*, pp. 71–88. Eighteen of the sixty-nine electoral associations that submitted slates failed to present lists of voters' signatures to the Central Electoral Commission. The remaining eight exclusions were on technical and procedural grounds. When the commission created controversy by refusing to register two well-known political movements, one liberal (Yabloko) and one nationalist (Derzhava, or Great Power), the Russian Supreme Court overturned those decisions. Laura Belin and Robert W. Orttung, *The Russian Parliamentary Elections of 1995: The Battle for the Duma* (Armonk, N.Y.: M. E. Sharpe, 1997), p. 60.

20. I take the term "party family" from the extensive literature on West European parties.

21. Chernomyrdin, first named head of government in December 1992 and not active in the 1993 parliamentary election, was ousted by Yeltsin in March 1998, continuing as leader of Our Home Is Russia. The president nominated him for reappointment as prime minister in August 1998, but parliament refused to confirm him. Sergei Kiriyenko served as prime minister from April to August 1998, Yevgenii Primakov from September 1998 to May 1999, and Sergei Stepashin from May 1999 to August 1999, when he was replaced by Vladimir Putin.

22. Yeltsin distanced himself from Russia's Choice after its defeat in the 1993 Duma election. The group renamed itself Russia's Democratic Choice in 1994. At the end of that year its leader, Yegor Gaidar, broke off personal relations with Yeltsin over the war in Chechnya, saying he had gone "into opposition."

23. Anthony Downs, *An Economic Theory of Democracy* (New York: Harper and Row, 1957), p. 77.

24. The phrase is from Samuel P. Huntington, *The Third Wave: Democratization in the Late Twentieth Century* (Norman: University of Oklahoma Press, 1991).

25. Guillermo O'Donnell and Philippe C. Schmitter, *Transitions from Authoritar-*

ian Rule: Tentative Conclusions about Uncertain Democracies (Baltimore: Johns Hopkins University Press, 1986), p. 3.

26. For general discussion of the all-encompassing nature of transitions in the ex-Communist countries, see Claus Offe, "Capitalism by Democratic Design? Democratic Theory Facing the Triple Transition in Eastern Europe," *Social Research*, 58 (Winter 1991), pp. 865–890, and Juan J. Linz and Alfred Stepan, *Problems of Democratic Transition and Consolidation: Southern Europe, South America, and Post-Communist Europe* (Baltimore: Johns Hopkins University Press, 1996), chaps. 15–21.

27. The RSFSR (Russian Soviet Federative Socialist Republic) was established in 1918, four years before entering the USSR as one of its "union republics." Its federal character was confined to symbolic trappings and to the granting of some administrative autonomy to areas designated as the homelands of ethnic minorities. The RSFSR was renamed the Russian Federation, or simply Russia, in December 1991.

28. Boris Yeltsin, *The Struggle for Russia*, trans. Catherine A. Fitzpatrick (New York: Times Books, 1994), p. 103.

29. Valerie Bunce and Maria Csanádi, "Uncertainty in the Transition: Post-Communism in Hungary," *East European Politics and Society*, 7 (Spring 1993), pp. 272–273.

30. Kenneth Jowitt, *New World Disorder: The Leninist Extinction* (Berkeley: University of California Press, 1992), p. 266.

31. Mary McAuley, *Russia's Politics of Uncertainty* (Cambridge: Cambridge University Press, 1997), p. 4.

32. David D. Laitin, *Identity in Formation: The Russian-Speaking Populations in the Near Abroad* (Ithaca: Cornell University Press, 1998), p. 85.

33. "The outcome of a free election is uncertain before the election occurs because voters can change their minds at the last minute." Downs, *An Economic Theory of Democracy*, p. 77.

34. Adam Przeworski, *Democracy and the Market: Political and Economic Reforms in Eastern Europe and Latin America* (Cambridge: Cambridge University Press, 1991), pp. 12–13.

35. In both 1995 and 1996, armed Interior Ministry personnel could be seen patrolling polling stations in Moscow, keeping vehicles well away from entrances. Officers told me they feared disruption of the voting by Chechen terrorists. Several unexplained bombings and armed attacks on officials took place in Moscow in the summer of 1996, including a midnight explosion that killed three passengers in a subway car just blocks away from where I was staying at the time.

36. As throughout the book, I express votes for Russian parties or candidates as a proportion of the valid ballots cast, excluding invalid or spoiled ballots

(nedeistvitel'nyye byulleteni). In reckoning turnout levels in Chapter 2, however, I include the invalid ballots.

37. These proportions do not sum to 100 percent: 2.8 percent of voters in 1995 voted against all parties on the ballot, as the electoral law entitled them to do. Such an expression of preference is considered a valid ballot in Russia, as opposed to an intentional or unintentional spoiling of the ballot form. The thirty-five first-time participants in 1995 include one party created in 1994 and three organizations which originated before the 1993 election but did not take part in it. Three of the eight holdover parties had been re-registered in different legal form since the 1993 election—Yabloko (which changed from a bloc into an association), Russia's Democratic Choice (a bloc formed around the remnants of the Russia's Choice movement), and KEDR (formerly a movement, now a registered party).

38. The 1995 Russia's Democratic Choice entry was a bloc spanning the eponymous political movement (as the original Russia's Choice movement was renamed in 1994) and three smaller groups.

39. Information about the vote in 1993 was collected in our 1995 pre-election survey, and about the vote in 1995 in the post-election survey. Voters' recall of their 1993 decisions may contain errors and distortions. But, if anything, the tendency to project present preferences into the past would understate between-election flux. For an attempt to make ecological inferences about individual-level volatility from aggregate data, see Mikhail Myagkov, Peter Ordeshook, and Alexander Sobyanin, "The Russian Electorate, 1991–1996," *Post-Soviet Affairs,* 13 (April-June 1997), pp. 134–166.

40. Hilde T. Himmelweit, Patrick Humphreys, and Marianne Jaeger, *How Voters Decide,* 2nd ed. (Milton Keynes, U.K.: Open University Press, 1985), chap. 3; Philip E. Converse and Roy Pierce, *Political Representation in France* (Cambridge, Mass.: Harvard University Press, 1986), pp. 51–54; Donald Granberg and Sören Holmberg, *The Political System Matters: Social Psychology and Voting Behavior in Sweden and the United States* (Cambridge: Cambridge University Press, 1988), chap. 8; Anthony Heath, Roger Jowell, and John Curtice, "Can Labour Win?" in Heath, Jowell, and Curtice, eds., *Labour's Last Chance? The 1992 Election and Beyond* (Aldershot, U.K.: Dartmouth, 1994), p. 22. Compare with the aggregate analysis in Peter Mair, "Party Systems and Structures of Competition," in LeDuc, Niemi, and Norris, *Comparing Democracies,* pp. 83–106.

41. The allegations cannot be conclusively verified, but the burden of evidence suggests that electoral fraud was not a central factor in 1993. See the brief discussion in Colton, "Introduction," pp. 23–26.

42. Fear among supporters of Yeltsin that he might lose to Zyuganov "led to an orchestrated series of statements calling for the suspension of the election and

the formation of a government of national unity." These came from members of his government, confidential advisers, and parliamentarians. Stephen White, Richard Rose, and Ian McAllister, *How Russia Votes* (Chatham, N.J.: Chatham House, 1997), p. 254. For an insider's account of the intrigue, see Aleksandr Korzhakov, *Boris Yel'tsin: Ot rassveta do zakata* (Moscow: Interbuk, 1997). An opinion poll in January 1996 found 96 percent of Russians saying they believed a presidential election should be held on schedule. Richard Rose and Evgeny Tikhomirov, "Russia's Forced-Choice Presidential Election," *Post-Soviet Affairs*, 12 (October–December 1996), p. 360.

43. For the association between the two five-point scales, $r = .37$ ($p \leq .01$).

44. *Rossiiskiye vesti*, December 11, 1993, p. 1.

45. Grigorii Yavlinskii, quoted in White, Rose, and McAllister, *How Russia Votes*, p. 244.

46. Yu. A. Levada, "'Chelovek politicheskii': Stsena i roli perekhodnogo perioda," in VTsIOM, *Ekonomicheskiye i sotsial'nyye peremeny: Monitoring obshchest-vennogo mneniya*, July–August 1996, p. 8.

47. Supporters of the main contenders accused one another of using threats of civil war to fortify their political positions. A pro-Zyuganov handbill given me on a street corner in Moscow, titled "Communists Against Civil War," said the Yeltsin campaign "should bear responsibility under the law for inciting war and the use of force and for intentionally destabilizing society."

48. Data from the 1993 election project that is summarized in Colton and Hough, *Growing Pains*.

49. As a benchmark, in British parliamentary elections the proportion of voters who make up their minds at any time during the campaign has ranged from 11 percent to 28 percent. Ivor Crewe, Anthony Fox, and Neil Day, *The British Electorate 1963–1992: A Compendium of Data from the British Election Studies* (Cambridge: Cambridge University Press, 1995), p. 141. Compare with the U.S. figures in Samuel L. Popkin, *The Reasoning Voter: Communication and Persuasion in Presidential Campaigns* (Chicago: University of Chicago Press, 1991), pp. 120–122. One study found that Americans who make up their minds in the last two weeks of a campaign "behave in a near-random fashion in casting votes for president." J. David Gopolan and Sissie Hadjiharalambous, "Late-Deciding Voters in Presidential Elections," *Political Behavior*, 16 (March 1994), p. 58.

50. The differences in decision timing between 1993 and 1995 seem to reflect a secular change in the direction of greater certainty. The pattern of early choice in 1996 is probably a result of the high visibility of the presidential election more than of any deepening of the changes of 1993 to 1995.

51. Pearson's *r* is .19 between sense of the election's importance and fear of loss of political freedoms, .20 between importance and fear of economic collapse, and

.14 between importance and fear of civil war (in each instance, $p \leq .01$). With citizens' political awareness, the only significant connection is with fear of loss of freedom ($r = .15, p \leq .01$).

52. The improvised 1993 election, in which some of the rules were varied by presidential decree, fits this claim less well than the elections of 1995 and 1996. See Michael Urban, "December 1993 as a Replication of Late-Soviet Electoral Practices," *Post-Soviet Affairs*, 10 (April–June 1994), pp. 127–158, and my introduction to Colton and Hough, *Growing Pains*.

53. See in particular R. Michael Alvarez, *Information and Elections* (Ann Arbor: University of Michigan Press, 1997). Alvarez's main explanatory variable, once the effects of information are taken into account, is the match between citizens' normative opinions on public issues and their perceptions of candidates' issue stands.

54. Valid votes cast for the Duma party lists totaled 53.8 million in 1993 and 67.9 million in 1995. Several million voters died between the elections. New voters would thus have amounted to about one-quarter of the 1995 electorate.

55. Bunce and Csanádi, "Uncertainty in the Transition," pp. 253, 254, 266 (emphasis added).

56. Richard Sakwa, *Russian Politics and Society*, 2nd ed. (London: Routledge, 1996), p. 115 (emphasis added).

57. Geoffrey Evans and Stephen Whitefield, "Identifying the Bases of Party Competition in Eastern Europe," *British Journal of Political Science*, 23 (October 1993), p. 539.

58. White, Rose, and McAllister, *How Russia Votes*, pp. 272–273 (emphasis added).

59. Morris P. Fiorina, "Voting Behavior," in Dennis C. Mueller, ed., *Perspectives on Public Choice* (Cambridge: Cambridge University Press, 1997), p. 391.

60. Consensus has been elusive even in the study of American elections, where the investment of resources has been colossal: "One might expect that the combination of sophisticated methodology, high-quality data, and effective theories would yield a commonly accepted understanding of voting and elections. This has not been the case. Controversy remains: controversy over the reasons that more people do not vote; over how people think about politics; over the relative importance of issues and candidates in presidential elections; over whether congressional elections are primarily national or local elections; over how stable partisan attachments are; over the nature of recent changes in the party system." Richard G. Niemi and Herbert F. Weisberg, "Introduction," in Niemi and Weisberg, eds., *Controversies in Voting Behavior*, 3rd ed. (Washington, D.C.: Congressional Quarterly Press, 1993), p. 10.

61. Quotation from Paul F. Lazarsfeld, Bernard Berelson, and Hazel Gaudet, *The People's Choice: How the Voter Makes up His Mind in a Presidential Campaign*, 3rd ed. (New York: Columbia University Press, 1968), p. 27; original 1944. The

ensuing discussion can be followed in Seymour M. Lipset and Stein Rokkan, "Cleavage Structures, Party Systems, and Voter Alignments: An Introduction," in Lipset and Rokkan, eds., *Party Systems and Voter Alignments: Cross-National Perspectives* (New York: Free Press, 1967), pp. 1–64; Richard Rose, ed., *Electoral Behavior: A Comparative Handbook* (New York: Free Press, 1974); Mark N. Franklin et al., *Electoral Change: Responses to Evolving Social and Attitudinal Structures in Western Countries* (Cambridge: Cambridge University Press, 1992); and Roy Pierce, *Choosing the Chief: Presidential Elections in France and the United States* (Ann Arbor: University of Michigan Press, 1995), chap. 8.

62. The original statement is Angus Campbell, Philip E. Converse, Warren E. Miller, and Donald E. Stokes, *The American Voter* (New York: John Wiley and Sons, 1960). The controversy over party identification and its applicability to Russia will be discussed in Chapter 4.

63. Consult especially V. O. Key, Jr., *The Responsible Electorate* (Cambridge, Mass.: Harvard University Press, 1966); Norman H. Nie, Sidney Verba, and John R. Petrocik, *The Changing American Voter* (Cambridge, Mass.: Harvard University Press, 1976); Franklin et al., *Electoral Change*; Russell J. Dalton, Scott C. Flanagan, and Paul Allen Beck, eds., *Electoral Change in Advanced Industrial Democracies: Realignment or Dealignment?* (Princeton: Princeton University Press, 1984); and Ronald Inglehart, *Culture Shift in Advanced Industrial Society* (Princeton: Princeton University Press, 1990). The theoretical inspiration for much issue-oriented research is Downs, *An Economic Theory of Democracy.*

64. Converse and Pierce, *Political Representation in France*, p. 174. De Gaulle was popularly elected to the presidency only once, in 1965, but was a focal player in national politics from 1940 to 1969.

65. A very good summary of thinking in this area is Helmut Norpoth, "The Economy," in LeDuc, Niemi, and Norris, *Comparing Democracies*, pp. 299–318. For further discussion, see Chapter 3.

66. The clearest short guide to how these considerations interweave is Warren E. Miller and J. Merrill Shanks, *The New American Voter* (Cambridge, Mass.: Harvard University Press, 1996), chaps. 11–14. Scholars have recently been as curious about the ideological issues as about the more applied.

67. An excellent summary is Ivor Crewe and Anthony King, "Are British Elections Becoming More 'Presidential'?", in M. Kent Jennings and Thomas E. Mann, eds., *Elections at Home and Abroad: Essays in Honor of Warren E. Miller* (Ann Arbor: University of Michigan Press, 1994), pp. 181–206. There is fuller discussion in Chapter 6.

68. See the review essay and articles reprinted in Richard G. Niemi and Herbert F. Weisberg, eds., *Classics in Voting Behavior* (Washington, D.C.: Congressional Quarterly Press, 1993), pp. 99–102, 119–159.

69. To repeat, other authors have worked with multistage models, though not as

systematic as Miller and Shanks'. Besides the studies of American politics cited in the previous note, see Pierce, *Choosing the Chief*, and Richard Johnston, André Blais, Elisabeth Gidengil, and Neil Nevitte, *The Challenge of Direct Democracy: The 1992 Canadian Referendum* (Montreal and Kingston: McGill-Queen's University Press, 1996).

70. Miller and Shanks, *The New American Voter*, p. 189.

71. The most important change is the deletion of "issue proximity" scores, which gauge the distance between voters' positions on policy questions and their beliefs about the stances of the election contestants. Critics argue that citizen assessments of where parties or politicians stand on issues are contaminated by their views and voting preferences. For discussion with Russian data, see Chapter 5.

72. Miller and Shanks, *The New American Voter*, p. 212. As they explain more fully on p. 208, the exogenous variables "are included in our analysis because of their own independent effects *and* because of the possibility that they represent shared antecedents that may 'confound' any relationship observed between other explanatory variables and the vote. We 'control' them statistically, thereby removing their confounding influence on the apparent impact of these variables."

73. There are, of course, some studies of elections in such conditions, but they must rely on qualitative analysis and on aggregate data. An imaginative example is Thomas Childers, *The Nazi Voter: The Social Foundations of Fascism in Germany, 1919–1933* (Chapel Hill: University of North Carolina Press, 1983).

74. Richard Johnston, André Blais, Henry E. Brady, and Jean Crête, *Letting the People Decide: Dynamics of a Canadian Election* (Stanford: Stanford University Press, 1992), p. 252.

75. The most comprehensive and informative work is White, Rose, and McAllister, *How Russia Votes*. The analysis there incorporates a number of social characteristics, perceptions of current economic conditions, and issue opinions as independent variables. But it skims partisan attachments and images, defines the relevant issue opinions to be mostly those about alternative regimes, and does not systematically examine such factors as assessments of the performance of incumbent parties and leaders, the personal qualities of leaders, and anticipated performance in office.

76. See White, Rose, and McAllister, *How Russia Votes*, passim but especially pp. 290–292; also Timothy J. Colton, "Determinants of the Party Vote," in Colton and Hough, *Growing Pains*, pp. 75–114, which makes a halfhearted stab at multistage analysis. Briefly in *How Russia Votes* and more extensively with other collaborators, Rose uses a classification technique known as discriminant functional analysis to sort through data about the 1995 election. He identifies five "functions," which are combinations of political, economic

and social "influences," and places Russian parties on the dimensions they define. Richard Rose, Evgeny Tikhomirov, and William Mishler, "Understanding Multi-Party Choice: The 1995 Duma Election," *Europe-Asia Studies,* 49 (July 1997), pp. 799–824. The analysis is quite informative but does not reconstruct the process which produced the agglutination of the functions or the consequent choices of voters. A similar approach is employed in Rose and Tikhomirov, "Russia's Forced-Choice Presidential Election," pp. 351–379, which comes up with four functions that explain that vote.

77. Miller and Shanks, *The New American Voter,* p. 192. Miller and Shanks put "stable social and economic characteristics" in the first stage of their model; "partisan identification" and "policy-related predispositions" next; "current policy preferences" and "perceptions of current conditions" in the third stage; "retrospective evaluations of the president concerning governmental 'results'" in the fourth stage; "impressions of the candidates' personal qualities" in the fifth stage; and "prospective evaluations of the candidates and the parties" in their last stage.

78. I experimented with several other classes of explanatory variables—including political awareness, popular fears about instability resulting from elections, and exposure to the mass media—but did not find them to be theoretically satisfying or systematically related to voting outcomes once other variables were taken into account.

79. Seymour Martin Lipset, *Agrarian Socialism: The Cooperative Commonwealth Federation in Saskatchewan* (Berkeley: University of California Press, 1950). If diverse political doctrines can promote diverse outcomes, so can the same doctrine, differently interpreted. For example, the Keynesian approach to macroeconomic management "acquired multiple meanings in the political and economic arenas of different nations." Peter A. Hall, "Introduction," in Hall, ed., *The Political Power of Economic Ideas: Keynesianism across Nations* (Princeton: Princeton University Press, 1989), p. 5.

80. For example, a woman may be a feminist in part because of her gender, but she cannot be a woman because she is a feminist.

81. Miller and Shanks, *The New American Voter,* p. 379. The same assertion is made for France and the United States in Pierce, *Choosing the Chief.*

82. See the treatment of current conditions as an influence on attitudes in Raymond M. Duch, "Tolerating Economic Reform: Popular Support for Transition to a Free Market in the Former Soviet Union," *American Political Science Review,* 87 (September 1993), pp. 590–608; Arthur H. Miller, Vicki L. Heslie, and William M. Reisinger, "Reassessing Mass Support for Political and Economic Change in the Former USSR," *American Political Science Review,* 88 (June 1994), pp. 399–411; Arthur H. Miller, William M. Reisinger, and Vicki L. Hesli, "Understanding Political Change in Post-Soviet Societies," *American Political Science Review,* 90 (March 1996), pp. 153–166; James L. Gibson, "Politi-

cal and Economic Markets: Changes in the Connection Between Attitudes Toward Political Democracy and a Market Economy Within the Mass Culture of Russia and Ukraine," *Journal of Politics,* 58 (November 1996), pp. 954–984; Robert J. Brym, "Re-evaluating Mass Support for Political and Economic Change in Russia," *Europe-Asia Studies,* 48 (July 1996), pp. 751–766; and William L. Miller, Stephen White, and Paul Heywood, *Values and Political Change in Postcommunist Europe* (London: Macmillan, 1998), chap. 13.

83. Miller and Shanks, *The New American Voter,* p. 496.

84. I assume that the causal sequencing here should not be qualitatively different from that traced in ibid.

85. I put these two sets of causal factors at the same developmental stage because I can find no basis for placing one prior to the other.

86. In addition to the fact that political parties and not groups of parties are on the ballot in Russian parliamentary elections, several of the analytical categories I use—about party leaders and anticipated performance in office—can be related only to parties as such.

87. The party claims its line of descent from the Russian branch of the CPSU, which was formed in June 1990 and was banned along with the rest of the CPSU after the abortive reactionary putsch of August 1991.

88. See Veljko Vujacic, "Gennadii Zyuganov and the 'Third Road,'" *Post-Soviet Affairs,* 12 (April–June 1996), pp. 118–154; Joan Barth Urban and Valerii D. Solovei, *Russia's Communists at the Crossroads* (Boulder, Co.: Westview, 1997); and Evelyn Davidheiser, "The CPRF: Towards Social Democracy or National Socialism?", in Matthew Wyman, Stephen White, and Sarah Oates, eds., *Elections and Voters in Post-communist Russia* (Cheltenham, U.K.: Edward Elgar, 1998), pp. 240–271.

89. As Jerry Hough reminds us, many feared at the time that the LDPR's showing "foreshadowed a Hitler-like breakthrough" in Russia. Hough, "The Failure of Party Formation and the Future of Russian Democracy," in Colton and Hough, *Growing Pains,* p. 669.

90. Of the several candidates who might be classified as centrist, the most successful, Svyatoslav Fedorov, received 0.94 percent of the popular vote in the first round.

91. The comparative literature on electoral systems is immense. Noteworthy contributions are Rein Taagepera and Matthew Soberg Shugart, *Seats and Votes: The Effects and Determinants of Electoral Systems* (New Haven: Yale University Press, 1989); Arend Lijphart, *Electoral Systems and Party Systems: A Study of Twenty-Seven Democracies, 1945–1990* (Oxford: Oxford University Press, 1994); and Gary W. Cox, *Making Votes Count: Strategic Coordination in the World's Electoral Systems* (Cambridge: Cambridge University Press, 1997).

92. Many methodologists would disagree, pointing out that the mathematical as-

sumptions of OLS regression are inconsistent with a binary choice such as voting for one of two presidential candidates. Miller and Shanks defend the method on pragmatic grounds.

93. Two recent studies that use multinomial logit to investigate voting in multiparty elections are Jorge I. Domínguez and James A. McCann, *Democratizing Mexico: Public Opinion and Electoral Choices* (Baltimore: Johns Hopkins University Press, 1996), and Denise V. Powers and James H. Fox, "Echoes from the Past: The Relationship between Satisfaction with Economic Reform and Voting Behavior in Poland," *American Political Science Review*, 91 (September 1997), pp. 617–634.

94. Miller and Shanks, *The New American Voter*, pp. 194, 196.

95. Ibid., p. 195.

96. Gary King, Robert O. Keohane, and Sidney Verba, *Designing Social Inquiry: Scientific Inference in Qualitative Research* (Princeton: Princeton University Press, 1994), p. 29.

2. Transitional Citizens and the Electoral Process

1. Look no further than Article 3(3), which mentions referendums in the same breath with free elections as a "supreme authority" in the land. Not a single national referendum has been held in Russia since the constitution was promulgated in 1993.

2. Voting after the Russian Revolution of 1917 was done by show of hands at public meetings. Stalin instituted a ballot paper system in the late 1930s, but it worked in such a way as to deprive the individual of privacy as relentlessly as before. Any ballot dropped unmarked into the box was tallied as being in favor of the official candidate. Someone could vote against the candidate by crossing out the candidate's name with a pencil, but that required entering a curtained polling stall—a tipoff to prying eyes that the person was abjuring the party line.

3. Theodore H. Friedgut, *Political Participation in the USSR* (Princeton: Princeton University Press, 1979), p. 146. For details on the evolution of the electoral controls, see Timothy J. Colton, *Moscow: Governing the Socialist Metropolis* (Cambridge, Mass.: Harvard University Press, 1995), pp. 88–89, 179–181, 299–300.

4. Valerie Bunce and Maria Csanádi, "Uncertainty in the Transition: Post-Communism in Hungary," *East European Politics and Society*, 7 (Spring 1993), p. 272.

5. For broad comparative perspectives on campaigning, see David Butler and Austin Ranney, eds., *Electioneering: A Comparative Study of Continuity and Change* (Oxford: Clarendon Press, 1992); Shaun Bowler and David M. Farrell,

eds., *Electoral Strategies and Political Marketing* (New York: St. Martin's, 1992); David M. Farrell, "Campaign Strategies and Tactics," in Lawrence LeDuc, Richard G. Niemi, and Pippa Norris, eds., *Comparing Democracies: Elections and Voting in Comparative Perspective* (Thousand Oaks, Calif.: Sage, 1996), pp. 160–183; and David Swanson and Paolo Mancini, *Politics, Media and Modern Democracy* (New York: Praeger, 1996).

6. Russell J. Dalton, *Citizen Politics: Public Opinion and Political Parties in Advanced Western Democracies,* 2nd ed. (Chatham, N.J.: Chatham House, 1996), pp. 43–45.

7. Local electoral commissions post lists of residents/voters on community bulletin boards and at mass transit stops several weeks before voting day. Persons not on the list can ask to be added, provided they have valid identification papers and are not registered as resident in some other place. The *propiska* system, instituted in 1932 as a means of keeping tabs on individuals and restricting rural migration into Soviet cities, has been partially but not fully dismantled in Russia since the late 1980s.

8. Unlike figures reported elsewhere in the book on voting for parties and candidates, these turnout numbers include invalid or spoiled ballots *(nedeistvitel'nyye byulleteni),* which averaged 1.06 percent of the total ballots cast in the four elections. According to official data (Tsentral'naya izbiratel'naya komissiya Rossiiskoi Federatsii, *Vybory deputatov gosudarstvennoi dumy 1995: Elektoral'naya statistika* [Moscow: Ves' Mir, 1996], p. 89), 371,125 of 1,320,619 spoiled ballets for the national party lists in December 1995 were unmarked. The rest were checked off for more than one party, in violation of the rules, or were unintelligible.

9. In Switzerland, women were not entitled to vote until 1971, and many policies are determined by regional governments. In the United States, voter registration laws do much to depress turnout.

10. One preliminary and selective look at evidence from post-Communist countries (Mark N. Franklin, "Electoral Participation," in LeDuc, Niemi, and Norris, *Comparing Democracies,* p. 218) has Russian turnout falling short of most, but more systematic work needs to be done on this question.

11. Russian turnout was in fact higher in the late Soviet period, after the Gorbachev electoral reforms, than since. Some 70 percent of eligible participants voted in the parliamentary elections of March 1990 and 75 percent in the election of Yeltsin as president in June 1991. One study, citing official returns and survey data, found Soviet voting at this time to be "high compared to the norm in the United States and many other industrialized countries." Cynthia S. Kaplan, "New Forms of Political Participation," in Arthur H. Miller, William M. Reisinger, and Vicki L. Hesli, eds., *Public Opinion and Regime Change: The New Politics of Post-Soviet Societies* (Boulder, Co.: Westview,

1993), p. 159. Kaplan explained the result in part in terms of "the pressure to vote enhanced by years of [Soviet] political socialization."

12. See in particular Sidney Verba, Norman Nie, and J. O. Kim, *The Modes of Democratic Participation* (Beverly Hills: Sage, 1971); Samuel H. Barnes and Max Kaase, eds., *Political Action: Mass Participation in Five Western Democracies* (Beverly Hills: Sage, 1979); Ronald Inglehart, *Culture Shift in Advanced Industrial Society* (Princeton: Princeton University Press, 1990), chap. 10; Sidney Verba, Kay Lehman Schlozman, and Henry E. Brady, *Voice and Equality: Civic Voluntarism in American Politics* (Cambridge, Mass.: Harvard University Press, 1995); Richard Topf, "Beyond Electoral Participation," in Hans-Dieter Klingemann and Dieter Fuchs, eds., *Citizens and the State* (Oxford: Oxford University Press, 1995), pp. 52–91; and Dalton, *Citizen Politics*, chaps. 3–4.

13. Ruy A. Teixeira, *The Disappearing American Voter* (Washington, D.C.: Brookings Institution, 1992), pp. 188–189. Respondents in the state-of-the-art study of political participation in the United States over-reported voting in the 1988 presidential election by a whopping 21 percent. For discussion and review of the methodological literature, see Verba, Schlozman, and Brady, *Voice and Equality*, appendix E, and Brian D. Silver, Barbara A. Anderson, and Paul R. Abramson, "Who Overreports Voting?" *American Political Science Review*, 80 (June 1986), pp. 613–624.

14. Scholars have been greatly aided by the fact that "overreporters look a lot like truthful reporters," both in the electoral realm and in other areas, and hence cross-group comparisons involving them are acceptable (Verba, Schlozman, and Brady, *Voice and Equality*, p. 616).

15. The national survey done after the 1993 Duma election and reported in Timothy J. Colton and Jerry F. Hough, eds., *Growing Pains: Russian Democracy and the Election of 1993* (Washington, D.C.: Brookings Institution, 1998), overstated voting by 16 percentage points.

16. Scholars have done more work on the attitudes underlying participation in the former USSR than on participation. But see the useful information in Kaplan, "New Forms of Political Participation," pp. 153–167; Matthew Wyman, *Public Opinion in Postcommunist Russia* (New York: St. Martin's, 1997), pp. 126–128; Donna Bahry and Lucan Way, "Citizen Activism in the Russian Transition," *Post-Soviet Affairs*, 10 (October–December 1994), pp. 330–366; and William M. Reisinger, Arthur H. Miller, and Vicki L. Hesli, "Public Behavior and Political Change in Post-Soviet States," *Journal of Politics*, 57 (November 1995), pp. 941–970. Bahry and Way, relying on a 1992 survey by the Moscow firm ROMIR, found that over the previous three years—going back to the late Soviet period—67 percent of Russians said they had voted in all elections, 11 percent had participated in an election campaign (defined more narrowly than I do, that is, excluding informal attempts to influence others' votes), 13 percent

had contacted a public official, and 15 percent had participated in protest activity. Reisinger, Miller, and Hesli do not examine voting.

17. Verba, Schlozman, and Brady, *Voice and Equality,* p. 51, and, for rather higher numbers for Britain, Geraint Parry, George Moyser, and Neil Day, *Political Participation and Democracy in Britain* (Cambridge: Cambridge University Press, 1992), chap. 3.

18. Contacting officials was legitimate and widely practiced under Soviet rule. See Wayne DiFranceisco and Zvi Gitelman, "Soviet Political Culture and 'Covert Participation' in Policy Implementation," *American Political Science Review,* 78 (September 1984), pp. 603–621, and Donna Bahry, "Politics, Generations, and Change in the USSR," in James R. Millar, ed., *Politics, Work, and Daily Life in the USSR: A Survey of Former Soviet Citizens* (Cambridge: Cambridge University Press, 1987), pp. 76–84. Reisinger, Miller, and Hesli, "Public Behavior and Political Change," pp. 953–954, state that at the beginning of the 1990s contacting of public officials and newspapers in Russia was similar to Western levels.

19. Dalton, *Citizen Politics,* pp. 54, 74. The most frequent participants in rallies, boycotts, and the like were the residents of eastern Germany, formerly the Communist-ruled German Democratic Republic. Fifty-two percent of the adults there had participated in a challenging act of protest and 67 percent had signed a petition. Reisinger, Miller, and Hesli, "Public Behavior and Political Change," p. 954, report survey results from 1990 to 1992 giving a much higher incidence of lifetime protest behavior in Russia.

20. For the purposes of Figure 2.1, voting includes a self-reported vote in either the 1995 or the 1993 election.

21. An interesting essay on turnout in Russia refers to such individuals as "principled abstainers." Ian McAllister and Stephen White, "To Vote or Not to Vote: Election Turnout in Post-communist Russia," in Matthew Wyman, Stephen White, and Sarah Oates, eds., *Elections and Voters in Post-communist Russia* (Cheltenham, U.K.: Edward Elgar, 1998), p. 23. The value of McAllister and White's study is diminished by the fact that their data come entirely from a pre-election survey in 1993. They thus have no information on who among the principled abstainers actually abstained. The citizens they call "uncommitted abstainers" are individuals who said in the interview they did not know for whom they were going to vote—an attitude that is not necessarily indicative of even the intent to abstain.

22. For comparative analysis of sociological and other determinants of nonvoting, see G. Bingham Powell, Jr., "Voting Turnout in Thirty Democracies: Partisan, Legal, and Socio-Economic Influences," in Richard Rose, ed., *Electoral Participation: A Comparative Analysis* (Beverly Hills: Sage, 1980), pp. 5–34; Raymond E. Wolfinger and Steven J. Rosenstone, *Who Votes?* (New Haven: Yale Univer-

sity Press, 1980); G. Bingham Powell, Jr., "American Voting Turnout in Comparative Perspective," *American Political Science Review*, 80 (March 1986), pp. 17–43; Robert W. Jackman, "Political Institutions and Voter Turnout in the Industrial Democracies," ibid., 81 (June 1987), pp. 405–423; Steven J. Rosenstone and John Mark Hansen, *Mobilization, Participation, and Democracy in America* (New York: Macmillan, 1993); Richard Topf, "Electoral Participation," in Klingemann and Fuchs, *Citizens and the State*, pp. 39–43; Joan Font and Rosa Virós, eds., *Electoral Abstention in Europe* (Barcelona: Institut de Ciències Politiques i Socials, 1995); Franklin, "Electoral Participation," pp. 216–235; Teixeira, *The Disappearing American Voter;* and Richard J. Timpone, "Structure, Behavior, and Voter Turnout in the United States," *American Political Science Review*, 92 (March 1998), pp. 145–158.

23. The correlation between age group (categories described in Table 2.12) and voting in 1995 is .11 ($p \leq .01$), but it rises to .17 ($p \leq .01$) if persons seventy and older are excluded.

24. In a related phenomenon, former members of the CPSU vote at higher rates in post-Soviet elections. In 1995 turnout among ex-CPSU members was 12 percentage points higher than turnout among persons who never belonged to the party ($r = .10$, $p \leq .01$). The difference existed among all age and educational groups.

25. Bahry and Way ("Citizen Activism in the Russian Transition," p. 349) argue convincingly from indirect evidence that pressure from the Soviet authorities to vote in single-candidate elections made participation a personal habit for many older people: "Mobilization brought people to the polls, and seems to have left them there." For a similar claim that ingrained deference brings about higher turnout among rural dwellers, and also greater support for conservative candidates, see Gavin Helf and Jeffrey Hahn, "Old Dogs and New Tricks: Party Elites in the Russian Regional Elections of 1990," *Slavic Review*, 51 (Fall 1992), pp. 511–530. In the 1996 presidential campaign, Boris Yeltsin's team used flashy television and billboard ads to try to persuade young people to come to the polls. The drive met with some success. Among our survey respondents, the gap in turnout between young and middle-aged voters decreased by about 5 percentage points as compared to 1995.

26. Cf. an important comparative study of the social psychology of modernization, which found that regardless of curriculum persons who had been in school longer were "better informed and verbally more fluent . . . [had] a stronger sense of personal and social efficacy . . . [and] participated more actively in communal affairs." Alex Inkeles and David H. Smith, *Becoming Modern: Individual Change in Six Developing Countries* (Cambridge, Mass.: Harvard University Press, 1974), p. 143.

27. All told, persons with less than five years of formal schooling, most of whom

are in the older age groups, were about 7 percentage points less likely than the average citizen to vote in 1995. Russians with elementary, secondary, and technical educations voted at about the mean rate. Those with a higher education were 6 percent more likely than average to vote. Correlation between a five-point education index (see Table 2.12) and turnout to vote in 1995 is .08 ($p \leq$ .01). The correlation goes down for citizens sixty-nine or younger, to .05 ($p \leq$ .01).

28. The number of persons in our sample who were born in 1925 or earlier and completed a higher education is only twenty-eight. Some of these individuals may well have graduated after 1953. There are some other differences in voting participation by social background, but none as great as those for age and education. Residents of villages and small towns were 5 percent more likely than average to vote in December 1995, and Russians with family incomes in the top fifth were 4 percent more likely. There was no measurable difference between the sexes, even though men vote more frequently than women in many countries.

29. See the review of the U.S. data in Warren E. Miller and J. Merrill Shanks, *The New American Voter* (Cambridge, Mass.: Harvard University Press, 1996), pp. 100–106. As measures of connectedness, Miller and Shanks use married status and four other indicators: home ownership, years in the home, years in the community, and church attendance. Home ownership has a radically different meaning in the Russian context. Years in the community has some relationship to turnout in Russia, but it disappears once you control for age, and church attendance is wholly unrelated to turnout. We did not ask respondents about years in the home.

30. For the association of voting in 1995 with both married status and neighborliness, $r = .11$ ($p \leq .01$).

31. Rosenstone and Hansen, *Mobilization, Participation, and Democracy in America*, pp. 164–171; Gary W. Cox, Frances M. Rosenbluth, and Michael F. Thies, "Mobilization, Social Networks, and Turnout: Evidence from Japan," *World Politics,* 50 (April 1998), pp. 447–474.

32. The answers for nonvoting in the second round of the presidential election are not given here because they are for most informants very close to the first-round answers.

33. Any Russian whose domicile is other than where he is on the official ledger, as kept by the local constabulary, runs the risk of being left off the voters' list there and also being unable to gain access to the polling station near his approved place of residence.

34. In the original formulation of the idea: "'Internal efficacy' is the individual's belief that means of influence are available to him. 'External efficacy' is the belief that the authorities or regime are responsive to influence attempts." George

I. Balch, "Multiple Indicators in Survey Research: The Concept 'Sense of Political Efficacy,'" *Political Methodology*, 1 (Spring 1974), p. 24. I am grateful to James Gibson for this reference.

35. Some of these questions were administered in one of the first systematic mass surveys of Russian opinion, done in the city of Yaroslavl in 1990. The responses were somewhat less cynical than those we evoked in 1995. See Jeffrey W. Hahn, "Continuity and Change in Russian Political Culture," *British Journal of Political Science*, 21 (October 1991), pp. 393–421. See also Stephen White, Richard Rose, and Ian McAllister, *How Russia Votes* (Chatham, N.J.: Chatham House, 1997), pp. 50–54; Wyman, *Public Opinion in Postcommunist Russia*, pp. 123–131; and William Mishler and Richard Rose, "Trust, Distrust and Skepticism: Popular Evaluations of Civil and Political Institutions in Post-Communist Societies," *Journal of Politics*, 59 (May 1997), pp. 418–451.

36. Seventy-one percent of Russian respondents in 1995 said they follow political events sometimes or all the time, and the same percentage said they were interested or very interested in the Duma campaign. Compare to Dalton, *Citizen Politics*, pp. 26–27 (covering the United States, Britain, Germany, and France), and Warren E. Miller and Santa Traugott, *American National Election Studies Data Sourcebook, 1952–1986* (Cambridge, Mass.: Harvard University Press, 1989), pp. 297–298.

37. Miller and Traugott, *American National Election Studies Data Sourcebook*, pp. 264.

38. Ibid., pp. 264–265. Cf. John E. Hughes and M. Margaret Conway, "Public Opinion and Political Participation," in Barbara Norrander and Clyde Wilcox, eds., *Understanding Public Opinion* (Washington, D.C.: Congressional Quarterly Press, 1997), pp. 193–197, and Ola Listhaug, "The Dynamics of Trust in Politicians," in Klingemann and Fuchs, *Citizens and the State*, pp. 272–277, which analyzes Norway, Sweden, Denmark, and the Netherlands from the late 1960s to the late 1980s. About one-third to two-thirds of citizens in all these countries except Denmark disagreed with versions of the "Don't care" statement, with large fluctuations over time. In Denmark, only 15 to 20 percent disagreed—still higher than in Russia—but the Danish question is worded in such a way as to incur a more cynical response.

39. In our survey after the 1995 Duma election, expressions of distrust outnumbered expressions of trust by 59 percent to 29 percent for the president, by 51 percent to 39 percent for the Russian government, and by 47 percent to 35 percent for parliament. Trust prevailed by 45 percent to 42 percent for the respondent's regional government, by 48 percent to 41 percent for local government, by 45 percent to 39 percent for the courts, and by 70 percent to 17 percent for the army. The Russian Orthodox Church was more trusted than any state agency—by 72 percent to 11 percent.

40. Differences of question wording and variation from country to country in the West impede precise comparison. But see U.S. data on whether the federal government can be trusted "to do what is right" in Miller and Traugott, *American National Election Studies Data Sourcebook,* p. 260, and the West European figures given in Ola Listhaug and Matti Wiberg, "Confidence in Political and Private Institutions," in Klingemann and Fuchs, *Citizens and the State,* pp. 304–306. See also the multisided discussion in Joseph S. Nye, Jr., Philip D. Zelikow, and David C. King, eds., *Why People Don't Trust Government* (Cambridge, Mass.: Harvard University Press, 1997).

41. Such questions would be appropriate in other countries in which democracy is but half-built. See especially Jorge I. Domínguez and James A. McCann, *Democratizing Mexico: Public Opinion and Electoral Choices* (Baltimore: Johns Hopkins University Press, 1996), chap. 6. See also the scattered data in *The People Have Spoken: Global Views of Democracy* (Washington, D.C.: U.S. Information Agency, Office of Research and Media Reaction, January 1998).

42. For an account of the first steps with these techniques in the late Soviet period, see Colton, *Moscow,* pp. 603–630.

43. I set aside here work through members of political parties, who make up only 1 percent of adult Russians. Affective ties with parties are thoroughly discussed in Chapter 4.

44. The wording of the question was carefully chosen here, since advertising is often stuffed illegally into mailboxes in Russian apartment buildings in addition to being delivered through the post. Our post-election interviews in 1995 and 1996 did not ask about the quantity of materials seen by voters, only whether they had encountered such materials or not. But the pre-election survey in 1995 asked about the quantity of posters encountered in the vicinity of the respondent's home in the preceding seven days. Five percent of respondents said they had seen many posters, 30 percent that they had seen a few, and 64 percent that they had seen none. More politically engaged Russians seem to have a keener eye for visual propaganda. In 1995, 79 percent of citizens in the lowest quintile of the population by political awareness said they had noticed no campaign posters in the previous week, whereas 51 percent of the most aware individuals said they had noticed none.

45. Yeltsin's advantage was greater on both counts in the seventeen-day interval between the first round and the runoff vote. Sixty-four percent of respondents who received mailbox materials said they received more from the Yeltsin campaign, and 77 percent gave Yeltsin the edge in materials distributed or displayed on the street. We did not ask questions about the source of campaign materials in connection with the 1995 parliamentary campaign.

46. An average of 20 percent of American voters report being contacted by a polit-

ical party (Hughes and Conway, "Public Opinion and Political Participation," p. 194). About 30 percent of British voters were contacted in the election of 1983, down from over 50 percent in 1951 (Dennis Kavanagh, "The United Kingdom," in Butler and Ranney, *Electioneering*, p. 232). In France, though, door-to-door canvassing "is unknown" (Jean Charlot and Monica Charlot, "France," in Butler and Ranney, *Electioneering*, p. 151).

47. The correlation between the size of the citizen's community of residence and receipt of some printed materials is .32 in 1995 and .27 in 1996 (for both, $p \leq$ .01); for being canvassed, it is .12 ($p \leq .01$) and .05 ($p \leq .05$).

48. In the United States in 1992, 3 percent of citizens worked for a party or candidate (no lower than the Russian figures), but 8 percent went to campaign meetings, 6 percent gave money, and 11 percent wore a button or had bumper stickers on their cars. In some other Western democracies, campaign participation may be less. See Dalton, *Citizen Politics*, pp. 47–51. In the United States at the turn of the century, though, one acute observer of campaigns described "a continuous series of meetings of every kind, of every shade of importance, and in every place . . . Wherever there is, and whenever it is possible to collect, a gathering of human beings, floods of oratory are poured forth on behalf of the parties, day after day, during the whole of the campaign." He estimated that about 90 percent of American citizens attended such meetings in presidential election years. M. Ostrogorski, *Democracy and the Organization of Political Parties* (New York: Macmillan, 1902), vol. II, p. 308.

49. In 1995 more attempts were made to influence the party-list vote (20 percent) than the district vote (14 percent). There was much overlap, partly because so many district candidates were party nominees.

50. In the United States, for instance, 32 percent of citizens tried to affect someone else's vote in 1984, 29 percent in 1988, and 38 percent in 1992. Dalton, *Citizen Politics*, p. 49.

51. For the association between political awareness and attempts to influence in the 1996 presidential election, $r = .13$ ($p \leq .01$). Thirty-nine percent of respondents in the most aware quintile said they tried to exert influence, but only 18 percent of persons in the bottom quintile.

52. See especially Robert D. Putnam, *Making Democracy Work: Civic Traditions in Modern Italy* (Princeton: Princeton University Press, 1993). The mobilizing role of secondary associations, especially labor unions, was brought out in some early studies of American elections (in particular, Bernard R. Berelson, Paul F. Lazarsfeld, and William N. McPhee, *Voting: A Study of Opinion Formation in a Presidential Campaign* [Chicago: University of Chicago Press, 1954], chap. 3), but has not been scrutinized recently. There is good discussion in a different country setting in Scott C. Flanagan et al., *The Japanese Voter* (New Haven: Yale University Press, 1991).

53. This is precisely the same proportion found in a leading American survey. Verba, Schlozman, and Brady, *Voice and Equality,* p. 147.

54. We repeated the question about attempts by management to influence voting, but not about whether the advice was taken, after the presidential election in 1996. More employees, 13 percent, said leaders of their work unit had favored a candidate; only 8 percent of this subgroup of employees had experienced similar pressure in 1995. For about four-fifths of them, the candidacy promoted in both rounds of the election was that of the incumbent, Yeltsin. Management efforts were in vain, as the proportion of workers pressured to vote for Yeltsin in the first round who did vote for him (34 percent) was exactly equal to the Yeltsin vote in our whole sample.

55. We asked about organizational memberships in closed-ended questions. Of 2,774 respondents (in the post-election survey), 1,136 were union members, but the biggest enrollment after that was the 76 persons in home and school committees. Other organizational types were athletic and recreational (31 members), religious (31), entrepreneurs (20), cultural (16), street patrols (16), community improvement (13), women's (13), charitable (12), environmental (8), patriotic (4), and ethnic (2). Bahry and Way, "Citizen Activism in the Russian Transition," p. 335, found that 40 percent of Russians in 1992 had participated in at least one of sixteen kinds of public organization over the past three years. They excluded persons who were members of an organization but were not active in it.

56. See Verba, Schlozman, and Brady, *Voice and Equality,* pp. 58–65, 79–81, and James E. Curtis, Edward G. Grabb, and Douglas E. Baer, "Voluntary Association Membership in Fifteen Countries: A Comparative Analysis," *American Sociological Review,* 57 (April 1992), pp. 139–152. Verba, Schlozman, and Brady found 79 percent of Americans to belong to at least one association in the late 1980s and 41 percent to be in four or more associations.

57. Compare with the 14 percent of organizational members—in a much larger associational pool—asked to vote in the authoritative study of the United States (Verba, Schlozman, and Brady, *Voice and Equality,* p. 147).

58. Sixty-four percent of citizens who said an association gave them advice on the vote identified a trade union as the source, followed by women's organizations (6 percent) and charitable organizations (4 percent).

59. Farrell, "Campaign Strategies and Tactics," in LeDuc, Niemi, and Norris, *Comparing Democracies,* pp. 173–175.

60. Figures in Lawrence LeDuc, Richard G. Niemi, and Pippa Norris, "Introduction: The Present and Future of Democratic Elections," in LeDuc, Niemi, and Norris, *Comparing Democracies,* pp. 45–48. For background on the Soviet and post-Soviet mass media, see Mark W. Hopkins, *Mass Media in the Soviet Union* (New York: Pegasus, 1970), and Ellen Mickiewicz's two books, *Split Signals:*

Television and Politics in the Soviet Union (New York: Oxford University Press, 1988), and *Changing Channels: Television and the Struggle for Power in Russia* (New York: Oxford University Press, 1997).

61. See the informative analysis in Laura Roselle Helvey, "Television and the Campaign," and Joel M. Ostrow, "The Press and the Campaign," both in Colton and Hough, *Growing Pains.* See also my chapter "The Mass Media and the Electorate" in the same volume, pp. 267–290.

62. In the week of the Duma campaign in which our respondents were interviewed, 29 percent of them had not discussed politics with friends or family (see Table 2.7), whereas only 15 percent had not seen something about the campaign on television.

63. Our 1996 survey found 94 percent of our respondents watched some television, 68 percent listened to the radio, and 61 percent read newspapers. For each medium a certain portion of the population—7 percent for television, 13 percent for radio, and 9 percent for newspapers—is attentive in general but says it does not receive campaign information from it.

64. Fifty-one percent of survey respondents said in the post-election interview that they had watched news programs about the campaign often. Thirty-two percent had watched TV advertising often and 33 percent said they had watched speeches and debates often. In the United States, recent research, revising previous interpretations, shows television news programs to be a more important source of campaign-related information than political advertising. See Xinshu Zhao and Steven Chaffee, "Campaign Advertisements versus Television News as Sources of Political Issue Information," *Public Opinion Quarterly,* 59 (Spring 1995), pp. 41–65.

65. Survey respondents were asked which station they watched "most often" *(chashche vsego).* Most insisted on volunteering more than one channel. Eighty-nine percent of television viewers said they got campaign news often from Channel One, 49 percent from Channel Two, and 18 percent from NTV. For information about news viewing from 1996 broken down by newscast, see the Russian survey reported in VTsIOM, *Ekonomicheskiye i sotsial'nyye peremeny: Monitoring obshchestvennogo mneniya,* January-February 1997, p. 54. According to that source, 57 percent of Russian adults regularly viewed *Vremya* (Time), the main evening news show on Channel One, followed by 51 percent who watched Channel Two's *Vesti* (News) and 20 percent who watched NTV's *Segodnya* (Today).

66. Since newspapers are perused one at a time, we had readers recite all national papers in which they had read stories on the election. *Komsomol'skaya pravda* was a regular source for 32 percent of readers of the national press, *Argumenty i fakty* for 30 percent, *Trud* for 19 percent, and *Izvestiya* for 16 percent. Russian surveys indicate that *Argumenty i fakty* is the most widely read national news-

paper in Russia, followed by *Komsomol'skaya pravda,* but *Komsomol'skaya pravda*'s daily distribution probably makes it a more useful source of campaign news. On newspaper readership, see VTsIOM, *Ekonomicheskiye i sotsial'nyye peremeny: Monitoring obshchestvennogo mneniya,* January–February 1997, p. 54.

67. For fuller analysis from 1993 data, see Colton, "The Mass Media and the Electorate," pp. 272–276. The data for 1995 and 1996 show little change from 1993.

68. Pearson's *r* for the association between community size and regular exposure to political information in the media in the 1996 campaign is .13 for radio ($p \leq$ .01), $-.07$ for the local press ($p \leq .01$), and does not attain significant values for television and the national press.

69. A pathbreaking study is Shanto Iyengar and Donald R. Kinder, *News That Matters: Television and American Opinion* (Chicago: University of Chicago Press, 1987). See more generally Diana C. Mutz, Paul M. Sniderman, and Richard A. Brody, eds., *Political Persuasion and Attitude Change* (Ann Arbor: University of Michigan Press, 1996).

70. Regional and municipal governments also have much influence over the print and electronic media at the local level.

71. Statistics from Tsentral'naya izbiratel'naya komissiya Rossiiskoi Federatsii, *Vybory deputatov gosudarstvennoi dumy 1995,* p. 57; White, Rose, and McAllister, *How Russia Votes,* p. 215; Sarah Oates and Laura Roselle Helvey, "Russian Television's Mixed Messages: Parties, Candidates, and Control in Election Campaigns, 1995–1996," paper presented at annual meeting of American Political Science Association, Washington, D.C., August 1997; Michael McFaul, *Russia's 1996 Presidential Election: The End of Polarized Politics* (Stanford: Hoover Institution Press, 1997), pp. 20, 33–34. See also Mickiewicz, *Changing Channels,* chap. 8, and Laura Belin and Robert W. Orttung, *The Russian Parliamentary Elections of 1995: The Battle for the Duma* (Armonk, N.Y.: M. E. Sharpe, 1997), chap. 6.

72. Forty-three percent of our survey respondents in 1995 and 41 percent in 1996 expressed distrust in the media. Especially in 1996, scores for trust of the media were highly correlated with degree of trust or distrust in the Russian government and in President Yeltsin (for both dyads *r* was .33 in 1995 and .47 in 1996).

73. The exact proportion of survey respondents saying media coverage was unbalanced was 38 percent in 1995, 52 percent for the first round of the 1996 presidential election, and 53 percent for the second round. Ninety-five percent of those who detected imbalance in 1996 said it operated in President Yeltsin's favor in the first round of the election, and 98 percent said it did so in the second round.

74. Pearson's $r = .18$ in 1995 and .16 in 1996 (for both, $p \leq .01$).

75. See the general discussion of the difficulty of translating money into electoral and other political influence in Daniel Treisman, "Dollars and Democratization: The Role and Power of Money in Russia's Transitional Elections," *Comparative Politics*, 31 (October 1998), pp. 1–21.

76. The politically aware are more likely to be exposed to media information to begin with but are also more likely to be influenced by what they consume. This latter effect is more noticeable for newspaper readers, especially in the 1995 election. For 1996, $r = -.06$ between political awareness and interpersonal influence, .06 between awareness and influence by television, and .15 between awareness and influence by the press. For all three dyads, $p \leq .01$.

77. For the political parties, respondents were handed a card showing a drawing of a glass thermometer with 0, 50, and 100 degrees marked and told: "Our thermometer has a scale from 0 to 100 degrees. Zero degrees denotes that you very much dislike this party or [electoral] bloc, 50 degrees denotes that you like and dislike this party or bloc in equal measure, and 100 degrees that you like the party or bloc a great deal. The part of the scale from 0 to 50 degrees denotes that to a greater or lesser degree you dislike the party or bloc, and from 50 to 100 degrees it denotes that to a greater or lesser degree you like the party or bloc." The respondent was then asked which number from 0 to 100 best reflected his attitude toward each party. The questions for district and presidential candidates were reworded accordingly.

78. Walter Lippmann, *Public Opinion* (New York: Free Press, 1965); original 1922.

3. Society in Transformation

1. Parties and quasi-parties named after social groups include the Agrarians, Women of Russia, and KRO (the Congress of Russian Communities), all of which fell a percentage point or two shy of the 5 percent threshold in the 1995 Duma election, and the more obscure Union of Labor, NUR Moslem Movement, Association of Lawyers, and Union of Housing and Municipal Workers. Two blocs in the 1995 parliamentary election courted various have-not groups, including pensioners, veterans, invalids, neglected children, and swindled stockholders. The broader-gauged KPRF made gestures to pensioners and industrial workers and the LDPR to Russian Orthodox believers. A youth-oriented movement called Future of Russia/New Names participated in the 1993 Duma election and got about 1 percent of the votes. Boris Yeltsin has sought the votes of young people and the liberal parties have serenaded intellectuals, the "technical intelligentsia," and entrepreneurs. A Movement in Defense of the Army and Defense Industry was formed in 1997.

2. This point is deftly made in Stephen White, Richard Rose, and Ian McAllister, *How Russia Votes* (Chatham, N.J.: Chatham House, 1997), p. 147.

3. Mark N. Franklin et al., *Electoral Change: Responses to Evolving Social and Attitudinal Structures in Western Countries* (Cambridge: Cambridge University Press, 1992), pp. 4–5.

4. Seymour M. Lipset and Stein Rokkan, "Cleavage Structures, Party Systems, and Voter Alignments: An Introduction," in Lipset and Rokkan, eds., *Party Systems and Voter Alignments: Cross-National Perspectives* (New York: Free Press, 1967), pp. 1–64.

5. Russell J. Dalton, "Political Cleavages, Issues, and Electoral Change," in Lawrence LeDuc, Richard G. Niemi, and Pippa Norris, eds., *Comparing Democracies: Elections and Voting in Comparative Perspective* (Thousand Oaks, Calif.: Sage, 1996), pp. 319–342 (quotation at p. 331). For further discussion along these lines, see especially Russell J. Dalton, Scott C. Flanagan, and Paul Allen Beck, eds., *Electoral Change in Advanced Industrial Democracies: Realignment or Dealignment?* (Princeton: Princeton University Press, 1984); Martin Harrop and William Miller, *Elections and Voters: A Comparative Introduction* (New York: New Amsterdam Books, 1987), chaps. 6–7; Franklin et al., *Electoral Change;* and Paul Nieuwbeerta, *The Democratic Class Struggle in Twenty Countries, 1945–1990* (Amsterdam: Thesis Publishers, 1995). Spirited defenses of the continued importance of social structure are offered in Herbert Kitschelt, *The Transformation of European Social Democracy* (Cambridge: Cambridge University Press, 1994), chap. 2; Roy Pierce, *Choosing the Chief: Presidential Elections in France and the United States* (Ann Arbor: University of Michigan Press, 1995); and Jeff Manza, Michael Hout, and Clem Brooks, "Class Voting in Capitalist Democracies since World War II: Dealignment, Realignment, or Trendless Fluctuation?" *Annual Review of Sociology,* 21 (1995), pp. 137–162.

6. Warren E. Miller and J. Merrill Shanks, *The New American Voter* (Cambridge, Mass.: Harvard University Press, 1996), p. 215.

7. The clearest statement is Valerie Bunce and Maria Csanádi, "Uncertainty in the Transition: Post-Communism in Hungary," *East European Politics and Society,* 7 (Spring 1993), pp. 240–275. A qualified claim that electoral politics "may have no stable basis in sets of interests derived from social structural locations" is in Geoffrey Evans and Stephen Whitefield, "Identifying the Bases of Party Competition in Eastern Europe," *British Journal of Political Science,* 23 (October 1993), pp. 521–548 (quotation at p. 539). See also White, Rose, and McAllister, *How Russia Votes,* pp. 64–67, and Stephen E. Hanson, "Ideology, Uncertainty and the Rise of Anti-System Parties in Post-Communist Russia," in John Löwenhardt, ed., *Party Politics in Post-Communist Russia* (London: Cass, 1998), pp. 101–104.

8. Most early studies of Russian voting include social variables, although not in the kind of multistage analysis I undertake here. For instance, White, Rose, and McAllister in *How Russia Votes* search out the electoral effects of sex, religion, age, education, book ownership, ethnicity (Russian versus non-Russian), ur-

banization, and geography (European versus Asian Russia). My analysis of the 1993 State Duma election incorporates eleven sociological variables. Timothy J. Colton, "Determinants of the Party Vote," in Colton and Jerry F. Hough, eds., *Growing Pains: Russian Democracy and the Election of 1993* (Washington, D.C.: Brookings Institution, 1998), pp. 75–114.

9. See especially Iván Szelényi, Éva Fodor, and Eric Hanley, "Left Turn in PostCommunist Politics: Bringing Class Back in?" *East European Politics and Societies,* 11 (Winter 1997), pp. 190–224; and Petr Matĕjů and Blanka Řeháková, "Turning Left or Class Realignment? Analysis of the Changing Relationship Between Class and Party in the Czech Republic, 1992–96," ibid. (Fall 1997), pp. 501–542.

10. According to published statistics, 72.9 percent of Russia's 147.6 million people in December 1995 lived in towns and cities and 27.1 percent in the countryside.

11. The most recent Russia-wide data on educational levels (from the 1989 Soviet census) put individuals with a completed higher education at 11.2 percent of the population aged fifteen and older. In our full 1995 sample, which was of persons aged eighteen and up, the ratio was 17 percent. This undoubtedly overestimates the actual level by several percentage points. Seven percent of our respondents had zero to four years of school, 17 percent had more than four years but no secondary diploma, 48 percent had a secondary education, and 11 percent had a specialized secondary education or an incomplete higher education.

12. Herbert Kitschelt argues this in *The Transformation of European Social Democracy* and in his *Party Systems in East Central Europe: Consolidation or Fluidity?,* Studies in Public Policy no. 241 (Glasgow: University of Strathclyde, 1995).

13. Our interviewers asked respondents two open-ended questions about their work: the name of their profession or occupation and the name of their job or position. The verbatim answers were assigned four-digit occupation codes according to the International Labor Office's International Standard Classification of Occupations, amended to fit local conditions. The "worker" designation includes active and retired employees in the general categories of agricultural and fishery workers, craft and related trades, plant and machine operators and assemblers, and elementary (unskilled) occupations. "Managers and professionals" covers senior economic managers, government officials, and persons in a variety of professions (among them engineering, medicine, teaching, and scientific research).

14. See Bertram Silverman and Murray Yanowitch, *New Rich, New Poor, New Russia: Winners and Losers on the Russian Road to Capitalism* (Armonk, N.Y.: M. E. Sharpe, 1997), and Harley Balzer, "Russia's Middle Classes," *Post-Soviet Affairs,* 14 (April–June 1998), pp. 165–186.

15. Fifty-five percent of our sample said they were religious believers or leaned to-

ward belief ("more a believing than a nonbelieving person") and gave their faith as Russian Orthodox. Thirty-nine percent of the Orthodox attended religious services at least once a month.

16. The 1989 Soviet census put ethnic Russians at 81.5 percent. Russians are 85 percent of our survey sample.

17. This overestimates the actual proportion in the population by several percentage points, even though one might have suspected that some former members of the CPSU would conceal this fact from interviewers.

18. Blair A. Ruble, *Money Sings: The Changing Politics of Urban Space in Post-Soviet Yaroslavl* (Washington, D.C.: Woodrow Wilson Center Press, 1995).

19. Respondents were asked how much money they and their families had pocketed in the month preceding the interview. Fourteen percent did not answer the question about family income in 1995 and 7 percent did not disclose their individual incomes. Thirteen percent said they had received *no* personal income the preceding month, and 3 percent that their family had received no income. Alone of the social-background questions, the income questions were asked afresh in 1996. Discussion of social variables in the presidential election relies on the 1996 data about income, but on 1995 measures for all other indicators. For related discussion, see Richard Rose, "Is Money the Measure of Welfare in Russia?" *Review of Income and Wealth,* 42 (March 1996), pp. 75–90.

20. I set these firms apart from Soviet-era state firms which have gone through a form of privatization since 1992. The Russian government still owns shares in many of the latter, and their employees often do not know who controls them.

21. Twenty-six percent of our respondents said they owned their dwellings before 1992. About two-thirds of these lived in villages and towns of under 100,000. Housing privatization has gone on quite evenly across community size, but state-owned flats still prevail in the big cities, a legacy of the Soviet past.

22. Geoff Garrett, "Popular Capitalism: The Electoral Legacy of Thatcherism," in Anthony Heath, Roger Jowell, and John Curtice, eds., *Labour's Last Chance? The 1992 Election and Beyond* (Aldershot, U.K.: Dartmouth, 1994), p. 116.

23. Scott C. Flanagan et al., *The Japanese Voter* (New Haven: Yale University Press, 1991), pp. 57, 60.

24. Kendall L. Baker, Russell J. Dalton, and Kai Hildebrandt, *Germany Transformed: Political Culture and the New Politics* (Cambridge, Mass.: Harvard University Press, 1981), p. 179.

25. Females were 53 percent of the entire population in 1995 and 57 percent of our sample.

26. See the survey evidence in Colton, "Determinants of the Party Vote," p. 90.

27. See in particular Laura Belin and Robert W. Orttung, *The Russian Parliamentary Elections of 1995: The Battle for the Duma* (Armonk, N.Y.: M. E. Sharpe, 1997), chap. 8. Russia is divided into eleven macroregions for census purposes.

The KPRF's portion of the party-list vote in 1995 ran from 31.1 percent in the Central Black Earth census region (south and southwest of Moscow) to 17.3 percent in the Urals. The nationalist LDPR received the most votes in the Volga-Vyatka census region (15.2 percent) and least in the Northwest (7.4 percent). Yabloko was strongest in the Northwest (12.4 percent) and weakest in the Central Black Earth (3.6 percent). Our Home Is Russia did best in the Volga census region (13.2 percent) and worst in the Far Eastern region (5.6).

28. Besides ibid., see Ralph S. Clem and Peter R. Craumer, "The Geography of the April 25 (1993) Russian Referendum," *Post-Soviet Geography,* 34 (August 1993), pp. 481–496; Darrell Slider, Vladimir Gimpel'son, and Sergei Chugrov, "Political Tendencies in Russia's Regions: Evidence from the 1993 Parliamentary Elections," *Slavic Review,* 53 (Fall 1994), pp. 711–732; Gavin Helf, "All the Russias: Center, Core, and Periphery in Soviet and Post-Soviet Russia" (Ph.D. dissertation, University of California at Berkeley, 1994); Nikolai Petrov, "Elektoral'nyi landshaft Rossii i yego evolyutsiya," in Michael McFaul and Nikolai Petrov, eds., *Politicheskii al'manakh Rossii 1995* (Moscow: Moscow Carnegie Center, 1995), pp. 28–44; and Ralph S. Clem and Peter R. Craumer, "Urban-Rural Voting Differences in Russian Elections, 1995–1996: A Rayon-Level Analysis," *Post-Soviet Geography and Economics,* 38 (September 1997), pp. 379–395. Territorially aggregated data have also been used to analyze elections in other post-Communist countries. See, for example, Andrew Wilson, "The Ukrainian Left: In Transition to Social Democracy or Still in Thrall to the USSR?" *Europe Asia Studies,* 49 (November 1997), pp. 1263–1292.

29. For an argument that the southern part of European Russia has a distinctively traditionalist political culture, see Ye. V. Morozova, "Sovremennaya politicheskaya kul'tura Yuga Rossii," *Polis,* no. 6 (1998), pp. 112–131.

30. The point can be rephrased in terms of the composition of the KPRF subelectorate. For example, only 10 percent of KPRF supporters in 1995 were in the top quintile of the whole electorate by community size and 12 percent were in the top quintile by family income. Twenty-three percent of KPRF voters were age thirty-nine or younger, but 41 percent of the supporters of other parties were in that age range.

31. All liberal parties combined, by testimony of our survey, took 33 percent of the votes in the largest communities (versus 8 percent in the smallest), 36 percent among persons with a higher education (versus 9 percent among the least educated), 24 percent among persons with the largest family incomes (versus 9 percent among voters with the smallest incomes), and 21 percent among eighteen-to-twenty-year-olds (versus 11 percent for persons seventy or older).

32. The curvilinear line of support for Yeltsin by age group is not apparent from Figure 3.2, which graphs only upper and lower categories of the sociodemographic variables. In our survey sample, 43 percent of voters under

the age of thirty voted for Yeltsin; this proportion fell to 31 percent for voters in their fifties, then increased to 38 percent for voters aged seventy and older.

33. Like the LDPR in 1995, Lebed in 1996 was most popular neither among the least educated voters nor among the most educated, but among persons with technical or vocational training (a "specialized secondary" diploma, in Soviet parlance). The KPRF and Zyuganov did best among voters with less than five years of school. The liberal Yabloko party and both Yeltsin and Yavlinskii in 1996 had their greatest appeal among individuals with a higher education, whereas the government party in 1995, Our Home Is Russia, was strongest among graduates of a vocational school.

34. Nor was Yabloko's following internally homogeneous in 1995. Thirty-seven percent of Yabloko voters had a completed higher education, but 63 percent did not.

35. For example, in spite of the connection between family income and support for Yeltsin, 52 percent of voters in the highest income bracket voted for other candidates in the first round of the presidential election. As for Zyuganov, his 50-percent share in the lowest income bracket left half of the votes to be shared by other candidates—including Yeltsin, who took 23 percent of the votes of persons in the bottom quintile by family income.

36. The index, adumbrated in Robert Alford, *Party and Society* (Chicago: Rand McNally, 1963), measures the percentage of the working-class vote for a party of the left minus the percentage of the middle-class vote for the same. Although the terms "working class" and "middle class" fit post-Soviet life imperfectly, the exercise is still helpful. In the first round of the 1996 election, support for Zyuganov was 36 percent among manual workers and 26 percent among other citizens, giving a modified Alford index of 10 points. Counting votes for either the KPRF or for all the socialist parties in 1995, the index was 11 points. These results would put Russia toward the bottom of the Western range. See Dalton, "Political Cleavages, Issues, and Electoral Change," pp. 322–325.

37. "How can social determinism explain why Catholics voted 54 percent for Eisenhower in 1956 and 83 percent for Kennedy in 1960? Evidently, the relationship between social characteristics and vote choice varies over time. Whatever the importance of social characteristics, other factors mediate or override such characteristics and determine the outcome of elections." Morris P. Fiorina, "Voting Behavior," in Dennis C. Mueller, ed., *Perspectives on Public Choice* (Cambridge: Cambridge University Press, 1997), p. 394.

38. The family income question was asked separately in 1995 and 1996, so some respondents' position on the scale shifts. But among citizens in the top quintile in 1995, 45 percent voted for Yeltsin in 1996, which is 28 percentage points more than the turnout for Our Home Is Russia in 1995.

39. Russian society is of course changing, but not so fast as to engender the discontinuities in electoral behavior we see from 1995 to 1996.

40. Education, for instance, is negatively related in our survey sample to age ($r = -.31$) and positively to 1995 family income ($r = .30$) and community size ($r = .22$). For all pairings, $p \leq .01$.

41. Women of Russia, which is not included in out multivariate analysis because of the smallness of its vote, polled 11 percent among women in our survey sample but 3 percent among men. Its vote share is over-reported in the sample.

42. Age is tied with urbanization for total effect on the Zyuganov vote in the 1996 runoff, but has a larger apparent effect in the first round.

43. The best of the early studies said that in most U.S. elections grand issues are not at stake and citizens "with no clear directives from stimuli outside themselves . . . are likely to fall back on directive forces within themselves. This means that voters are likely to fall back on early allegiances, experiences, values, and norms—for example, those associated with being raised as a member of the working class or a minority group." Bernard R. Berelson, Paul F. Lazarsfeld, and William N. McPhee, *Voting: A Study of Opinion Formation in a Presidential Campaign* (Chicago: University of Chicago Press, 1954), p. 115. The authors did not explain why other motivational forces, such as partisan allegiance or economic self-interest, would play second fiddle to social background under such conditions.

44. They are for the most part pared-down versions of the total effects. For the residual effects of all fourteen social variables, see Tables D.1 and D.2 in Appendix D. There is one big surprise there—the residual effects of family income on the first round presidential vote for Yeltsin and Lebed. The first difference in predicted probability is .13 ($p \leq .01$) for Lebed and *minus* .09 ($p \leq .10$) for Yeltsin, for whom the parameter is *plus* .14 ($p \leq .01$) when only social characteristics are taken into account. The best interpretation of this anomaly is that those better-off Russians who did not manifest the attitudes commonly associated with high income were more likely to vote for Lebed and against Yeltsin.

45. Current conditions are tied with issue opinions in our transmission estimates for the first round of the presidential election, but come out ahead in the parliamentary election and in the presidential runoff.

46. Helmut Norpoth, "The Economy," in LeDuc, Niemi, and Norris, *Comparing Democracies*, p. 318. Especially important works include Edward R. Tufte, *Political Control of the Economy* (Princeton: Princeton University Press, 1978); Donald R. Kinder and D. Roderick Kiewiet, "Sociotropic Politics: The American Case," *British Journal of Political Science*, 11 (April 1981), pp. 129–161; D. Roderick Kiewiet, *Macroeconomics and Micropolitics: The Electoral Effects of Economic Issues* (Chicago: University of Chicago Press, 1983); Michael S. Lewis-Beck, *Economics and Elections: The Major Western Democracies* (Ann Ar-

bor: University of Michigan Press, 1988); Helmut Norpoth, Michael S. Lewis-Beck, and Jean-Dominique Lafay, eds., *Economics and Politics: The Calculus of Support* (Ann Arbor: University of Michigan Press, 1991); and Christopher Anderson, *Blaming the Government: Citizens and the Economy in Five European Democracies* (Armonk, N.Y.: M. E. Sharpe, 1995). One scholar (Martin Paldam, "How Robust Is the Vote Function? A Study of Seventeen Nations over Four Decades," in Norpoth, Lewis-Beck, and Lafay, *Economics and Politics*, p. 9) lists more than 200 titles about economics and voting as of the early 1990s.

47. Quotations from Kinder and Kiewiet, "Sociotropic Politics," pp. 130, 132.

48. For American and West European cases, see especially Kiewiet, *Macroeconomics and Micropolitics;* Lewis-Beck, *Economics and Elections*, pp. 57–63; Anthony Heath et al., *Understanding Political Change: The British Voter, 1964–1987* (Oxford: Pergamon Press, 1991), chap. 9; and Bruno Paulson, "The Economy and the 1992 Election," in Heath, Jowell, and Curtice, eds., *Labour's Last Chance*, pp. 93–101.

49. Jeffrey Sachs, "Life in the Economic Emergency Room," in John Williamson, ed., *The Political Economy of Policy Reform* (Washington, D.C.: Institute for International Economics, 1994), pp. 503–523.

50. Adam Przeworski, *Democracy and the Market: Political and Economic Reforms in Eastern Europe and Latin America* (Cambridge: Cambridge University Press, 1991), pp. 136, 138. There is fuller discussion in Dani Rodrik, "Understanding Economic Policy Reform," *Journal of Economic Literature*, 34 (March 1996), pp. 9–41.

51. See especially Raymond M. Duch, "Tolerating Economic Reform: Popular Support for Transition to a Free Market in the Former Soviet Union," *American Political Science Review*, 87 (September 1993), pp. 590–608, which is based on a representative survey of residents of the European territory of the USSR done in May 1990. See also John P. Willerton and Lee Sigelman, "Perestroika and the Public: Citizens' Views of the 'Fruits' of Economic Reform," in Arthur H. Miller, William M. Reisinger, and Vicki L. Hesli, eds., *Public Opinion and Regime Change: The New Politics of Post-Soviet Societies* (Boulder, Co.: Westview, 1993), pp. 205–223, and Matthew Wyman, *Public Opinion in Postcommunist Russia* (New York: St. Martin's, 1997), chap. 2.

52. The change from late Soviet to early post-Soviet attitudes is brought out with special clarity in Arthur H. Miller, Vicki L. Heslie, and William M. Reisinger, "Reassessing Mass Support for Political and Economic Change in the Former USSR," *American Political Science Review*, 88 (June 1994), pp. 402–405. They inferred from a 1992 survey in Russia, Lithuania, and Ukraine that citizens' sense of private economic well-being was somewhat predictive of support for market reform, but popular pessimism about the economy in general was almost uniform. For corroboration from 1995 Russian data, see Robert J. Brym,

"Re-evaluating Mass Support for Political and Economic Change in Russia," *Europe-Asia Studies,* 48 (July 1996), pp. 754–757. A dissenting view is in Geoffrey Evans and Stephen Whitefield, "The Politics and Economics of Democratic Commitment: Support for Democracy in Transition Societies," *British Journal of Political Science,* 25 (October 1995), pp. 503–507. The All-Russian Center for Public Opinion Research (VTsIOM) monitors trends in Russian attitudes toward the economy in its bulletin *Ekonomicheskiye i sotsial'nyye peremeny: Monitoring obshchestvennogo mneniya.*

53. See Timothy J. Colton, "Economics and Voting in Russia," *Post-Soviet Affairs,* 12 (October-December 1996), pp. 289–317, and White, Rose, and McAllister, *How Russia Votes,* especially pp. 58–64. Neither work fits the economic variables into a multistage model of voting choice. There is brief discussion, resting on aggregate data, in Yitzhak M. Brudny, "In Pursuit of the Russian Presidency: Why and How Yeltsin Won the 1996 Presidential Election," *Communist and Post-Communist Studies,* 30 (1997), pp. 272–273. For evidence from other post-Communist countries, see A. C. Pacek, "Macroeconomic Conditions and Electoral Politics in East Central Europe," *American Journal of Political Science,* 38 (August 1994), pp. 723–744; Janice Bell, "Unemployment Matters: Voting Patterns during the Economic Transition in Poland, 1990–1995," *Europe-Asia Studies,* 49 (November 1997), pp. 1263–1291; and Denise V. Powers and James H. Cox, "Echoes from the Past: The Relationship between Satisfaction with Economic Reform and Voting Behavior in Poland," *American Political Science Review,* 91 (September 1997), pp. 617–634. See also the special issue of *Comparative Political Studies,* 29 (October 1996), on "Public Support for Market Reforms in Emerging Democracies," edited by Susan C. Stokes. Most of the material in the issue is about support through forms other than voting.

54. For a clear if overly rhapsodic chronology of economic reform, see Anders Åslund, *How Russia Became a Market Economy* (Washington, D.C.: Brookings Institution, 1995). A more balanced account is Thane Gustafson, *Capitalism Russian-Style* (Cambridge: Cambridge University Press, 1999).

55. Sixty-two percent of our informants named an economic problem in 1995 and 64 percent in 1996. Seventy-one percent of Russians surveyed at the time of the Duma election of 1993 pointed to an economic problem as the country's most important (Colton, "Determinants of the Vote," p. 93). The slight drop in salience of economic issues is almost entirely because of the war in Chechnya, which 10 percent of citizens in 1995 and 13 percent in 1996 identified as Russia's worst problem.

56. The question referred to the "material position" *(material'noye polozheniye)* of the family over the past twelve months, which in Russia includes monetary income and economic welfare more generally.

57. Thirty-two percent of respondents with personal experience of unemploy-

ment said it was Russia's gravest problem, as compared with 15 percent of others.

58. Monitoring surveys by a leading domestic polling firm show the trend. Sixty-two percent of Russians in the work force interviewed in a national sample in March 1993 reported being paid fully and on time in the preceding month. This proportion declined to roughly 40 percent in 1994 and 1995 and stood at 29 percent in November 1996. In the 1996 survey, 31 percent said they had been paid either with delays or with reductions in wage, while 39 percent said they had not been paid at all. VTsIOM, *Ekonomicheskiye i sotsial'nyye peremeny: Monitoring obshchestvennogo mneniya,* January-February 1997, p. 50.

59. Respondents in Russian monitoring surveys saying the economy was in bad or very bad condition held steady at about 75 to 80 percent in polls conducted from 1993 to 1996. Ibid., p. 55.

60. As discussed in Chapter 6, Russians' votes are affected by blanket assessments of the performance of incumbents. But the analysis here relies upon survey questions about current conditions as such, without reference to any party or leader.

61. The correlation between sociotropic and pocketbook evaluations of the economy was .32 in 1995 and .47 in 1996; between assessments of democratization and of the national economy it was .23 in 1995 and .41 in 1996; and between assessments of democratization and family finances it was .15 in 1995 and .32 in 1996. In all cases, $p \leq .01$.

62. The total effect of unemployment experience on the probability of voting for Our Home Is Russia in 1995 is .06, and the residual effect is almost the same (.05). In 1996 the influence of experience with arrears on the first-round Yeltsin vote declines from .11 at the total-effect stage to .08 at the residual stage. Robustness is exactly what recent work has found for the electoral effect of layoffs in the household in the United States. See Miller and Shanks, *The New American Voter,* chap. 13.

63. For Our Home Is Russia in 1995, evaluations of party leaders are approximately equally significant.

64. This point is well made in Michael McFaul, *Russia's 1996 Presidential Elections: The End of Polarized Politics* (Stanford: Hoover Institution Press, 1997), chaps. 1–2.

65. G. Bingham Powell and Guy D. Whitten, "A Cross-National Analysis of Economic Voting: Taking Account of the Political Context," *American Journal of Political Science,* 37 (May 1993), pp. 398–399. Cf. Anthony Heath and Bruno Paulson, "Issues and the Economy," *Political Quarterly,* 63 (October-December 1992), pp. 432–337.

66. In keeping with presidential responsibility, the strongest effect found in studies

of U.S. congressional elections tends to be the influence of national economic assessments on the vote for a congressional candidate from the sitting president's party (see Kiewiet, *Macroeconomics and Micropolitics*, pp. 102–108).

4. Partisanship in Formation

1. Maurice Duverger, *Political Parties*, 3rd ed., trans. Barbara and Robert North (London: Methuen, 1964), p. xxiii.
2. Leon D. Epstein, *Political Parties in Western Democracies* (New York: Praeger, 1967), pp. 13–14.
3. Otto Kirchheimer, "The Transformation of the Western European Party System," in Robert A. Dahl, ed., *Political Oppositions in Western Democracies* (New Haven: Yale University Press, 1966), p. 178.
4. Party identification, three reviewers declared with some chagrin in the 1970s, "has become as pervasive a concept as power, authority, legitimacy, stability, or any other element in the professional political scientists' vocabulary." "Introduction," in Ian Budge, Ivor Crewe, and Dennis Farlie, eds., *Party Identification and Beyond: Representations of Voting and Party Competition* (London: John Wiley and Sons, 1976), p. 3. This book contains what is still the shrewdest critique of the theory of party identification.
5. For informed general discussion, see M. Steven Fish, *Democracy from Scratch: Opposition and Regime in the New Russian Revolution* (Princeton: Princeton University Press, 1995); M. Steven Fish, "The Advent of Multipartism in Russia, 1993–1995," *Post-Soviet Affairs*, 11 (October–November 1995), pp. 340–383; Michael Urban, with Vyacheslav Igrunov and Sergei Mitrokhin, *The Rebirth of Politics in Russia* (Cambridge: Cambridge University Press, 1997); Michael Urban and Vladimir Gel'man, "The Development of Political Parties in Russia," in Karen Dawisha and Bruce Parrott, eds., *Democratic Changes and Authoritarian Reactions in Russia, Ukraine, Belarus, and Moldova* (Cambridge: Cambridge University Press, 1996), pp. 175–219; Matthew Wyman, Stephen White, and Sarah Oates, eds., *Elections and Voters in Post-communist Russia* (Cheltenham, U.K.: Edward Elgar, 1998); and John Löwenhardt, ed., *Party Politics in Post-Communist Russia* (London: Cass, 1998).
6. Many parties acquired the signatures "by paying enterprising individuals to collect signatures or by outright fraud." Laura Belin and Robert W. Orttung, *The Russian Parliamentary Elections of 1995: The Battle for the Duma* (Armonk, N.Y.: M. E. Sharpe, 1997), p. 59.
7. John H. Aldrich, *Why Parties? The Origin and Transformation of Party Politics in America* (Chicago: University of Chicago Press, 1995), p. 286.
8. "Privileged representation for parties in the future parliament was a valuable and low-cost organizational resource for ambitious politicians, and the auto-

matic translation of a certain share of the vote for a particular leader or party into parliamentary seats would help allow the heads even of embryonic partisan movements to offer their followers sufficient incentives to accept their leadership." Thomas F. Remington, "Political Conflict and Institutional Design: Paths of Party Development in Russia," in Löwenhardt, *Party Politics in Post-Communist Russia*, p. 216.

9. Yeltsin flirted with establishing a party of his own, but repeatedly pulled back. His senior political aide in the early 1990s, Gennadii Burbulis, told an American scholar in an interview "that Yeltsin feared a party would limit him, that it would commit him to a policy position and limit his freedom of action." Jerry F. Hough, "Institutional Rules and Party Formation," in Timothy J. Colton and Jerry F. Hough, eds., *Growing Pains: Russian Democracy and the Election of 1993* (Washington, D.C.: Brookings Institution, 1998), p. 52.

10. Duverger, *Political Parties*, pp. 63–64.

11. Exactly 0.9 percent of our survey respondents said in 1995 they belonged to a political party or movement. This would work out to approximately 1 million members in the electorate at large. The parties' own estimates of their memberships are unreliable. In 1993, for example, the LDPR claimed to have 100,000 members, but observers "put the actual number closer to 1,500." Evelyn Davidheiser, "Right and Left in the Hard Opposition," in Colton and Hough, *Growing Pains*, p. 189.

12. Fish, "The Advent of Multipartism in Russia," p. 359.

13. Richard S. Katz, "Party Organizations and Finance," in Lawrence LeDuc, Richard G. Niemi, and Pippa Norris, eds., *Comparing Democracies: Elections and Voting in Comparative Perspective* (Thousand Oaks, Calif.: Sage, 1996), p. 119. The phrase dates back to Otto Kirchheimer in the 1960s. A variation on Kirchheimer's type, the "electoral-professional party," is outlined in Angelo Panebianco, *Political Parties: Organization and Power*, trans. Marc Silver (Cambridge: Cambridge University Press, 1988), pp. 262–267.

14. D. A. Levchik, "Politicheskii 'kheppening,'" *Sotsiologicheskiye issledovaniya*, 8 (August 1996), pp. 51–56. Levchik cites as a pioneer of this approach one Vladimir Pribylovskii, who unsuccessfully sought a Duma seat in a Moscow district in 1993 on a platform he called "Subtropical Russia," in which he promised if elected to raise the average air temperature in Russia to 20° Celsius and to lower the boiling temperature of water to 50°. To be fair to the Beer Lovers' Party, the young Moscow intellectuals who headed it did publish a pro-private enterprise economic program. I classify it as a liberal opposition party.

15. The 17 percent indicating trust or complete trust in parties is a worse result than for any state institution about which we asked similar questions in 1995 and 1996. In a survey by a Russian polling firm in 1993, only 6 percent of respondents gave favorable ratings to political parties on a seven-point trust

scale. Stephen White, Richard Rose, and Ian McAllister, *How Russia Votes* (Chatham, N.J.: Chatham House, 1997), p. 53. A survey in nine post-Communist countries, not including Russia, found parties the most distrusted of all institutions. William Mishler and Richard Rose, "Trust, Distrust and Skepticism: Popular Evaluations of Civil and Political Institutions in Post-Communist Societies," *Journal of Politics,* 59 (May 1997), p. 422.

16. The optimal number is lower—2.5—if respondents who preferred more than twenty parties are excluded. The same question in France elicited an average of 2.9 parties desired in 1958 and 2.5 in 1967. Philip E. Converse and Roy Pierce, *Political Representation in France* (Cambridge, Mass.: Harvard University Press, 1986), p. 56. Our question was open-ended. Answers that gave a numerical range were coded at the mean of the range. For comparative data on support for multiparty politics, see William L. Miller, Stephen White, and Paul Heywood, *Values and Political Change in Postcommunist Europe* (London: Macmillan, 1998), pp. 162–166, 410–411.

17. For age group and number of parties desired, $r = -.09$ ($p \le .01$). For education group and parties, $r = .12$ ($p \le .01$). Compare Russia to France in 1967, where uneducated citizens preferred 2.3 parties on average and persons with a higher education an average of 2.9 parties (Converse and Pierce, *Political Representation in France,* p. 57). In Russia, where the experience with multiparty politics is shorter and more exasperating, the poorly educated can stomach fewer parties than the French did a generation ago, while the well-educated tolerate more parties.

18. For the original statement of the problem, see Anthony Downs, *An Economic Theory of Democracy* (New York: Harper and Row, 1957), chaps. 11–14.

19. This is an improvement over the state of knowledge about the Russian parties in 1993, as reported in Miller, White, and Heywood, *Values and Political Change in Postcommunist Europe,* p. 169.

20. Pearson's r between the number of parties evaluated and our raw political awareness score is .50. With interest in politics the correlation is .38, with interest in the 1995 campaign it is .29, and with formal education it is .32. For all pairings, $p \le .01$. Citizens who eventually voted in December 1995 recognized more parties in the pre-election interview. The mean number of parties evaluated for voters was 6.1 and for nonvoters 4.4.

21. Pearson's r between recognition of the parties and acceptance of multiparty competition is .06 ($p \le .01$). Survey respondents who strongly agreed with the benefits of competition among the parties were able to evaluate an average of 6.7 parties in 1995; for persons who strongly disagreed, the figure was 6.2. Ignorance of the parties was most evident among those who were not able to answer the question about competition; they evaluated 3.2 parties each.

22. Angus Campbell, Philip E. Converse, Warren E. Miller, and Donald E. Stokes, *The American Voter* (New York: John Wiley and Sons, 1960), p. 133.

23. Warren E. Miller and J. Merrill Shanks, *The New American Voter* (Cambridge, Mass.: Harvard University Press, 1996), p. 117.

24. See especially Martin Harrop and William Miller, *Elections and Voters: A Comparative Introduction* (New York: New Amsterdam Books, 1987), chap. 6; Converse and Pierce, *Political Representation in France*, chap. 3; Sören Holmberg, "Party Identification Compared Across the Atlantic," in M. Kent Jennings and Thomas E. Mann, eds., *Elections at Home and Abroad: Essays in Honor of Warren E. Miller* (Ann Arbor: University of Michigan Press, 1994), pp. 93–122; and Roy Pierce, *Choosing the Chief: Presidential Elections in France and the United States* (Ann Arbor: University of Michigan Press, 1995), chap. 3. Kendall L. Baker, Russell J. Dalton, and Kai Hildebrandt, *Germany Transformed: Political Culture and the New Politics* (Cambridge, Mass.: Harvard University Press, 1981), chaps. 8–9, adapt the concept to the circumstances of postwar West Germany. A very important older work is David Butler and Donald E. Stokes, *Political Change in Britain: Forces Shaping Electoral Choice* (London: Macmillan, 1969), which used the term "partisan self-image" to refer to identification. Attempts to study party identification in non-Western locales have been rare, but see Samuel J. Eldersveld, "Party Identification in India in Comparative Perspective," *Comparative Political Studies,* 6 (October 1973), pp. 271–295.

25. On question wording and its pitfalls, consult Max Kaase, "Party Identification and Voting Behaviour in the West German Election of 1969," in Budge, Crewe, and Farlie, *Party Identification and Beyond*, pp. 81–102; Converse and Pierce, *Political Representation in France*, pp. 72–77; and Paul R. Abramson and Charles W. Ostrom, "Question Wording and Partisanship: Change and Continuity in Party Loyalties During the 1992 Election Campaign," *Public Opinion Quarterly,* 58 (Spring 1994), pp. 21–48.

26. Samuel L. Popkin, *The Reasoning Voter: Communication and Persuasion in Presidential Campaigns* (Chicago: University of Chicago Press, 1991), pp. 50–60. Information shortcuts may be especially needed in the United States, where there are so many elected offices.

27. Morris P. Fiorina, *Retrospective Voting in American National Elections* (New Haven: Yale University Press, 1981), p. 85–91, 102.

28. Lawrence LeDuc, "The Dynamic Properties of Party Identification: A Four-Nation Comparison," *European Journal of Political Research,* 9 (September 1981), pp. 257–285; James E. Alt, "Dealignment and the Dynamics of Partisanship in Britain," in Russell J. Dalton, Scott C. Flanagan, and Paul Allen Beck, eds., *Electoral Change in Advanced Industrial Democracies: Realignment or Dealignment?* (Princeton: Princeton University Press, 1984), pp. 298–329; Harold D. Clarke, Marianne C. Stewart, and Paul F. Whiteley, "New Models for New Labour: The Political Economy of Labour Party Support, January 1992–April 1997," *American Political Science Review,* 92 (September 1998), pp. 559–576.

29. Paul Allen Beck and M. Kent Jennings, "Family Traditions, Political Periods, and the Development of Partisan Orientation," *Journal of Politics*, 53 (August 1991), p. 757. For summaries of earlier phases of the project, see M. Kent Jennings and Richard G. Niemi's two books: *The Political Character of Adolescence: The Influence of Families and Schools* (Princeton: Princeton University Press, 1974), and *Generations and Politics: A Panel Study of Young Adults and their Parents* (Princeton: Princeton University Press, 1981). For older arguments that partisanship solidifies over the life cycle and across generations, see Philip E. Converse, "Of Time and Partisan Stability," *Comparative Political Studies*, 2 (July 1969), pp. 139–171, and William Claggett, "Partisan Acquisition versus Partisan Intensity: Life-Cycle, Generational, and Period Effects, 1952–1976," *American Journal of Political Science*, 25 (May 1981), pp. 193–214. Converse predicted it would take three generations for the level of partisan identification in a new political system to reach equilibrium and level off at about 70 percent of the electorate.

30. Richard G. Niemi and M. Kent Jennings, "Issues and Inheritance in the Formation of Party Identification," *American Journal of Political Science*, 35 (November 1991), pp. 970–988. For a similar argument, see Edward G. Carmines and James A. Stimson, *Issue Evolution: Race and the Transformation of American Politics* (Princeton: Princeton University Press, 1989), chap. 6.

31. White, Rose, and McAllister, *How Russia Votes*, p. 137.

32. William L. Miller, Stephen White, and Paul Heywood, "Twenty-Five Days to Go: Measuring and Interpreting the Trends in Public Opinion During the 1993 Russian Election Campaign," *Public Opinion Quarterly*, 60 (Spring 1996), p. 124. Related surveys at around the same time uncovered 38 percent of citizens showing identification in the Czech Republic, 33 percent in Slovakia, and 28 percent in Hungary. See also Miller, White, and Heywood, *Values and Political Change in Postcommunist Europe*, p. 411.

33. Geoffrey Evans and Stephen Whitefield, "The Politics and Economics of Democratic Commitment: Support for Democracy in Transition Societies," *British Journal of Political Science*, 25 (October 1995), pp. 499–500.

34. Arthur H. Miller, Gwyn Erb, William M. Reisinger, and Vicki L. Hesli, "Emerging Party Systems in Post-Soviet Societies: Fact or Fiction," paper presented at annual meeting of International Society of Political Psychology, July 1996; Arthur H. Miller, William M. Reisinger, and Vicki L. Hesli, "Leader Popularity and Party Development in Post-Soviet Russia," in Wyman, White, and Oates, *Elections and Voters in Post-communist Russia*, p. 103.

35. Respondents who claimed to be partisans but could not name the party that was the apple of their eye, or who named more than one party, were coded as nonpartisans.

36. For further discussion, see Chapter 5. Note that in the two-party United States the problem does not occur. By convention, researchers use a seven-point scale

consisting of three strength-related values for each of the two parties and an independent category in the middle.

37. Besides the seven parties shown in Figure 4.6, the parties clearing an even 1 percent of the partisan electorate were the liberal Forward Russia (4 percent), Russia's Democratic Choice (4 percent), Pamfilova Bloc (2 percent), and Common Cause (1 percent); the centrist Employees' Self-Management Party (4 percent) and KEDR (1 percent); the nationalist Derzhava (1 percent) and Govorukhin Bloc (1 percent); and the socialist Communists for the Soviet Union (1 percent) and Power to the People (1 percent).

38. The ratios were 33 percent scoring as strong, moderate, or weak partisans among persons who had discussed politics often in their childhood, the exact same for occasional discussions, and 30 percent for persons who had never discussed politics at home.

39. Pearson's r between past membership in the CPSU and possession of partisanship in 1995 is .10 ($p \leq .01$).

40. Between age group and partisanship, $r = .09$ ($p \leq .01$).

41. Between educational index and partisanship, $r = .08$ ($p \leq .01$).

42. The data also show some other mild associations with social background. Married persons were more likely than single persons to be partisans in 1995 ($r = .09$, $p \leq .01$), white-collar workers more likely than blue-collar workers ($r = .08$, $p \leq .01$), and persons who socialize with their neighbors more likely than loners ($r = .06$, $p \leq .01$). There are no consistent correlations between partisanship in Russia and either sex or community size.

43. Pearson's $r = .16$ ($p \leq .01$). Causality is probably two-way here, with partisanship breeding the attitude that the citizen would never vote for a party or parties as well as the other way around. Multiple answers were permitted to our "would never vote" question. Respondents on average named 2.2 parties for which they would never vote. The LDPR was named in 65 percent of the cases, followed by the Communist Party (28 percent), the Beer Lovers' Party (27 percent), and Russia's Democratic Choice (20 percent).

44. "Voters who have difficulty handling the cacophony of varying political claims and arguments need some sort of guide in deciding how to vote . . . A standing decision to identify with one or another party may provide that guide." W. Phillips Shively, "The Nature of Party Identification: A Review of Recent Developments," in John C. Pierce and John L. Sullivan, eds., *The Electorate Reconsidered* (Beverly Hills: Sage, 1980), p. 227. Partisanship may in this light be counted as one of the "selection principles" for coping with political information whose importance was first discussed in Downs, *An Economic Theory of Democracy*, chap. 7.

45. The transitional environment, it has been said, "is unusually full of information, and confusing information at that, given the deregulation of politics and

economics . . . and . . . the absence of such filters as class, institutions, roles, and interests to sort out environmental cues." Valerie Bunce and Maria Csanádi, "Uncertainty in the Transition: Post-Communism in Hungary," *East European Politics and Society*, 7 (Spring 1993), p. 269.

46. We have this information for 1996 only, as the question about trust in parties was not asked in 1995. Fifty-four percent of partisan respondents as well as of nonpartisans said they did not trust the political parties. But the proportion who said they did trust the parties was rather higher among partisans (23 percent versus 14 percent). "Don't know" responses were higher among non-partisans.

47. Correlations for all of these associations are significant at the .01 level.

48. Converse and Pierce, *Political Representation in France*, p. 69.

49. The exceptions, as can be seen in columns 2 and 3, were two nationalist parties (Derzhava and KRO) and the centrist Women of Russia. Our Home Is Russia is omitted from column 2 because the government party family consists of that one party only.

50. The only questions omitted in 1996 were those asking respondents to name the leaders of the party they said they were enthused about.

51. Bear in mind that the proportions in Figure 4.12 are of a partisan segment which itself shrank as a proportion of the whole electorate by 18 percentage points from 1995 to 1996. Vis-à-vis the electorate, only the socialist bloc held its own, at 17 percent. All the others decreased. The fall was most precipitate for the nationalist and centrist parties (off 12 percentage points each) and less for the liberal and government parties (off by 4 percentage points each).

52. All references are to proportions among respondents interviewed in both the first and third waves of the survey.

53. Fiorina in *Retrospective Voting in American National Elections* was impressed by information from panel studies that 15 to 20 percent of American voters altered identification categories over two-year intervals in the 1950s and the 1970s.

54. For each party, the four values on the scale incorporate nonpartisanship and weak, moderate, and strong partisanship as directed at that party.

55. This context-driven explanation of the attenuation of partisanship prompts a question about the attitudes of the partisans-turned-nonpartisans—who by our calculation were only 2 percentage points less numerous in the summer of 1996 than were partisan citizens. A proposition worth testing in future is that such individuals entertain latent partisanship which may be activated as circumstances change. In 1996 their ratings of the parties and leaders they had supported in 1995 were noticeably higher than those of other citizens, though lower than those of partisans of the given party. For example, KPRF partisans in 1996 assigned to their party an average feeling-thermometer score of 89

points and all others gave it an average score of 37, but the mean score given by 1996 nonpartisans who *had* been partisans of the KPRF in 1995 was 56 points. For Zyuganov, the party's presidential candidate, mean thermometer scores in the three categories were 85, 39, and 58 points.

56. Shifting preferences on political issues, such as economic reform or foreign policy, might also be tested for influence on partisanship, along the lines tried out in the United States by Jennings, Niemi, and others. But at the present rudimentary state of expertise about transitional politics I am not sure how we would model this relationship.

57. The table does not show the effects of 1995 partisanship on the likelihood of affiliation in 1996 with other political parties. These effects are mostly small.

58. For instance, Miller and Shanks, *The New American Voter,* p. 482, a study which puts great emphasis on partisan identification, concludes that in the 1992 presidential election citizen perceptions of current national conditions and evaluations of President Bush's performance in office were about equal in combined influence on voting decisions to party identification.

59. For this association, $r = .10$ ($p \le .01$).

60. Differentiating partisanship for individual parties by strength produces multicategory variables with very small numbers in some categories. Strength-modulated measures of Russian partisanship rarely yield a better fit with the data in multivariate analysis than do the dichotomous measures.

61. In addition to the four closely observed parties, the full regression equation includes four other partisanship dummies—for any one of the centrist parties, socialist parties other than the KPRF, nationalist parties other than the LDPR, and liberal parties other than Yabloko. For brevity, I omit the estimates of their electoral influence.

62. In a survey conducted in January-February 1998, nowhere near a federal election, a research group of which I was part asked Russians the same battery of questions about partisanship as in the 1995 and 1996 election surveys. Thirty-two percent of them identified themselves as partisans—9 percent strong partisans, 10 percent moderate partisans, and 13 percent weak partisans. The poll was of 1,541 adults in a national probability sample. Because the work was done on a consulting basis, the data are proprietary.

63. Compare with the United States, where the estimate of the influence of party identification on the presidential vote in 1992 loses almost 40 percent of its value between the bivariate and total-effect stages (Miller and Shanks, *The New American Voter,* p. 286). Precise comparison of the two countries is impossible, owing to the different metrics used in the analysis, but the gross contrast is still evident.

64. The candidates not nominated by political parties were Yeltsin, Lebed, and Gorbachev. Zyuganov was officially proposed by a "bloc" representing a number of socialistic organizations, but his campaign was to all intents and pur-

poses run by the KPRF. I can testify from experience that most election propaganda, pro and con, stressed his stewardship of the KPRF.

65. Due to swings in partisanship, many 1996 partisans had been nonpartisans in 1995 or, less frequently, the partisans of other parties or of parties in other families. For example, 50 percent of socialist partisans in 1996 had been socialist partisans in 1995, 31 percent had been nonpartisans, and 19 percent had been supporters of parties in other families.

66. Lebed parted company with Yurii Skokov and the rest of the KRO leadership after briefly entering Yeltsin's administration in July 1996. He founded his own political movement in 1997.

67. The dummy variables for partisanship are the same as for the 1995 Duma election, with the difference that KRO, not the LDPR, is the nationalist party represented. As in 1995, four dummies for categories other than the four parties given in the table—for centrist parties, socialist parties other than the KPRF, nationalist parties other than KRO, and liberal parties other than Yabloko—are included.

68. M. Ostrogorski, *Democracy and the Organization of Political Parties*, (New York: Macmillan, 1902), vol. I, p. liii.

5. Opinions, Opinions . . .

1. Walter Lippmann, *Public Opinion* (New York: Free Press, 1965), p. 18.

2. Anthony Downs, *An Economic Theory of Democracy* (New York: Harper and Row, 1957), p. 46.

3. Downs emphasized this point, saying his model of the issue-driven voter "leaves room for altruism in spite of its basic reliance upon the self-interest axiom." He gave as an example the possibility that some Americans would feel satisfied "if the government increased taxes upon them in order to distribute free food to starving Chinese." Ibid., p. 37.

4. See the works cited in the Preface, n. 8.

5. Twenty-one of the questions were about economic and socioeconomic issues, three about law and order, three about constitutional issues, one about Russian imitation of the West, and eight about foreign policy. There were additional questions in the post-election interview.

6. The correlation *(r)* between the number of opinions and our political awareness score is .36. For interest in politics the correlation is .32, for interest in the 1995 parliamentary campaign it is .14, and for educational level it is .27. In every instance, $p \leq .01$. Compare with the higher coefficients for association with the number of political parties evaluated in 1995 (Chapter 4, n. 17).

7. John R. Zaller, *The Nature and Origins of Mass Opinion* (Cambridge: Cambridge University Press, 1992), p. 28.

8. Ibid.

9. There is no one best yardstick for gauging attitudinal stability. But compare Table 5.1 with the examples in ibid., pp. 28–29. And see the extended discussion in Benjamin I. Page and Robert Y. Shapiro, *The Rational Public: Fifty Years of Trends in Americans' Policy Preferences* (Chicago: University of Chicago Press, 1992), who emphasize continuity in American mass opinion, and William G. Mayer, *The Changing American Mind: How and Why American Public Opinion Changed between 1960 and 1988* (Ann Arbor: University of Michigan Press, 1992), where the stress is more on change.

10. See especially Zaller, *The Nature and Origins of Mass Opinion,* chap. 4.

11. If we partition the sample into quintiles by political awareness, the difference between the least and the most aware group is 4 percentage points for ability to answer the question on full employment, 24 points on protection of industry, 8 points on food prices, 37 points on foreign investment, 22 points on land ownership, and 13 points on incomes policy.

12. This is the metaphor used in Philip E. Converse and Roy Pierce, *Political Representation in France* (Cambridge, Mass.: Harvard University Press, 1986), chap. 4.

13. Besides ibid., consult Angus Campbell, Philip E. Converse, Warren E. Miller, and Donald Stokes, *The American Voter* (New York: John Wiley, 1960), chap. 9; Philip E. Converse, "The Nature of Belief Systems in Mass Publics," in David E. Apter, ed., *Ideology and Discontent* (New York: Free Press, 1964), pp. 206–261; Jean A. Laponce, "Note on the Use of the Left-Right Dimension," *Comparative Political Studies,* 3 (January 1970), pp. 481–502; Hans D. Klingemann, "Measuring Ideological Conceptualizations," in Samuel Barnes et al., *Political Action: Mass Participation in Five Western Democracies* (Beverly Hills: Sage, 1979), pp. 215–253; Dieter Fuchs and Hans D. Klingemann, "The Left-Right Schema," in Kent Jennings et al., *Continuities in Political Action* (Berlin: de Gruyter, 1989), pp. 203–234; Ronald Inglehart, *Culture Shift in Advanced Industrial Society* (Princeton: Princeton University Press, 1990); Mayer, *The Changing American Mind;* and Warren E. Miller and J. Merrill Shanks, *The New American Voter* (Cambridge, Mass.: Harvard University Press, 1996), chap. 11.

14. I describe one family of Russian parties in this book as the "liberal opposition." Quite a few Moscow and St. Petersburg academics and journalists, but few others in Russia, would be at home with that label.

15. In a survey of the European parts of the USSR in May 1990, about 60 percent of respondents could place themselves on a left-right scale, and those seeing themselves as on the left were more likely than rightists to favor radical reforms. Lauren M. McLaren, "Ideology in the Former Soviet Union: Defining Left and Right in a Non-Western Context," unpublished paper, Department of Political Science, University of Houston, 1994. Eurobarometer surveys in Russia in 1991 and 1992 found the same correlation between leftist self-location and support for a market economy; in many East European countries the re-

verse was true. Jürgen Hofrichter and Inge Weller, "On the Application of the Left-Right Schema in Central and Eastern Eurobarometer Surveys," report prepared for Eurobarometer Unit, Commission of the European Community (Mannheim, April 1993). I am grateful to Stephen White and Sarah Oates for acquainting me with these papers. See also evidence of the earlier orientation persisting as late as 1993 in Geoffrey Evans and Stephen Whitefield, "The Evolution of Left and Right in Post-Soviet Russia," *Europe-Asia Studies,* 50 (September 1998), p. 1030.

16. Jerry F. Hough, Evelyn Davidheiser, and Susan Goodrich Lehmann, *The 1996 Russian Presidential Election,* Brookings Occasional Papers (Washington, D.C.: Brookings Institution Press, 1996), p. 47.

17. The correlation *(r)* of ideological self-knowledge (as a dichotomous variable) with the awareness score is .20 ($p \le .01$). Ideological consciousness is also correlated with certain social traits, and in particular education ($r = .18, p \le .01$), male gender ($r = .12, p \le .01$), and past membership in the CPSU ($r = .04, p \le .05$).

18. Compare with William L. Miller, Stephen White, and Paul Heywood, *Values and Political Change in Postcommunist Europe* (London: Macmillan, 1998), pp. 307–312, which compares Russians' consciousness of left and right with Ukrainians, Czechs, Slovaks, and Hungarians, and Evans and Whitefield, "The Evolution of Left and Right," pp. 1027, 1041, which provides important information on the trend in Russian thinking from 1993 to 1996. Questions of interpretation are raised, however, by several aspects of the analysis. Evans and Whitefield's 1993 questionnaire did not contain a "Don't know" response. Their respondents from 1995 and 1996 who were unable to answer—the number is unclear—are coded at the midpoint. Strictly speaking, their ten-point scale does not have a neutral center point.

19. Left-right self-identifiers placed an average of 3.9 of the 5 candidates somewhere on the seven-point scale; others placed 0.8 candidates on average.

20. In the most knowledgeable quintile of the electorate, the mean score ascribed to Yeltsin was 4.8 points and to Zyuganov 2.7, for a difference of 2.1 points. In the least knowledgeable quintile, the values were 4.5 and 3.5, making the difference 1.0 points.

21. In France in the 1960s, 24 percent of the electorate was unable to answer such a question. In the United States around the same time, nonresponses for a question about the meaning of the liberal-conservative distinction were 37 percent. Converse and Pierce, *Political Representation in France,* pp. 136–137.

22. For further discussion of the qualitative evidence, see Timothy J. Colton, "Ideology and Russian Mass Politics: Uses of the Left-Right Continuum," in Matthew Wyman, Stephen White, and Sarah Oates, eds., *Elections and Voters in Post-communist Russia* (Cheltenham, U.K.: Edward Elgar, 1998), pp. 161–183.

23. Thirty-one percent of respondents in the most aware quintile of the electorate

offered an ideological definition of the left-right distinction; 19 percent in the middle quintile and 7 percent in the bottom quintile did the same.

24. This is not to deny that some elite players have strong belief systems, including beliefs about criteria for membership in the political community. See Stephen E. Hanson, "Ideology, Uncertainty and the Rise of Anti-System Parties in Post-Communist Russia," in John Löwenhardt, ed., *Party Politics in Post-Communist Russia* (London: Cass, 1998), pp. 98–127. I direct my comments to the incoherence of frameworks for political beliefs in the rank-and-file population.

25. Miller and Shanks, *The New American Voter,* chap. 11. For related discussion on issue hierarchies, see Paul M. Sniderman, Richard A. Brody, and Philip E. Tetlock, *Reasoning and Choice: Explorations in Political Psychology* (New York: Cambridge University Press, 1991), chaps. 3–5, and Anthony Heath et al., *Understanding Political Change: The British Voter, 1964–1987* (Oxford: Pergamon Press, 1991), chap. 11.

26. Miller and Shanks, *The New American Voter,* p. 291.

27. Richard Rose, Evgeny Tikhomirov, and William Mishler, "Understanding Multi-Party Choice: The 1995 Duma Election," *Europe-Asia Studies,* 49 (July 1997), pp. 799–824.

28. Sarah Oates, "Party Platforms: Towards a Definition of the Russian Political Spectrum," in Löwenhardt, *Party Politics in Post-Communist Russia,* p. 81.

29. M. Steven Fish, "The Advent of Multipartism in Russia, 1993–1995," *Post-Soviet Affairs,* 11 (October–November 1995), p. 367.

30. The LDPR set the tone in 1993 when it "called for a gradual approach to economic reforms," attacked both the Yeltsin program and the Soviet command system, and demanded a transfer of economic power into "the hands of the average citizen." Evelyn Davidheiser, "Right and Left in the Hard Opposition," in Timothy J. Colton and Jerry F. Hough, eds., *Growing Pains: Russian Democracy and the Election of 1993* (Washington, D.C.: Brookings Institution, 1998), p. 189.

31. Michael McFaul, *Russia's 1996 Presidential Election: The End of Polarized Politics* (Stanford: Hoover Institution Press, 1997), p. 52.

32. We also asked about state versus individual responsibility for social welfare and about the war for secession in the republic of Chechnya. In neither case do the answers add much to the analysis of property and a crackdown on crime and corruption. Information relating the candidates to the Chechen war is hopelessly compromised by the flurry of peace activity immediately after the second round of the 1996 election, before many of the interviews were held. Both President Yeltsin and Aleksandr Lebed had key roles in the negotiations.

33. Compare to John H. Aldrich, John L. Sullivan, and Eugene Borgida, "Foreign Affairs and Issue Voting: Do Presidential Candidates 'Waltz Before a Blind Audience?'" in Richard G. Niemi and Herbert F. Weisberg, eds., *Controversies in*

Voting Behavior, 3rd ed. (Washington, D.C.: Congressional Quarterly Press, 1993), pp. 184–185. They found 65 to 80 percent of American voters able to place both themselves and both presidential candidates on scales for domestic and foreign-policy issues in the 1984 U.S. election.

34. Pearson's *r* between political awareness and knowledge of the four parties' issue positions in 1995 is .35 ($p \le .01$) and between awareness and knowledge of the presidential candidates' positions in 1996 it is .28 ($p \le .01$).

35. A third factor which may be of relevance is the timing of the survey questions. The issue-position questions were asked in the pre-election interview in 1995 but after the presidential election in 1996, when respondents may have absorbed more information about the contenders than they had before the election. Learning may indeed have taken place over a more protracted period, going back to (or even before) the 1995 election. But I doubt that either of these learning effects is enough to explain the contrast between 1996 and 1995 values. There is some corroboration in the data concerning familiarity with the political parties. We asked our basic feeling-thermometer question in 1996 about seven of the ten parties included in the original 1995 interview. Among panel members interviewed both times, the number of parties recognized and evaluated on the thermometer increased from 4.2 (of 7) in 1995 to 4.8 in 1996. This is a much more modest difference than that observed in the recognition of parties' and candidates' issue positions.

36. The number of parties whose positions were recognized (2.9 on property and 4.0 on crime and corruption) was about equal to those recognized for presidential candidates in 1996, but we asked the locational questions about ten parties, as compared to five presidential candidates.

37. Scholarly discussion dates back to Benjamin I. Page and Richard A. Brody, "Policy Voting and the Electoral Process: The Vietnam War Issue," *American Political Science Review,* 66 (September 1972), pp. 979–995.

38. Dichotomizing the electorate into voters for and against any one party or candidate actually muffles the bias built into the location indicators. The effects of selective imputation come through more strongly when we look closely at groups of voters. In the presidential election, for example, Table 5.7 shows citizens who voted against Yeltsin in the first round giving him a score of 2.05 on the property issue and 2.95 on the civil rights issue. What it does not show is that the subset of anti-Yeltsin voters who voted for his main antagonist, Zyuganov, assigned to Yeltsin a considerably higher pro-privatization score than to others on the property issue (1.85) and a considerably more pro-repression score on the rights issue (2.66). By the same token, Yeltsin supporters gave Zyuganov a slightly more pro-state score on property (4.32) but a substantially more pro-repression score on rights (2.34). If the gap between Yeltsin and Zyuganov on the property issue was 1.99 points among all voters, among

Yeltsin voters it was 1.74 points and among Zyuganov voters it was 2.26 points. On the rights issue, Yeltsin was assigned an average location at an inconsequential 0.17 points higher (more pro-individual rights) than Zyuganov by all voters, yet Yeltsin voters placed the president 1.25 points higher than his challenger, while Zyuganov voters placed Zyuganov 1.27 points higher (that is to say, in the *liberal* direction!) than they placed Yeltsin.

39. Criticism of issue proximity scores has increased. The case is ably rehearsed in Miller and Shanks, *The New American Voter,* pp. 14–15, 206–207, and Sniderman, Brody, and Tetlock, *Reasoning and Choice,* pp. 167–168. For discussion using data from the 1993 Russian election, see Timothy J. Colton, "Determinants of the Party Vote," in Colton and Hough, *Growing Pains,* pp. 98–104.

40. My standard for inclusion is lenient: a total-effect statistic standing for an impact on the probability of voting for any one of the four top-flight parties, the five party families, or the four chief presidential candidates of no less than .05 (5 percentage points).

41. In 1995 the correlation (r) between attitudes on full employment and food prices was .42, between full employment and incomes .30, and between food prices and incomes .41; in 1996 the correlations were .42, .29, and .47. In every case, $p \le .01$.

42. We also asked a question about the respective rights of Russia's ethnic-based "republics" and its other regions, but the responses were not related to voting behavior.

43. Readings of this variable were also volatile over time. The intertemporal correlation between 1995 and 1996 values is .17 ($p \le .01$.), which is lower than for any of the variables described in Tables 5.2 and 5.4.

44. "Mass orientations toward economic and political reform are not independent of each other: they do not oppose but rather reinforce one another in the former Soviet Union." Arthur H. Miller, Vicki L. Hesli, and William M. Reisinger, "Reassessing Mass Support for Political and Economic Change in the Former USSR," *American Political Science Review,* 88 (June 1994), p. 409. See also Raymond M. Duch, "Tolerating Economic Reform: Popular Support for Transition to a Free Market in the Former Soviet Union," *American Political Science Review,* 87 (September 1993), pp. 590–608; William Zimmerman, "Markets, Democracy, and Russian Foreign Policy," *Post-Soviet Affairs,* 10 (April–June 1994), pp. 103–126; Geoffrey Evans and Stephen Whitefield, "The Politics and Economics of Democratic Commitment: Support for Democracy in Transition Societies," *British Journal of Political Science,* 25 (October 1995), pp. 485–514; James L. Gibson, "Political and Economic Markets: Changes in the Connection Between Attitudes Toward Political Democracy and a Market Economy Within the Mass Culture of Russia and Ukraine," *Journal of Politics,* 58 (November 1996), pp. 954–984; and Miller, White, and Heywood, *Values and Political Change in Postcommunist Europe,* chap. 12.

45. Sentiment against foreign investment yields a relatively large total effect for the Lebed vote (.10), but it is not statistically significant at the .05 level.

46. The other difference we can note in passing is about the electoral effect of attitudes toward the former Soviet republics. Nostalgia for the USSR is most rampant among pro-Communist voters, but in 1996 it was the anti-Communist Yeltsin who was favored on the emotion as it meshes with post-Soviet diplomacy. In a bivariate analysis (see Table D.4), integrationism lines up positively with the first-round Zyuganov vote and negatively with the Yeltsin vote. But at the total-effect stage (see Table 5.11), the upper hand goes to Yeltsin, for reasons that must be related to his stature as final arbiter of foreign policy. The total effect, though, is statistically significant at the .10 level only.

47. Yeltsin's support in fact peaked among voters who preferred the present political system. In the first round he took 66 percent of their votes and 47 percent among those who wanted a full-fledged Western democracy. In the runoff he polled 92 percent among devotees of the existing system and 83 percent among supporters of a Western democracy.

48. Richard G. Niemi and Herbert F. Weisberg, eds., *Classics in Voting Behavior* (Washington, D.C.: Congressional Quarterly Press, 1993), p. 99.

6. Performance, Personality, and Promise

1. Anthony Downs coined the phrase in *An Economic Theory of Democracy* (New York: Harper and Row, 1957). He also wrote (p. 41), "In effect, every election is a judgment passed upon the record of the incumbent party."

2. Jerry F. Hough, "The Failure of Party Formation and the Future of Russian Democracy," in Timothy J. Colton and Jerry F. Hough, eds., *Growing Pains: Russian Democracy and the Election of 1993* (Washington, D.C.: Brookings Institution, 1998), p. 675.

3. This is so even when the party head has led it to repeated defeats. I have several times discussed this subject with Grigorii Yavlinskii of Yabloko. The party and its leader have reaped between 7 and 8 percent of the popular vote in two parliamentary elections and one presidential election, but Yavlinskii sees these results as vindicating his leadership and presses forward without apology. The LDPR arguably suffered a defeat in the 1995 State Duma election, when its share of the popular vote was cut in half from 1993, but its leader, Zhirinovskii, came out of the election more dominant in the party than ever.

4. Michael McFaul, *Russia's 1996 Presidential Election: The End of Polarized Politics* (Stanford: Hoover Institution Press, 1997), p. 84.

5. In the 1995 Duma campaign, party posters and leaflets "generally featured the party leader in a statesmanlike pose." Stephen White, Richard Rose, and Ian McAllister, *How Russia Votes* (Chatham, N.J.: Chatham House, 1997), p. 215.

6. S. N. Pshizova, "Kakuyu partiinuyu model' vosprimet nashe obshchestvo," *Polis,* no. 4 (1998), p. 106.

7. White, Rose, and McAllister, *How Russia Votes,* the fullest treatment of Russian voting, does not explicitly analyze the candidate effect. There is a brief discussion of it for the 1993 Duma election in Timothy J. Colton, "Determinants of the Party Vote," in Colton and Hough, *Growing Pains,* pp. 105–108.

8. Warren E. Miller and J. Merrill Shanks, *The New American Voter* (Cambridge, Mass.: Harvard University Press, 1996), p. 389. Miller and Shanks cite the revealing discussion in Wendy M. Rahn, John H. Aldrich, and Eugene Borgida, "Individual and Contextual Variations in Political Candidate Appraisal," *American Political Science Review,* 88 (March 1994), pp. 193–199.

9. The same would hold for positive assessments of current developments. A voter might see the economy as trending upward and praise the government for facilitating the recovery—or, alternatively, feel an improvement but not link it to public policy. For related discussion, see Miller and Shanks, *The New American Voter,* pp. 393–397. Voters' selective apportionment of guilt for national problems is one of the points best developed in White, Rose, and McAllister, *How Russia Votes.*

10. In the presidential runoff, *100 percent* of the persons who approved fully of Yeltsin's record voted for his re-election.

11. Eighteen percent of voters who completely trusted the government in 1995 voted for Our Home Is Russia, as opposed to 4 percent of the most distrustful voters, but 27 percent of the most trustful voters voted for the KPRF, Our Home's harshest antagonist. For approval of the president, though, Our Home Is Russia outpolled the KPRF 37 percent to 15 percent among voters giving Yeltsin the highest rating.

12. Timing of the interviews may conceivably have been a factor, yet it cannot have been decisive. All questions in 1996 were asked after the second round of the election. In 1995 approval of Yeltsin was tested in the pre-election interview and trust in the government in the post-election interview. The apparent causal importance of confidence in the government is much greater in 1996 than in 1995, even though in both cases the information was obtained after the vote.

13. Philip E. Converse and Georges Dupeux, "De Gaulle and Eisenhower: The Public Image of the Victorious General," in Angus Campbell, Philip E. Converse, Warren E. Miller, and Donald E. Stokes, *Elections and the Political Order* (New York: John Wiley and Sons, 1966), p. 292.

14. Miller and Shanks, *The New American Voter,* p. 415, say that media consultants and pollsters, who have a big stake in the thesis that U.S. presidential politics revolves around candidates, have promoted it so avidly that it has become "a self-fulfilling prophecy."

15. Wendy M. Rahn, John H. Aldrich, Eugene Borgida, and John L. Sullivan, "A Social-Cognitive Model of Candidate Appraisal," in Richard G. Niemi and Herbert F. Weisberg, eds., *Controversies in Voting Behavior,* 3rd ed. (Washington, D.C.: Congressional Quarterly Press, 1993), p. 189. Fine digests of this literature are Carolyn L. Funk, "Understanding Trait Inferences in Candidate Images," in Michael X. Delli Carpini, Leonie Huddy, and Robert Y. Shapiro, eds., *Research in Micropolitics,* vol. 5 (Greenwich, Conn.: JAI Press, 1996), pp. 97–123, and Ian McAllister, "Leaders," in Lawrence LeDuc, Richard G. Niemi, and Pippa Norris, eds., *Comparing Democracies: Elections and Voting in Comparative Perspective* (Thousand Oaks, Calif.: Sage, 1996), pp. 280–298. Donald R. Kinder, "Presidential Character Revisited," in Richard R. Lau and David O. Sears, eds., *Political Cognition* (Hillsdale, N.J.: Lawrence Erlbaum, 1986), pp. 233–256, is an especially important reference.

16. See especially Brian Graetz and Ian McAllister, "Party Leaders and Election Outcomes in Britain, 1974–83," *Comparative Political Studies,* 19 (January 1987), pp. 484–507; Clive Bean and Anthony Mughan, "Leadership Effects in Parliamentary Elections in Australia and Britain," *American Political Science Review,* 83 (December 1989), pp. 1165–1179; Marianne C. Stewart and Harold D. Clarke, "The (Un)Importance of Party Leaders: Leader Images and Party Choice in the 1987 British Election," *Journal of Politics,* 54 (May 1992), pp. 447–470; Clive Bean, "The Electoral Influence of Party Leader Images in Australia and New Zealand," *Comparative Political Studies,* 26 (April 1993), pp. 111–132; Ivor Crewe and Anthony King, "Are British Elections Becoming More 'Presidential'?" in M. Kent Jennings and Thomas F. Mann, eds., *Elections at Home and Abroad: Essays in Honor of Warren E. Miller* (Ann Arbor: University of Michigan Press, 1994), pp. 181–206; Ivor Crewe and Anthony King, "Did Major Win? Did Kinnock Lose? Leadership Effects in the 1992 Election," in Anthony Heath, Roger Jowell, and John Curtice, eds., *Labour's Last Chance? The 1992 Election and Beyond* (Aldershot, U.K.: Dartmouth, 1994), pp. 125–147; Michael J. Harrison and Michael Marsh, "What Can He Do for Us? Leader Effects on Party Fortunes in Ireland," *Electoral Studies,* 13 (December 1994), pp. 289–312; David J. Lanoue and Barbara Headrich, "Prime Ministers, Parties, and the Public: The Dynamics of Government Popularity in Great Britain," *Public Opinion Quarterly,* 60 (Spring 1996), pp. 106–127; and Richard Nadeau, Richard G. Niemi, and Timothy Amato, "Prospective and Comparative or Retrospective and Individual? Party Leaders and Party Support in Great Britain," *British Journal of Political Science,* 26 (April 1996), pp. 245–258.

17. Graetz and McAllister, "Party Leaders and Election Outcomes in Britain," and Bean and Mughan, "Leadership Effects in Parliamentary Elections in Australia and Britain."

18. The slate of KRO (the Congress of Russian Communities) had two co-heads,

Aleksandr Lebed and Yurii Skokov. I utilize only the information about Lebed, the better known of the pair.

19. Ability to evaluate the five 1995 party leaders who ran for president in 1996—Zyuganov, Lebed, Yavlinskii, and Zhirinovskii, whose parties we evaluated in the 1995 survey, and Svyatoslav Fedorov, whose party was not evaluated in 1995—was an average of 12 percentage points greater than in the previous winter.

20. The data on parties in Figure 6.3 duplicate information already presented in Figure 4.4 in Chapter 4.

21. The point is made repeatedly in studies of older democracies: "It goes without saying that personality images and party images are bound to affect each other" (Crewe and King, "Did Major Win? Did Kinnock Lose?" p. 127). For extended discussion with Russian data, see Arthur H. Miller, William M. Reisinger, and Vicki L. Hesli, "Leader Popularity and Party Development in Post-Soviet Russia," in Matthew Wyman, Stephen White, and Sarah Oates, eds., *Elections and Voters in Post-communist Russia* (Cheltenham, U.K.,: Edward Elgar, 1998), pp. 100–135.

22. This difference is exactly one-and-a-half times the average standard deviation (30 points) of the leaders' scores.

23. The Russian-language terms had to be chosen carefully. We translated "intelligent and knowledgeable person" as *umnyi, znayushchii chelovek;* "strong leader" as *sil'nyi rukovoditel';* "decent and trustworthy person" as *chestnyi chelovek, zasluzhivayet doveriya;* "vision of the country's future" as *svoye predstavleniye o budushchem strany;* and "really caring about people like you" as *deistvitel'no zabotitsya o takikh lyudyakh, kak Vy.*

24. Kinder, "Presidential Character Revisited," p. 238.

25. Lebed from 1992 to 1995 commanded the Russian Fourteenth Army, stationed in now independent Moldova. After siding with ethnic Slavs in the Transdniester area against the republic's government, he brokered a truce between the warring parties.

26. The group averages depicted in Figure 6.4 are a visually satisfying but imprecise way of capturing the relationships. Correlation coefficients (r) between assessments of recent economic trends and ratings of candidate integrity are .41 for Yeltsin and $-.29$ for Zyuganov. For preference for state ownership, the correlations are $-.28$ for Yeltsin and .30 for Zyuganov. For Yeltsin's record as president, they are .65 for Yeltsin and $-.36$ for Zyuganov. In all cases, $p \leq .01$.

27. My interpretation of the causal ordering is similar to that advanced for the 1992 presidential rivals in the United States, George Bush and Bill Clinton, in Miller and Shanks, *The New American Voter,* pp. 420–422.

28. Again, individual-level correlation coefficients give a more precise reading. For Yavlinskii, r is .09 for economic trends ($p \leq .05$), .10 for the Yeltsin record

($p \leq .05$), and .04 for property ownership ($p > .10$). For Lebed, the coefficients are .23 ($p \leq .01$), .24 ($p \leq .01$), and .09 ($p \leq .05$), respectively.

29. The thermometer scores are perhaps biased somewhat by their proximity to the voting decision. And, although the survey question asks how much the respondent likes or dislikes the individual politician, the responses may be affected by other feelings and opinions, over and above the attitude toward the politician. Nevertheless, the inclusion of partisanship, issue opinions, and other pertinent variables as controls in the statistical analysis should guard against extreme bias in the associations estimated.

30. The total effects shown in Table 6.9 are for the influence of the leader of the party specified in the column on the tendency to vote for that particular party. Parameters for the influence of the reputations of leaders of the other parties were computed, but are not displayed for brevity's sake. The same applies to appraisals of the personal characteristics of presidential candidates in Table 6.10.

31. Comparisons such as this are hostage to the statistical models behind them. If we were to assume that evaluations of party leaders are causally *antecedent* to partisanship—which has not been my assumption—the multistage analysis would yield different estimates of effect. Look back at Table 4.6 in Chapter 4 and imagine that the eighth row down, not the sixth row, was highlighted and that the total effect of partisanship on the 1995 party-list vote had to be computed with controls in place for party leaders and retrospective evaluations of incumbents, in addition to the blocs of variables in the first through sixth rows. That would lower the total effect of partisanship on the KPRF vote from .50 to .36, for the LDPR from .76 to .28, for Our Home Is Russia from .51 to .32, and for Yabloko from .66 to .40. By the same logic, the total-effect row in Table 6.9 would be the fifth, not the eighth, and the total effects for evaluations of the party's leader would be .54, .60, .36, and .31. (I disregard here retrospective evaluations of incumbents, whose role in mediating leadership assessments is minor.) Leadership effects would thus still be less than partisanship effects for Yabloko (by .40 to .31), but would exceed partisanship effects for the KPRF (by .54 to .36), the LDPR (by .60 to .28), and Our Home Is Russia (by .36 to .32). For Our Home Is Russia, the difference in leadership's favor would be slight. For the KPRF, the entire exercise is farfetched, as I know no one who believes the KPRF's reputation is an offshoot of Gennadii Zyuganov's. For the LDPR, the results of the alternate method of estimation have a certain satisfying ring to them. But to vary the causal sequence for one party or one leader would ruin the internal cohesion of our voting model and create insuperable problems for statistical estimation. And even the LDPR, which has had a caucus in the Duma since 1993, is more than the plaything of its leader, in my opinion.

32. The data summarized in the figures are for the four leading candidates only—
Yeltsin, Zyuganov, Lebed, and Yavlinskii. But the comparisons on which they
are based involve them and a fifth leader, Zhirinovskii.

33. Miller and Shanks, *The New American Voter,* p. 392.

34. The feeling-thermometer question supplies the data for the interparty comparisons in Figures 4.3, 4.4, and 6.3

35. A question about the Chechnya problem was also posed, but the responses, as
with other questions about the war, are unusable because post-election peace
negotiations, led by Aleksandr Lebed, were already under way when the survey
was done. For what it is worth, 51 percent of our respondents believed Lebed
would do best with the issue.

36. On each issue, several percent of our respondents gave more than one candidate as best able to handle the issue. Such persons were classified in the "Don't
know" category.

37. As with the analysis of leadership characteristics above, the total effects listed
in Tables 6.13 and 6.14 are for the electoral influence of the prospective evaluations of the party or presidential candidate specified. Parameters for the other
parties and candidates were estimated, but are not tabulated here.

38. As mentioned in Chapter 1, in our survey panel 57 percent of first-round
Lebed voters and 67 percent of first-round Yavlinskii voters supported Yeltsin
in the second round. Twenty-four percent of Lebed voters and 15 percent of
Yavlinskii voters sided with Zyuganov in the runoff, while 19 percent and 18
percent, respectively, abstained. Previous supporters of Lebed and Yavlinskii
made up 27 percent of Yeltsin's support in the second round, and previous
supporters of other candidates another 6 percent.

7. Tying the Strands Together

1. In Russian, the noun for "election" *(vybory)* is the plural of "choice" *(vybor).*

2. In American politics, with its stable two-party system, scholars usually distill
the voter's choices to the Democrat/Republican dichotomy. In the multiparty
systems of Western Europe, the availability of the left-right scale allows analysts to express electoral alternatives as points on a continuum. Neither option
applies for now to Russia.

3. The logit-based statistical model dictates only that the predicted probabilities
of all categories of the dependent variable, including the base category, must
sum to one, and that accordingly the differences in predicted probabilities reported for the effect of any independent variable under analysis must sum to
zero. These constraints leave vast room for variation, as can be seen by looking
at any of the elaboration tables in Chapters 3, 4, 5, and 6.

4. Warren E. Miller and J. Merrill Shanks, *The New American Voter* (Cambridge,

Mass.: Harvard University Press, 1996), chap. 17 (going by conclusions about the importance of "general themes" for individual voting decisions). Miller and Shanks found a rather different balance of causes in the 1988 presidential election, in which Bush defeated Michael Dukakis.

5. A similar conclusion about social characteristics and modeling the vote is reached in ibid.

6. For example, a KPRF partisan cannot be an LDPR or a Yabloko partisan. But someone who prefers state to private ownership could in principle take a liberal stance on a political or cultural issue, and a citizen who thought his family's material position was in decline could give a positive assessment of the national economy or of democratization.

7. The values of the total effects are identical to those in the elaboration in Table 4.6.

8. Unlike the simpler analysis in Chapter 6, the shifts in values of the leadership variables utilized in this statistical test encompass changes in opinion of all four of the parties. See the explanation in Table B.1, Appendix B.

9. I make this point without reference to the process of electing deputies to the Duma from territorial districts, which I did not try to examine in the book. It too has many idiosyncrasies, to which we should all be attentive in future work.

10. Angus Campbell, Philip E. Converse, Warren E. Miller, and Donald E. Stokes, *The American Voter* (New York: John Wiley and Sons, 1960), p. 25. Warren Miller, who died in 1999, was, of course, a co-author of both books.

Appendix B

1. See the review in Cynthia J. Buckley, "Social Science Surveys in the Russian Federation," *American Behavioral Scientist,* 42 (October 1998), pp. 223–236.

2. Interviews were thus conducted in thirty-two of the eighty-nine administrative units of the Russian Federation: the two cities directly subordinated to the central government (Moscow and St. Petersburg); nineteen oblasts (Amurskaya, Chelyabinsk, Kaluga, Kurgan, Leningrad, Lipetsk, Moscow, Nizhnii Novgorod, Orenburg, Penza, Perm, Rostov, Saratov, Smolensk, Tambov, Tomsk, Tula, Tver, and Volgograd); five territories or krais (Altai, Krasnodar, Krasnoyarsk, Primorskii, and Stavropol); five republics (Chuvashiya, Kabardino-Balkariya, Komi, Tatarstan, and Udmurtiya); and one autonomous district (Khanty-Mansiiskii).

3. The second-stage units were in 160 towns and villages, including Moscow, St. Petersburg, and 10 localities in Moscow oblast.

4. See Leslie Kish, *Survey Sampling* (New York: Wiley, 1965), pp. 398–404.

5. Many miscellaneous considerations got in the way of interviews. For example,

ten of our first-wave interviewees had died by the time of the third-wave interview. Health problems kept twenty-seven persons from being interviewed in the first wave and six in the third wave. Six individuals were too drunk to be interviewed in the first wave and six in the third wave.

6. The dependent variable in the regression for the 1995 parliamentary election took five categorical values, representing a vote for the KPRF, the LDPR, Our Home Is Russia, or Yabloko or, fifthly, any other voting choice (including a vote against all parties). For the first round of the 1996 presidential election, the categories were a vote for Yeltsin, Zyuganov, Lebed, or Yavlinskii, or any other voting choice. For the 1996 runoff, the categories were a vote for Yeltsin, a vote for Zyuganov, and a vote against both candidates.

7. To estimate influences on a dependent variable like voting choice in a multiparty or multicandidate election with linear or ordinary least-squares regression, it is necessary to disaggregate the outcome into separate dichotomous variables, one for each category of the outcome, and to do separate procedures for the relationships with the independent variables. The base category for the regression will differ from estimation to estimation. Predicted probabilities for the outcome, not being mathematically bounded, will in some instances be negative or greater than one, which are meaningless as probabilities. And the predicted probabilities for all categories of the outcome will not sum to one.

8. See Gary King, Michael Tomz, and Jason Wittenberg, "Making the Most of Statistical Analyses: Improving Interpretation and Presentation," paper presented at annual meeting of American Political Science Association, Boston, August 1998. The statistical package is Michael Tomz, Jason Wittenberg, and Gary King, CLARIFY: Software for Interpreting and Presenting Statistical Results, Version 1.2 (Cambridge, Mass., Harvard University, September 16, 1998—at http://gking.harvard.edu). CLARIFY is used in conjunction with the STATA package.

9. The variables for the personal characteristics of Lebed and Zyuganov were also dropped from the second-round estimations.

Appendix C

1. The Russian term used in the questionnaires, *koleblyus'*, literally means "I waver," and can also be broadly translated as "I agree some and disagree some."

Acknowledgments

I have incurred many debts in the course of researching and writing this book. William Zimmerman, my main American collaborator in the survey work on which it rests, was a constant source of wisdom and good cheer. The Carnegie Corporation of New York and the John D. and Catherine T. MacArthur Foundation generously funded the project. Carnegie covered general costs and the surveys of the electorate bracketing the parliamentary election of 1995; MacArthur financed the 1996 presidential survey. David Speedie, Astrid Tuminez, Deana Arsenian, and Andrew Kuchins, the program officers of the foundations, followed the enterprise with sympathy and bore up stoically with its complications.

I warmly thank Polina Kozyreva and Mikhail Kosolapov of the Institute of Sociology for superintending the three Russian surveys with professionalism and with an unblinking eye to the fine points that separate a magnificent job from an OK one. Michael Swafford helped out with many aspects of the surveys. Yelena Artamonova was an especially valued member of the Moscow team. Maria Tarasova ably facilitated my frequent visits to the country.

I am deeply grateful to Gary King of the Harvard Government Department for pushing me to employ the best available procedures for interpretation and presentation of the evidence, and for his patience with my at times naive queries. Michael Tomz and, above all, Jason Wittenberg dispensed excellent programming and statistical support.

The Government Department and the Davis Center for Russian Studies have served as my joint Harvard home throughout the effort. Donna Griesenbeck, Melissa Griggs, London King, Judith Mehrmann, Christine Porto, and Elsa Ransom of the Davis Center skillfully handled many administrative chores, large and small, while Dmitry Gorenburg, Elsa Ransom, Graeme Robertson, Natalia Tsvetkova, and Joshua Tucker gave top-notch research assistance. St. Antony's College at Oxford University provided a congenial setting in 1995–96 for thinking through post-Soviet mass politics and managing the field research in Russia; Archie Brown and Alex Pravda were gracious hosts. Interested and forgiving audiences at Oxford, Cambridge, Manchester, Glasgow, Birmingham, and the London School of Economics let me try out some preliminary analysis. Subsequent presentations at Michigan, Princeton, Brown, Yale, and Columbia universities furnished opportunities to develop the argument.

The manuscript benefited hugely from thorough readings by Josephine Andrews, Yekaterina Antonyuk, James Gibson, Thane Gustafson, Thomas Remington, Randall Stone, Daniel Treisman, Stephen White, and William Zimmerman. They were good enough friends and colleagues not to spare my feelings in their commentary. My investigations of Russian elections and related questions have also gained from ideas and feedback shared by Graham Allison, James Alt, Vladimir Bokser, George Breslauer, Yitzhak Brudny, Ralph Clem, Evelyn Davidheiser, Geoffrey Evans, Jeffry Frieden, Carolyn Funk, Marshall Goldman, Sergei Grigoriev, Henry Hale, Stephen Hanson, Joel Hellman, Laura Roselle Helvey, Fiona Hill, Stephen Holmes, Jerry Hough, Debra Javeline, Richard Johnston, Anthony King, Mark Kramer, David Lane, Susan Goodrich Lehmann, David Laitin, John Marttila, Michael McFaul, Arthur Miller, Pippa Norris, Sarah Oates, Bradley Palmquist, Nikolai Petrov, Roy Pierce, William Reisinger, Richard Rose, Robert Shapiro, Lilia Shevtsova, Regina Smyth, Steven Solnick, Sidney Verba, Stephen Whitefield, and Matthew Wyman. At Harvard University Press, Jeff Kehoe and Anita Safran have been exemplary editors.

Index